Real-World Flash Game Development

Real-World Flash Game Development

How to Follow Best Practices and Keep Your Sanity

Second Edition

Christopher Griffith

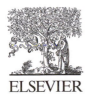

AMSTERDAM • BOSTON • HEIDELBERG • LONDON • NEW YORK • OXFORD
PARIS • SAN DIEGO • SAN FRANCISCO • SINGAPORE • SYDNEY • TOKYO

Focal Press is an imprint of Elsevier

Focal Press is an imprint of Elsevier
225 Wyman Street, Waltham, MA 02451, USA
The Boulevard, Langford Lane, Kidlington, Oxford, OX5 1GB, UK

Notices

Knowledge and best practice in this field are constantly changing. As new research and experience broaden our understanding, changes in research methods, professional practices, or medical treatment may become necessary.

Practitioners and researchers must always rely on their own experience and knowledge in evaluating and using any information, methods, compounds, or experiments described herein. In using such information or methods they should be mindful of their own safety and the safety of others, including parties for whom they have a professional responsibility.

To the fullest extent of the law, neither the Publisher nor the authors, contributors, or editors, assume any liability for any injury and/or damage to persons or property as a matter of products liability, negligence or otherwise, or from any use or operation of any methods, products, instructions, or ideas contained in the material herein.

Library of Congress Cataloging-in-Publication Data
Griffith, Christopher, 1979–
  Real-world Flash game development : how to follow best practices and keep your sanity / Christopher Griffith. – 2nd ed.
    p. cm.
  ISBN 978-0-240-81768-2 (pbk.)
  1. Computer games–Programming. 2. Computer animation. 3. Flash (Computer file) I. Title.
  QA76.76.C672G774 2011
  794.8'1526–dc22   2011006568

British Library Cataloguing-in-Publication Data
A catalogue record for this book is available from the British Library.

For information on all Focal Press publications
visit our website at *www.elsevierdirect.com*

11 12 13 14 5 4 3 2 1

Printed in the United States of America

Typeset by: diacriTech, Chennai, India

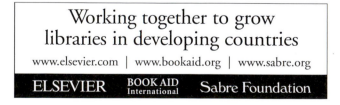

Working together to grow
libraries in developing countries

www.elsevier.com | www.bookaid.org | www.sabre.org

ELSEVIER   BOOK AID International   Sabre Foundation

CONTENTS

ONLINE CONTENTS: www.flashgamebook.com

INTRODUCTION

It feels like ages ago since I began the journey of writing this book. In its first year, more than 4500 copies were sold, and its reception exceeded my wildest expectations. I am thankful to all those who bought it and also to those who took the time to spread the word to others. Because technology develops at such an unrelenting pace, however, the work of a good author is never quite finished. In this revised edition of the book, you'll find most of the same material from the original (although some of it has found a permanent place online), as well as what I hope is new and exciting coverage of more advanced topics like mobile development for devices.

Game development is a strange hybrid of many skills and styles merged together. One can argue that games are the most complicated form of entertainment to create. They not only require solid coding, attractive design, and sound user interface decisions, but also the best games all share one particular aspect: they're fun to play. This "fun factor" can be especially elusive because it is so subjective. Different genres of games appeal to different people in different walks of life. Very few games, if any, are going to appeal to everyone, everywhere, all the time.

That said, the most popular type of game for players on the Internet are what have been termed "casual" games. If you're not familiar with this phrase, casual games are meant to appeal to a wide audience and focus on simplicity and approachability over depth and realism. This is not to say that some casual games are not deep and realistic, but the audience for a complicated tactical simulation on a console is very different from someone killing 10 minutes on his or her lunch break at work. Casual games can fall into any number of genres, from classic arcade-style games like Pac-Man to puzzle and logic games like Tetris. In fact, both of the titles I just mentioned have one thing in common: they are both products of an era in game development (from the late 1970s to mid-1980s), when the focus was not on spectacle and movie-quality graphics and audio, but rather on creating games that were first and foremost fun to play.

Games in Flash

Because you've picked up this book, I assume that you're not just interested in creating a game, but that you want to build it in Flash. Flash is an outstanding platform for developing games, particularly casual games for the Web. The file size and power of the plug-in, combined with the 98% install base around the world, make it a smart choice for getting your games seen by the largest possible audience. Historically, some Flash games have been thought of as glitchy, lacking in polish, and generally low-end. That is quickly changing, however, as Flash games become more and more sophisticated and get closer to "traditional" computer and video games.

Which Flash to Use?

I feel I should also take a moment to talk about versions of Flash. The first edition of this book was intended for use with Flash CS4. At the time, Flash CS4 had been out for almost a year, and it made sense to make that the version of choice. In the spring of 2010, Adobe released Flash CS5, which this book primarily uses as the default tool. All of the examples except the two mobile games at the end can be opened in CS5 and do not require anything later (and even those technically can—more in a moment about that). Throughout the writing of this book, I have also been on the beta for CS5.5, due to be released about the time this book appears on store shelves. Because of this, I felt it would be negligent of me to not include some mention of specific features in CS5.5. For the rest of this book, I will call out specific areas, where CS5.5 has introduced new workflows or options that will make your life easier. In addition, CS5.5 cleans up a number of the sloppier workflow options for Android and iOS development that exists in CS5, so I will be showing screenshots of CS5.5 because that will be the model going forward. The examples in Chapters 15 and 16 can both technically be created with CS5 (with some additional downloads from Adobe's Web site), but the performance, options, and ease-of-use of the tools in CS5.5 make it a much better choice.

How to Get the Most Out of This Book

This book further assumes either that you have at least intermediate experience with Flash (CS5, 5.5, or an earlier version) as an animation or Web site creation tool, or that you're entering Flash with game development experience on another platform. The purpose of this book is not to teach basic usage of the Flash environment from the ground up—that has been done many times over by other skilled authors and instructors. Rather, I hope that by the time you finish reading this book, you will feel totally comfortable tackling a game in Flash.

The first part of this book will discuss a lot of the terminologies and basic concepts you'll need to understand about game development, as well as how to map out a game from start to finish on a single page. In the second part, we'll discuss managing audio and visual assets in Flash, game logic (including dissecting an entire game script into its core components), and ways to architect your games to save you from headaches later. I'll share some best practices for both code and library organization.

A problem in Flash can usually be dissected any number of ways, and games are no exception. Sometimes, external forces (clients, deadlines, and so on) will dictate one approach over another. Part three will take what you've learned from the first half of the book and apply it in a number of real-world scenarios, showing how you don't have to sacrifice the ideals of sound game development just because your timeline got cut in half.

Finally, in this new edition, we'll look at Flash in a mobile setting and how to optimize for that medium. The examples will discuss both the Packager for iPhone, as well as deploying games on AIR for Android.

Resources on the Web Site

On the companion Web site to this book, www.flashgamebook.com, you'll find a bevy of resources to assist you, both in following the examples later in the book and in creating your own original work. All the source code from the examples I share is available there, as well as several chapters from the first edition that have been "retired" from the printed page. The site also provides a way for readers like you to ask questions and receive updates and clarifications as they become necessary. Be sure to check it out as you read and after you finish reading the book.

COMPUTER SCIENCE ISN'T FOR EVERYONE

A Little Groundwork

Before we get too far into Flash, it's important to lay a foundation for game development, so we understand the terminology that will be used throughout the rest of the book. Refer back to this chapter when you forget what a term means or how it applies in a particular situation. If you start to feel a little overwhelmed by all the long words and abstract concepts, don't worry! Game development (particularly efficient, well-executed development) is complicated, and there's nothing wrong in admitting it. Remember that anyone who has programmed a game has suffered the same anxieties and doubt. Like anything in life, it will require practice and real-world experience to become proficient in game development. So grab a cup of your favorite caffeine-infused beverage, and let's get started!

Common Game Types

There are many different types of games (and some games that pride themselves on being unable to be easily categorized), but most can be classified into one of the following genres.

Adventure

Adventure-style games are typically story-driven and have one or more central characters. These games are perceived the most like movies (some have been known to have the production budget of one) and can rely heavily on dialogue, exploration, and logical problem solving to move the player through the narrative. Adventure games were especially popular during the late 1980s and early 1990s, with LucasArts and Sierra producing some of the finest examples of the genre. This game type has had a resurgence of sorts in Flash due to its art-driven production pipeline and the typically lower system requirements.

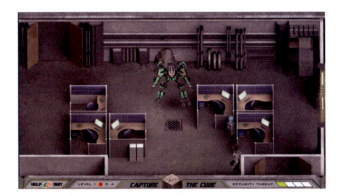

Figure 1.1 Mountain Dew—Capture the Cube Game.

Action

This category encompasses a large number of gameplay perspectives and subgenres, but usually action games consist of tests of players' dexterity, reaction time, and quick-wittedness under pressure. First-person shooters, side and vertical scrolling games, and fighting games all fall into the action genre. Flash lends itself very well to some of the subgenres of this category, particularly retro-style action games such as Space Invaders or Super Mario Brothers.

Puzzle

Think Tetris, Bejeweled, Sudoku, and the list goes on. Games that involve logic, problem solving, pattern matching, or all of the above fall into this game type. Flash thrives in this genre for a couple of reasons. First, there's generally a lower amount of art needed for a simple puzzle game, meaning individual developers can often do it themselves. Second, the core casual gaming audience on the Web tends to be older and appreciate the generally slower pace of puzzle games.

Word Games

This category could be considered a subgenre of puzzles, but the approach to building them can be different enough that I thought they deserved their own space. Word searches, crossword puzzles, spelling games, and anagrams all belong to this genre. Flash is a

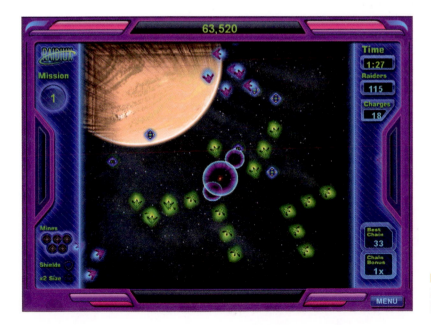

Figure 1.2 Raidiux © 2009, Blockdot, Inc. All Rights Reserved. www.blockdot.com.

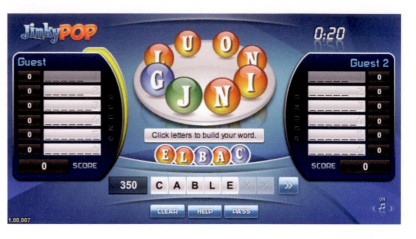

Figure 1.3 JinkyPOP © 2009, Blockdot, Inc. All Rights Reserved. www.blockdot.com.

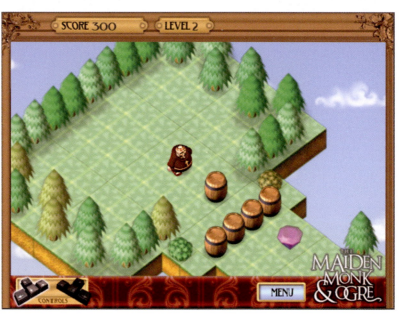

Figure 1.4 The Maiden, Monk, and Ogre © 2009, Blockdot, Inc. All Rights Reserved. www. blockdot.com.

popular medium for games of this type; for the same reasons, it is for other puzzle games as well.

Strategy and Simulation

I'm cheating a little by combining these two genres into one, but they share a number of common traits. Careful planning, resource management, and decision making, such as city planning or the creation of a large army, characterize strategy games. The level of minutia the player is expected to maintain usually defines a strategy or simulation game. Some games are so complex as to allow every possible option available to the player to be micromanaged.

More casual strategy games, like most created in Flash, simplify gameplay by reducing the number of options available and focusing on a couple of main tasks. A popular example of the casual strategy subgenre is tower defense games, where the player must stop enemies from getting past their defenses using a variety of different weapons placed strategically.

Role-Playing Game (RPG)

RPGs are similar to adventure games, but they are normally defined more by the growth of the main character throughout the course of the game's story. Traditionally, RPGs take place in a fantasy setting and center around the player's statistical development, such as improving traits such as strength, intelligence, agility. The most popular recent incarnation of these games has been in massively multiplayer online RPGs (MMORPGs), where players compete against and collaborate with each other to develop their characters. Because of the social and Web-based aspects, a few Flash MMORPGs have begun to emerge. However, these games are typically costly and have long-development cycles, making them riskier ventures for companies and infeasible for individual developers.

Vehicle Games

These games are pretty self-explanatory; they revolve around the operation of a vehicle on land, in water, in air, or in space. Traditionally, these games are played from a first- or third-person perspective to achieve a sense of realism. Because of system requirements and the complexity of building a full 3D environment in Flash, most casual games in this genre feature a two-dimensional game view.

Board/Card-Based Games

Usually a digital incarnation of a real-world game, this category can consist of games such as chess, checkers, blackjack, and poker. Because of the low system requirements, Flash is a great platform for creating most board and card games, as is evidenced by the large number of casino-style game sites on the Web.

General Development Terms

Computer science is a difficult field of study and definitely not for everyone who simply wants to make games. However, a fundamental understanding of some of the core concepts of programming helps later when we're dissecting a game piece by piece. Yes it's dry and occasionally tedious sounding, but I promise that fun stuff will follow!

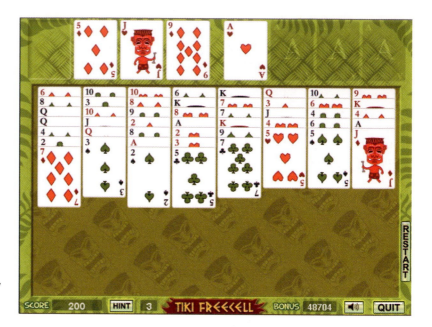

Pseudocode

Pseudocode is nothing more than a standard language explanation of a series of programmatic steps, which is like a summary of your logic. Throughout some of the examples in this book, you'll find that I sometimes break down the logic in a game in pseudocode before typing any actual ActionScript. It is easy to get too caught up in the syntax of programming and overlook a flaw in the logic, so it is almost always simpler to break down a problem in English before tackling it as actual code. Often my pseudocode will become the foundation for the names of my functions and properties.

Algorithm

An algorithm is nothing more than a series of instructions and decisions that define the solution to a problem. They are not code or language specific, and therefore they make sense in plain English. For instance, an algorithm could be as straightforward as the process that takes place when a program sorts a list of words by their length. Here is what that might look like in pseudocode:

```
for all in wordlist
        sort by length

sort by length (word A, word B)
        if A.length > B.length
                return B
        else
                return A
```

Procedural Programming

Many earlier programming languages, such as BASIC or Pascal, were what are known as *procedural* languages. You can think of them in the abstract as programming a list of tasks or subroutines. They can be executed in any order, but all the commands are driven by one main logic controller, sometimes referred to as the "main loop." The examples in this book will be a combination of procedural programming techniques and the next kind, object-oriented programming.

Object-Oriented Programming (OOP)

Unlike procedural programming, where the focus is on a set of tasks to be executed, OOP is centered around the concept of "objects" interacting with each other. OOP can be a very complicated subject to understand fully, but suffice it to say that each object is a self-contained entity that has defining properties, can send and receive messages from other objects, and can process its own internal logic. For example, in OOP, a person would be one object and his or her friend another. The persons will share some components, both being people, but they will also have characteristics unique to themselves. They communicate to each other through messages in a common language. Some of the aspects of ActionScript work in an OOP manner, and I will cover those at length later on in this book.

Design Patterns

Much is talked about these days with regard to design patterns in software engineering. There are many lengthy explanations, with whole books devoted to the subject in abstract. For the purposes of this book, think of a design pattern as the template for your code. It is the blueprint by which you can structure a game as you program it, particularly from an object-oriented approach. There are many accepted design patterns in the industry, some of which work well for Flash game development, and some that don't really have a place here. In Chapter 5, I'll discuss the most effective patterns I've found when working in Flash and how to implement them.

Classes

In OOP, classes are pieces of code that act as the building blocks of objects. You can think of them as templates from which all the objects used in an application are derived. A class defines all the properties and functions (known as *methods*) of an object. Using classes in Flash is important for a number of reasons. First of all, defining your code in classes requires you to put more planning into how you structure your game. This is a good thing; not having clearly defined blueprints leads to second guessing and duplication of work later on. If a carpenter went to build a house with no plans from the architect other than a single drawing, he would either quit or have to improvise continually along the way. The result would be a very inconsistent, possibly uninhabitable house. I'll cover class structure extensively later on, as most or all of our development will be centered on their use. In the mean time, here is an example of a simple class defining a player in a game.

```
package {

    import flash.display.MovieClip;

    public class Player extends MovieClip {

        public const jumpHeight:Number=10;//pixels
        public const speed:Number=15;//pixels per second

        public var health:Number=100;//percent
        public var ammo:int=20;//units

        public function Player() {
            //initialization
        }
    }
}
```

Not all the codes may make sense at this point, but hopefully you can see that we've just defined a player character with a predefined jumping height and movement speed, and variables for how much health and ammo he has. Granted, this little bit of code alone won't do anything, but it does create a foundation upon which to build more functionality and features.

Public, Protected, Private, and Internal

The four prefixes you can give to the properties and functions inside your classes, also known as *attributes*, define what items are available from one class to the next. All of them are documented in Flash's Help files, but here's a quick summary:

- Public methods and variables are accessible from anywhere and are the foundation for how classes interact with each other; when one class extends another, all public methods and variables are inherited.
- Protected methods and variables are accessible only from inside their class and are inherited.

- Private methods and variables are accessible only from inside their class and are *not* inherited.
- Internal methods and variables are accessible from all classes within their package.

There is one other attribute, known as *static*, which can work with any of the other four listed above. When a method or variable is static, there is only one copy of that item ever created and it is accessed through the class directly, not objects created from the class. In other words, a static property called "version" of the class Game would be accessed as Game.version. If you tried to access it from an instance of the game class, you would get an error.

Game-Specific Development Terms

Now, we move onto more interesting development terminology. This section covers concepts that we will be directly applying as we build games in future chapters.

Artificial Intelligence (AI)

AI refers generically to a set of logical decisions that a program can make to mimic human decision making. AI can be very simple (like having the computer move the paddle toward the ball in a game of Pong) or extremely complex (like having enemies duck for cover, understand when they're in danger, and react accordingly in Halo 2). For our purposes in this book, and because Flash would not be able to handle it otherwise, most of the AI we develop will be relatively uncomplicated.

Game Loop (or Main Loop)

This term generally refers to the main segment of code that determines the next course of action for a game based on input, AI, or some other arbitrary logic. It usually is nothing more than function calls to other pieces of logic and checking to see if certain conditions have been met (such as whether or not a player has won).

Here is an example of pseudocode describing a simple main loop from a game:

```
on enter frame
      move player
      move enemies
      check for collisions
      check for win or lose
```

In languages like C, a main loop is literally a coded loop (like a "while" or "for" loop) that runs until a condition is met. In some cases, this is also referred to as the *state machine* because it is the logic that determines which "state" the game is in, pregame, ingame, postgame, etc., and performs the corresponding functions. In ActionScript, it must be set up differently because a regular loop would lock up the Flash player waiting for the game to finish. Because of its animation heritage, Flash works in the context of frames, much like a movie. It has a frame rate, that is, number of frames per second that can be defined. When a frame passes, Flash updates the screen, making it the perfect time to perform logic. This can seem odd to developers used to other languages, but it quickly becomes second nature. I'll discuss game loops further later, as they will be the driving force behind our game code. In Chapter 16, I'll also cover explicit use of a finite state machine (one with a finite number of predefined states).

Game View

A game can take place from any number of views—often the genre of a game defines which view to use, but not necessarily. Many modern action games are first- or third-person views, in which you see the game world from your character's perspective or from just behind them. More casual action and adventure games utilize views from the side. Other genres such as strategy or racing may view the action from above. Part of what makes a game compelling and fun to play is the view you choose to employ. An action game with lots of fast movement and obstacles would be difficult and lackluster from a bird's-eye view, but from a first-person view, it has an immediacy and intensity that suspends the player's disbelief. Some game views work better in Flash than in others. Most any views involving a three-dimensional environment won't work well given Flash's technological performance limitations, but there are tricks and techniques I'll discuss later that can be used to "simulate" 3D in a convincing manner.

Scrolling

Often a game's environment extends beyond its viewable area. For instance, in Super Mario Brothers, the game world stretches on for some distance but only a small portion can be seen at a time. Because of this, the game scrolls back and forth horizontally with the player kept within the main viewable area. This same effect can be used both horizontally and vertically for driving games, strategy games, etc.

One technique to give a scrolling game environment more depth and look three-dimensional is to have multiple layers of the environment scroll at different speeds. This technique is known as *parallax scrolling*. Much like in the real world, objects that appear to be in the distance, such as mountains or buildings, can move at a slower speed than objects in the foreground. We'll discuss an example of side scrolling animation in Chapter 7.

Tile-Based Games

Some game environments can be broken up into a grid, such as a maze or strategy game. The artwork for the game can then be created as *tiles* of a predetermined size. Although it requires more work on the programming end to develop an efficient tile-mapping system, it opens up games to the creation of a level editor to allow end users to create custom maps. Starcraft and Warcraft are two strategy games that feature very well-implemented tile systems with editors. We'll look at a tile-based game engine in Chapter 14.

Flash Development Terms

Before I end this chapter, here are a handful of terms that I'll continue to refer to throughout the book. Understanding the way each of these items works will be key to architecting sound game code down the road. In Chapter 4, we'll dig into these concepts even more in-depth, but this will serve as a quick overview.

Stage

In Flash, the Stage is the main content area upon which everything is built. All other visual objects are placed on top of the Stage once they have been added to it. Think of it as your game's canvas.

Display Objects

A display object is any object that has a visual representation and can be placed onto the Stage. There are many different types of display objects in Flash; those most familiar to experienced developers will be Buttons, Sprites, and MovieClips. Even the Stage itself is a special kind of display object. The display objects all share some common traits; they all have an x, y, and z positions on screen, as well as scaling and rotation properties. Flash maintains lists of all the display objects on screen at any given time, making them easy to access and manipulate.

Events and Listeners

Events are the primary means of communication between objects in AS3. They are simply messages that objects in Flash can broadcast or *dispatch*. Any object that has been set up to listen for them receives events. They can be notifications of user input, information about external data being loaded, etc. Flash has many built-in events for common tasks, and it is entirely possible (and encouraged) to create new ones for custom objects like games. Events can carry with them any amount of data pertinent to their type, but all of them contain a few basic properties:

- A name or *type*
- A *target*: The object that dispatched the event
- A *current target*: The object that is currently listening to/handling the event

Events are an extremely powerful tool that we will make extensive use of in later chapters.

Packages

A package is a collection of classes and functions, used for organization purposes. Because there are so many different classes built into Flash, not to mention all the classes we will create, it is important to keep them grouped into logical collections. For instance, any classes in Flash that deal directly with display objects are in a package called flash.display. Most events are found in the flash.events package. The standard naming convention for a package is all lowercase. To use classes in a particular package, we use the *import* command to gain access to them:

```
package mypackage {

    import flash.display.MovieClip;

    public class MyClass() extends MovieClip {
    }
}
```

Author Time, Compile Time, and Runtime

These terms refer to the different stages when data in Flash is altered or verified. Throughout the book, I will make reference to things that happen inside the Flash-authoring environment—these are author-time events. Events or errors that occur during the process in which Flash creates a SWF file are known as compile-time events. Finally, runtime events occur once a SWF is running by itself.

You Can Wake Up Now

Whew. You made it! Although you may not fully understand the concepts I've presented here, you will start to see them in context in later chapters and they will start to click. Just think, now you can drop words like "polymorphism" in casual conversation and sound like a full-fledged nerd, er…software engineer!

2

THE BEST TOOL FOR THE JOB

Flash Back

Adobe (formerly Macromedia, originally FutureSplash) Flash has been around for a long time now and has come a long way from its humble beginnings. Starting in Flash 4, developers were given an impressive (at the time) set of scripting tools for what had previously been primarily a lightweight animation tool. The first games started to appear in Flash 4 and continued on into Flash 7 with the introduction of ActionScript version 2. Flash developers could now program in a fairly object-oriented way, albeit with some concessions and quirks.

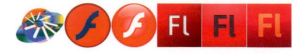

Fast forward to the newest release, Flash CS5.5. Since the version CS3, Flash users have had access to a powerful new version of the language: ActionScript 3 (AS3). Redesigned from the ground up, AS3 much more closely follows the standards and guidelines of modern programming languages (such as Java or C#), with a well-defined road map for new functionality in later versions. Flash CS4 introduced even more amazing new features to exploit games, such as basic 3D transformations, inverse kinematics (for realistic character manipulation), and an all-new animation toolset. In Flash CS5, Adobe delivered the ability to deploy to mobile platforms, a nice new version-control-friendly file format, and a number of nice workflow improvements to the IDE. CS5.5 has continued these improvements and fixed a number of stability and workflow issues with CS5.

Because Flash CS5/5.5 is our development environment of choice, AS3 is what we will cover in this book. If you're still making the transition from AS2 to AS3, or have yet to start, don't be discouraged. Where a programming convention or technique has changed significantly from AS2, I'll note it off to the side. AS3 can take some time to get used to, as some of its syntax has changed dramatically over AS2. However, before long, the changes will become second nature and you'll wonder how you ever got along without some of the best features of AS3. If you've already got AS3 development experience, you're a step ahead and should feel right at home in the language. And if you're coming from a game development background outside of Flash, you'll find some things familiar and some things very different from what you're used to.

The Case for Flash

The first thing to know about Flash is that it was never *designed* to develop games. There are a number of absent features that up to this day frustrate even a fan of Flash, like me. I'll further outline these strikes against it shortly, but first let's see what Flash has been doing.

Player Penetration

Roughly 98% of users on the Internet have some version of the Flash player, and usually within a year of a new version being released, about more than 80% have upgraded. The sheer size of the audience accessible to Flash developers is unprecedented in the games industry. Because it is available on machines running Windows, Mac OS, or Linux, it also bridges the gaps between all the major consumer platforms. Most game designers and developers that produce big-budget, retail titles have to settle for a much smaller demographic and have to make the conscious (and often costly) decision to include platforms other than their main target. This ubiquity is quickly spreading to other devices besides desktop computers; phones and tablets of all shapes and sizes are quickly adopting various flavors of Flash to enhance the user experience.

Flexibility

Flash is capable of being many things at once. You can create cartoons, postproduction effects, presentations, banner advertisements, all kinds of Web sites, Web and desktop-based applications, and, of course, games. Developers use Flash for any and all of these functions, and some may only be familiar with the one task they've learned to do. Because it is a very visual environment, Flash is also much more approachable to novices than most development packages. Unfortunately, this immense flexibility comes with a price. By not being designed specifically to do any one thing, Flash tends to take a very generic approach to its toolset and includes functionality that is useful to a number of applications, not just one niche. You can create additional tools, scripts, workflows, etc. that will help you in your particular task, but that is all up to your individual ingenuity. I'll cover some of these additions in a later chapter.

Speed to Market

Flash makes many tasks, which would require a great deal of code in other languages, much easier. Tasks, such as simple animation, basic playback of video and audio, are very streamlined in Flash and allow developers to get their products to market much faster than other solutions, with arguably more power. For instance, because of its animator heritage, Flash makes it very easy to display visuals on the screen. This may sound like an obvious statement, but compared with other development environments, this is a big advantage. C++, Java, and other languages render everything to the screen programmatically, so drawing a simple rectangle on screen requires many, many lines worth of code. All it takes in Flash is selecting the rectangle tool and placing one on the Stage, or writing a few lines of ActionScript. Flash takes care of rendering everything "under the hood," so you as the developer don't have to worry about it. Well, not too much anyway.

It Looks Good

While I'm sure we've all seen our share of hideous-looking Flash content over the years, some of the best-looking and most visually effective work I've ever seen on the Web was created in Flash. Because Adobe is such a design-centric company, they are equally concerned with tools that allow your work to look nice as they are with tools that make it run well. This has a tendency to frustrate both designers and developers from the hard-core ends of the spectrum, but it is exactly this marriage of technology and design that makes Flash unique.

Nobody's Perfect

For all that Flash has been doing, it is certainly not without its flaws when it comes to producing games. Don't get me wrong; the point of enumerating these flaws is so you as the developer will be aware of them, not to make a case against using Flash in the first place. The good news is that most of these downsides can be worked around with the right tools.

Flaw: The Code Editor

Although the Flash ActionScript editor has definitely evolved with the rest of the package over the years, it still lacks a handful of fundamental features that keep me from wholeheartedly recommending it as the coding tool of choice. The most aggravating omission is actually just a poor implementation: code hinting. As you write code, Flash tries to anticipate what you're going to want to type next and offers you a selectable list of options to try and speed up the process. The problem is that it only hints code when you get to the end of a word, so if you start to misspell a variable or function and don't receive a hint for it, you have no indicator of where you went wrong. With CS5, Adobe added the ability to introspect (look inside) custom classes, but the code editor is still inferior to both competing products.

Solution: Use an Additional Tool

The simplest solution (and the one I use) to this quandary is to use an additional application to handle all your ActionScript writing and use Flash for everything else. The two best options out there as of this writing are FlashDevelop, a free open-source code editor, and Flash Builder (formerly Flex Builder), Adobe's coding application based on Eclipse (another open-source editor). If you're on a tight budget or you don't intend to use the Flex framework to create Flash content, FlashDevelop is a great choice and what I use

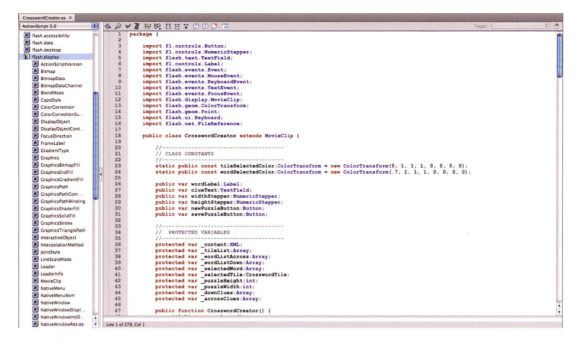

Figure 2.2 The built-in ActionScript editor in Flash CS5.

on a daily basis. If you want to create content in Flex, or you already own a copy of Flash Builder, it is an equally robust solution with some really great additional features such as "bookmarking" lines of code that you're actively working on. The extra step of switching back to CS5 to publish your SWF will pale in comparison with the amazingly good code hinting and other scripting enhancements these programs offer.

Flaw: Performance/Memory Management

As Flash games continue to grow in size and complexity, they require heftier hardware to run well. Most other modern development environments include tools for benchmarking a game's consumption of system resources such as CPU power and memory. Flash does not have any features like this, so it is harder to predict without real-world testing how well a game will perform on a range of systems or what its minimum requirements should be.

Solution: Use a Third-Party Solution or Roll Your Own

The Task Manager in Windows and the Activity Monitor on a Mac are great system-level tools that everyone has for monitoring the

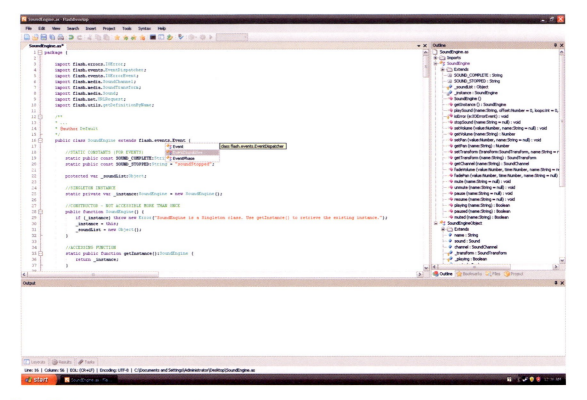

Figure 2.3 The free code editor FlashDevelop.

memory and CPU allocation of a given application. Unfortunately, there's no real way of getting the exact CPU usage of a Flash game because most ways of testing it involve running it inside another program, such as Flash CS5 or a Web browser. These programs can be running other tasks that consume system resources, and it's hard to know where the "container" ends and the game begins. That said, sometimes a simpler approach to this problem is more effective. Flash content is set to run at a predefined frame rate. If the player gets too bogged down with either code or whatever it's trying to render to the screen, it will bring the frame rate down. It is very easy to use a small component in your games to monitor the frame rate a particular machine is getting. You can then use this information during testing to determine the minimum level of machine required to play your game. Simply set a tolerance level (usually 85% or higher of a game's designed frame rate is acceptable) and then note which machines fall below this tolerance. Memory is a little more exposed in Flash, and there are ways of determining choke points in your game where memory usage gets out of hand, though it does require writing your own utility. This is done using the Sampler package, and we will discuss the

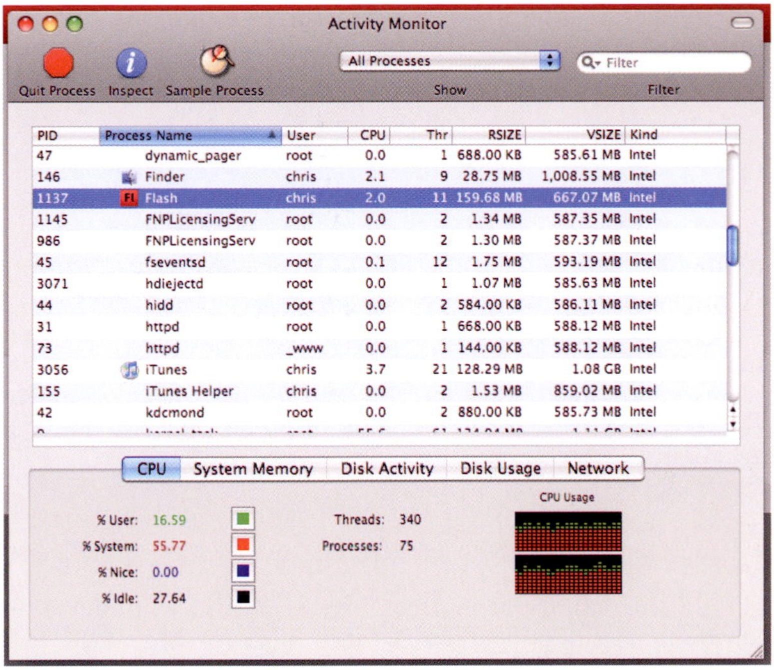

Figure 2.4 The Activity Monitor on a Mac.

package, the frame rate component, and other optimizations in Chapter 17.

Flaw: Debugging Content

Adobe greatly improved the debugger from AS2 to AS3, but it still has a number of flaws when it comes to working with larger projects. As projects get larger and larger and rely on external files, it becomes difficult to debug complex problems. You can remotely debug content running in a browser, but it is not always 100% stable, and any child SWFs that have not been exported for debugging (such as files that perhaps aren't under your control) won't have the necessary information needed to find the problem. I've had content that works fine within Flash and falls apart once it is on a Web server; the results of which are a bug hunt in the dark and a lot of head scratching. Needless to say this becomes even more frustrating with games, which rely so heavily on lots and lots of code.

Solution: Use Traces and Custom Tools

The single most helpful tool in debugging Flash content is the *trace* command; it has been around since Flash 4 and works essentially the same way it did those many years ago. All it does is display whatever information you tell it to at runtime. This becomes invaluable when attempting to watch something as complicated as a game execute in real time. You can have Flash trace out entire sequences of logic to determine where a bug is occurring, and you can use it to display messages to other developers who might be working with your code. Though traces work through the Output window in Flash, it is possible to capture them inside Firefox using an extension called FlashTracer and the debug version of the Flash player. Links to both can be found on this book's Web site. It works well for general debugging, but when a game works fine in Firefox but not other Web browsers it won't be of any help. Another option is to create even more robust tools you can use in any environment. We'll explore how to create and implement these tools in Chapter 17.

Flaw: Lack of Built-In Game Libraries and Tools

Up until this point, the shortcomings of Flash I've outlined are ones that affect developers of all kinds of Flash content. Because games tend to need more specific toolsets and lean toward the end of customized development, Flash lacks a number of code libraries that are readily available on other platforms. Examples of this type of library could be a physics simulator for doing realistic physical collisions or a sound manager that easily handles fading/panning sound effects in real time. These libraries must be written from scratch, which means they do not benefit from the speed boost of being implemented directly inside of Flash.

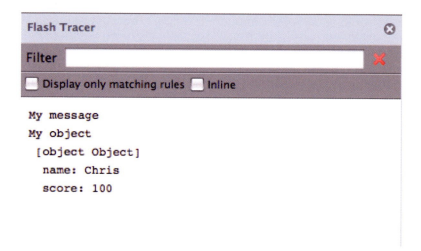

Figure 2.5 The FlashTracer extension running inside Firefox 3.

Solution: Write Your Own/Find Open Source Implementations

Unfortunately, until Adobe adds game-specific libraries to the Flash player, we are stuck building our own. Luckily, many developers in the Flash community are working to either port libraries such as these from other languages or write them from the ground up in ActionScript. Many of them are open-source projects that anyone can contribute to and improve. There are links to a number of these on this book's Web site, and we'll even explore one in Chapter 16 for doing 2D physics. To be fair to Adobe, there are a number of new capabilities coming in future versions of the Flash player that support such game-centric features as 3D hardware acceleration and control pads.

Stop Fighting It

Traditional game developers sometimes try to fight Flash's nature when they first make the transition, but often the best way to get the desired result out of Flash is to play to its strengths. Take, for example, a character in a game you want to animate depending on its state (idle, running, jumping, etc.). An artist has given you image sequences of each of these states. The character's state may be controlled by user input with the mouse or keyboard, or by AI. A conventional approach to this problem would be to write a script that updates the character with the correct frame of animation based on what the game is telling it to do. However, this requires the script to know how many animations there are, how many frames each animation is, and whether the animations loop or only play once. It also has to add the new image to the Stage and remove the old one. In addition, it adds overhead to any other code running in the game, which can become troublesome if you have many characters on screen at once.

This is a perfect example of an area where Flash shines over other game development tools. Because the environment is built around the concept of timelines and animation, you have a tremendous amount of flexibility when it comes to controlling player states, game states, or any other objects in your game that are more than a still image. The trick is in knowing what Flash does best and where you need to alter its behavior.

The flip side of the game development coin is that games *do* take code: often lots of it. A game built entirely around animation and fancy art would not likely be very interesting or reusable at a later date. Users who have previously built content in Flash with very little scripting may find themselves panicking at the sight of the amount of code we will encounter in later chapters. This is normal; take a deep breath. Development in Flash has always been a marriage of different disciplines, and games are possibly the ultimate example of this notion. Each task Flash has been designed to make easier has aspects that translate to game development.

Things Flash Was Built to Do

Animation versus Games

Possibly Flash's strongest use out of the box is as an animation application. Much like postproduction programs (like Adobe After Effects) or multimedia authoring tools (like Adobe Director), Flash is centered around the concept of a timeline. By default, events occur in a linear order, and objects on the timeline can have timelines nested within them. This allows for very complex animations to be built relatively quickly.

Consider for a moment an animation of a character walking. In order to look convincing, all the character's appendages would need to be separated and animated independently. Additionally, they need to move across the Stage so the character is not just walking in place. To move all the parts at the right speed would be very cumbersome and time consuming. Instead, with nested timelines, the walking sequence can be contained inside a clip that is moved at a different rate across the Stage. Although this concept is not at all new to anyone familiar with Flash, it speaks to a hierarchy that will prove very handy later.

Application versus Games

Though it started as an animation tool, Flash has grown into a number of other uses. Since the last few versions of Flash, Adobe has started marketing it (along with Adobe Flash Builder) to create what is referred to as Rich Internet Applications (RIAs). In brief, RIAs are applications that perform what were traditionally desktop-bound tasks from the Web. They can be anything from shopping cart applications to billing software to a weather forecast widget. To provide flexibility and to make rapid development of this kind of software possible, Adobe includes a number of components—prebuilt pieces of code designed for easy reuse. These components are items such as scrollbars, text boxes, radio buttons—devices you might see on a typical Web page in HTML. Although these components are great for RIAs, they serve little use directly in games (though I will show later how they can be very useful in tools that aid game development).

Arguably, a game *is* an application, since it performs certain functions based on user input. However, an application in the traditional sense is used to create something or deliver information; it receives input and gives output. The guidelines for producing an application like a word processor are very different from those used to create a game. This must be understood so as not to try to develop games like you would any number of other applications. Although applications tend to be used for productivity, games are used for entertainment, or in some cases, education. Games are experiential; they set a tone and create an environment for the user to have fun (or occasionally teach a concept or make a point).

Web Sites versus Games

Another area where Flash has flourished is in Web site development. I started using it at an ad agency, building branded Web sites for clients. Flash includes many features for working on the Web, including streaming support for content, the ability to load data from a variety of external sources, and of course, its browser-based player that places Flash content alongside anything else in HTML. Much like games, Web sites tend to be experiential, but they are also usually meant to be informative. When they are intended purely for entertainment, they can resemble a game on many levels, short of a score or accomplishment-based outcome. In fact, because of the similarities in how each type of content is produced, the line between Flash Web sites and games nested inside them has become very blurred.

Flash versus Traditional Game Development

Working with game developers coming from a background like C or Java has been an enlightening experience; many aspects of Flash's workflow that I take for granted are real stumbling blocks to outsiders. First of all, traditional game developers tend to keep all the code for a game and all the assets (art, sounds, video, etc.) separated completely. The code defines what assets are loaded and how they are used. In Flash, the standard way of managing assets is to import them into a single library file. To use an asset, you simply drag it onto the Stage and start working with it, or you give it a name that can be referenced later in the code. This interdependence of code and assets has often been of a criticism leveled against Flash by more traditionalist developers, as too heavily tying code to specific assets can render it hard to reuse later. Although there is some truth to this claim, there are ways (which we will cover later) to utilize the conveniences of Flash's asset management with largely reusable code.

Flash CS5 versus Flash Builder

Adobe Flash Builder is a tool for creating Flash content outside the CS5 environment, based on a preset framework of components and a layout language similar to HTML. It excels rapidly creating RIAs. It was conceived to try to win over developers to Flash from platforms such as Java or .NET. Flash CS5 stands out in terms of animation and motion graphics capabilities, whereas Flash Builder shines as a programmer tool. It is an outstanding code editor and has many features that make traditional programmers feel right at home, as it is based on the popular Eclipse IDE. The main reason I chose to cover Flash CS5 instead of Flash Builder as my development environment of choice is that I feel Flash is simply a better environment for making most games. There is no equivalent to be found in Flash Builder for Flash's animation toolset, but Flash can be augmented and used concurrently with other tools like Flash Builder to make up for its code shortcomings. The other reason to use Flash Builder is the Flex Framework, a set of classes for easily creating and skinning RIAs using a markup language called MXML, and it adds considerable bulk to your projects that in no way benefits game development. See above regarding alternate code editors for Flash.

The Best Tool for the Job

Perhaps one of Flash's greatest strengths is the fact that there are arguably so many ways to achieve the same end goal. There are definitely better and worse processes along the way, and in the chapters to come, I will outline what I've found works consistently and what to avoid.

A PLAN IS WORTH A THOUSAND ASPIRIN

I've built a lot of games in Flash over the years. Some have taken less than a week, and some have stretched on for several months. Whether they had huge budgets or practically no budget at all, one common thread has come back over and over again: the projects that were well planned out and clearly defined went smoothly and those that were not didn't. Planning a game thoroughly can be a tedious step, but it's much easier to change your mind or predict problems on paper than it is in the heat of development. How exactly you go about documenting and outlining your game is a matter of personal preference and a measure of just how anal-retentive you're willing to be. Here are some strategies that work for me.

Step 1

Be able to describe the game from a bird's-eye view in one to two sentences. Most any game idea, no matter how complex, can be summed up in this manner, even if it leaves out a lot of details. Being able to distill a game down to its most basic premise keeps you on track and acts as a "bigger picture" reminder of what you're building. If you work at a company building games for clients, you're likely dealing with marketing people, not gamers; they tend to appreciate this level of succinctness. For example, a summary of Pac-Man could be as follows:

Move through a maze collecting food while avoiding ghosts that are trying to kill you.

A game I once built for Mountain Dew's MDX drink would have a description like the following:

Drive a cab around the city at night and earn as much money as possible by delivering passengers to their destination in a timely manner. Pick up bottles of MDX for a speed boost.

Note the plug at the end outlining how the client's product will be showcased, which is very intentional.

Step 2

Outline or wireframe out the flow of all the game's screens. At its most basic, this includes the main menu, help panels, the core gameplay itself, and any results screen (client link, scoreboards, etc.). Note that this is not an outline of gameplay, but rather all the steps leading up to and surrounding it. Performing this step captures the user's progression through the game and helps identify touch points between different screens that might be tricky to integrate if you don't plan for them in advance. Figure 3.1 is an

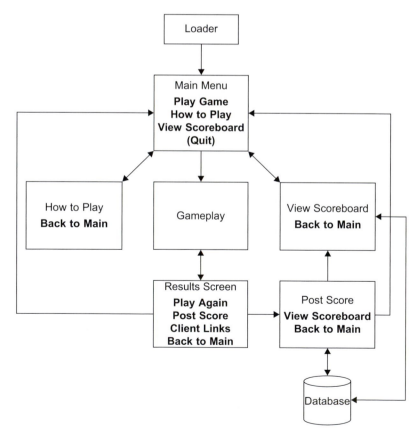

Figure 3.1 A very simple game flow, with a box representing each screen.

example of how a simple game with relatively few screens might look. In this example, bolded text represents buttons or links that can be clicked to access the associated screen. A simple wireframe like this is also often helpful to artists, reminding them of any necessary buttons, callouts, etc.

You might have noticed ( ) around the Quit button. This indicates that a Quit button is optional. It makes sense for games that a player will download to his/her computer, but for Web games in a browser, it doesn't really have a place. If you add the option to Quit from your game in a Web page, be sure you know where you're going to send them.

Step 3

With your description and basic wireframe in hand, it's time to outline the core mechanics that your game will utilize. This is more or less a feature list and can simply be in bulleted form, but the more detail you cover the less surprises you'll run into once you're in production. It allows you to break down the gameplay into its main pieces of functionality. These include components such as the game's rules, input mechanisms (such as the keyboard or mouse), movement and collision, and how the player's score or progress is determined and recorded. Once again referring back to Pac-Man as an example, here's how a mechanics list might read:

- Maze tile engine
  - Nothing can move through walls
  - Any open space is filled with food, power-ups, or bonus items (fruit)
  - One pass-through connecting left and right sides
  - Each tile has at least one and up to four possible connections to other tiles
- Collision management
  - Maze
  - Ghosts
  - Pick-ups
- Player
  - Keyboard input; directional arrows
  - Lives
    - Player has three lives at start of game
    - Player loses a life every time he is hit by a ghost without a power-up
    - When player dies, his progress in the current level is maintained
- AI
  - Normal behavior: chases player
  - Power-up behavior: avoids player

- Starts from a central location at beginning of level and is sent back there if caught by player in power-up mode
- Speed increases with each successive level
- Pick-ups
  - No pick-ups regenerate until the start of a new level or a new game
  - Food
    - All food pick-ups must be collected to win a level
    - Food contributes 10 points per item to the player's score
  - Power-ups
    - Each level of a game has four power-ups
    - Eating a power-up makes player invincible for five seconds and allows them to eat ghosts
  - Bonus food items
    - Appear on a random interval, one at a time, and only stay in place for a few seconds before disappearing
    - Contributes 100 points per item to the player's score
- Scoring
  - Pick-ups and eating ghosts contribute to overall score
  - Final score is used as ranking mechanism for scoreboards
- Winning criteria
  - Player wins a level when he picks up all food
  - Game continues until player runs out of lives, getting successively harder with each level (see AI)

As you can see, all the familiar features of Pac-Man have been outlined here, as well as their relationships to each other. Note that this list is not typically client facing, but in projects with a short timeline, it can be wise to put it in front of a client to get sign-off *before* you begin production. This can give you leverage when that last-minute client change comes down the line and threatens to derail the project. It also gets the client empowered and makes them feel like they have a say in the process, but at a point when a change in direction isn't catastrophic.

Step 4

Build an asset list. Whether you're working with an artist or you're building the entire game yourself, it's a best practice to make a list of all the art, sound, and copy (or text) assets you'll need. Working through this list after Step 3 is important because the game mechanics and any specific art pieces and animations you need should be fresh in your head. Following the Pac-Man theme, here is a sample asset list. You can reference your wireframe from Step 2 to help you remember what assets you'll need for the nongameplay screens.

- Game Animations
  - Pac-Man
    - Movement

- Power-up
- Death
  - Ghosts
    - Movement
    - Retreating movement
- Static Game Art
  - Maze walls
  - Food
  - Power-ups
  - Bonus food
  - Point displays
- Nongame Screens
  - Loader artwork
  - Main Menu
    - Title artwork
    - Play Button (three states: up, over, and down)
    - How to Play Button ("")
    - View Scoreboard Button ("")
  - How to Play
    - Rules copy
    - Rules artwork
    - Back to Main Button (three states: up, over, and down)
  - View Scoreboard
    - Scoreboard table artwork
    - Back to Main Button (three states: up, over, and down)
  - Results Screen
    - Score display artwork
    - Play Again Button (three states: up, over, and down)
    - Post Score Button ("")
    - Back to Main Menu Button ("")
  - Post Score Screen
    - Confirmation message
    - View Scoreboard Button (three states: up, over, and down)
    - Back to Main Menu Button ("")
- Audio
  - Sound effects
    - Eating food sound
    - Eating power-up sound
    - Eating bonus food sound
    - Eating ghost sound
    - Ghost attacking Pac-Man/death sound
    - Level begin sound
    - Level end sound
    - Game over sound
  - Music
    - None, it's Pac-Man!

You probably noticed that nothing in this list defines *how* any of these assets should look/sound, but this list defines just the objects and events they are associated with. What the assets look like should largely be irrelevant to you as the developer, provided they meet your or your company's quality standards and any technical requirements, which leads us to the next step.

Step 5

Make a list of technical requirements for your game. This will include two sets of criteria: (1) the system requirements of the end user playing the game and (2) any server-side requirements your game needs in order to function, such as a database and any scripts necessary to connect to it. For a simple game, these requirements should be fairly succinct, and if you are building the game for clients that are going to host it themselves, this list may have been provided to you entirely.

Let's start with the system requirements for the game's audience. Unless the game is an exact copy of another title you've already released, you probably won't know the exact machine requirements necessary to run the game smoothly. Any estimates you make will be vetted for accuracy during the testing process. At the very least, you can set a screen resolution and minimum version of the Flash player that is capable of running the game. One note about the Flash player is that Adobe now periodically releases minor updates that add features in addition to fixing bugs. As a result, you must be cognizant of any cutting-edge features that might necessitate a particularly patched version of the player.

Here is an example:

Flash player major version: 10

Flash player minor version: 10.0.2.13

Screen resolution: 1024 × 768 or higher

Connection speed: DSL or higher

RAM: 512 MB+

CPU: 1.5 GHz+

These are fairly modest requirements for Flash games on the Web. Obviously during the testing and QA (quality assurance) process, you can adjust your initial numbers as necessitated by the game's feature set. Games with a lot of motion and many objects moving on the screen at once are obviously going to need more computing horsepower than a single screen with static game pieces. Sometimes a feature can be compelling enough to justify a trade-off in higher system requirements and thus a reduced audience. This decision must not be made lightly, however. For instance, more robust AI that makes the game more enjoyable but taxes the CPU is more justifiable than a bunch of real-time special effects, such as shadows, glows, etc., which look nice but don't add any real gameplay value. You and your client's mileage may vary, but experience has shown me that the lower you set your technical barrier to entry the more people will play your game.

Next come the server-side requirements for your game. For simple games with no data that needs to be saved from session to session, this is probably as simple as having an HTML page to house your game's SWF file. More and more, however, players expect more robust functionality out of games on the Web. The ability to save their high scores and even maintain a profile for larger games is very popular, as it gives players bragging rights when they do well and often affords some level of personalization.

Depending on whether you're doing the back-end integration (server-side scripts, database work, etc.) or you work with a team, this list of requirements may look very different. If you work at a company with a team that already has a database infrastructure in place, your requirements may look something like the following:

Methods Required

Save score

Parameters: score—number, initals—string, security hash—string

Returns 0 for success, −1 for error

Load score table

Parameters: size—number

Returns list of initials and scores, highest to lowest

Based on the wireframe example, we have created throughout the previous steps, these two methods (or functions) are all you will need to post a player's score and load a table of high scores. The first method, saving the score, would receive the player's score, their initials, and a security hash (which is covered in-depth in the online bonus chapter "On Your Guard"). The second method, used when viewing the high-score table, would receive a table size (like 10, 20, etc.) for the number of results to return. Regardless of whether your team works in PHP, .NET, or some other back-end language, this simple listing will let them know what code they need to expose to Flash in order for the game to perform its operations.

If you will be building these scripts yourself, and don't already have a system in place for doing so, you'll need to set up a database structure to house all your game's data. If you are new to this area of development but want to learn, I recommend starting with PHP. It is free, it is fast, and it is relatively easy to pick up. There are also many resources in books and on the Web for how to save data into a database with PHP.

A BETTER PHP

If you're already familiar with PHP, I would highly recommend looking into AMFPHP; it allows you to send binary data in Flash's native format rather than name/value strings. Because of this, it allows you to send and receive typed results (i.e., a number comes back as a number, not as a string), and the chunks of data are much smaller and faster. There are examples of using AMFPHP in Chapter 15 and Appendix D.

Step 6 (Optional)

Diagram your classes using a UML Modeler. UML stands for Unified Modeling Language and is the standard for planning complex software through a visual process. Basically, it involves visually showing the hierarchy of the classes you intend to create alongside each other, with all the publicly available properties and methods listed along with what they accept and return. You may be wondering, "Why would I want to do that? Why can't I just get started typing code and build it as I go?" The answer is simple; a UML diagram takes your whole project into account in a single document. It is much easier to make changes and correct inconsistencies and confusion in naming conventions from this bird's-eye view than once you've got a dozen ActionScript files open and you're trying to remember what the name of the method you're trying to call from one to the next. You can keep the diagram handy as you work, and there are programs available, which will take your completed diagram and turn it into actual ActionScript class files complete with all the methods and properties ready to be used! Figures 3.2 and 3.3 demonstrate how a visual layout can become a set of ready-to-use class templates.

Now you're probably wondering, "Well, if this step is so important and helpful, why do you have it listed at the end as optional?" There are a couple of reasons for this. One reason is that for very simple games on a tight timeline, a full-blown UML diagram may yield low returns on time that could be better spent just knocking out the code. If you're pretty certain your game will only rely on a couple of class files, UML is probably overkill. I very rarely use it in my day-to-day work, but on occasion, it has been helpful. Second, although many UML tool options exist, with a large number of free offerings, I have yet to find one that I wholeheartedly recommend for Flash development. Well, I take that back. The best UML tool for ActionScript I've ever used is Grant Skinner's gModeler. It is streamlined especially for this use; it was created in Flash so it will run on any OS that supports the Flash player, and it will generate code, as well as documentation. Unfortunately, it is several years old and will only generate up to ActionScript 2 code, leaving AS3 developers like us in the cold. If you're still doing work in AS2, I *highly* recommend using it to model your classes.

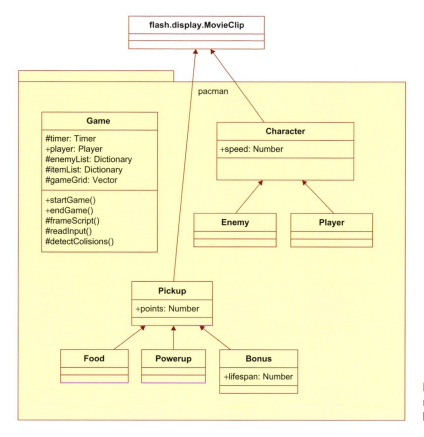

Figure 3.2 A UML diagram representing a game hierarchy.

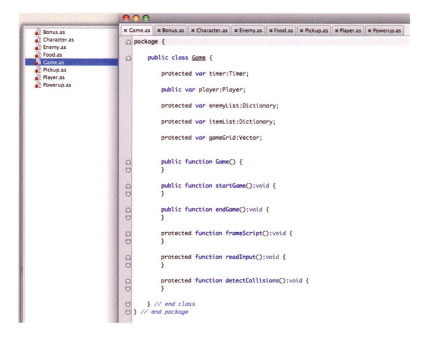

Figure 3.3 The generated classes that resulted from the UML diagram in Fig. 3.2.

Though I haven't found my equivalent for "gModeler AS3," I've found the free StarUML (www.staruml.com) to be a solid title and fairly straightforward. Also, an Adobe employee has created a tutorial showing how to generate stub code from your diagrams much the same way gModeler did. These resources are available on www.flashgamebook.com.

I know this seems like a lot of steps just to get started if you're not used to this level of planning. Trust me, it will not only get easier and more natural as you figure out what works best for you, but you will find that less surprises pop up down the road. Now that you have your plan firmly in hand, it's time to open that copy of Flash.

A quick review of the planning steps:

- One-two sentence description
- A game screen wireframe/flow
- List of game mechanics
- List of assets: art, animation, sound, video, and copy
- Technical requirements
- UML class diagrams

4

//COMMENTS FTW!

Real-World Flash Game Development, Second Edition.

In this chapter, we'll cover best practices to use when programming in ActionScript 3. This includes smart class utilization, using the event model, error handling, and data structures. We'll also cover a number of idiosyncrasies of Flash, which tend to trip up developers coming to Flash from other languages.

Fair Warning

It's worth mentioning that this chapter (like the rest of this book) assumes a familiarity with either ActionScript 1 or 2 or another programming language. If you have no idea what objects, variables, or functions are or have never used Flash at all, you will be lost very quickly. Some familiarity with ActionScript 3 is ideal since we'll also be moving pretty quickly through a wide variety of topics, but it's not absolutely necessary. The documentation that comes with Flash expounds on all of these topics, so if you find yourself confused or want to learn more, you can check out those examples. You can also always ask questions on any chapter in this book at www.flashgamebook.com. If you're an experienced AS3 user, be patient—we'll get through the basics as quickly as possible and move on to the fun stuff!

Part 1: Classes

As we learned in Chapter 1, classes are essentially the blueprints for objects in ActionScript (and many other object-oriented programming languages). They define the properties that are inherent to that object, as well as the methods that determine how that object functions on its own and as part of a larger context. When you create an object from a class, that object is known as an *instance* of that class. Every instance of a class may have different specific values for its properties, but they all share the common architecture, so Flash knows that all instances of a certain class will behave in the same way. In its simplest form, *instantiation*, or creation, of an object looks like the one shown below in ActionScript.

```
var myObject:MyClass = new MyClass();
```

As a standard naming convention, classes should start with a capital letter and then use InterCaps, or "CamelCase" from then on, denoting the start of a word with a capital letter. CamelCase makes names in code much easier to read—take, for example, the longest class name currently used in the Flash CS5 code base:

```
HTMLUncaughtScriptExceptionEvent
```

While this is something of an extreme example, note that it is much easier to read than:

```
htmluncaughtscriptexceptionevent
```

Packages

A set of classes with categorically similar or related functionality can be grouped together in packages. Classes within the same package can reference each other without any special code, whereas classes in different packages must *import* each other with a line of code, similar to the following:

```
import flash.display.MovieClip;
```

Note that in this case, the MovieClip class is inside the display package, which is part of the larger flash package. The standard naming convention for packages is all lowercase letters, which differentiates them from classes visually. Packages are represented in the file system as a series of nested folders. In the previous example, if the MovieClip class were not an included part of the Flash Player, you could find the MovieClip.as file inside a folder called display, inside another folder called flash.

Classes as Files

To create a class, you simply open Flash or a text editor like Flash-Develop and create a basic framework. All AS3 classes must have this minimal amount of code in order to function.

```
package flash.display {
        public class MovieClip {
        }
}
```

Note that the names in bold are the custom package and class names of your choice. All classes need a class definition wrapped by a package definition, placed in a folder structure that matches the package hierarchy. However, this class won't do anything, so next we'll cover adding properties and methods.

Constructors

Every class has a constructor, even if it does nothing and is not explicitly defined. It is the function, with the same name as the class, which is called when a new instance of the class is created. In the case of our last example, even if we leave it out, Flash adds the following to the class:

```
package flash.display {
        public class MovieClip {
                public function MovieClip() {
                }
        }
}
```

The constructor allows us to run any initialization code that the new instance might need, or it can do nothing, depending on how your class is to be used.

Constants, Variables, and Methods

A class without any data or functionality inside it is not of very much use, so we can define variables or properties, of the class that will store information, and methods, or functions that will perform actions. I'm going to assume you already know how to use variables and methods, from either earlier versions of Action-Script or another language. Constants are entirely new to AS3 but are not a complicated concept. Essentially, they are variables that can only be assigned a value once. When you declare a constant or variable, it is best to give it a *type*, which tells Flash which class to use as the blueprint for that variable. Below are few examples:

```
const myInt:int = -3; //WILL ALWAYS BE -3 AND CANNOT BE MODIFIED
var myBoolean:Boolean = true;
var myString:String = "Hello World";
var myObject:Object = new Object();
```

Giving a variable a type also saves memory because Flash knows the maximum amount of memory it needs to store an instance of a specific class. If you don't type a variable, as in the following example, Flash must reserve a larger amount of memory to accommodate any possible value.

```
var myMystery:* = "?";
```

Once you assign a value to an untyped variable, it *becomes* typed from then on, so attempts to change its type (like you could in earlier versions of ActionScript) will result in runtime errors, such as the following example.

```
var myMystery:* = "?";
myMystery = 5; //WILL CAUSE A RUNTIME ERROR
```

What's worse, the above example *won't* be caught during compilation, so it might get missed until your game is deployed live for real users. Unless absolutely unavoidable (like an instance where you simply don't know what will be assigned to a variable), *always* type your variables. You'll create far less headaches down the road for yourself.

When you define methods, there are similar practices to follow. It is best practice to define what parameters a method will receive and what, if anything, it will return.

```
function myFunction (myParam:String):void {
      //COMMANDS HERE
}
```

In this example, the method accepts a single parameter, myParam, and returns nothing. If you have a case where a method needs to accept an unknown number of parameters, a slightly different syntax can be used.

```
function myFunction (...params):void {
      //COMMANDS HERE
}
```

Here, the single parameter, params, is prefixed by three dots. This signifies to Flash that the parameter should be treated like an Array of values, so getting to each parameter that was passed must be done through array syntax:

```
function myFunction (...params):void {
      trace(params[0]);
}
```

It's important to remember that when accepting a variable number of parameters, type checking during compilation will not catch any attempts to pass invalid data to the method. In this instance, it's best to do some type of manual checking and generate errors at runtime. We'll cover more on errors shortly.

```
function myFunction (...params):void {
      for (var i:int = 0; i < params.length; i++) {
            if (!(params[i] is DisplayObject)) {
                  throw new ArgumentError("Only DisplayObjects
                   can be used in myFunction.");
            }
      }
}
```

The keyword *void* is used to denote a function that does not return anything (and will cause an error if it attempts to), and all other types that variables can use can also be used here. If you leave off the return value altogether, you can opt to return something or not, depending on some piece of internal logic. However, as a best practice, a method should always declare what it will return as it helps to catch errors and maintains consistency.

Getter and Setter Methods

There are two special types of methods you can create when you want to expose a variable outside its class but want to control how the variable is used. They are known as accessor—or getter and setter—methods, and they are called like normal variable assignments but act like functions underneath. You can use them to make read-only variables or to perform actions on a value before it is set as a variable. There are a few rules to follow when using these special methods: getter methods never accept any parameters and must specify a return type and setter methods may only have one parameter and never return anything. Let's look at a couple of examples in a single script.

```
package {
    public class MyClass {
        protected var _maxNameLength:int = 8;
        protected var _name:String;
        protected var _lives:int = 3;

        public function get name():String {
            return _name;
        }
        public function set name(value:String):void {
            name = value.substr(0,maxNameLength);
        }

        public function get lives():int {
            return _lives;
        }
    }
}
//OUTSIDE CLASS
var myInstance:MyClass = new MyClass();
myInstance.name = "CHRISTOPHER";
trace(myInstance.name); //OUTPUTS "CHRISTOP";
trace(myInstance.lives); //OUTPUTS 3;
myInstance.lives = 10; //THROWS ERROR
```

The name getter and setter functions return the protected value of _name, which would otherwise be inaccessible, and it also forces any attempts to assign a value to the _name property to a fixed length of eight characters. The lives getter is an example of a read-only property—there is no accompanying setter function. Any attempts to set the value will cause an error. This is very useful when you need to use values inside the class but also want external classes to be able to read the value.

**The standard convention for variable and method names is to start lowercase and then use CamelCase for all subsequent words in the name. There is some debate over how to delineate public variables from protected, private, or internal. My preference is to follow Adobe's convention, which is to use an underscore ("_") at the beginning of the name of any property that is not expressly public. Doing so allows you to use getter and setter methods like the previous example, where _name was the protected variable and name was used for the pair of methods. This yields continuity in your naming and makes your code easier for others (and yourself) to follow.

AN ALTERNATE NAMING CONVENTION

Since writing the first edition of this book, I've had the privilege of working directly with some game industry veterans and picked up some new patterns and conventions that they commonly use. While I think there's still value in Adobe's method if you're a beginner or if you're *only* working in Flash, I wanted to mention this alternate convention because it is particularly helpful if you're intending to try to leverage code across platforms outside AS3. It's also what I now use as my standard and believe it is only fair to disclose that. Basically, it does not differentiate between private and public properties but rather prefixes them all with "m" as *members* of a class. There's no real reason for public or private members to have different conventions because the compiler will catch illegal access of either kind—it's not like you can really mess it up. Also, it has the added benefit of grouping all member variables in a class alphabetically when using code hinting. For instance, a player's speed would be mSpeed rather than _speed, regardless of being public, protected, or private. Method names and names of accessors are still used as normal, but method parameters are all prefixed with an underscore so as to denote them clearly inside the method as temporary and local. You could use something other than a prefix—some people like "p" instead. Don't use a dollar sign "$" like in some other languages; an Adobe engineer has mentioned in his blog that this could cause problems in certain circumstances because it conflicts with internal Flash Player naming. The last example in Chapter 16 will use these more recent conventions, so you can see how they compare to Adobe's standard and decide if you prefer it. Ultimately, the important thing to remember when working on any project is to pick a method that makes sense and stick with it consistently.

Class Identifiers

Classes can use few different identifiers to determine how they are exposed to other classes. The four available identifiers are as follows:

- *Public*: The public attribute defines that a class can be accessed or used from anywhere else.
- *Internal*: The internal attribute allows a class to only be accessed by other classes in the same package—by default, classes are internal unless specified public, so internal does not actually have to be used.
- *Dynamic*: If a class is dynamic, it can have properties and methods added to it at runtime—by default, classes are static and can only use the properties and methods defined inside themselves.
- *Final*: If a class is final, it cannot be extended by another class—more on this shortly will be discussed when we cover inheritance—by default, classes can be extended and are *not* final.

All of these identifiers can be used with each other, except that public cannot be used with internal. Similarly, variables and methods can have their own set of identifiers used to define how they are exposed outside the class.

- *Public*: Like the class attribute, this denotes that a variable or method can be accessed from anywhere, including outside the class.
- *Internal*: Also similar to classes, this denotes that a variable or method can only be accessed from inside its package.
- *Private*: The private attribute prevents a variable or method from being accessed outside its individual class.
- *Protected*: A protected attribute is pretty much like private, except that protected variables and methods can also be accessed by classes that extend the current class (more on inheritance shortly).
- *Static*: If a method or variable is static, it is part of the class and not instances of the class, meaning there is only ever one value or functionality defined, and it is accessed via the class name rather than an instance (i.e., MovieClip.staticVar rather than myMovieClip.staticVar)—note that static properties and methods are not inherited by subclasses.

The first four attributes in this list cannot be used with each other, as they would conflict, but *static* can be used in combination with any one of them.

Inheritance and Polymorphism

These two concepts were touched on in brief in Chapter 1, but we'll expound on them a little more here. When you need to create a class that has the same functionality as another class, but needs some additional properties or methods, a good option to save time and coding is to extend the first class to a new class, known as a *sub-class*. All public and protected methods and variables that are not static will be available to the new class. To clarify, any static properties of the parent, or *superclass*, must be prefaced with the class name (as in the example below). In addition, any internal methods or variables will be available to the subclass if it is in the same package as its superclass. To illustrate, let's look at an example below:

```
package {
        public class SuperClass {
                static public var className:String = "SuperClass";
        }
}


package {
        public class SubClass extends SuperClass {
                public function SubClass() {
                        trace(SuperClass.className); //OUTPUTS
                          "SuperClass"
                        trace(className); //THROWS ERROR
                }
        }
}


//FROM OUTSIDE EITHER CLASS
trace(SuperClass.className); //OUTPUTS "SuperClass"
trace(SubClass.className); //THROWS ERROR
```

Occasionally, you'll need to change the functionality of a method in a subclass from the way it behaves in the superclass. This change in functionality through inheritance is known as *polymorphism*. You can do this using the *override* keyword before the beginning of the method, albeit with a number of caveats.
- Only methods may be overridden; no properties
- Only public, protected, and internal methods may be overridden
- Internal methods may only be overridden in subclasses in the same package as the superclass
- The new overriding method must match the composition of the original method, with the same parameters and return value
Let's look at an example.

```
package {
        class SuperClass {
                public var name:String = "SuperClass";
                protected var _number:Number = 5;
                internal var _packageNumber:Number = 7.5;
                private var _secretNumber:Number = 10;
```

```
                        public function helloWorld():void {
                                trace("HELLO WORLD");
                        }
                }
        }

package {
        class SubClass extends SuperClass {
                public function SubClass() {
                        trace(name); //OUTPUTS "SuperClass"
                        trace(_number); //OUTPUTS 5;
                        trace(_packageNumber); //OUTPUTS 7.5
                        helloWorld(); //OUTPUTS "HI WORLD";
                        super.helloWorld(); //OUTPUTS "HELLO WORLD";
                        trace(_secretNumber); //THROWS ERROR;
                }

                override public function helloWorld():void {
                        trace("HI WORLD");
                }
        }
}
```

When SubClass traces out properties it has inherited from SuperClass, they stay intact, with the exception of the private variable. Also, when helloWorld is run from SubClass, it traces a different message than when run from SuperClass. That said, there is a way to get at the SuperClass implementation of helloWorld through the use of the *super* keyword. Super returns a reference to the superclass of the current class, allowing you access to any methods you may have overridden.

Interfaces

One of the most commonly misunderstood (including by myself for a long time) aspects of object-oriented programming (OOP) is the concept of *interfaces*. It is confusing for a few reasons, not the least of which is the confusion of an OOP interface with a graphical user interface (like operating systems provide). An interface does not contain any code, outside of declaring the public methods that a class will use and what each will accept as parameters and what each will return. If a class is like a blueprint of the specific directions for creating a new instance of that class, an interface is like a checklist for that blueprint to make sure it adheres to a certain specification. Perhaps the best way to understand how an interface is structured is to see one in code.

```
public interface IEventDispatcher {
    function addEventListener(type:String, listener:Function,
      useCapture:Boolean=false, priority:int=0,useWeakReference:
      Boolean = false):void;
    function removeEventListener(type:String, listener:Function,
      useCapture:Boolean=false):void;
    function dispatchEvent(event:Event):Boolean;
    function hasEventListener(type:String):Boolean;
    function willTrigger(type:String):Boolean;
}
```

Note the differences between an interface and a class. Interfaces are always public or internal, just like their class counterparts, but none of the methods have any attributes because they are all assumed to be public. Interfaces cannot include variables, but they can include getter and setter methods, which can substitute for variables.

At this point, you might very well be asking, "Why would I ever bother to use an interface when I can simply extend a class to make sure all the subclasses have the available methods?" The answer is that unlike some other languages, classes in Flash cannot inherit from multiple superclasses. This poses a problem when you need to extend one class but include functionality from another class in a different inheritance hierarchy.

A good example of a situation like this is the *IBitmapDrawable* interface that is part of the Flash display package. When you want to draw something to a BitmapData object, you can use either another BitmapData object, or a DisplayObject. In order to keep just any object from being passed to the draw method, both BitmapData and DisplayObject implement an interface called IBitmapDrawable. This interface actually doesn't do anything but enforce this compatibility between two classes that have nothing to do with each other. The draw method can then look like the following:

```
public function draw(source:IBitmapDrawable, matrix:Matrix = null,
  colorTransform:ColorTransform = null, blendMode:String = null,
  clipRect:Rectangle = null, smoothing:Boolean = false):void
```

When an object is passed for the *source* parameter, Flash checks to see if the object implements the IBitmapDrawable interface and can throw an error to let the developer know. Here is another example of a class implementing an interface while extending an unrelated class.

```
package {
        import flash.events.IEventDispatcher;
        import flash.events.EventDispatcher;
```

```
import flash.events.Event;
import flash.geom.Rectangle;

public class RectangleDispatcher extends Rectangle
  implements IEventDispatcher {
        private var _dispatcher:EventDispatcher;

        public function RectangleDispatcher() {
                _dispatcher = new EventDispatcher(this);
        }

        override public function set width(value:Number) {
                super.width = value;
                dispatchEvent(new Event(Event.CHANGE));
        }

        override public function set height(value:Number) {
                super.height = value;
                dispatchEvent(new Event(Event.CHANGE));
        }

        public function addEventListener(type:String,
          listener:Function, useCapture:Boolean=false,
          priority:int=0,useWeakReference:Boolean =
          false):void {
                _dispatcher.addEventListener(type, listener,
                    useCapture, priority, useWeakReference);
        }

        public function removeEventListener(type:String,
          listener:Function, useCapture:Boolean=false):void {
                _dispatcher.removeEventListener(type,
                    listener, useCapture);
        }

        public function dispatchEvent(event:Event):Boolean{
        _dispatcher.dispatchEvent(event);
        }

        public function hasEventListener(type:String):Boolean{
                return _dispatcher.hasEventListener(type);
        }

        public function willTrigger(type:String):Boolean{
                return _dispatcher.willTrigger(type);
        }
    }
  }
```

In this example, the class being extended is Rectangle, which has no ties to the EventDispatcher hierarchy. By implementing the IEventDispatcher interface and creating an instance of the Event-Dispatcher class, we can enjoy both the functionality of a Rectangle and an EventDispatcher. When the width or height of this special rectangle changes, it will dispatch an event to anything that is listening. We will cover more on events in an upcoming section.

So, the question now is probably "When should I use interfaces?" Unlike some OOP proponents who believe the answer is "always," I believe it really depends on the breadth of the game or application you are building. Sometimes, in quick games where I am the sole developer, I prefer inheritance because I usually have the luxury of defining my entire inheritance chain and I don't have to work within a preexisting framework. I find interfaces to be most helpful when working with other developers (particularly those at other companies where we're not eager to share specific code with each other) because we can agree upon an interface for our common class elements and integration of our respective components is far more likely to work without a hitch as a result. Interfaces are also extremely useful in creating flexible, reusable game engines for more complex games, as we will see in later chapters. In the end, interfaces are just a tool, and like any tool, it should be used when called for and left alone the rest of the time. In fact, in the mobile examples, we'll look at toward the end of this book, where performance is a key factor, and interfaces are often *not* the answer.

Linking Classes to Assets in Flash

A common staple of my game development (and arguably one of the biggest advantages of developing games in Flash) is the ease with which you can link a Flash class to an item in your FLA library. Any item in your library can have an associated class linked to it, but the ones you will probably use the most are the DisplayObject sub-classes Sprite and MovieClip. First, how Flash creates classes for library items should be understood.

If you set the linkage property of a symbol in the library, it has a class created for it when the SWF is compiled, regardless of whether or not one was explicitly defined. For instance, take a Sprite in an FLA library named "square," with a simple blue square inside it. Because the symbol is not a Sprite directly but rather an extension of Sprite, a new class with the name "square" will be created at compile time that extends Sprite and looks like the following:

```
package {
    import flash.display.Sprite;
    public class square extends Sprite {}
}
```

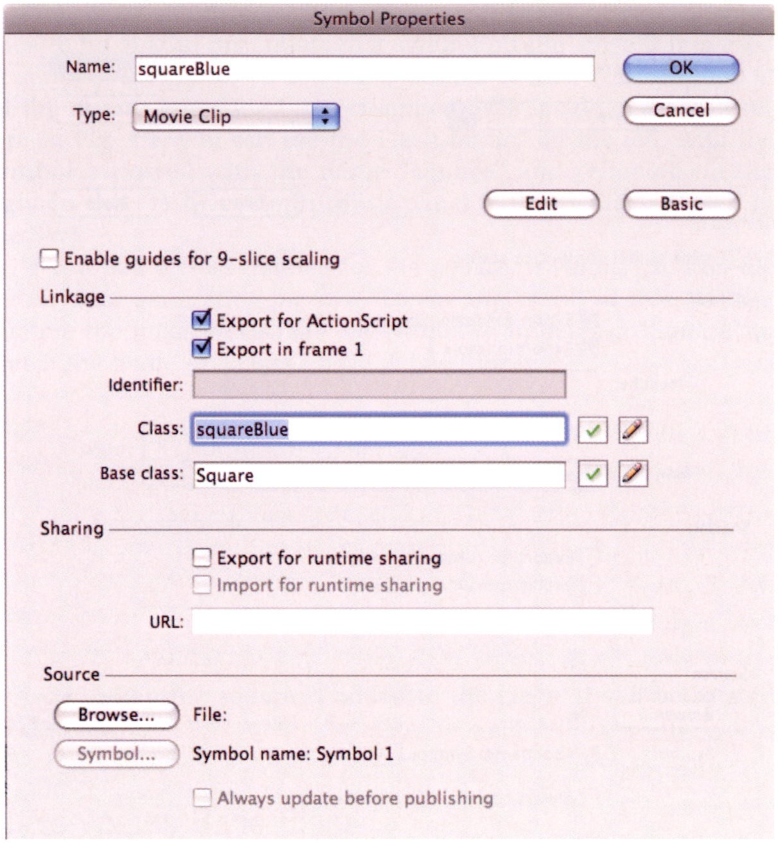

Figure 4.3 The base class can be set to use a class for multiple symbols with different assets.

name like you would any other. For instance, if I had a document class for the previous example, it might look something like the following:

```
package {
        import flash.display.Sprite;
        public class ClassesExample extends Sprite {
                public function ClassesExample() {
                        var blue:Square = new squareBlue();
                        addChild(blue);
                        var green:Square = new squareGreen();
                        addChild(green);
                }
        }
}
```

You can use it like a normal class because when Flash compiles the SWF, it *will* be a normal class, just as though you'd written it yourself.

getDefinitionByName and Casting

Suppose you needed to instantiate a series of symbols or classes that followed a numeric sequence, say for the purposes of our example "square1" through "square10." It would be very tedious to have to instantiate them one at a time and create a lot of extra codes. It would probably look something like the following:

```
var square:Square = new square1();
addChild(square);
square = new square2();
addChild(square);
...
square = new square10();
addChild(square);
```

Luckily, Flash gives us the ability to "look up" a class by its name. In the flash.utils package, there is a method called *getDefinitionByName*, which accepts said name as a string parameter.

```
for (var i:int = 1; i <= 10; i++) {
        var squareClass:Class = getDefinitionByName("square" + i)
          as Class;
        var square:Square = new squareClass();
        addChild(square);
}
```

It returns a generic object that is a reference to the class, if it exists. That object can then be converted to a class through an operation known as *casting*. Casting is the process of telling ActionScript to treat one object like a different kind of object. It is most often used to treat a subclass like its superclass, which is known as "safe" casting because all of the functionality will be guaranteed to carry over from the superclass. An example of this would be with Sprite and MovieClip. MovieClip extends Sprite, so it is *safe* to cast a MovieClip as a Sprite because their public methods and variables will match. If we were to do the opposite, cast a Sprite as a MovieClip, it would be considered an "unsafe" casting because a Sprite does not contain all of the methods and variables of a MovieClip. While Flash will let you cast either direction, it's generally a good idea to avoid casting to a subclass unless you know for certain that the methods and variables you want to call will be available. In the case of the above example, converting a base object to a class is technically an unsafe casting, but the Class class (a confusing nomenclature to be sure) contains no additional public methods or variables, so there is no danger of causing an error. We'll use casting and getDefinitionByName regularly later in game examples.

Part 2: Events

A core component of ActionScript 3 is the use of events. Event objects can be believed as messages that are sent between objects to notify each other of, well, events. When an object is set up to receive events, it is known as *listening*. When an object sends an event, it is known as *dispatching*. In their most basic form, events contain a type (the name of the event being sent), a target (the object that dispatched the event), and a currentTarget (the object currently processing the event after receiving it). A basic event is merely a notification that something happened, and you'll need to access the object that sent the event in order to get any more information. However, events can be customized to send any amount of data along with the message, but we'll get to that shortly. First, let's look at how objects can send events.

dispatchEvent

Many of the core classes of AS3 dispatch events. In order to dispatch an event, an object must either extend the Event-Dispatcher class in some way or implement the IEventDispatcher interface (see the interface example in the previous section on classes). If it meets one of these two criteria, you simply call the *dispatchEvent* method and pass it an event object. Event objects are created from the Event class or a sub class of it. The basic Event class has a number of predefined names, or *enumerations*, of event types, but you can use any name you want.

```
var event:Event = new Event(Event.COMPLETE);
```

or

```
var event:Event = new Event("myCustomEventName");
```

However, it is a good idea to define your event names as constants somewhere so that you can avoid misspellings. For instance, if my game class needed to tell another object when the game had started and ended, it would be wise for me to define these event names, so they can be referenced later. The typical event naming scheme is to use all capital letters, with underscores between words, for the property name and CamelCase for the actual value, as in the next example.

```
package {
        import flash.display.Sprite;
        import flash.events.Event;
        public class Game extends Sprite {
                static public const GAME_START:String = "gameStart";
                static public const GAME_OVER:String = "gameOver";
```

```
protected function startGame():void {
        //START GAME LOGIC
        dispatchEvent(new Event(GAME_START));
}

protected function gameOver():void {
        //GAME OVER LOGIC
        dispatchEvent(new Event(GAME_OVER));
}
    }
}
```

There are a few things to note about that example. First, event names are not only public constants but they're static, which makes them easily accessible from anywhere. Next, the Sprite class extends EventDispatcher, so all my methods are ready for me to use without defining anything extra, which is *very* convenient. Finally, I often create and dispatch my events in a single line. You'll rarely need to keep a reference to an event object after you create it, unless you're adding a bunch of extra data to it, so I prefer this method for basic events because it's one less line to type and one less variable to assign. Now, let's look at how another class might listen to these events.

addEventListener, removeEventListener, and Event Phases

There are a couple of different ways to listen for events, and these depend on the *phase* an event is in. When a DisplayObject on the stage dispatches an event, it goes through three phases: capture, target, and bubble. In the *capture* phase, the event travels all the way from the Stage down through the display list chain to the DisplayObject that sent the event. Once the event reaches its "owner," it enters what is known as the *target* phase. Finally, the event travels back up the display list to the Stage called the *bubbling* phase. Any object along the path of the display list can listen for these types of events, assuming the event is created that way. The reason for this particular sequence is that objects in the display list can easily listen for events further down the chain, such as mouse or keyboard input. For non-DisplayObjects (or Display-Objects that are not on the stage), events have only one phase, the target phase. In other words, the only way to listen for these events is to listen to the object directly. Let's look at some examples to make this a little clearer.

We'll start with a generic object first since their events are simpler and can only be listened to in one way. This is also the most common way to listen for messages, during the target phase. To listen for an object's events, you simply call its *addEventListener* method and pass it a number of parameters. We'll use the example of the Game class from above, assuming that there is an instance of this class in the document class of an FLA.

```
package {
        import flash.display.Sprite;
        import flash.events.Event;
        public class Document extends Sprite {

                public var game:Game;

                public function Document() {
                        game = new Game();
                        game.addEventListener(Game.GAME_START,
                          gameStart);
                        game.addEventListener(Game.GAME_OVER,
                          gameOver);
                        addChild(game);
                }

                protected function gameStart(e:Event):void {
                        trace(e);
                }

                protected function gameOver(e:Event):void {
                        trace(e);
                }
        }
}
```

The two required parameters of the addEventListener method are an event type (as a string) and a method to call when that event occurs. Note that I can use protected (or private, or internal) methods as my event listeners—this is the only time where something that occurs outside this class can access an otherwise off-limits method. A method that is set up to receive events must accept a single parameter, the event object. There are few other parameters that are optional when setting up a listener, and I actually like to assign them, control freak that I am. The third parameter is *useCapture*, which is false by default. We will cover it momentarily as it deals with event phases and display list. The fourth parameter is the listener priority, which is 0 by default. The priority level tells Flash which listeners should get the event first—the higher the number, the higher the priority. If it is critical for one object to receive an event before another, this is the best way to ensure that. I usually leave it at 0.

Finally, the fifth parameter is *useWeakReference*, which might be the coolest feature of events, and is false by default. To fully appreciate what it does, you first need to understand how garbage collector of Flash (the mechanism that removes unused objects from memory) works. We'll cover the garbage collector more in depth when we reach the section on Flash idiosyncrasies, but suffice it to say for the moment that by setting useWeakReference to true, the listener will automatically be removed when the object it is listening to is deleted from memory. Unless you have a specific reason you do not want the listener to be removed automatically, I recommend always setting useWeakReference to true. The following is a modification of the two lines from the above example, written to use weak references.

```
game.addEventListener(Game.GAME_START, gameStart, false, 0, true);
game.addEventListener(Game.GAME_OVER, gameOver, false, 0, true);
```

When you no longer need to listen for an event (or if you are not using weakly reference listeners), you can use the *removeEventListener* method with the same first three parameters you called in addEventListener to disengage a listener from an object. For the example above, once the Document class was done listening to the game for events, it could call the following two lines:

```
game.removeEventListener(Game.GAME_START, gameStart, false);
game.removeEventListener(Game.GAME_OVER, gameOver, false);
```

Like addEventListener, the third parameter is optional, depending on whether you're using the capture phase, which we will cover now.

As I mentioned earlier, if you're passing events between DisplayObjects, you have a few different options available to you, depending on where your objects are in relation to each other. Here are some different situations:

Scenario #1: The object you want to listen to is a child object, either directly or through the display chain, of your current object.

In this instance, you can listen to the target object in all three phases. When you listen during the capture or bubbling phases, you don't add the listener to the object itself, but rather the object that is listening, as the event will be broadcast to your object as it "passes through." By default, most events do not bubble unless explicitly told to do so. To be able to listen to the events of Game class from all three phases, we would first have to modify the dispatchEvent calls to look the following:

```
dispatchEvent(new Event(GAME_START, true));
dispatchEvent(new Event(GAME_OVER, true));
```

The second parameter when creating a new event tells the event whether or not to bubble. Now that these events are bubbling, we can modify the listeners in the Document class to account for all three event phases:

```
//CAPTURE PHASE
addEventListener(Game.GAME_START, gameStart, true, 0, true);
//TARGET PHASE
game.addEventListener(Game.GAME_START, gameStart, false, 0,
  true);
//BUBBLE PHASE
addEventListener(Game.GAME_START, gameStart, false, 0, true);
```

Note the subtle differences between how the listeners are added. The capture and bubbling listeners are identical, except for the useCapture parameter, and the target listener is attached to the game object directly. There are few times when you'd probably use all of these listener types at once. I almost always listen at the target phase because I usually know which object I need to receive events and which don't matter. One scenario where it is very helpful, though, is when you need to stop an event from being broadcasted.

Event Propagation and Cancellation

By default, events, particularly those in DisplayObjects, will move through their hierarchy uninterrupted, notifying each listener in the chain as the event reaches it. However, there might be some scenarios where you would want to stop certain events from reaching their destination. A common example is with mouse input. Say you had an application or a game with a side panel containing some buttons and other information. If you were displaying a message and wanted to disable input to the panel while the message was being shown, you could tell the panel to disable itself, which would in turn disable each of the buttons. However, there are a lot of codes to write, and it is more easily handled by canceling events.

When one of the buttons in the panel is clicked on by the mouse, for example, it generates an event (specifically, a MouseEvent) that moves through each display list level until it reaches the object that was clicked. If you listen for that event during the capture phase in some parent object of the panel, you can stop that event from proceeding any further and ever reaching its destination. You do this through the use of a couple of methods of event objects: *stopPropagation* and *stopImmediatePropagation*. They both do virtually the same thing but with minor differences. The former stops any objects further down the display chain from receiving the event. The latter stops those objects, as well as any other listeners, in the current DisplayObject.

Custom Events

If you find during development that you need an event type that contains more information than a generic event, you can easily extend the Event class to make custom events. Let's look at one quick example:

```
package {
        import flash.events.Event;

        public class GameEvent extends Event{
                static public const GAME_START:String = "gameStart";
                static public const GAME_WIN:String = "gameWin";
                static public const GAME_LOSE:String = "gameLose";

                public var score:Number;
                public var timeLeft:Number;
                public var level:int;
                public var difficulty:int;

                public function GameEvent(type:String,
                    score:Number = 0,
                    timeLeft:Number = 0,
                    level:int = 1,
                    difficulty:int = 1,
                    bubbles:Boolean = false,
                    cancelable:Boolean = false) {
                this.score = score;
                this.timeLeft = timeLeft;
                this.level = level;
                this.difficulty = difficulty;
                super(type, bubbles, cancelable);
        }

        override public function clone():Event {
                return new GameEvent(type, score, timeLeft, level,
                    difficulty, bubbles, cancelable);
                }
        }
}
```

Since we've created a custom event class, it makes more sense to keep the event type names here, rather than in the Game class. In this case, GAME_OVER has been split into GAME_WIN and GAME_LOSE for more specific events. Also, we've included holder variables for the game's current score, time left, difficulty, and current level if they were applicable. Obviously, you would tailor these properties to your specific game. In the Game class, we would now dispatch events like the following:

```
dispatchEvent(new GameEvent(GameEvent.GAME_START));
```

There are a couple of things to remember when extending the Event class. One is that any additional properties you want to store must have variables created for them, so the constructor can assign them or they can be re-assigned after the event object is created. Another point to keep in mind is that you need to explicitly call the Event superclass constructor through super() and pass it at least the first parameter (and preferably all of them). The final aspect of events to remember is that you should provide a clone method to override the original. The clone method is automatically used by Flash when events are re-dispatched from a listener object. If an override is not provided, it will return a generic event rather than your custom type. While it is not mandatory to provide it, it is a best practice and will prevent problems from cropping up down the road where your data gets lost along the way.

That completes this section on events. While there are even more aspects of the event model in Flash which we could explore, what we've learned represents the core functionality that you will likely use when developing games.

Part 3: Errors

No one likes errors in their code. In fact, no one likes their mistakes being pointed out by others, let alone a computer. It may sound like an absurd statement, but errors in Flash really are your friends. In ActionScripts 1 and 2, errors were passive—if they occurred, things might break, but you wouldn't necessarily know where or why. When I first switched to AS3, I couldn't stand how many errors I got and it drove me nuts. Now that I've gotten used to it, I'm very appreciative when Flash presents me with a batch of errors; I would much rather know that something happened and be able to fix it rather than have it fail silently and have no idea why my application isn't running as expected. And really, though my ego might not like to admit it, those errors were probably in my AS1 and AS2 codes; I just didn't know it. As some of you may already know, errors in ActionScript 3 make themselves known by bringing your program (or at least method) to a screeching halt and displaying a message in the output window. Anyone first developing in AS3 is bound to cause quite a few errors. You'll also note quickly that the Flash documentation tends to refer to them in a couple of different ways. Sometimes errors are referred to as *exceptions*. Also, because errors are derived from the Error class, there are a number of subclasses that extend from it, such as ReferenceError or ArgumentError. These subclasses give you more detailed information about what went wrong. There are two main kinds or errors you'll run into during development.

The first are compile-time errors, which crop up when you go to publish your SWF. These are my favorite errors because they let you know immediately that you did something flat-out *wrong*. The SWF won't even work correctly as a result, so you're forced to go back and fix them. The most common errors are typographic: mistyped variable names, assigning the wrong type of value to a variable, and calling a method that doesn't exist. While they can be annoying if there are many of them, it's always better to know about problems up front and fix them.

The other kind is a runtime error, which occurs while your SWF is running. These are equally helpful, but they have to be discovered and are most likely to crop up during testing. They'll only occur when you run the piece of code with the problem in it. The other trick with runtime errors is that they're not always mistakes, per se. Sometimes, an error occurs when certain events are dispatched and nothing is listening to them. In this case, the error acts as a notification that something went wrong and that you need to account for the scenario in which it took place.

Regardless of the type, errors should always be handled. There are a couple of ways to fix errors. Most of the time, the error is the result of a coding mistake or omission. However, sometimes an error can occur because a piece of functionality has other dependencies, like external files, which are not available during development. In this case, you can prevent the errors from bringing the rest of your code to a halt by *catching* them.

try, catch, finally

If you want to trap an error and keep it from halting the rest of your code, you should wrap the code inside what a *try* statement block.

```
try {
        //ERROR-INDUCING CODE HERE
}
```

If an error occurs inside of a try block, it will attempt to be caught by an adjacent *catch* block.

```
try {
        //ERROR-INDUCING CODE HERE
} catch (error:Error) {
        //NOTIFY DEVELOPER OF ERROR
        trace(error);
}
```

If no error occurs, the code in the catch block will not execute. You can also use multiple catch blocks to catch different kinds of errors rather than catching all errors with one lump block.

```
try {
        //ERROR-INDUCING CODE HERE
} catch (error:ArgumentError) {
        //CATCHES JUST ARGUMENT ERRORS
        trace(error);
} catch (error:ReferenceError) {
        //CATCHES JUST REFERENCE ERRORS
        trace(error);
} catch (error:Error) {
        //CATCHES ALL OTHER ERRORS
        trace(error);
}
```

If you want some type of code to run regardless of whether an error occurs, you can put it in a *finally* block, which appears after all catches. If no error occurs, the sequence will be try > finally. If an error occurs, it will follow try > catch(es) > finally.

```
try {
        //ERROR-INDUCING CODE HERE
} catch (error:Error) {
        //NOTIFY DEVELOPER OF ERROR
        trace(error);
} finally {
        trace("MADE IT THROUGH TO THE END");
}
```

Throwing Your Own Errors

Sometimes, you may want to cause errors yourself to let you or another developer using your code to know that they're attempting to perform an illegal operation. Creating an error is known as *throwing* to coincide with the *catch* metaphor. To throw an error, you simply use the throw statement, which is a core part of AS3.

```
throw new Error("This is a custom error message.");
```

You don't actually have to specify a message for your error, particularly if you intend to create your own Error subclass (where the message could be predetermined by the class), but I find it very helpful to do so. If you're working in a complex application that has a lot of opportunities for errors, you can also define error codes to provide differentiation as a second parameter to the Error constructor. I don't tend to throw errors as much in my game-specific classes, but I use them frequently when creating utility classes that may be shared among a number of projects or other developers.

Creating custom error classes is even more straightforward than custom event classes, so I'll give only a brief example of how to do so. I have found that the basic included error types are more than enough to handle the errors I need to create. Here is a quick example of a GameError class that you could use to hold a number of predefined error messages.

```
package {
        public class GameError extends Error {
                static public const INVALID_INPUT:String = "That is
                    not a valid form of input for this game.";
                static public const GAME_NOT_READY:String = "The game
                    object is not yet initialized. Run init() before
                    starting game.";

                public function GameError(message:String="") {
                        super(message);
                }
        }
}
//IN GAME CLASS
public function startGame():void {
        if (!initialized) throw new GameError(GameError.
          GAME_NOT_READY));
        //OTHER CODE
}
```

In this example, the GameError class (much like an Event subclass) predefines the error messages the game will use for easy access and syntax checking. If the game is not initialized when start-Game is called, it will throw a GAME_NOT_READY error. For more information about error handling, check out the online chapter "Bugs: Squash 'Em If You've Got 'Em," available on the book's Web site.

Part 4: Data Structures and Lists

One of the most important abilities in programming is being able to group similar objects together in lists for easier tracking. For example, a game might have a player, a number of different kinds of enemies, and a number of pickup items. It is inefficient, or even impossible in some scenarios, to keep track of the enemies and pickups with individual variables, so we need more complex data structures to store them and make them easily accessible. AS3 gives us four main containers for this type of data, and depending on what type of information you're trying to store, a fifth one as well. We'll look at each of these structures, their pros and cons, the best tasks for them, and how to *iterate*, or step through, each of them.

Objects

At the root of all the different classes in ActionScript are basic Objects. They are the building blocks for every other more complex data type. They are also dynamic and therefore useful by themselves as lists. Every variable added to them is indexed by a string name. Here is an example that stores a Sprite in a list by its name:

```
var enemyList:Object = new Object();
var enemy:Sprite = new Sprite();
enemy.name = "BadGuy1";
enemyList [enemy.name] = enemy;
```

Now let's say you had a whole batch of enemies. You could use a *for* loop to add them to the list.

```
var enemyList:Object = new Object();
for (var i:int = 0; i < 10; i++) {
        var enemy:Sprite = new Sprite();
        enemy.name = "BadGuy" + i;
        enemyList [enemy.name] = enemy;
}
```

Later on, if you need to perform an action on all your enemies, you could simply run another *for* loop, but this time a *for...in* loop.

```
for (var i:String in enemyList) {
        var enemy:Sprite = enemyList[i];
        //DO SOMETHING TO ENEMY SPRITE
}
```

It's worth noting that when you iterate through an object using a *for...in* loop that it goes through the object in reverse order from newest item added to oldest, so you can't count on an object for your items to be in a particular order. However, when order doesn't matter in your list, this is a powerful tool because you can gain direct access to any item in the list. If you need to remove an item from an object list, you simply use the *delete* command along with the item's key. Items in objects are "keyed off" a string value. In the example above, each enemy in the list is indexed by its name, and future attempts to access this enemy can only be done if you know its name or run through a loop to find it. Suppose when the user clicks on an enemy, it should be destroyed and therefore be removed from the list. Once the enemy is clicked on, you have a reference to it through a MouseEvent. You could then remove it from the list like the following example.

```
protected function enemyClicked(e:MouseEvent) {
        var enemy:Sprite = e.target as Sprite;
        delete enemyList[enemy.name];
        //REMOVE DISPLAY OBJECTS, ETC
}
```

Pros: Easy to access items, fast to iterate through, easy to garbage collect

Cons: Unordered, must have a unique string property such as a name associated with whatever you're storing (using the same string twice will override the first one)

When to use: Best used when you're not interested in the order of a group of items and when you have a unique string identifier like a name to use

Arrays

Up until AS3, Objects and Arrays were the only two native types of data storage available in Flash. An Array is an ordered list of items that are indexed by number, starting from 0. Arrays can have an unlimited number of items added to them using the *push, unshift,* and *splice* commands. When an item is removed using the *pop, shift,* or *splice* commands, the array size, or *length,* is reduced. Items in the list can be set to null values, but the null still occupies a slot in the array. Like Objects, Arrays are easy to set up and use. Once an Array is created, the *push* command is used to add items to the end of it. Likewise, the *unshift* command can be used to insert items at the front.

```
var enemyList:Array = new Array();
for (var i:int = 0; i < 10; i++) {
        var enemy:Sprite = new Sprite();
        enemyList.push(enemy);
}
```

One big advantage of Arrays is the ability to easily combine them. Say you had separate lists of enemies, obstacles, and pickups, and you needed to perform an operation on all of them and also keep them in their discrete lists. You can use the *concat* method to concatenate the Arrays together into one list and only loop through one larger Array.

```
var combinedList:Array = enemyList.concat(obstacleList,
  pickupList);
for (var i:int = 0; i < combinedList.length; i++) {
        var item:Sprite = combinedList[i];
        //PERFORM SOME OPERATION ON EACH ITEM
}
```

Another advantage of using Arrays is the availability of sorting options. Because it is an ordered list, the order can be changed dependent on almost criteria you specify using the *sort* and *sortOn* commands. The *sortOn* method is particularly helpful when you have an Array of DisplayObjects such Sprites. Say you wanted to sort the list by their "x" positions from left to right. The code would probably look something like the following:

```
enemyList.sortOn("x");
```

There are also special constants built into the Array class that allow you to specify sorting order. By default, Arrays will sort in ascending order, that is, from smallest to largest. You can add a second parameter to the *sortOn* method to specify a different order.

```
enemyList.sortOn("x", Array.DESCENDING);
```

For all this flexibility in ordering, Arrays are not without their shortcomings. Unlike the Object example where we were able to pinpoint an item in the list based on its name, there is no safe way to do that with Arrays. You could theoretically store each item's index in the Array in the item itself, but that would assume that the Array order would never change at all—a largely unsafe assumption to make. In order to find an item in an Array, you must iterate through it, compare each item to the one you're looking up, and break out of the Array once you've found it to minimize processing cycles.

```
protected function enemyClicked(e:MouseEvent) {
        var enemy:Sprite = e.target as Sprite;
        for (var i:int = 0; i < enemyList.length; i++) {
                if (enemyList[i] == enemy) {
                        enemyList.splice(i, 1);
                        break;
                }
        }
}
```

The larger the Array is, the longer this process takes, and it is obviously a way less efficient than simply keying off a value like in an Object. AS3 added two methods that simplify the coding of this considerably: *indexOf* and *lastIndexOf*. These two methods basically do the search for you, simplifying your code to

```
protected function enemyClicked(e:MouseEvent) {
        var enemy:Sprite = e.target as Sprite;
        var index:int = enemyList.indexOf(enemy);
        enemyList.splice(index, 1);
}
```

The *lastIndexOf* method does exactly the same search but starts at the end of the Array and counts down. While this is definitely less to type and is cleaner than a *for* loop, the underlying process is still the same and large arrays are still taxing on Flash.

Pros: Ordered, lots of sorting options, ease of combining Arrays
Cons: Slower to access specific items (requires iteration), slightly slower to iterate through than objects

When to use: The best time to use an Array is when you need your items to be able to be sorted and their order matters. Arrays also do not have to store all of the same type of item, making them a little bit more flexible for general-purpose use (see section "Vectors," below)

Vectors

A Vector is simply a typed Array, meaning that all items in the list must be of the same type. By enforcing typing, Vectors are faster to iterate through and process and take up less memory. They also have the option to be of a fixed length, that is, no more items can be added to them. They are slightly differently than Arrays, but all their other methods are the same.

```
var enemyList:Vector.<Sprite> = new Vector.<Sprite>();
for (var i:int = 0; i < 10; i++) {
        var enemy:Sprite = new Sprite();
        enemyList.push(enemy);
}
```

Pros: All of the pros of Arrays except ability to combine differently typed Vectors, faster to iterate through than Arrays
Cons: Still requires iteration to access specific items, so a little slower than objects, requires Flash Player 10 (not available if you're still publishing for Player 9)
When to use: If at all possible, you should always use Vectors over Arrays if all of your items are of the same type. Typically, in a game, your lists will already be homogeneous anyway, so switching to a Vector give you some extra performance

Dictionaries

Just as the Vector object improved on Arrays for ordered storage, AS3 added a new class to improve on basic Objects for storing unordered lists: the Dictionary object. Unlike regular Objects, which require a string to be used as the key for an item, Dictionaries can use any data type, including the item itself. This makes them even easier to use for complex data types because you don't have to have a unique string to identify items. The Dictionary constructor also contains one parameter called *weakKeys*, which defaults to false. When a Dictionary uses weakKeys if an item in the list and its key are one in the same, and you remove the item from the list, the key is removed as well. For this reason, I like to set weakKeys to true. Here is the enemyList example, using a Dictionary object.

```
var enemyList:Dictionary = new Dictionary(true);
for (var i:int = 0; i < 10; i++) {
```

```
        var enemy:Sprite = new Sprite();
        enemyList[enemy] = enemy;
}
```

As you can probably already tell, getting access to a specific item in a Dictionary is also easier than with a traditional object. With Dictionary objects, it is necessary to use the new *for each* loop in AS3.

```
for each (var enemy:Sprite in enemyList) {
        //DO SOMETHING TO ENEMY SPRITE
}
```

The *delete* command applies here the same way it does with regular objects.

```
protected function enemyClicked(e:MouseEvent) {
        delete enemyList[e.target];
}
```

Pros: Ability to key off any value, including items themselves; fast, direct access of an object to individual items; can store items of any type together

Cons: Unordered, not as helpful for lists of primitive values like strings or numbers

When to use: As much as possible! Outstanding for storing all unordered lists of complex objects

ByteArrays

Although not useful for storing lists of objects, the ByteArray class is designed to store raw binary data, making it a perfect (in fact, the only) candidate container for things such as image or sound data. We won't really use ByteArrays in this book, but they are very fast and worth mentioning since they are often overlooked.

So What Should I Use For My Lists?

That answer, as with so many questions, is, "Depends." I tend to like to use Dictionaries to keep track of all my object lists in a game and then use Arrays or Vectors only when I need their sorting abilities. You really can't beat a Dictionary for ease of use or speed. If I must have an ordered list, I would prefer a Vector to an Array due to its slight edge in speed. This is not to say that basic Objects and Arrays are no longer useful. Objects are still great containers for dynamic data but not as fast for lists as Dictionaries. Arrays are great to fall back on if you can't guarantee that all your list items will be of the same type or if you're working with older classes that aren't configured to handle Vectors.

Custom Data Structures

In the event that you need even more functionality than these built-in classes afford, you can of course extend any of them to a new class. One important thing to remember about all of these classes is that they are *dynamic*, allowing them to have any properties added to them at runtime. In order for your subclasses to inherit this same functionality, they must also be dynamic. We'll look at an example of a custom data structure (though not an extension of any of these) in Chapter 14.

Part 5: Keep Your Comments to Everyone Else!

Probably the single-most overlooked task of any developer, particularly in crunch time, is commenting code. Comments are invaluable when handing code off to another developer, or even just returning to it later. The convention is usually "the more comments, the better," but this can actually sometimes make code harder to read. Here are a few tips for commenting your code.

- Don't comment the obvious: If a line of code simply declares a variable called "player," it should be fairly self-explanatory what is happening; extra comments like "//CREATING PLAYER OBJECT" simply clutter up the code.
- Be thorough, but concise: Explain as much as you can in as few words as you can; if comments break onto multiple lines or trail off so the reader has to scroll sideways, it breaks the overall flow of the code.
- When possible, use the ASDoc formatting standards of commenting classes: This primarily means creating comment blocks in a specific format (established by Adobe) just prior to properties and methods; by creating your comments this way, documentation can easily be generated for your code and many script editors such as FlashDevelop can use the comments in tooltips to help remind you of proper syntax (see below for example).
- Keep comments correct: This may sound like an unnecessary statement, but if you write your comments for a piece of functionality and later than functionality has to change, your comments must be updated, too.
- Use header comment blocks: Sometimes a simple, complete explanation in one place is more effective than a bunch of lines spread out over a file; if you can explain everything that a class does in a few sentences at the top of a file, don't hesitate to do so.

Here is an example of ASDoc formatting—more precise standards and style guides are available on Adobe's Web site. This is taken from a SoundEngine class, which we will look at in a later chapter.

```
/**
 * Plays the sound specified by the name parameter. Checks for the
   sound internally first, and then looks for it as an external file.
 * @param    name   String The name of the linked Sound in the
   library, or the URL reference to an external sound.
 * @param    offset  Number    The number of seconds offset the
   sound should start.
 * @param    loops    int    The number of times the sound should
   loop. Use -1 for infinite looping.
 * @param    transform    transform    The initial sound transform
   to use for the sound.
 * @return    SoundChannel    The SoundChannel object created by
   playing the sound. Can also be retrieved through getChannel
   method.
 */
public function playSound(name:String, offset:Number = 0, loops:
    int = 0, transform:SoundTransform = null):SoundChannel
```

Note that the comment block is placed just before the method itself. It starts with a description of the method and then a list of parameters it accepts and what it returns. When using an editor like FlashDevelop or compiling documentation, the method itself will be used to define things such as the default values of parameters and specific data types.

The Bottom Line

It is better to comment some than none at all, so even if you're pressed for time, you'll thank yourself later for having put *something* in, even if later on it takes you a minute to remember what you were thinking.

Part 6: Why Does Flash Do That?

Flash and ActionScript have a number of idiosyncrasies that can throw even seasoned developers off track. Some of these oddities are instances where the language breaks form with similarly constructed languages like Java or C#, much to the chagrin of developers coming to Flash from these languages. Others have to do with the processing order in which Flash performs commands; sometimes, a bug is simply the result of a misunderstanding of this "order of operations." We'll cover a number of these quirks in this section.

Event Flow

One of the common misunderstandings that I've witnessed with developers first utilizing Flash's event model is the difference between DisplayObject-generated events and all other events. As we discussed earlier, events in ActionScript have three phases: capture, target, and bubbling. Objects that dispatch events but are not in the display list (which can include DisplayObjects that have not been added to the stage) generate events only at the target phase. In other words, other objects may listen for these events only by attaching themselves directly to the dispatching object.

DisplayObjects that are active somewhere in the display list are capable of dispatching events that pass through all three phases. When a DisplayObject that is on the Stage dispatches an event, it actually originates at the Stage level and progresses through each subsequent child to effectively "tunnel" down to the originating object—this is the capture phase. The event then enters the target phase and any listeners attached directly to the DisplayObject will receive the event. Finally, if the event is set to bubble, it will reverse its direction back up to the same display hierarchy it traversed in the capture phase.

Frame Scripts

Before I go any further, I should go ahead and state for the record that coding on the timeline should be avoided at all costs. There is basically nothing that you can't do with classes to control your DisplayObjects at this point, and forcing your code into classes imposes better architecture and less sloppy shortcuts, which will later come back to bite you.

Now, I say basically because until AS3 (Flash CS3, specifically), you still had to put a stop() action on the last frame of any Movie-Clip you didn't want to loop. Since switching to all-class scripting architecture, I found it very frustrating to not be able to easily remove this last bit of straggling timeline code from my FLA once and for all. Then, I discovered an undocumented method of Movie-Clips. It's called addFrameScript, and it's a complete mystery to me why Adobe hasn't documented it or encouraged its use because it is a fantastic piece of code. Basically, it allows you to tell a particular function to run when a certain frame of a MovieClip is hit. Unlike all the other MovieClip functions, it is zero-based rather than one-based, so you must subtract one from the desired frame number to use it correctly. Here is its syntax in the context of a MovieClip class.

```
public function MyMovieClip() {
        addFrameScript(totalFrames-1, stop);
}
```

Now, when the clip reaches the last frame, it will call its stop() method and not loop. Obviously, this has further-reaching implications and uses than simply stopping a MovieClip from playing. In fact, I have come up with a way to use this method to overcome a defect in ActionScript with regards to MovieClips and frame labels. Since early versions of Flash, you could put string labels on any frame in the timeline and use them as reference points for navigation. Starting from AS3, Adobe finally introduced the ability to see what label you're currently on in a clip (with the *currentLabel* property), as well as a list of all the labels in a clip (the *currentLabels* property). I've long thought that Flash should dispatch an event whenever a frame label is hit, so you could trigger actions based on label markers. With *addFrameScript*, you can! Let's look at an example.

Here is an architecture I like to use for my document class in a Flash file. It involves placing labels on the main timeline to denote sections of a game; they might be things such as "loader," "title-Screen," "game," "resultsScreen,"and so on. Figure 4.4 illustrates this arrangement.

In my document class, I create constants to match these frame labels, so I can reference them easily and don't risk misspelling them. I also import the FrameLabel class, as I will be using it shortly.

```
package {
        import flash.display.MovieClip;
        import flash.display.FrameLabel;
        public class FrameScriptExample extends MovieClip {
                static public const FRAME_LOADER:String = "loader";
                static public const FRAME_TITLE:String = "title";
                static public const FRAME_GAME:String = "game";
                static public const FRAME_RESULTS:String = "results";
                public function FrameScriptExample() {
                        stop();
                }
        }
}
```

Once I have all my labels established, I create two functions that will control my frame events.

```
private function enumerateFrameLabels():void {
        for each (var label:FrameLabel in currentLabels)
                addFrameScript(label.frame-1, dispatchFrameEvent);
}
```

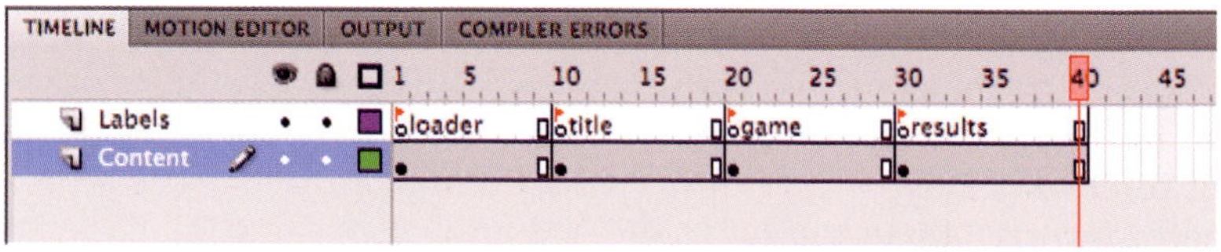

Figure 4.4 For my main timeline, I set up labels denoting each section of the game experience.

```
private function dispatchFrameEvent():void {
      dispatchEvent(new Event(currentLabel));
}
```

The *enumerateFrameLabels* method iterates through the list of FrameLabel objects in the Array *currentLabels* and adds a frame script to every frame that has a label. The function it adds is called *dispatchFrameEvent*, and all it does is to generate a new event with the same name as the frame label. Now, every time a frame label is hit, an event with that label name will be dispatched. By using events, any number of objects can listen for these frame events. The rewritten constructor for this class now looks something more like the following:

```
public function FrameScriptExample() {
      stop();
      enumerateFrameLabels();
      addEventListener(FRAME_TITLE, setupTitle, false, 0, true);
}


protected function setupTitle(e:Event):void {
      //PERFORM TITLE FUNCTIONS
}
```

It is worth noting that only one function can be assigned to a frame at a time, so any subsequent *addFrameScript* calls to the same frame number will replace the existing script. If you're at all nervous about using undocumented features in your work, *addFrameScript* is a pretty safe bet—it's what the CS5 IDE uses internally when you place code on the timeline. Let's say you put a script on the last frame of the main timeline called *stop()*. When you compile the SWF, Flash takes each of these frame scripts and converts them into functions with names such as "frame30" to ensure they are unique. Then, in the constructors for any clips with frame scripts, Flash calls *addFrameScript* to attach these functions to their respective frames. It looks something like the following:

```
addFrameScript(30, frame30);
```

I'm sure there are many other good applications of this method, so continue to explore it and let's collectively push Adobe to support and document it. If it's good enough for Flash, it should be good enough for you. One other minor sticking point is that very early versions of Flash Player 9 prior to Flash CS3's release (specifically, 9.0.28 and earlier) do not support *addFrameScript*. The command is ignored entirely. Because of this issue, other security issues, bug fixes, and performance improvements, I recommend you to only build for Flash Player 9.0.115 or higher. If you're building for Flash Player 10 (which is the default for CS5), you don't need to worry about it at all.

Working with Multiple SWF Files

At some point, you'll probably be in the position of using multiple SWF files to support a game. Perhaps you have multiple game levels, each in their own SWF, or you have externalized all your audio a separate file. To load external SWF files at runtime, you'll need to use a Loader object, which is part of the display package. The syntax looks like the following:

```
package {
        import flash.display.Loader;
        import flash.display.Sprite;
        import flash.display.MovieClip;
        import flash.events.Event;
        import flash.net.URLRequest;
        public class LoaderExample extends Sprite {
                protected var resourceLoader:Loader;
                protected var resources:MovieClip;
                public function LoaderExample() {
                        loadResources();
                }
                protected function loadResources():void {
                        if (!resourceLoader) resourceLoader = new
                           Loader();
                        resourceLoader.load(new URLRequest
                           ("resources.swf"));
                resourceLoader.contentLoaderInfo.addEventListener
                   ( Event.COMPLETE, resourcesComplete, false, 0, true);
                }
                protected function resourcesComplete(e:Event):void {
                        resources = e.target.content as MovieClip;
                }
                protected function unloadResources():void {
                        resourceLoader.unloadAndStop();
                }
        }
}
```

In the *loadResources* method of this example, a new Loader object is created (if one doesn't already exist) and is used to load a SWF named "resources.swf." A listener is then added to the Loader's *contentLoaderInfo* object, which will dispatch events about the Loader's progress. Once the load has completed, the resources variable is assigned to the content of the Loader. If at some point the data needs to be unloaded, the method *unloadResources* can be called to dump the SWF. Developers familiar with AS3 already will note that the new *unloadAndStop,* introduced in CS4, is a big improvement over the previous (and still available) *unload* method. It makes sure that all listeners and sounds connected to the loaded content are properly removed and garbage collected to prevent any of the assets lingering in memory.

One thing to note about classes in separate SWFs is that, by default, every SWF has its own "sandbox" to store classes known as its *ApplicationDomain*. This is to prevent classes in one SWF colliding with those in another, which is helpful if two SWF files have similarly named classes that are actually completely different in their implementation. Most of the time, this is the behavior you will want, as it protects your class integrity and keeps you from thinking about how any other content may be built. However, occasionally, you want to be able to merge a loaded SWF's ApplicationDomain with its container. A good example of this is a SWF that contains nothing but sounds exported in the library. In order to easily get access to the classes for these sounds, you would have to go a roundabout way of looking them up. If you know that none of the class names in your loaded SWF file will conflict with those in the container, you can tell Flash to merge the two when the SWF is loaded. Using the previous example, the *loadResources* method would have to change.

```
protected function loadResources():void {
        if (!resourceLoader) resourceLoader = new Loader();
        var loaderContext:LoaderContext = new LoaderContext
          (false, ApplicationDomain.currentDomain);
        resourceLoader.load(new URLRequest("resources.swf"),
          loaderContext);
        resourceLoader.contentLoaderInfo.addEventListener
          (Event.COMPLETE, resourcesComplete, false, 0, true);
}
```

The new code uses two classes from the system package: LoaderContext and ApplicationDomain. When you perform a load, you can specify the context under which the file is loaded. Inside that context, you can determine which ApplicationDomain the loaded file should use. By specifying the current domain, any class definitions in the loaded SWF file will be combined with and accessible to those in the container. In Chapter 14, we'll look at a variation on this process when loading a set of assets.

One point to remember about using Loader objects is that you *must* call unloadAndStop to fully unload any content you want to get rid of. Simply setting the Loader object to *null* will only eliminate the reference to it, and there is no guarantee that it will be automatically garbage collected correctly. Fewer things are worse in Flash than a memory leak that can't be fixed because there is no attainable reference to the offending object.

Garbage Collection

AS3's garbage collection (GC) system, or the mechanism that removes unused objects from memory, has some peculiarities that are likely to throw off AS2 developers though they are likely nothing new to devs from other memory-managed languages. Ideally, a garbage collector is always keeping track of which objects are in use and which are not, freeing up as much memory as possible. In reality, it is not so perfect, but there are ways to make sure your code conforms to how the GC will work. First, it's important to understand in brief how the Flash GC performs its functions.

The AS3 GC uses two techniques to clean up your objects. The first is known as reference counting; all the objects in memory have a number representing how many references there are to that object. For example, the following code creates three different references to a single object.

```
var obj1:Object = new Object;
var obj2:Object = obj1;
var obj3:Object = obj2;
```

Anytime the number of references to an object changes, Flash checks to see if that number is zero. If it is, the object is purged from memory. In this case, as long as we set obj1, obj2, and obj3 to *null*, the original object will be deleted. Sounds easy and effective enough, right? Unfortunately, there are a number of scenarios where a "parent" object may no longer reference its child objects, but they reference each other, as in the following example.

```
var obj1:Object = new Object();
var obj2:Object = new Object();
obj1.otherObject = obj2;
obj2.otherObject = obj1;
obj1 = null;
obj2 = null;
```

In this instance, while we've nulled out the references to obj1 and obj2, they now reference each other. As a result, the garbage collector will not purge them as it does not discriminate between *what* is referencing the objects, only that *something* is. This brings us to the second method the GC uses to get rid of unused objects. It is known as *mark sweeping*. In this process, Flash creates a tree hierarchy of how all objects are connected to each other that links back to what is essentially the root of the SWF. Any objects that are not connected to the main tree in some way, even if they are connected to each other, are marked for deletion from memory.

At this point, you're probably thinking, "Okay, great. Sounds like Flash has it covered." Once again, it is not quite that simple. The reference counting technique of the GC happens automatically and immediately when the number of references to an object changes. However, because mark sweeping requires running the entire length of the object tree in memory, it is very intense on the system and is only run *periodically*. In my experience, this is usually pretty frequently on decent machines, but it cannot be counted on for split-second accuracy. Don't worry, though—there are a few things you can do to help the garbage collector run thoroughly and effectively.

1. Be diligent about removing your references to objects.

    If you have multiple references to objects in your classes, I suggest writing a function called *cleanUp* in classes that contain a lot of references. This function can perform tasks like setting references to *null* and emptying Arrays. By helping the reference counting mechanism of the GC, you'll make the entire process easier on Flash and therefore less taxing on your game.

2. Use weakly referenced listeners.

    Event listeners are a commonplace for memory leaks because developers add them and then neglect to remove them. Any object that is dispatching events contains a list of all the objects listening to those events. Even if the listening object has all of its external references set to *null*, it will still be in this listener list. Luckily, there is an option when adding an event listener to use what are known as weak references. Weak references are not counted as part of the reference counting mechanism of the GC, so if only the remaining references to an object are weak, it will be deleted. Simply set the fifth parameter of the *addEventListener* method to true to use weak references. I recommend *always* using them as they will save you endless headaches, and there is not a scenario I have come across yet where using weak references had a negative impact.

3. Avoid using dynamic objects other than for lists.

    As a best practice, you should always use statically typed classes, as opposed to dynamic classes, which allow you to add new properties and methods at runtime. By forcing yourself to intentionally declare the variables and object references you want to use in your classes, you keep better track of them. Also, statically typed classes require less memory as instances because they do not require a lookup table to hold the dynamically created properties and methods. Dynamic objects are a common way references to other objects get lost so that they're not effectively garbage collected.

4. Use the unloadAndStop method in Flash Player 10.

    Like I mentioned a brief while before in the section on loading external files, unless you're still developing Flash Player 9 content, always use the unloadAndStop method for getting rid of loaded content. It does a far more effective job of preparing all the objects in the content for garbage collection and will save you a lot of time trying to manually purge all those references yourself.

The garbage collector in Flash has many nuances, and Adobe will surely continue to improve it with each new version of the Flash Player, hopefully eventually giving developers the ability to delete an object outright without having to wait for the GC to do it.

Conclusion

Hopefully, this chapter has been an effective rundown on all the basics you need to know about using AS3 in Flash. This foundation will allow us to explore new classes and features in later chapters as we begin to build games. If you're interested in learning more about the fundamentals of ActionScript, a good place to start is Adobe's documentation on Flash. It is very thorough and covers all of these subjects and more in detail. Many thanks to Grant Skinner for his blog posts on garbage collection—they were an invaluable resource.

5

THE LEAST YOU CAN DO VERSUS AN ARCHITECT'S APPROACH

The subtitle of this book may be *How to Follow Best Practices*, but it's only fair to cover some "worst practices" and basic pitfalls you should avoid when getting started. As such, the first half will look at the bare minimum any Flash game developer should do, regardless of the circumstances. Once you have the basics known, you can "graduate" to the second half of this chapter where we'll examine how to look at your games like an architect from day one.

One of the most common phrases I hear developers (including myself from time to time) use to justify lackluster coding is, "Well, this project just didn't afford me the time." The implication here is that if the developer had more time to do the work, it would have been done better. I certainly don't disagree with that premise. Before I worked at a game company, I was employed by an interactive ad agency. Anyone who has ever worked at an ad agency knows that there is never enough time on any project, *ever*. Forget formalized design patterns and wireframes, we're talking about timelines in which it's hard to find time to use the bathroom. I have built the core mechanics for a game in less (but not much less) than 24 hours; it wasn't pretty but it got the job done. I believe most reasonable people could agree that a day or two turnaround for any game, regardless of complexity, is utterly absurd, and any project manager or account executive who agrees to such a timeline should be flogged publicly.

Despite all of this, I do think that abandoning all sense of standards, forward thinking, or just reasonable programming principles because you were given a ridiculous schedule is not a good practice. In my experience, coding a game rigidly and badly saves no more real time than coding it in a halfway decent way, so why not strive for the higher standard? In this chapter, I'll outline some examples of "the least you can do," even when you don't have much time on your hands. If you follow these basic principles when you're in crunch time, you (and anyone else who has to look at your code) will be thanking yourself later on down the road.

Basic Encapsulation: Classes and Containers

I once had to make edits to a game in which the developer had, for the supposed sake of simplicity and speed, put virtually all of the codes for the game, menu screens, and results screen in the same document class. Needless to say, it was an organizational nightmare. There was absolutely nothing separating game logic from the navigational structure or the leaderboard code. I'm sure at that time, this kept the developer from switching between files, but at an ultimately very high cost. The code was an ugly step up from just having it all tossed on the first frame of the timeline. Here are the steps the developer should have taken to improve the readability and editability of his or her code, in order of importance:

- Move all game logics to its own class. At the bare minimum, any code that controls the mechanics of a game should be encapsulated by itself, away from irrelevant information. This is the core of the game, and the most likely candidate for re-use—it should not be lumped in with everything else.
- Move code for each discrete screen or state of the game to its respective class. If the game has a title screen, rules screen, gameplay screen, and results screen, there should be a class for each. In addition, the document class should be used to move between them and manage which one is active.

This doesn't sound unreasonable, does it? It's hardly a formalized structure, but it can be up to far more scrutiny than the previous "structure."

Store Relevant Values as Variables and Constants

If you work with string or numeric properties that represent a value in your code (such as the speed of a player, the value of gravity in a simulation, or the multiplier for a score bonus), store them as a variable or a constant. "Well, duh," you're probably thinking right now, "Who wouldn't do that?!?" Sadly, I have to say I've seen a lot of codes over the years which were hurriedly thrown together, and the same numeric values were repeated all over the place instead of using a variable. Here's an example:

```
player.x += 10 * Math.cos(angle);
player.y += 10 * Math.sin(angle);
```

In their haste, a developer was probably testing values to determine the proper speed at which to move the player Sprite and just used the number directly in the equation. It would have been virtually no extra time to simply assign the number to a variable, speed, and then use the variable in the code instead.

```
var speed:Number = 10;
//
player.x += speed * Math.cos(angle);
player.y += speed * Math.sin(angle);
```

Now if something changes in the game before it's finished which requires a change in player speed, it will require altering only a single line of code versus how ever many places that value was used. Although this seems like a very simple exercise, a number of otherwise good developers have been guilty of this at one time or another because they were rushing. While this example is obvious, there are other instances of this phenomenon, which might not occur to developers immediately. One example that comes to mind is the names of event types. Many Flash developers with a background in ActionScript 2 are used to name events using raw strings:

```
addEventListener("init",initMethod);
```

In ActionScript 3, Adobe introduced constants: values that will never change but are helpful to enumerate. One of the key uses of constants is in naming event types.

```
public static const INIT:String = "init";
addEventListener(INIT, initMethod);
```

There are a number of reasons for following this syntax. The first is that it follows the above example: if you are going to use a value more than once *anywhere* in your code, it should be stored in memory to change it easier. The second reason is that by declaring event types and other constants in all capital letters, they stand out in your code if someone else is looking at them. Perhaps the most important reason, however, is compile-time checking. When Flash compiles your SWF, it runs through all the codes to look for misuse of syntax and other errors.

```
addEventListener("init", method1);
addEventListener("inti", method2);
```

If I had the previous two lines of code in different parts of the same class, Flash would not throw an error when I compiled it.

```
public static const INIT:String = "init";
addEventLister(INIT, method1);
addEventLister(INTI, method2);
```

However, had I used a constant value from above and misspelled the name of the constant, Flash would have warned me about my mistake when I tried to compile it. This type of checking is utterly invaluable at the eleventh hour when you're trying to get a project out the door and don't have time to debug inexplicable errors.

Don't Rely on Your Stage

When a developer is working on a game in a crunch, it is often in a vacuum. He or she can take certain things for granted, such as the size of the Stage of their SWF. However, if that SWF is loaded into another container of different dimensions, the game's mechanic can be adversely affected. For instance, the following lines of code center an object horizontally and vertically on the stage, assuming its container lines up with the upper left-hand corner of the stage and its registration point is in its center.

```
player.x = stage.stageWidth/2;
player.y = stage.stageHeight/2;
```

If the SWF containing this code is loaded into a larger SWF, it is unlikely it will still have the desired effect. The better option in this case is to use the less-frequently known width and height values in the LoaderInfo object for the SWF. Every SWF knows what its intended stage size should be and that information is stored in an object that is accessible to every DisplayObject in the display list. The two lines above would simply become:

```
player.x = loaderInfo.width/2;
player.y = loaderInfo.height/2;
```

These values will stay consistent even if the stage does not. One exception to this is if you are working with scalable content (like a universal iPhone/iPad app) and the original size of the stage is irrelevant to how elements on the screen need to be laid out.

Don't Use Frameworks or Patterns You Don't Understand or That Don't Apply

This may sound like an odd item in a list of bad practices to avoid when you're pressed for time, but it is yet another very real scenario I've witnessed with my own eyes. It is the opposite of gross underengineering—obscene overengineering—and it is every bit as much a crime … as development crimes go. An example might be trying to apply a complex design pattern to a very simple execution. Some developers are tempted by many OOP frameworks that exist because of the generosity of the Flash community as a way to speed up development in a crunch. However, if the developer doesn't really understand the framework and how to implement it effectively, they will have essentially added an enormous amount of bulk to their project for no reason and will often end up "rewiring" how the framework is intended to function because it should never have been used in the first place.

Another project I recently had to make edits was created with a model-view-controller (MVC) framework designed to force adherence to the design pattern of the same name. However, because of the architecture of the framework, it meant that related code was scattered over at least 20 different class files. Some of the classes only had one or two methods or properties associated with it, making it a bread-crumb trail to attempt to debug. It was a classic example of overengineering; the game was not complicated or varied enough to warrant such a robust system, but the developer equated using an OOP framework with good programming, so they used it anyway. As a result, it took probably twice as long to fix bugs in the game because it was hard to track down where the logic for different parts of the game was stored.

Know When It's Okay to Phone It In and When It Definitely *Isn't*

If you're producing games independently of an employer or client, either for profit or for an experiment, the stakes are much lower. Fewer people, if any, are ever going to see your code, let alone have to work with it. You can get away with some sloppier standards or rushed programming. In fact, some of the best foundations for games I've seen have been born out of hastily thrown together "code brainstorms." In experimentation, all you're interested about is the "idea" behind a mechanism.

However, the moment you start answering to anyone else about your code, be it a client or a coworker, it is vital to take the time to do it *right*. No one is perfect, and no one's code is perfect either, but there's a huge visible difference between someone who made a genuine effort and someone who did not. Even if you're independent now, don't turn a blind eye to your coding practices—you might want to get a job someday and many employers like to see code samples. Now that we've looked at the bare minimum, let's look at higher ideals toward which we should strive.

Transitioning to Architecture

Ever since ActionScript 3 was introduced, there has been a flurry of interest regarding architecture and design patterns. If you read Chapter 1, you will know that design patterns are basically a blueprint or template for solving development problems. They are meant to provide re-usable architecture when building applications. In some areas of the programming community, design patterns are an essential part of application development. That said, more often than not, design patterns implemented in ActionScript tend to hamper development because they work against the natural grain of the language. One reason for this is that AS3 is already somewhat designed as a language to work in a certain way, specifically with *events*. In this chapter, we'll explore some of the basic fundamentals of object-oriented programming to keep in mind as we develop, some programming styles and design patterns that work, and when you should ignore the hype.

OOP Concepts

As I mentioned in Chapter 1, object-oriented programming (OOP) is a model of software design centered around the concept of objects interacting with each other. To put it into game terms, every character on the screen in a game would be a unique object, as well as interactive elements around them. They would all have commands they accept and messages they can broadcast to each other. By having each object responsible for its own behavior, programming becomes much more modular and flexible. Abstractly, this is probably not too a difficult concept to grasp. In practice, it can be difficult to achieve without a certain amount of planning and forethought. This is where design patterns arose; by using an "approved" style of software design, planning an application became easier because the template was already designed. Note, I said *application*. Many of the accepted design patterns in the industry work extremely well for applications that perform specific tasks, such as productivity apps, utilities, design software, and so on. However, design patterns aren't always the answer for game development, because games are meant to feel more like "experiences" than rigid, predictable business software. The best solution to develop a game engine may not follow an "accepted" pattern at all, and that's perfectly okay. However, some basic principles should be followed when using OOP so that your code is modular and scalable.

Encapsulation

One of the most fundamental OOP concepts is encapsulation. Briefly, encapsulation is the notion that an object (or class, in ActionScript) should be entirely self-managed and contained. An object should not have to know anything about the environment in which it exists to carry out its functions, and it should have a prescribed list of functions (or interface) that other objects can use to tell it what to do. In order to send information to objects outside, it should send messages that can be "listened to" by other objects. You can think of a well-encapsulated object like a soda vending machine. All of the inner workings are hidden away from you, and its functionality is distilled down to the buttons you can press to select a drink and the bin in which you can "listen" to receive your purchase. There is no reason for you to know what is going on inside the machine; it might be a couple of gnomes brewing and canning the soda right there on the spot or it might just be a series of tubes. Either way, all you're interested in is getting your tasty sugar water through an interface that is easy to understand and use. If you look at any of the built-in classes in Flash, they follow this same pattern. The only information listed about a class in the documentation is its public methods, properties, and events. There is certainly more going on "under the hood" than what we're exposed to, but we don't need to know about all of it. Your goal should be the same in developing your classes for games.

Inheritance

Say we have two classes, Chair and Sofa. Each of these classes share similar traits such as weight, size, number of legs, number of people they can seat, and so on because they both are types of sitting furniture. Instead of defining all of these traits in both classes, we could save ourselves time by creating a class called Furniture and adding the common traits to those. We could then say that Chair and Sofa *inherit* those properties by being (or *extending*) Furniture. This is the concept of inheritance; all objects in the real and virtual worlds have a hierarchy. When programming in an object-oriented style, the key to maximizing efficiency is to recognize the relationships of one object to another and the features they share. Adding a property to both Chair and Sofa then becomes as simple as adding that property to Furniture. When you extend a class, the new class becomes its *subclass* and the original is now referred to as the *superclass*; in the previous example the Furniture is the superclass and the Chair and Sofa are subclasses. There are some practical limitations to pure inheritance (namely that a class can only extend one other class) that we'll discuss shortly.

Polymorphism

Although it sounds like an affliction one might develop in a science fiction novel, polymorphism is basically the idea that one class can be substituted in code for another and that certain behaviors or properties of inherited objects can be changed or *overridden*. ActionScript only allows for a basic type of polymorhpism, so that's all we'll cover here. Take the Chair from the previous example on inheritance. Now, let's say that we extend Chair to make a High-Chair for an infant. Certain properties of the chair may not apply or behave differently in the HighChair versus the normal Chair. We can override the features that are different in the HighChair but continue to inherit those that are similar. In practice, this process is not as complicated as it sounds, and I will point it out when it is used.

Interfaces

A core principle of object-oriented programming is the separation between an *interface* and an *implementation*. An interface is simply a list of public methods and properties, including their types. An implementation would be a class that uses that interface to define what methods and properties will be publicly available to other classes. This concept can be initially confusing, so let's look at an example. Note in this example (and throughout the rest of this book) that interface names in ActionScript start with a capital I by convention.

In the section "Inheritance," we used an example of a Chair and Sofa extending from Furniture. However, if you were to introduce another piece of furniture, a Table for instance, you would now be presented with a problem. While all three of these objects are Furniture, they have very different uses. The Table has no need for methods that involve people sitting down, and the other two have no need for methods that set dishes on them. Theoretically, you could create a whole structure of inheritance, breaking down Furniture into SeatingFurniture, DisplayFurniture, SupportFurniture, etc., but you can see that this is becoming extremely unwieldy. Also, any changes that are made in large inheritance structures can "ripple" down to subclasses and create problems where none existed before. This is where interfaces come in very handy.

For these three classes, you can simply define distinct interfaces that support each one's specific needs. You could break down the interfaces as such:

- IFurniture: contains move() method
- ISeatedFurniture: contains sitDown() method
- ILayingFurniture: contains layDown() method
- ITableFurniture: contains setDishes() method

Unlike inheritance, where a class can only inherit directly from one other class, you can use, however, many interfaces you like with a single class. The Chair would implement IFurniture and ISeatedFurniture. The Sofa would contain those two, as well as ILayingFurniture, and the Table would contain IFurniture and ITableFurniture. Also, because interfaces can extend one another, the latter three interfaces could all extend the first one as well, making implementation even simpler. Now that you have some basic interfaces defined for different furniture purposes, you can mix and match them as needed to apply to a particular piece of furniture.

Don't worry if some of this abstract terminology gets confusing. When we build a full-scale game in Chapter 14, you'll be able to see these concepts in practice.

Practical OOP in Game Development

By default, AS3 supports OOP and good encapsulation through the use of events to send messages between objects. I've heard AS3's event model described as being akin to the *Observer* design pattern, but regardless of the niche it falls into, it is the native way in which the language operates. Remember that despite the advantages other patterns may offer, all of them are altering the default behavior of the language if they deviate from this model. Figure 5.1 shows the relationship of objects to each other in AS3's hierarchy.

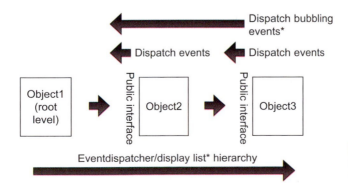

Figure 5.1 The basic event and communication model for AS3.

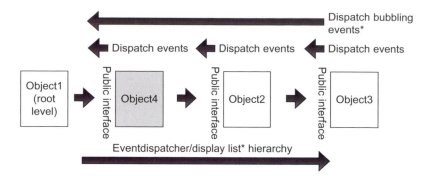

Figure 5.2 A model similar to Fig. 5.1, but with a new object inserted into the hierarchy.

In this illustration, Object1 is at the top of the hierarchy either as the root DisplayObject or just as a generic data EventDispatcher. It has a reference to Object2 and can give it commands directly via its public interface because it knows Object2's type. However, Object2 has no way of knowing its parent without breaking encapsulation. In fact, Object2 should be able to function regardless of what its parent object is. In order to send information out, it dispatches events. If Object1 adds itself as a listener to Object2, it will receive these events. The same is true between Object2 and Object3. If all of these are DisplayObjects, any events Object3 sets to bubble will eventually reach Object1 if it is listening for them. You can think of these objects as a line of people all facing one direction. The person at the back of the line can see all the other people and address each one directly, even if it has to go through the people directly in front of them. However, everyone has no way of knowing whom, if anyone, is directly behind him or her or if they are even listening. All they can do is say something (dispatch an event); they don't have to care whether it is heard. By avoiding a reliance on knowing the hierarchy above any particular object, adding new objects to the hierarchy becomes relatively trivial.

In Fig. 5.2, we have added Object4 to the second level of the hierarchy. All that needs to change is that Object1 needs to know the correct type of Object4 to properly address its public interface, and Object4 needs to know the same information about Object2. Granted, this is a very abstract and simple example, but a well thought-out structure will allow you to make changes like this without dire consequences to the rest of your application. Because games can vary so widely in their mechanics and behavior and because elements of gameplay tend to change throughout playtesting, having a flexible system is a requirement when building a game engine.

The Singleton: A Good Document Pattern

Although I don't subscribe to anyone about the design pattern for game development, I do like to use one particular pattern for the document class of my games. That pattern is known as the Singleton. The name sort of implies the concept behind it. A class that is a Singleton will only ever have one instance of itself in memory and provides a global point of access to that instance. In the context of a document or top-level class in a site, it ensures that there is always an easy way to get back to some basic core functionality. Say, for instance, that all the text for my game is loaded in from an external XML file because it is being localized into other languages. I don't want to load the XML over and over again whenever I need it, so it makes sense for my document class to be responsible for loading it and then make it available to all the objects down the display list. The Singleton pattern provides a good way of doing this because it essentially creates a global access point from anywhere, even non-DisplayObjects. However, this is a double-edged sword because abuse of this pattern to store too much data or rely too heavily on references back to the main class will break your encapsulation. In practice, you should never put references to a Singleton class inside an *engine* component you intend to re-use as this will make it too rigid. It should be reserved for classes that are being built for that specific game. Let's look at an example of a class set up as a Singleton. This file can be found in the Chapter 5 folder under SingletonExample.as.

```
package {

    import flash.display.MovieClip;

    public class SingletonExample extends MovieClip {

        static private var _instance:SingletonExample;

        public function SingletonExample(se:SingletonEnforcer) {
            if (!se) throw new Error("The SingletonExample
              class is a Singleton. Access it via the static
              getInstance method.");
        }

        static public function getInstance():SingletonExample {
            if (_instance) return _instance;
            _instance = new SingletonExample(new
              SingletonEnforcer());
            return _instance;
        }
    }
}

internal class SingletonEnforcer {}
```

Traditionally in other languages, a Singleton class would have a private constructor function, preventing you from calling it. However, in AS3, all constructors must be public, so we have to put in an error check to enforce proper use. The class keeps a static reference to its only instance, and the static getInstance method returns it. To prevent someone from arbitrarily instantiating the class, we create a secondary private class that is only accessibly to the main document. Think of it like the secret password for the Singleton's constructor. Only the getInstance method knows how to properly create a new SingletonExample instance as it will fail without this private class. This is a pretty commonly accepted way of dealing with basic Singleton classes in AS3. However, this particular example will also break when used as a document class. This is because Flash will automatically try to instantiate the class to create the display list hierarchy. To get this, we must modify the time of instantiation, alter the way the constructor works, and eliminate the private class. This new version can be found in SingletonExampleDocument.as.

```
package {

    import flash.display.MovieClip;

    public class SingletonExampleDocument extends MovieClip {

        static private var _instance:SingletonExampleDocument;

        public function SingletonExampleDocument() {
            if (_instance) throw new Error("This class is a
                Singleton. Access it via the static
                SingletonExampleDocument.getInstance method.");
            _instance = this;
        addEventListener(Event.REMOVED_FROM_STAGE, onRemove,
          false, 0, true);
        }

        private function onRemove(e:Event):void {
            _instance = null;
        }

        static public function getInstance():SingletonExample-
          Document {
            if (_instance) return _instance;
            _instance = new SingletonExampleDocument();
            return _instance;
        }
    }
}
```

As you can see in this modified version, we allow instantiation through the constructor once, relying on Flash to do it for us. Once it is created, the constructor will throw an error from here on out. The other addition we made is in case this document is loaded into another SWF. If this game is loaded into a container that has the ability to load and unload it multiple times, it's best to have the Singleton cleanup by itself once it is removed from the stage. This will prevent persistence of the Singleton in memory.

For another example of a Singleton in practice, refer to Chapter 8 on audio. The SoundEngine class we will create there will follow the same pattern. These types of controllers, or "engines," are good candidates for Singletons because they need to be easily accessible from anywhere in your game.

Summary

If you are interested in learning more about design patterns to use in your game development, there are links to good articles and other books on this book's website, www.flashgamebook.com. The bottom line to remember is to always do what makes sense for your situation and don't go overboard with a solution that isn't applicable to what you're doing. Ultimately, if your game is no fun, no one will care that it is a perfectly implemented, flawlessly designed model-view-controller pattern. Learning to program well and effectively is a journey, and given the ever-changing landscape of new languages, technologies, and platforms, no one will ever reach a destination where they can say "I'm done!" Well, someone might, but they'll be left in the dust pretty quickly by everyone else.

6

MANAGING YOUR ASSETS AND WORKING WITH GRAPHICS

While code is certainly a huge part of most games, the assets the code manipulates (art, sounds, text) are usually equally important. In all previous versions of Flash, all binary resources were stored in a proprietary format known as FLA. Unlike most programming languages where such resources reside as individual files separate from the code, every Flash file has an associated library that contains all the assets that will get bundled into the SWF at compile time. Luckily for us, this is one of the biggest and most welcome changes in Flash CS5.

A Better File Format

The FLA source file format of Flash has been a source of consternation for many developers over the years. It is completely binary and proprietary and can often be bulky if uncompressed assets are imported into it. This makes it very unfriendly for version control systems, like subversion, as each time the file is versioned it must upload the entire file. When you're working with a 30- to 40-MB FLA file (due to large audio assets or bitmaps), checking that file just 10 times will use 300–400 MB of disk space. In CS5, Adobe introduced a new file format called XFL. It consists of an XML file that stores all of the information about your settings, library, and timelines, and all of the raw assets in your library zipped into one file. In addition, and

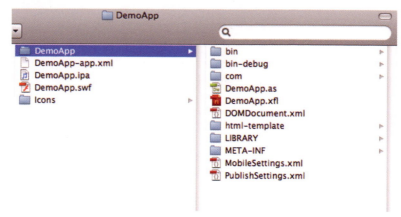

Figure 6.1 The new XML-based file structure of Flash CS5+.

even more importantly, Flash will now let you save the project in an uncompressed format. This means that instead of an FLA, you now have a folder with raw assets and the XML information file. Now when you use a version control system, only those elements that have changed will be updated. For example, if you only change the publish settings of an application in a minor way, only the settings of XML file will be versioned, and because it is text based, only the part of it that changed will be versioned. Another example would be when a developer receives an updated asset, such as a replacement sound file or bitmap. They can simply replace the file, republish the SWF, and check in the new file. This is a *huge* boon for projects with multiple developers and/or artists who work on the same files. Two people could theoretically work on the same project file, updating different parts of it, and a version control system would be able to merge their changes together (assuming there were no conflicts).

CONVERTING FLAs FROM CS4 AND EARLIER

If you save a CS4 FLA as an uncompressed XFL in CS5, you don't get an exposed folder of assets. Instead, because the assets were already converted to the own binary format of Flash, you get a folder of indistinguishable .dat files. This can be frustrating to discover if you're looking to update old files. If you plan to make more than minor edits to an older file, it might be worth taking the time to recreate it in a "fresh" CS5 file so that you can take full advantage of the format.

A Few Words about Organization

If you've worked in Flash for a very long time, you've probably had the opportunity to open someone else's Flash file from time to time. I've rarely found two developers who organize their library the same way. For a while, a popular convention was to sort library

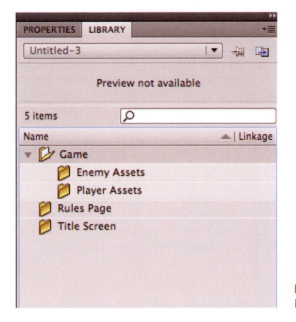

Figure 6.2 A library organized by "use."

assets by type, so there would be folders called MovieClips, Buttons, Bitmaps, etc. Some prefer to sort it by use, reflected in folder structures like Fig. 6.2.

The important thing to remember is that any organization is better than none, and often the complexity of the project will dictate the best structure to use. I typically use a hybrid of the two aforementioned methods. I will keep my visual assets (MovieClips, Images, Video) sorted by use and then by type inside their respective folders. I then keep items like sounds and font symbols organized strictly by type. My reasoning behind this is that having the items physically near each other in the library makes it easier to select and edit the properties of multiple items.

Working with Graphics

We're long past the days of Pong; the bar has been raised. With few exceptions, games are expected to have good-looking graphics and animation that feels natural and smooth, and Flash games are no different. In this section, I will outline the best formats to use for graphics in games and the use of the timeline for animation. I won't discuss creation of artwork for a couple of reasons. First, I am not an artist. Second, as Flash games become more and more sophisticated, it is less likely that one individual will be responsible for both the artwork and the code in a single game. If you work alone and/or you are interested in designing graphics for Flash games, I recommend checking out Robert Firebaugh's Flash

Professional 8 Game Graphics. While it's several versions behind now, it is still a great resource for learning how to design efficient artwork for use inside Flash.

Flash supports both vector and raster (bitmap) artworks. Each has its advantages and disadvantages in game development. Vector graphics are resizable without any quality loss, have usually much lower file size than raster, and they can be manipulated over the timeline to create seamless (if rather time-consuming) animations on the level of professional cartoons. However, vectors can be notoriously heavy on the CPU in large numbers or when used in large objects. Vector artwork is usually best created directly inside Flash though it can be done in a tool such as Adobe Illustrator. The upside of the first option is that Flash will automatically optimize vectors as they are drawn to use the least number of points possible. In a program like Illustrator where accuracy and pixel-perfect quality are valued over optimization, art tends to end up with bulkier vectors that must be cleaned up after they are imported into Flash. If you are working on a project with all vector artwork, less points translate to faster rendering and lower file size.

Most everyone will be familiar with and has used raster images, even if all you've ever done is use them as your computer's wallpaper. They have few advantages over vectors. First, they offer photorealism on a level that would not be possible without overly complex vector shapes. Many different art programs, including most 3D software, will render out images, where only a few will generate Flash-compatible vector files. They are also much less intense to render to the screen as Flash considers them on the level of complexity of a vector rectangle. They are not without their drawbacks, unfortunately. Raster images become exponentially heavy in file size as they increase in pixel size and cannot be resized inside Flash without a certain level of quality loss. Also, images with transparency are more taxing on the Flash renderer than ones without.

At this point, you may be saying "So, neither one is a clear winner. Which one should I use?" Once again, like library organization preferences, this is usually dictated by the project. There is no single right choice that will work across the board; very rarely I will use all one or the other. That said, I lean more heavily on raster images than I do vector when it comes to game development. Many games rely on the ability to render objects to the screen quickly to maintain a sense of excitement, and a significant number of detailed vectors will slow things down too much. As a general rule, the art for games I work on is usually about 80% raster and 20% vector. Characters, backgrounds, particle effects, etc. are all raster. Menus, in-game displays, and of course any text are vector.

Raster Formats to Use

The two best raster formats to use in Flash are JPEG and PNG. JPEGs are great when you don't need any transparency because the compression level and quality you can get out of external programs like Photoshop is better than what Flash will perform internally. Because of their lack of transparency, they also have a lower overhead on the Flash renderer. PNGs are the best solution when you need transparency in your images, but they cost more in file size and in processor power.

Most projects will be a blend of the two formats. Whenever possible, it's a good idea to use a JPEG for any assets that can function in a rectangular format without any transparency. This includes the following:

- Game and menu screen backgrounds
- Images that are going to be used as a texture in a bitmap fill
- Art that is going to get masked inside of another shape
- Overlays that will be used for some type of graphical effect over the game, like static or interference

PNGs are the best choice for clean transparency and are better for the smaller elements in a game, including as follows:

- Characters, especially those that are animated
- In-game elements that need to be separated from the background
- User interface elements like buttons and other irregular shapes
- Any image that has fine lines and needs pixel-perfect accuracy; JPEGs have a tendency to blur or muddy pixel-fine details in an image

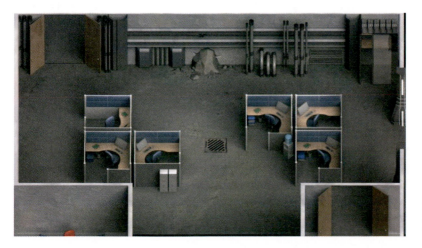

Figure 6.3 The background art for a game, saved as a JPEG file.

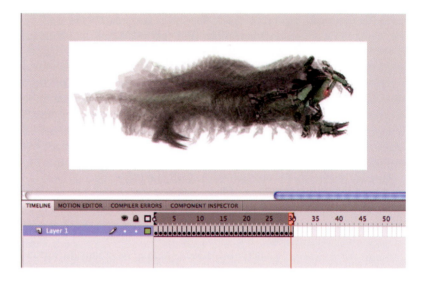

Figure 6.4 A character sequence of individual PNG files, with Onion Skinning turned on in Flash.

8-BIT PNGs WITH AN ALPHA CHANNEL

PNGs come in two flavors: 32 bit (or 16 million colors with a full 8-bit alpha channel) and 8 bit (256 colors). A seemingly little known fact about Adobe Fireworks is that it can generate a special type of PNG, which has an 8-bit color channel and an 8-bit alpha channel (sometimes called PNG8+8). If you're using artwork that has a fairly flat color palette or that won't degrade when the number of colors is reduced, this format is an outstanding option. It allows you to keep nice clean edges and transparency, thanks to a true alpha channel while reducing the file size by over 50%. In fact, this format is often smaller than the compressed version of a 32-bit PNG inside of Flash, and the resulting images look better. Hopefully, this format will eventually find its way into Photoshop's Save For Web feature. Until then, you can always use Fireworks to batch process your 32-bit PNGs to 8-bit PNGs.

Of course, these are just guidelines, not hard-and-fast rules, but using a combination of formats that take file size into account up front will save you time in the optimization phase. Another aspect of dealing with raster images is how Flash will handle them when compiling the game. Flash has a couple of different options when it comes to exporting images that can have an impact on how your game looks. Simply double-click on an image in your library to view its properties. You can also select multiple images at a time and adjust the properties of all of them at once.

Compression

When you import a JPEG file that has already been optimized in another application, Flash will use it "as-is" by default. But in case of PNGs, if the image has 256 colors or less, Flash will automatically

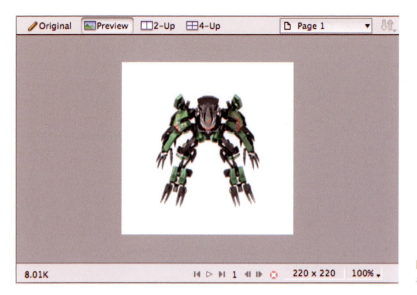

Figure 6.5 The result of saving a JPEG from Fireworks.

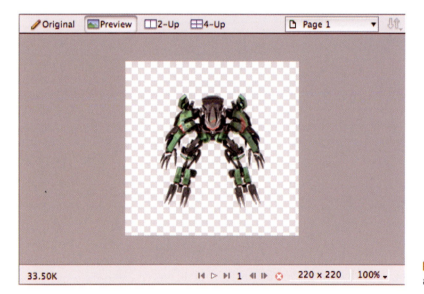

Figure 6.6 The result of saving a 32-bit PNG from Fireworks.

downconvert it to an 8-bit PNG file, and you get instant file size savings with no quality loss (also known as lossless compression). If the image has more than 256 colors, Flash will apply its own version of JPEG compression when your file is compiled. The level of this compression can be controlled at the document level in the Publish settings (where it defaults to 80%) and on a per-image basis. For any images that will be still on screen for any length of time, a setting of 70–80% is recommended to prevent too much degradation. For images that are used in a rapid sequence, like

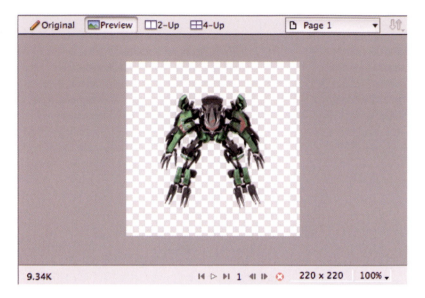

Figure 6.7 The result of saving an 8-bit PNG from Fireworks.

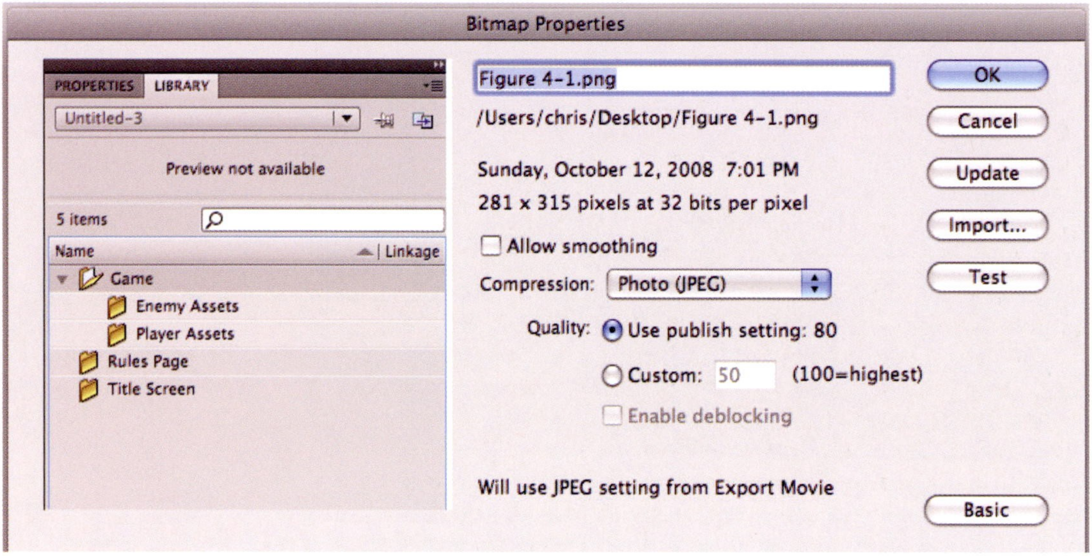

Figure 6.8 The Bitmap Properties panel will let you adjust the properties of a specific image or multiple images.

character animation, I've gotten away with as low as a setting of 50% without it being noticeable. In fact, at 30 frames per second, the human eye cannot perceive enough detail and the natural blurring effect of JPEG compression will create a nice sense of motion blur. Never use anything over 90% unless the game is going to be displayed on an enormous high-resolution display; you likely won't be able to tell the difference and the file size will jump up dramatically.

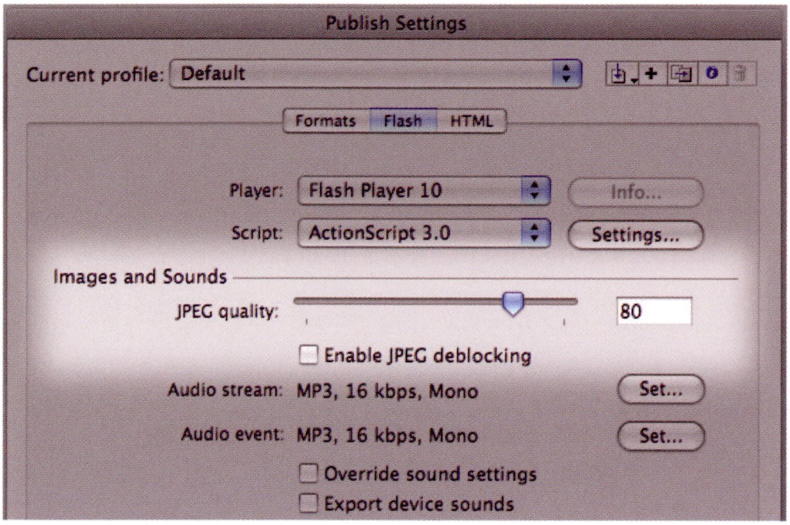

Figure 6.9 The Publish settings window allows you to set the default image quality.

Smoothing

By default, Flash does not re-render images as they are distorted in any form on the stage, including skewing, scaling, or even rotating (at any angle not divisible by 90). This causes a jagged, blocky effect that is very noticeable on any images that are not moving rapidly. If you have any raster elements in your game that need to be able to rotate or resize from time to time, consider checking the Allow smoothing box in the Bitmap Properties panel. While it looks considerably cleaner, this does tax the processor a little bit more per image, so use it sparingly and consider disabling it for some images if your game begins to stutter later on in testing.

Deblocking

Enabling deblocking will apply some extra smoothing to improve images that are set to an extremely low JPEG quality, as in 30 or less. Unless you are using many heavily compressed images, deblocking is probably not a feature you will need much.

External Image Tools

The artists I work with typically use Adobe Photoshop and Adobe Fireworks raster game art. They produce very good JPEG compression and very clean PNG files. If you're on a tight budget and can't afford (or don't need all the high-end features of) Photoshop, Fireworks by itself is a very satisfactory application. As of this writing, it is $300.

For vector art, I've known a number of artists who use the tools in Flash to great effect, which cost nothing extra and automatically optimize the vectors as they are created. Fireworks also has a very

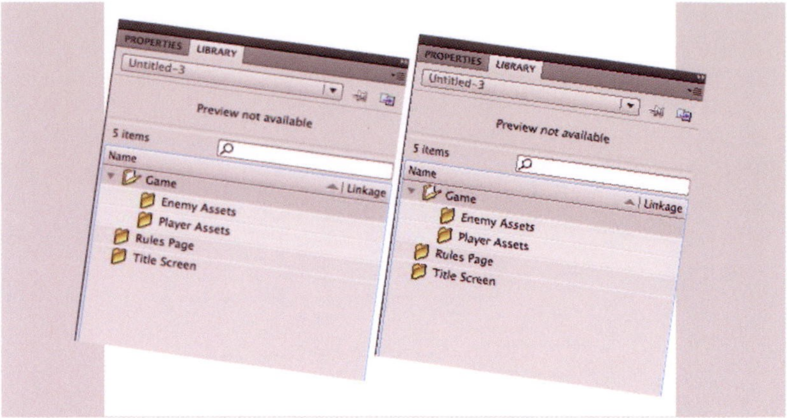

Figure 6.10 Bitmap Smoothing (on the left) can make a big difference, particularly in images with fine details.

nice set of vector tools that export easily into Flash. Over the years, I've also worked with artists who like Adobe Illustrator, but I find it to be overkill for the level of detail needed in most games and not all the effects (like complex blends and gradients) will translate well to Flash.

CS5.5 FEATURE: CONVERT TO BITMAP AND EXPORT TO BITMAP

Possibly, the two most exciting—and game development friendly—features to be included in Flash CS5.5 will change how you make the decision to use vector or raster assets. Although they have similar names, they behave very differently in practice. The first option, known as Convert to Bitmap, allows you to select any display object on stage, be it a raw shape or a symbol with lots of children, and convert it to a flattened bitmap. If the object is already a symbol in your library (recommended), you can still reference and modify the symbol. This is immensely helpful if you're working with game that was created in Flash using complex vector shapes, filters, etc., and all you really need is a nice clean bitmap at runtime. To use it, simply select the stage object you want to convert, right-click on it with the mouse, and select Convert to Bitmap, as shown in Figure 6.11. Because the bitmap is in your library now, you can also export it for use with ActionScript.

Alternatively, perhaps you need to maintain the fidelity of the original art because it is changing frequently and/or you don't need the bitmap data to be available in code. Under the Property Inspector for any symbol on the stage, where you used to set the Cache as Bitmap option, you can now select Export as Bitmap (shown in Figure 6.12). This will maintain the fidelity of the object in Flash but flatten it to a bitmap when the SWF is created. This is an extremely powerful tool because it allows you to create user interface elements in vector format that you can scale and size as necessary and have it ultimately output a more efficient bitmap in the SWF. It should be pointed out that this option

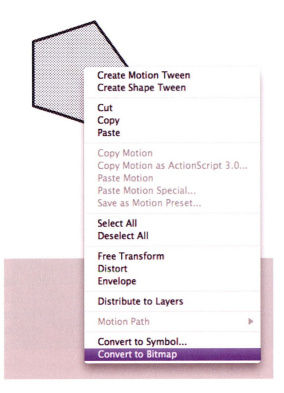

Figure 6.11 Using Flash CS5.5's new Convert to Bitmap option.

actually outputs is a Sprite or MovieClip object that contains a shape with a bitmap fill. I presume this was done to allow you to give the symbol a name on the stage and have that name still reference it correctly at runtime. However, it has the drawback that if you wanted to try to extract the BitmapData from it at runtime, and it's not an option because it is not a true Bitmap object.

Key Points to Remember

It's very easy when working with a lot of images in a game for users to get out of hand quickly, both in disorganization and file size.

- Be vigilant about keeping tabs on your images throughout the development process.
- Keep series of images organized in folders in your library.
- Keep images organized in the file system, so you can do "updates" in Flash rather than having to re-import them all over again if anything changes.
- Err on the side of smaller, both in dimension and file size, particularly with full-framerate animations.

will call a method named *createProjectile*. We will look at this method shortly. The function that runs every frame, *frameScript*, performs three tasks. It moves the player, moves all of the projectiles, and updates the position of the foreground and background tiles.

```
protected function movePlayer():void {
        player.x = mouseX;
        player.y = mouseY;
        if (mouseX > 0 && mouseX < _stageWidth && mouseY > 0 &&
            mouseY < _stageHeight) {
                Mouse.hide();
        } else Mouse.show();
}


protected function moveProjectiles():void {
        for each (var projectile:Projectile in _projectileList) {
                projectile.x += projectile.speed;
                if (projectile.x - projectile.width > _stageWidth) {
                        removeProjectile(projectile);
                }
        }
}
```

In the *movePlayer* function, the player's *x* and *y* positions are updated to match with those of the mouse. In addition, we check to make sure the mouse cursor is within the bounds of the stage. If it is, we hide the cursor so it does not cover up the player; otherwise, we show it. The *moveProjectiles* method iterates through the list of projectiles and updates each according to its speed. If the projectile has moved too far off the screen, it is removed.

```
protected function moveForeground():void {
        foreground.x -= _speed;
        var right:int = foreground.getRect(this).right;
        if (right <= _stageWidth) {
                foreground.x = right - _stageWidth;
        }
}


protected function moveBackground():void {
        background.x -= _speed/3;
        var right:int = background.getRect(this).right;
        if (right <= _stageWidth) {
                background.x = right - _stageWidth;
        }
}
```

These two functions are almost identical. The only real difference is that the background moves at one-third the rate of the foreground. This will give the impression that the background is much further away from the player.

```
protected function createProjectile(e:MouseEvent):void {
        var projectile:Projectile = new Projectile
            (_projectileSpeed);
        projectile.x = mouseX;
        projectile.y = mouseY;
        _projectileList.push(projectile);
        addChildAt(projectile, getChildIndex(player));
}


protected function removeProjectile(projectile:Projectile):
    void {
        if (projectile.parent == this) removeChild(projectile);
        _projectileList.splice(_projectileList.indexOf
            (projectile),1);
}
```

The last two functions in this class control are the creation and removal of projectiles. The *createProjectile* method is called when the mouse is pressed. It generates a new projectile object, moves it to the mouse's position, adds it to the vector list, and places it on the stage underneath the player. In *removeProjectile*, we simply pass any projectile instance as a parameter, and it is removed from the stage and spliced from the list.

When you run this example, you can see that the animation behind it is very basic, but effective. It conveys a continual sense of motion and gives the impression that we're traveling very quickly. It is also a good base on which to add components like enemies animating in the same direction as the foreground and background. In the next example, we will look at a very different kind of game, in which tweening is a more effective method of animation.

Memory: Tweening Animation

The following example is a simple memory game. There are six pairs of matching cards that have a gray back and one of six different colors on their front. The player clicks any two cards to flip over; if they match, they stay face up. If they do not match, they are flipped back over. In this instance, the game mechanic involves no motion by default, so we'll need to add animation to liven the experience up. This is when a tweening library like TweenMax comes in. We'll use TweenMax, combined with the 3D DisplayObject properties, to make the cards look like they're being flipped over. Like the last example, this game has two classes that control its functionality. The files can be found in the Chapter 6 examples folder; the main file is

Memory.fla and the two class files are Memory.as and MemoryCard. as. If you open the FLA file, you will see 12 instances of the Memory-Card class arranged on the stage. We'll look at this file first.

The MemoryCard Class

Each MemoryCard object is a MovieClip derivative that contains the face-down state on the first frame and all the other faces on subsequent frames. Every card needs to know what its value is so that it can display the correct frame, and so that the game can compare any two cards to determine a match. The card numbers start at one and go up, in this case to six.

```
package {

    import flash.display.MovieClip;

    public class MemoryCard extends MovieClip {

        protected var _cardNumber:int;

        public function MemoryCard() {
            stop();
        }

        public function get cardNumber():int {
            return _cardNumber;
        }

        public function set cardNumber(value:int):void {
            _cardNumber = value;
        }

        public function show():void {
            gotoAndStop(_cardNumber + 1);
        }

        public function hide():void {
            gotoAndStop(1);
        }
    }
}
```

Once a card has an assigned *cardNumber*, the *show* and *hide* methods are the two main functions in play. The *hide* method returns the card to its first frame, and the *show* method jumps to its respective cardNumber plus one. The rest of the functionality for this game is in the Memory class.

The Memory Class

```
package {

        import flash.display.Sprite;
        import flash.events.Event;
        import flash.events.MouseEvent;
        import gs.TweenMax;
        import gs.easing.*;

        public class Memory extends Sprite {
```

Because we're making use of the TweenMax classes here, we need to be sure to import them for our use. In this example, we import the main class, TweenMax, and the entire easing equation set. We won't use every equation, but it's helpful to have them all available so we can select just the right look and feel.

```
protected var _cardList:Vector.<MemoryCard>;
protected var _selectedCards:Vector.<MemoryCard>;

public function Memory() {
        addEventListener(Event.ADDED_TO_STAGE, addedToStage,
            false, 0, true);
}

protected function addedToStage(e:Event):void {
        _cardList = new Vector.<MemoryCard>();
        _selectedCards = new Vector.<MemoryCard>(2);
        for (var i:int = 0; i < numChildren; i++) {
                if (getChildAt(i) is MemoryCard) {
                        _cardList.push(getChildAt(i) as MemoryCard);
                }
        }
        shuffleCards();
        activateCards();
}
```

When the class is instantiated, it creates a list of all the cards on the stage and stores them in a vector. It also creates another vector of length 2 that will store up to two cards that have been clicked. The game then shuffles and activates the cards, which we will look at next.

```
protected function shuffleCards():void {
        var shuffledList:Vector.<MemoryCard> = new Vector.
            <MemoryCard>();
        while (_cardList.length > 0) {
                var rand:int = Math.round(Math.random()*(_cardList.
                    length-1));
```

```
                    var index:int = shuffledList.push(_cardList[rand])-1;
                    _cardList[rand].cardNumber = Math.floor(index / 2)+1;
                    _cardList.splice(rand, 1);
            }
            _cardList = shuffledList;
    }

    protected function activateCards():void {
            for each (var card:MemoryCard in _cardList) {
                    card.addEventListener(MouseEvent.CLICK,
                        selectCard, false, 0, true);
                    card.buttonMode = true;
            }
    }

    protected function deactivateCards():void {
            for each (var card:MemoryCard in _cardList) {
                    card.removeEventListener(MouseEvent.CLICK,
                        selectCard);
                    card.buttonMode = false;
            }
    }
```

The *shuffledCards* method does very much what you would expect; it creates a new list having randomly pulled from the original list. The two activation methods enable and disable mouse input, respectively. This is so the game can manage user input more easily and prevent impatient clicking from breaking the game logic.

```
    protected function selectCard(e:MouseEvent):void {
            deactivateCards();
            if (_selectedCards[0] == null) { //NO CARD SELECTED
                    _selectedCards[0] = e.target as MemoryCard;
                    flipCard(_selectedCards[0]);
            } else if (_selectedCards[0] == e.target) { //SAME CARD
                        SELECTED
                    flipCard(_selectedCards[0], false);
                    _selectedCards[0] = null;
                    activateCards();
            } else { //NEW CARD SELECTED
                    _selectedCards[1] = e.target as MemoryCard;
                    flipCard(e.target as MemoryCard);
            }
    }

    protected function flipCard(card:MemoryCard, show:Boolean =
        true):void {
```

```
    if (show) {
            TweenMax.to(card, .5, { onComplete:card.show,
                rotationY:90, ease:Back.easeIn });
            TweenMax.to(card, .4, { onComplete:checkCards,
                rotationY:0, ease:Quad.easeOut, delay:.5 });
    } else {
            TweenMax.to(card, .4, { onComplete:card.hide,
                rotationX:90, ease:Quad.easeIn });
            TweenMax.to(card, .5, { rotationX:0, ease:Bounce.
                easeOut, delay:.4 });
    }
}
```

When a card is clicked, the *selectCard* method is called. If no cards are selected, the clicked card becomes the first of a comparison pair. If the same card is selected again, it is flipped back over. Finally, if a second card is clicked, it is added to the pair and flipped. The *flipCard* method is the first place we use any TweenMax functionality. By default, this function will show the card face; if the second parameter is false, it will hide the card again. The most basic TweenMax syntax involves the two static methods *to* and *from*. The *to* method creates a TweenMax object that will be automatically disposed of when the tween finishes. The first parameter is the object that you want to tween, and the second parameter is the amount of time you want it to take in seconds. The final parameter is an object containing all the properties you want the tween to change, as well as information about which easing equation to use and what function to call when the tween is finished. TweenMax also supports a full event listener model, but it's a little overkill in this very simple instance.

When a card is flipped to be shown, the game first animates its *rotationY* property to appear to flip horizontally. Note that the easing method for this first tween is part of the *Back* class. The card will appear to turn the opposite direction for a brief moment before snapping toward its intended direction. When this tween is complete, it calls the card's *show* method and begins a tween restoring it to its original state. Once this second tween is complete, the *checkCard* method is called, which we will examine next. If the card is being hidden, the tween animates the card's *rotationX* property to flip the card vertically. When the card finally returns to its hidden state, the tween animates it using the *Bounce* easing class. This will give the effect of the card hitting a rubber surface.

```
protected function checkCards():void {
    if (!_selectedCards[1]) {
            activateCards();
    } else {
```

```
                    if (_selectedCards[0].cardNumber == _selectedCards
                        [1].cardNumber) {
                            _cardList.splice(_cardList.indexOf
                                (_selectedCards[0]),1);
                            _cardList.splice(_cardList.indexOf
                                (_selectedCards[1]),1);
                            TweenMax.to(_selectedCards[0], 1,
                                { rotationZ:180, ease:Elastic.easeOut });
                            TweenMax.to(_selectedCards[1], 1,
                                { rotationZ:-180, ease:Elastic.easeOut });
                    } else {
                            flipCard(_selectedCards[0], false);
                            flipCard(_selectedCards[1], false);
                    }
                    _selectedCards[0] = null;
                    _selectedCards[1] = null;
                    activateCards();
            }
        if (!_cardList.length) {
                trace("WON GAME");
        }
    }
```

The final method in the Memory class is *checkCards*. It looks at the *_selectedCards* list and checks to see if they have the same card number. If the cards are not a match, it flips them back over. If they are a match, they are removed from the main card list and have a final tween run on them. This tween uses *Elastic* easing to spin the cards with a rubber-band-like motion. Once the entire card list vector is empty, the game has been won.

Obviously, the tweens I chose to use here are largely arbitrary. One of the great things about TweenMax is how easy it is to change the values to experiment with different equations and timing. We are also not limited to simple position, rotation, and scale tweens. TweenMax has support for color and filter animation effects as well, so you can really go wild experimenting, and the syntax is still very straightforward. Feel free to explore the full library with this game example.

Summary

However, if you ultimately choose to execute animation in your game, make sure you consider how it affects the gameplay and what is most appropriate for the subject matter. A game that is intended for older adults or those who have vision difficulties should have more subtle, smooth animation to not become distracted. However, a game intended for most kids can't really ever have enough animation; and the wackier the animation the better! Remember, the wrong kind of animation is almost as bad as not having any at all because it breaks the tone you're trying to set. Just keep your theme in mind and tween away!

TURN IT UP TO 11: WORKING WITH AUDIO

Sound is the most sorely overlooked component in the world of Flash games. Because it can't be seen, it's very often tacked on at the end of a project, when someone realizes "this game really needs sound." It can mean the difference between a completely flat experience and a very rich one. Most of the best Flash games I've played had excellent sound design. It's not just that they used sound effects and/or music; it's that they paid attention to how the sounds blended together in the final mix. In this chapter, I'll outline the best formats to use for audio in games and different approaches to control sound within a game.

Formats to Use

I've heard many schools of thought from different developers on what formats they prefer. Some like nothing but WAV or AIFF files, both uncompressed formats. Others prefer MP3s that have already been compressed and are ready for export. The source format for audio doesn't matter quite as much as it does for graphics because audio is almost always re-encoded, when Flash exports a SWF. The export settings, which I will outline shortly, become very important at this point because they will determine how the audio ultimately sounds in a game. Much like graphic formats, I find that a blend of the two types based on how they're being used is the best way to make format decisions.

For sound effects, which I categorize as sounds that are event-triggered (like a punch or an explosion) and last no more than a few seconds, I prefer WAV files that have been saved with the following settings from a sound editor:

- Bit depth: 16
- Sample rate: 22 kHz
- Channels: Mono

This combination keeps the file size of each sound effect down, but also provides enough flexibility and quality for anyone but the most attentive audiophile.

For music or ambient sound (background sounds that provide atmosphere), I prefer MP3 files. There are a couple of reasons for this. First, music tracks for games should be fairly long (one minute or more) to avoid being too repetitive, and long sounds begin to create very large files. A one minute music track at the settings I described above for sound effects would be 2.5 MB. This doesn't seem like very much in this day and age, but consider if you had multiple music tracks and they started to get longer than one minute. This would add up pretty quickly and become cumbersome to manage and taxing on Flash's memory footprint. I've found that the following settings yield good-sounding music tracks:

- Constant bit rate (Flash doesn't like variable bit rate)
- Bitrate: 64 kbps

Depending on how prominent the music is in a game, a higher quality setting might be more appropriate. The same audio that would have been 2.5 MB as a WAV is 480 k; less than one-fifth the size.

Voice-over audio is a case where the context should determine the format. A computer voice speaking the name of a button when the user rolls over it is akin to a sound effect, so treat it like one. Narration, or any extended dialog, makes more sense to treat like music given its length.

Export Settings to Use

In the early days of Flash, when keeping SWF file size low was overwhelmingly important, developers got used to setting all their sounds to use the lowest possible quality. All the sounds were muddy and often indistinct, but no one seemed to care because everyone was doing it. Now, with ever-increasing audio and visual fidelity in games (both commercial and on the Web), the lowest common denominator won't usually cut it. Let's examine the Sound Properties window for a clip inside an FLA.

In this case, I have opened a file that was imported as an MP3. Flash automatically chose MP3 compression as the best option to use, and selected an option only available to MP3s: use imported

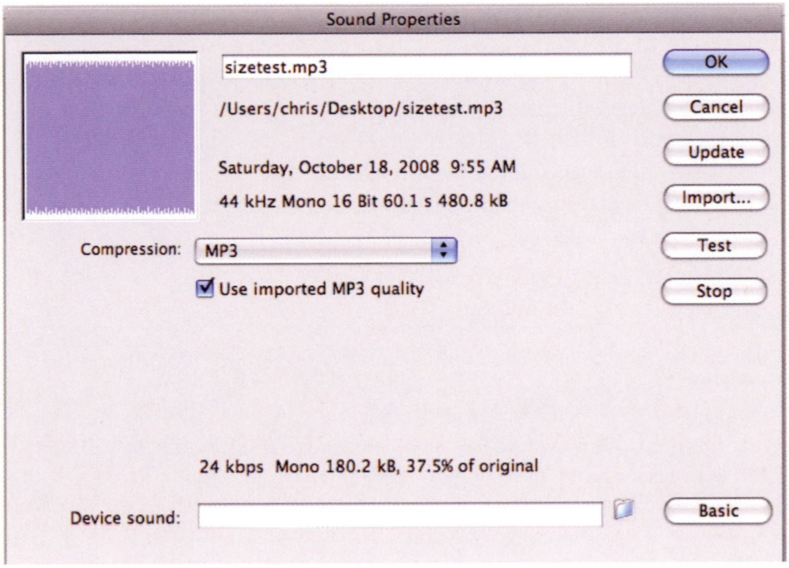

Figure 8.1 The Sound Properties window allows you to set the export settings for each individual sound in your library.

MP3 quality. This is a great option and not only means that the sound won't experience any further quality loss, but also the SWF will export faster than Flash if Flash had to recompress it.

CS5.5 Feature—Incremental Compilation

A new behind-the-scenes feature included in CS5.5 is something called incremental compilation. What this does is take assets that haven't changed since the last SWF file was created (specifically audio files set to export at MP3 and fonts, although hopefully Adobe will eventually extend this to all asset types) and cache the last compiled version of them. What this means, in practice, is that, large sounds that used to take upward of 10 seconds to export to MP3 will now take a fraction of a second. This cache is created the very first time you export a SWF in a session of CS5.5, so the very first export will take the original amount of time. However, every subsequent export you do until you close the Flash IDE or alter the audio asset's properties will benefit from this huge speed boost. Best of all, this happens automatically—you don't have to do anything to get the benefit!

You may be thinking at this point that it would simply make sense to use MP3 compression for every sound effect in a game and forego WAV files altogether. The problem with this approach is that it is taxing on the Flash Player to start the process of playing an MP3 file because it must be uncompressed in real time. A music track that only loops every one to two minutes isn't noticeable, but if you have many sound effects occurring in rapid succession, this can cause a bog down on the processor that hurts the game's performance. This is where a different form of compression comes in very handy.

ADPCM is a lower level of compression and sounds much closer to the source audio than an MP3. As you can see from Fig. 8.2, a one-second sound file that was 44 k in size becomes just 11 k, using a sample rate of 22 kHz and a bit depth of 4. Not only is this very small, but also it will cause far less overhead in the Flash Player.

OBSESSING OVER SOUND QUALITY

I tend to like to tweak the sound properties throughout the course of a project. Sometimes, a compressed sound will be noticeable garbled or distorted, when played by itself, but in the context of all the other sounds, it works fine. The opposite is also sometimes, true. I've often found that for short sound effects that exist in within a specific frequency range (beeps, clicks, and so on), you can even get away with lowering the bit depth to three without a noticeable difference, and squeeze out a few extra kilobytes. Your mileage may vary.

There is one other setting that is useful, specifically, for voice-over sounds: Speech. It has no options to set other than a sample rate (22 kHz is usually fine), and is a special variant of MP3 compression designed by Adobe to work best with a human voice. It also exports relatively quickly and doesn't seem to carry quite the overhead of a regular MP3.

If you only have a few sounds in your game, or you know most of your sounds are of the same type and will use the same form of compression, you can leave the individual sound properties set to Default and change them globally in the Publish Settings. You'll be most interested in the Audio Event settings; Audio Stream isn't

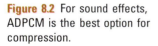

Figure 8.2 For sound effects, ADPCM is the best option for compression.

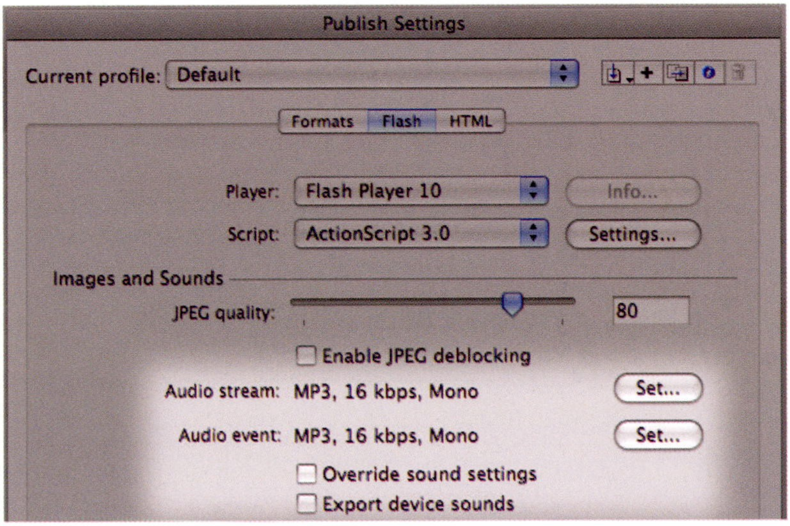

Figure 8.3 You can set the audio quality for all your sounds that don't use custom settings within the Publish Settings window.

commonly used within games—but later we'll look at a method for using it in an unorthodox way to maintain frame rate.

Using External Files

Flash isn't limited to playing sounds that are embedded within the FLA. External MP3 files can be loaded in and played at runtime. Although this feature doesn't really make sense for individual sound effects, music or other long sounds can work very well this way. The SWF isn't loaded down with the extra file size of the audio and can stream it in over time, once the rest of the game is loaded. Because you don't have to worry about how it impacts your initial load, it also makes increasing the quality (and, therefore, the file size) of the sound less of a concern. Below is a simple bit of ActionScript that loads in an external sound.

```
var sound:Sound = new Sound(new URLRequest("mySound.mp3"));
sound.play();
```

The one main drawback to this method is that it exposes your MP3 file to anyone with an activity viewer in his or her browser. Although you can copyright any assets of your game to prevent others from using them commercially, it does not prevent someone from stealing the individual files.

Tools for Working with Sounds

Probably the best choice for working with sound in Flash is Adobe's SoundBooth. It is cross-platform, and it supports multiple tracks for doing more complex mixing. It is reasonably priced and integrates nicely with Flash. Sony's Sound Forge is another excellent application, but it is expensive and is applicable only for Windows. If you are budget strapped (and on a Mac), HairerSoft's Amadeus Pro and Freeverse's Sound Studio are great options. Audacity is a free, cross-platform, open-source editor with a number of options, but if you need to do any level of sound manipulation greater than cropping and normalizing, it's really worth the money to spring for a higher end program. Links to the apps just mentioned are available on this book's Web site.

Scripting Sounds

Sounds are handled differently from all other media in Flash because they have no visual representation. There are two ways you can add sound to your game: through script and by, directly, placing sounds on the timeline. This is the case with most elements in Flash, except that when you add a button to the stage, for instance, you can also access it through script. The same is not true for sounds. A sound on the timeline is not accessible from ActionScript and, therefore, cannot be controlled. This forces developers to carefully choose how they are going to handle sounds.

At first, the obvious choice would be to always play sounds through script because it provides the most flexibility and control, and for games, this is almost always the case. The exception comes, however, when working with some animation. If a game has any segments that consist of long sequences of animation, like cutscenes, it makes more sense to play any accompanying sound effects on the timeline. This helps during sequencing to line up music or sound effects with the animation, and it's also just plain easier.

The reason it's all right to use timeline sound effects this way is because sequences like this are linear and noninteractive. The sounds are not likely to get stuck in a loop or linger around in memory because they weren't disposed of properly.

The rest of the time, scripting is the best way to control sounds. Because sounds don't need to adhere to the hierarchical structure of Display Objects, the best strategy is to create a generic sound controller that can play any type of sound and control its basic properties from anywhere in the game. To create this sound controller, we'll dive into some ActionScript.

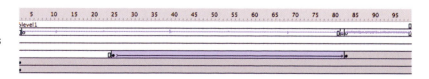

Figure 8.4 When creating long sequences of animation, it makes sense to use sound effects played through the timeline.

Understanding the Sound Classes

Scripting sounds has gotten slightly more complicated in AS3 than it was in AS2. As with many aspects of AS3, the increased complexity is matched by increased flexibility, but it can initially be confusing. Objects of the *Sound* class are really just containers for the actual sound data. When played, they generate a *SoundChannel* object, and any subsequent commands should be issued to this channel. As a result, you have to keep track of multiple objects to have any level of control over the sound you trigger.

Another way in which sounds are handled differently is that adjustable properties of sounds (like volume and panning) are no longer individually assignable components. They are handled through a new class known as the *SoundTransform*. To set the volume and pan of a sound, you need to change its channel's sound transform object. The following code starts a sound playing and then creates a transform at 100% volume (1) and centered pan (0):

```
var soundChannel:SoundChannel = mySound.play();
soundChannel.soundTransform = new SoundTransform(1, 0);
```

The SoundEngine Class

We'll create a class called SoundEngine that will manage playing all the sounds in a game and take care of storing all the pertinent objects. It will also provide us with easy methods to call for setting volume and pan without having to, manually, create new transforms. One other great feature it will afford us is the ability to call either internal sounds (found in the library) or external sound files. It will follow what is known as a Singleton design pattern, which you learned about in Chapter 5. Suffice it to say that there will only be one instance of the SoundEngine, and it will be accessible from anywhere. This will make playing sounds as simple as a line or two of code.

CODE IMPROVES FROM USE

The version of the SoundEngine I created in the first edition of this book was a good starting place, but it was the first iteration of that code. I, subsequently, started using it at my day job and encouraged others to do so as well. Almost immediately we discovered limitations in it and potential spots for bugs to arise. For a while, it became the most heavily edited library in our workplace, often the butt of a joke: "Something's broken: must be the SoundEngine." I'm pleased to say that thanks to the diligent work of several amazing developers, I am presenting this new, improved "SoundEngine 2.0" for this second edition. Most of the public interface has stayed the same from the first version, so if you've been using it, you should be able to easily replace your old files with this one without introducing any bugs. I'll note in the coming pages any significant changes between the two versions.

There are three class files we'll need to establish to create this engine. The first is the engine itself, SoundEngine.as. The second class is an internal "helper" class called SoundEngineObject. This object will store information about each individual sound as it is created in order to keep track of them. In the original version of this engine, I kept this class inside of the SoundEngine.as file, which, while tidy, left extensibility of the engine inflexible. It is still marked *internal*, but by being in its own file, other classes in the same package can access it. We'll discuss more about this class in a moment. The other file is a special type of event, SoundEngine-Event.as. This is the type of object the SoundEngine will dispatch when certain events, such as a sound reaching its end or an error in playing or loading a sound, occur within the engine.

Here's a quick rundown of the functionality this class will contain:

- Start sounds, both internal and external
- Stop sounds
- Pause/resume sounds
- Mute/unmute sounds
- Set and retrieve the volume of sounds
- Set and retrieve the pan of sounds
- Set and retrieve the entire active SoundTransform of sounds
- Retrieve the SoundChannel object that an active sound is using
- Add listeners that will be notified of events within the SoundEngine
- Retrieve the current status of a sound, such as whether it is playing, paused, or muted

All of this information can currently be retrieved from sounds, albeit with several lines of code. Our goal is to simplify this process and not have to rewrite this code every time we want to play a sound.

We'll begin in the SoundEngine.as file and set up the class definitions we'll be using.

```
package
{
        import flash.events.EventDispatcher;
        import flash.events.IOErrorEvent;
        import flash.media.Sound;
        import flash.media.SoundChannel;
        import flash.media.SoundMixer;
        import flash.media.SoundTransform;
        import flash.net.URLRequest;
        import flash.system.ApplicationDomain;
        import flash.utils.getDefinitionByName;

    public class SoundEngine extends EventDispatcher {
        }
    }
```

We'll need access to parts of the events package to be able to dispatch events, as well as the media package, where all the sound-related classes are stored. We'll also need the *URLRequest*-class to load external files, and the *ApplicationDomain* class and *getDefinitionByName* method to look up sounds in the library.

Inside the SoundEngine class, we'll add some basic properties and the constructor for the class:

```
protected var _soundList:Object;
protected var _allMuted:Boolean = false;
protected var _debug:Boolean = false;
static private var _instance:SoundEngine;

public function SoundEngine(validator:SoundEngineSingleton) {
       if (_instance) throw new ArgumentError ("SoundEngine is a
         Singleton class. Use getInstance() to retrieve the existing
         instance.");
       _soundList = new Object();
}

static public function getInstance():SoundEngine {
       if (!_instance) _instance = new SoundEngine(new SoundEngine-
         Singleton());
       return _instance;
}
```

The top five lines are variable declarations for the properties that we are going to store in the engine. The _soundList property will be used to keep track of all the SoundEngineObjects the engine creates. The _allMuted property will help us determine if the engine is currently muted, so that any new sounds played will be muted as well. There is a _debug flag that can be set to toggle debug information printing to the output window—one of the additions of my coworkers. Finally, the _instance property is also static; it will be used to store the one SoundEngine object that gets created, so we can always access it.

The constructor of a Singleton should technically be private, so that nothing outside the class can instantiate it. However, Action-Script 3 does not support private constructors, so we have to use a work-around, which I will discuss momentarily. First, let's look at the getInstance method. It is static, so it will be accessible from anywhere as SoundEngine.getInstance(). If an instance of the engine has not yet been created, it stores a new one in the _instance property I mentioned earlier. It then simply returns the instance it has created. You probably noticed that both the methods make use of a class called SoundEngineSingleton. This is an empty class that we will define internally to prevent any other class outside of the engine from creating a new one. Without access to this internal class, only the SoundEngine is capable of creating itself. We will accomplish this with an additional line at the bottom of the file:

```
class SoundEngineSingleton {}
```

Flash infers that a class declared this way is internal, so we're done. Now anyone who uses the class has only one way of getting to the SoundEngine and is prevented from accidentally breaking some of its functionality or creating more than one engine. Think of it as the key to the engine; without it the engine won't start.

Now that we've defined the basic properties of the engine and established a way to create and access it, we should jump over to the SoundEngineObject class to define exactly what each object will do, when created.

```
static private var _canPlaySound:Boolean = Capabilities.hasAudio;

public var name:String;
public var sound:Sound;
public var channel:SoundChannel;

protected var _transform:SoundTransform;
protected var _playing:Boolean = false;
protected var _muted:Boolean = false;
protected var _paused:Boolean = false;
protected var _pauseTime:Number;
protected var _loops:uint;
protected var _offset:Number;

public function SoundEngineObject(name:String, sound:Sound) {
        this.name = name;
        this.sound = sound;
}
```

The first property is a static flag called _canPlaySound, which reads the system's ability to play sound files. What we discovered through testing was that on a machine with a broken or missing sound card, any requests to play sound by Flash will cause a runtime error. While Adobe should have just chosen to suppress any such errors, we introduced this flag to do an initial check and make sure that no sounds are played if such a scenario exists. Before performing any sound-based operations, the class will check this value to make sure no error will be caused. Each engine object stores the basic information about the sound it creates, such as the channel, the transform, the number of times it should loop, and so on. Additionally, each object has a name property, which is how the engine will keep track of, or index, them. Now, we'll add some methods to the object, so that it can perform actions and give information.

```actionscript
public function play(offset:Number = 0, loops:int = 0, transform:
  SoundTransform = null):SoundChannel {
      if (_canPlaySound) {
              _offset = offset;
              if (loops < 0) loops = int.MAX_VALUE;
              _loops = loops;
              channel = sound.play(_offset, _loops, transform);
              if (channel == null) {
                      _canPlaySound = false;
                      return null;
              }
              _transform = channel.transform;
              if (isMuted) { //In case this sounds was muted,
                paused, and then resumed
                      mute(true);
              }
        channel.addEventListener(Event.SOUND_COMPLETE, complete,
          false, 0, true);
              _playing = true;
              return channel;
      } else {
              return null;
      }
}


public function stop():void {
      if (_canPlaySound && channel != null) {
              channel.stop();
              _loops = 0;
              _playing = false;
              dispatchEvent(new SoundEngineEvent
                (SoundEngineEvent.SOUND_STOPPED, name));
      }
}


protected function complete(e:Event):void {
      if (_canPlaySound && channel != null) {
              _playing = false;
              dispatchEvent(new SoundEngineEvent(SoundEngineEvent.
                SOUND_COMPLETE, name));
      }
}


public function get isPlaying():Boolean {
      return _playing;
}
```

The *play* and *stop* methods start and stop the sound object, respectively, and store the information about how the sound is to be played. They also set up a listener for the SOUND_COMPLETE event, which is dispatched when the sound finishes. You'll probably notice I used a lot of the same syntax Sound and SoundChannel objects so as to stay consistent with ActionScript's conventions. If the same sound is called multiple times before it is able to finish, as might well be the case in a game in which a player fires some type of projectile, any currently playing channel should be allowed to finish and then remove itself. Also, we allow the option for sound to loop endlessly by passing in a negative number (preferably −1) and then setting the number of loops to the largest possible integer. In the original version of the engine, I used the SOUND_COMPLETE event to check and start the sound looping again. However, this led to a "hiccup" every time the sound looped because of the delay between the event and the sound actually restarting. The only way to get a smooth, seamless loop is to pass in a loop count to the play method. There is also one public "getter," which will return whether or not the sound is currently playing; this functionality does not exist in the basic Sound classes in ActionScript and is very helpful information to have in a game. If background music is already playing, for example, then you don't want to accidentally start it a second time.

```
public function get volume():Number {
        if (_canPlaySound && channel != null) {
                return channel.soundTransform.volume;
        } else {
                return 0;
        }
}


public function set volume(value:Number):void {
        if (_canPlaySound && channel != null) {
                var tf:SoundTransform = _transform;
                tf.volume = value;
                _transform = tf;
                if (!_muted) channel.soundTransform = _transform;
        }
}


public function get pan():Number {
        if (_canPlaySound && channel != null) {
                return channel.soundTransform.pan;
        } else {
                return 0;
        }
}
public function set pan(value:Number):void {
```

```
        if (_canPlaySound && channel != null) {
                var tf:SoundTransform = _transform;
                tf.pan = value;
                _transform = tf;
                if (!_muted) channel.soundTransform = _transform;
        }
}

public function get transform():SoundTransform {
        if (_canPlaySound && channel != null) {
                return channel.soundTransform;
        } else {
                return null;
        }
}

public function set transform(value:SoundTransform):void {
        if (_canPlaySound && channel != null) {
                _transform = value;
                if (!_muted) channel.soundTransform = _transform;
        }
}
```

These six methods allow us to set the individual properties controlling volume and pan of the sound, as well as the raw transform object. Note that if the sound is muted, the transforms are stored but not applied; when they are unmuted, they will reference this stored transform.

```
public function mute(value:Boolean):void {
        if (_canPlaySound && channel != null) {
                _muted = value;
                if (_muted) {
                        channel.soundTransform = _transform;
                } else {
                        channel.soundTransform = new SoundTransform
                          (0, 0);
                }
        }
}

public function get isMuted():Boolean {
        return _muted;
}

public function pause(value:Boolean):void {
        if (_canPlaySound && channel != null) {
                _paused = value;
                if (_paused) {
                        var normalOffset:Number = _offset;
```

```
                                    play(_pauseTime, _loops, _transform);
                                    _offset = normalOffset;
                        } else {
                                    _pauseTime = channel.position;
                                    channel.stop();

                        }

            }

}


public function get isPaused():Boolean {
        return _paused;
}
```

The final methods in the class control the pausing and muting of the sound, as well as information about each. In the pause method, we store where the sound is when it is paused and stop it, using this information as the offset when we resume. In the mute method, we simply toggle between a zeroed-out SoundTransform object and the one stored in our _transform property. Note that, in the original version, these methods took no parameters and simply toggled the value of the internal property. This led to inconsistencies where some objects could get set to muted and some not and then toggling would just invert both sets; there was no way to force *all* of them to mute. By making the passing of a value explicit this solves the issue.

Now that we have an understanding of how each object will work in the engine, we can return to the main class and see how each is accessed. Back in the SoundEngine class:

```
public function playSound(name:String, offset:Number = 0, loops:
    int = 0, transform:SoundTransform = null, applicationDomain:
    ApplicationDomain = null):SoundChannel {
        if (!_soundList[name]) { //SOUND DOES NOT EXIST
                var sound:Sound;
                var soundClass:Class;
                try {
                        soundClass = (applicationDomain != null) ?
                          applicationDomain.getDefinition(name) as
                          Class : getDefinitionByName(name) as Class;
                } catch (err:ReferenceError) {
                        if (_debug)
                                trace("SoundEngine Message: Could
                                  not find sound object with name
                                  " + name + ". Attempting to load
                                    external file.");
                }
                if (soundClass) { //INTERNAL REFERENCE FOUND -
                  CREATING SOUND OBJECT
                        sound = new soundClass() as Sound;
```

```
        } else { //NO INTERNAL REFERENCE FOUND - WILL
          ATTEMPT TO LOAD
            sound = new Sound(new URLRequest(name));
            sound.addEventListener(IOErrorEvent.
              IO_ERROR, onIOError, false, 0, true);
        }
        _soundList[name] = new SoundEngineObject(name, sound);
    _soundList[name].addEventListener(SoundEngineEvent.
      SOUND_COMPLETE, onSoundEvent, false, 0, true);
    _soundList[name].addEventListener(SoundEngineEvent.
      SOUND_STOPPED, onSoundEvent, false, 0, true);
    }
    var channel:SoundChannel = _soundList[name].play(offset,
      loops, transform);
    if (channel == null) {
        return null;
    }
    if (_allMuted) _soundList[name].mute(true);
    return channel;
    }

protected function onIOError(e:IOErrorEvent):void {
    if (_debug)
        trace("SoundEngine Error Message: Failed to load
          sound: " + e.text);
    delete _soundList[e.target.url];
    dispatchEvent(new SoundEngineEvent(SoundEngineEvent.
      SOUND_ERROR, e.target.url));
}

protected function onSoundEvent(e:SoundEngineEvent):void {
    dispatchEvent(e);
}

public function stopSound(name:String = null):void {
    if (name) {
        if (_soundList[name]) {
            _soundList[name].stop();
        } else if (_debug) {
            trace("Sound "+ name + " was not found,
              ignoring stop command.");
        }
    } else {
        for (var i:String in _soundList) {
            _soundList[i].stop();
        }
    }
}
```

The *playSound* method is the largest and most important in the entire class. It checks to find whether the sound requested has ever been played (created) before. If it hasn't, the getDefinitionByName method is used to look up the sound by name in the library. If a custom *ApplicationDomain* was specified (which we'll further discuss in Chapter 14), it attempts to look up the sound name in that domain instead. We found this to be necessary, when loading asset SWF files with sounds embedded in them, so this is a considerable improvement in flexibility over the original version. If the sound cannot be found, the assumption is made that an external file was requested, and the sound uses the name as the URL to load the sound. Once the sound engine object has been created, listeners are attached to it to be notified, when the sound completes or is stopped. An additional listener is also added if the sound is in an external file and loading it fails. The two additional protected methods, *onIOError* and *onSoundEvent*, are for dispatching events to anything listening to the engine. The *stopSound* method does what you would expect; it stops the sound passed in for the name parameter. However, we've added an extra feature—if no sound name is passed in, the engine will stop all the sounds. During a game, you might often need to kill every sound that's playing, and this prevents you from having to name them individually.

Next, we move on to the volume, pan, and transform methods:

```
public function setVolume(value:Number, name:String = null):void {
        if (name) {
            if (_soundList[name]) {
                _soundList[name].volume = Math.max
                    (0, Math.min(1, value));
            } else {
                throw new Error("Sound " + name + "
                    does not exist.");
            }
        } else {
            for (var i:String in _soundList) _soundList[i].
                volume = Math.max(0, Math.min(1, value));
        }
    }

public function getVolume(name:String):Number {
        if (_soundList[name]) {
            return _soundList[name].volume;
        } else {
            throw new Error("Sound " + name + " does not exist.");
        }
        return 0;
    }
```

```
public function setPan(value:Number, name:String = null):void {
        if (name) {
                if (_soundList[name]) {
                        _soundList[name].pan = value;
                } else {
                        throw new Error("Sound " + name + " does not
                          exist.");
                }
        } else {
                for (var i:String in _soundList) _soundList[i].pan
                  = value;
        }
}

public function getPan(name:String):Number {
        if (_soundList[name]) {
                return _soundList[name].pan;
        } else {
                throw new Error("Sound " + name + " does not
                  exist.");
        }
        return 0;
}

public function setTransform(transform:SoundTransform, name:
    String = null):void {
        if (name) {
                if (_soundList[name]) {
                        _soundList[name].transform = transform;
                } else {
                        throw new Error("Sound " + name + " does not
                          exist.");
                }
        } else {
                for (var i:String in _soundList) _soundList[i].
                  transform = transform;
        }
}

public function getTransform(name:String):SoundTransform {
        if (_soundList[name]) {
                return _soundList[name].transform;
        } else {
                throw new Error("Sound " + name + " does not exist.");
        }
        return null;
}
```

Note how each of the "setter" functions follows the form of the *stopSound* method; if no specific sound is passed in, the method runs on all of them.

```
public function mute(value:Boolean = false, name:String = null):
  void {
        if (name) {
                if (_soundList[name]) {
                        _soundList[name].mute(value);
                        if (!_soundList[name].isMuted) _allMuted
                          = false;
                } else {
                        throw new Error("Sound " + name + " does not
                          exist.");
                }
        } else {
                _allMuted = value;
                for each (var i:SoundEngineObject in _soundList) {
                        i.mute(_allMuted);
                }
        }
}

public function pause(value:Boolean = true, name:String = null):void {
        if (name) {
                if (_soundList[name]) {
                        _soundList[name].pause(value);
                } else {
                        throw new Error("Sound " + name + " does not
                          exist.");
                }
        } else {
                for (var i:String in _soundList) _soundList[i].
                  pause(value);
        }
}

public function isPlaying(name:String):Boolean {
        if (_soundList[name]) {
                return _soundList[name].isPlaying;
        }
        else if (_debug) {
                trace("Sound " + name + " does not exist.");
        }
        return false;
}

public function isPaused(name:String):Boolean {
```

```
        if (_soundList[name]) {
            return _soundList[name].isPaused;
        }
        else {
            throw new Error("Sound " + name + " does not exist.");
        }
            return false;
}
public function isMuted(name:String = null):Boolean {
        if (name) {
            if (_soundList[name]) {
                    return _soundList[name].isMuted;
            } else throw new Error("Sound " + name + " does not
              exist.");
            return false;
        } else {
            return _allMuted;
        }
        return true;
}
```

The *pause* and *mute* methods work the same way as their
SoundEngineObject counterparts, simply applying the setting to all
sounds or just one. If any sounds attempt to play when _allMuted
is true, they are created and then immediately muted as well. The
isMuted method reflects this as well—if no sound is specified, then
it will return the value of _allMuted. Also worth noting is that for
all of these methods (except *isPlaying*), an error is thrown if the
sound named doesn't exist. That concludes the functionality of the
SoundEngine class.

You most likely noticed that the type of event dispatched by the
SoundEngine was of the type SoundEngineEvent, referring to the file
mentioned earlier. We'll now take a quick look at that custom event.

```
package {

import flash.events.Event;

public class SoundEngineEvent extends Event {
        static public const SOUND_COMPLETE:String =
          "soundComplete";
        static public const SOUND_STOPPED:String = "soundStopped";
        static public const SOUND_ERROR:String = "soundError";
        protected var _name:String;

        public function SoundEngineEvent( type:String, name:
          String, bubbles:Boolean=false, cancelable:Boolean=
          false ){
```

```
                    _name = name;
                    super(type, bubbles, cancelable);
            }
            override public function clone() : Event {
                    return new SoundEngineEvent(type, name, bubbles,
                        cancelable);
            }

            public function get name():String {
                    return _name;
            }
    }
}
```

The three constants defined at the top of the class are used to clearly define the types of events that the SoundEngine can dispatch. The SoundEngineEvent is just like a normal event, except that it contains one extra piece of data: the name of the sound that generated the event. Without this, there would be no distinguishing of one sound event from the next, especially when many were occurring all at once.

Using the Class

Now that we have the class complete, we'll set up a test file to ensure that it is working. Create a new ActionScript 3 FLA. Import the test sound effect provided to the library. To set up the sound to be available to ActionScript, double-click it to pull up its Properties panel. Under the Linkage area, select the checkbox to export the Sound for ActionScript. In the Class field, type "Explosion"; this is how you'll refer to this sound from this point on. Flash will automatically fill in the Base Class as an object of type Sound.

Save the FLA alongside the SoundEngine class file so Flash will know how to find it. Open the Actions panel and type the following in frame 1:

```
var se:SoundEngine = SoundEngine.getInstance();
se.playSound("Explosion");
```

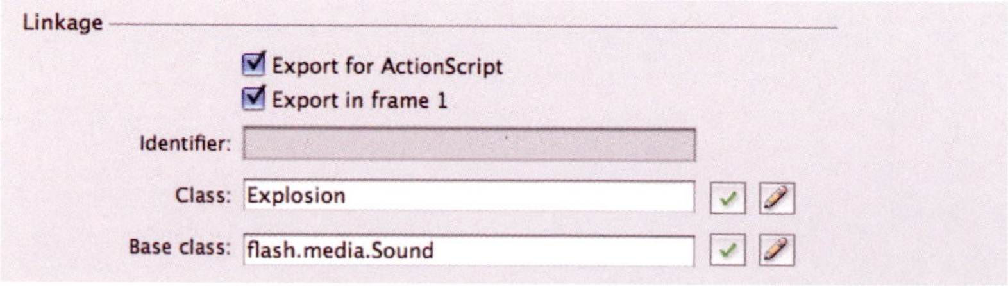

Figure 8.5 Use the Linkage properties to set up a sound for export.

When you test your SWF, you should hear the sound effect play. Note that we create a reference to the SoundEngine for convenience. If you were merely calling a single sound effect in a script and had no reason to store a reference, you could shorten the call this way:

```
SoundEngine.getInstance().playSound("Explosion");
```

Because this engine only exposes the existing functionality of the Sound classes in a simpler and more convenient way, there is plenty of other functionality that could be added in companion classes. For instance, the ability to fade out sounds over time or crossfade sounds to create musical transitions are both features that don't make sense in a basic sound engine but are very useful in games. In fact, we'll now look at a companion class, which a coworker of mine created based on the SoundEngine. Many thanks to Curry McKnight for this code! It makes use of TweenLite, just as the example in Chapter 7.

```
public class SoundTweener
{
      public static function allFrom( _duration:Number, _vars:
        Object ):TweenGroup
      {
            var soundList:Object = SoundEngine.getInstance().
              soundList;
            var soundArray:Array = new Array();
            for each( var soundObj:SoundEngineObject in soundList)
                    soundArray.push( soundObj );
            if( soundArray.length )
            {
                    return TweenGroup.allFrom( soundArray,
                      _duration, _vars, TweenLite );
            }
            else
            {
                    return null;
            }
      }

      public static function allTo( _duration:Number, _vars:
        Object ):TweenGroup
      {
            var soundList:Object = SoundEngine.getInstance().
              soundList;
            var soundArray:Array = new Array();
            for each(var soundObj:SoundEngineObject in soundList)
                    soundArray.push( soundObj );
```

```
                if( soundArray.length )
                {
                        return TweenGroup.allTo( soundArray,
                          _duration, _vars, TweenLite );
                }
                else
                {
                        return null;
                }
        }

public static function from( _sound:String, _duration:
  Number, _vars:Object ):TweenLite
{
        var soundObj:SoundEngineObject = SoundEngine.
          getInstance().soundList[ _sound ];
        if( soundObj )
        {
                return TweenLite.from( soundObj, _duration,
                  _vars );
        }
        else
        {
                return null;
        }
}

public static function to( _sound:String, _duration:Number,
  _vars:Object ):TweenLite
{
        var soundObj:SoundEngineObject = SoundEngine.
          getInstance().soundList[ _sound ];
        if( soundObj )
        {
                return TweenLite.to( soundObj, _duration,
                  _vars );
        }
        else
        {
                return null;
        }
}

public static function killAllTweens( _complete:Boolean =
  false ):void
{
        var soundList:Object = SoundEngine.getInstance().
          soundList;
```

```
            for each( var soundObj:SoundEngineObject in
              soundList )
                      TweenLite.killTweensOf( soundObj,
                        _complete );
      }


      public static function killTweensOf( _sound:String,
        _complete:Boolean = false ):void
      {
              var soundObj:SoundEngineObject = SoundEngine.
                getInstance().soundList[ _sound ];
              if( soundObj )
              {
                      TweenLite.killTweensOf( soundObj,
                        _complete );
              }
      }
}
```

This class consists of a set of static methods that directly interface with the SoundEngineObjects and the list of them contained in the SoundEngine. Simply provide the name of the sound you want to control and pass it parameters the same way you would any other kind of tween object. Here's how it would look in practice.

```
var se:SoundEngine = SoundEngine.getInstance();
se.playSound("EngineHum");
SoundTweener.from("EngineHum", 1, { volume:0 } );
```

This will start an engine sound and then tween it to its normal value starting at 0. Just like a normal TweenLite object, you can also pass any custom-easing functions to give your sound just the effect you're looking to achieve.

The SoundMixer Class

One other class worth mentioning in the audio section of Flash is the SoundMixer. It is the global sound controller for the Flash Player and has its own SoundTransform. If you need to do something basic like simply mute all the sounds in your game outside of the SoundEngine, you can accomplish it with a very simple script.

```
SoundMixer.soundTransform = new SoundTransform(0);
```

You can also use the SoundMixer to stop every sound that is playing inside of Flash, the descendant of *stopAllSounds*() from all the way back in Flash 3. While I recommend using a class like the SoundEngine to manage playback and control of your sounds, SoundMixer is a nice fallback if you are loading in content created by someone else and you need to control any rogue sounds.

FLASH HACK: THE SOUND OF SILENCE

At a conference I once heard a Flash cartoonist reveal a secret for how he made sure that Flash could keep up with the set frame rate and slow down on older machines. Although it applied to Flash 5, I've found it can still help in a pinch today. Basically, he would put a clip on the main timeline that had a one-second sound with total silence in it, set to stream, and loop it 9 or 10 times. The way Flash is designed to work is that it will skip rendering frames in order to keep in sync with streaming sounds on the timeline. It will, however, continue to process frame scripts, meaning that any scripts that are reliant on the frame rate will still run. In essence, it may make gameplay choppier on slow computers, but it will play at the correct speed. The reason he looped it a number of times is that each time a streaming sound restarts the Flash player will stutter momentarily if the processor is maxed out. The clip will play straight through and only have to restart the stream every 10 seconds or so. At this rate, it is barely noticeable and makes a huge impact on the playability of complex games. Because the sound is made up of silence, you can use the highest compression settings possible that would turn any other sounds to utter garbage, and it won't make a difference. It won't add more than a few kilobytes to your end file and is worth the peace of mind that the game will, at least, keep up on older machines.

The bottom line to remember with sounds is to not to forget them. There is almost no game experience that cannot be enhanced by a well-implemented soundtrack. Make audio a priority, and your game will be stronger as a result.

PUT THE VIDEO BACK IN "VIDEO GAME"

Video is probably used more than you might initially think in Flash games. Video is a great format for noninteractive cutscenes because the performance is consistently satisfactory (Adobe has put a great deal of effort into making sure that video plays smoothly in Flash), and it can be created and stored completely externally to a game. In this chapter, we'll see how it is also an excellent container for character animations, particle effects, and other small in-game animations. We'll also explore the Adobe Media Encoder that comes with Flash CS5 and the different settings to use for each type of video.

Video Codecs

Flash can handle a few different formats of video, all of which cater to different uses. The first, and the oldest, is Sorenson Spark. Although it tends to show the most compression artifacts on a higher-resolution video, its processor requirements are modest, and it requires the least horsepower of any of Flash's codecs. It works well for a game that needs to support older machines and where the video isn't going to get very large. In Flash 8, Flash introduced the On2 VP6 codec. The compression quality and file size are much improved over Spark, albeit at a higher cost of CPU overhead. The best feature of VP6 is that it can be encoded with an alpha channel, so parts of the video can be transparent. For larger videos an alpha channel can begin to drag down the performance, whereas at smaller dimensions it is a lifesaver for both the performance and file size (which we will discuss momentarily). The final and the most recent addition to Flash is H.264 (or MPEG-4 based) video. It is by far the best-looking video available in Flash and rivals the quality of either QuickTime or Windows Media Player. The two drawbacks are that it is very processor intensive and it does not support an alpha channel, so you can think of it as more of an upgrade to Spark than a replacement for VP6. I would recommend it for cutscenes in games in which the target machine is relatively new; the quality cannot be beaten. In addition, in some current and future iterations of the Flash Player, H.264 video will be hardware accelerated, meaning it will utilize the end users' GPU on their video card to deliver lightning fast performance and leave the CPU free up to run your code and other rendering tasks.

External Video Uses: Cutscenes and Menus

With console and commercial computer games reaching awe-inspiring levels of graphical sophistication, the bar is naturally raised on even simple Web-based games to look polished and "modern." This feel can be achieved through the use of cutscenes in games that are story driven. When used wisely (and not overused), such as between levels or as a payoff at the end, they add a very cinematic quality to a game.

Another way of effectively incorporating video is in menus. Most players of Flash games are used to just static buttons and text on a menu screen. By utilizing even a simple video loop created in Adobe After Effects (or even created in Flash and then exported as a movie),

Figure 9.1 Video cutscenes can add a very immersive element to a game and can make Flash games look more polished and modern on a par with commercial games.

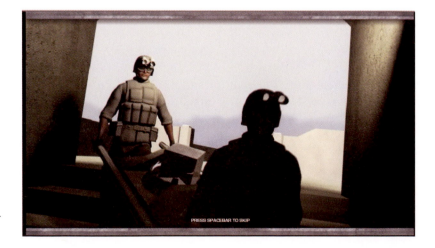

a menu can be much more dynamic and hold players' visual interest enough to get them into the game. Because these two uses of video are passive, or noninteractive, it makes the most sense to load the video files externally rather than embedding them in the game SWF. We'll now discuss how to encode the video and after that how we load that video and play it as a cutscene using ActionScript.

Encoding a Cutscene

Adobe has replaced the Flash Video Encoder that came with earlier versions of Flash with the far more robust and completely redesigned Media Encoder. It takes any video, audio, or image sources and converts them into one of the basic Flash-compatible video formats. It can be intimidating to use at first, as there are many options to consider. Luckily, most of the presets will work well for our needs, some with only minor modifications. We'll now walk through the process of encoding a couple of videos using different settings, based on how we would use the video in a game.

To walk through this example, you'll need the video support files for this chapter from this book's Web site. Since it comes with Flash CS5 and CS5.5, I'll assume you have the Media Encoder. Launch the program and drag the video file named *Cutscene.mov* into the program. This will add it to the list of media to be encoded.

Once you have added your video, you'll see that there are a few columns of settings. Second from the left is the Format column. If it is not already set to FLV/F4V, toggle it to that setting now. To the right

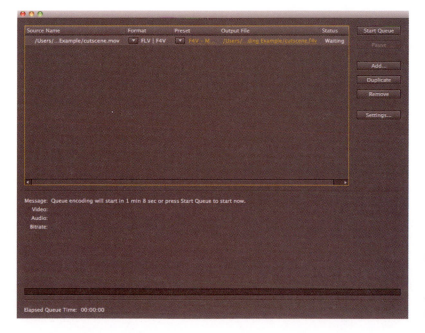

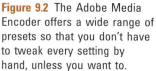

Figure 9.2 The Adobe Media Encoder offers a wide range of presets so that you don't have to tweak every setting by hand, unless you want to.

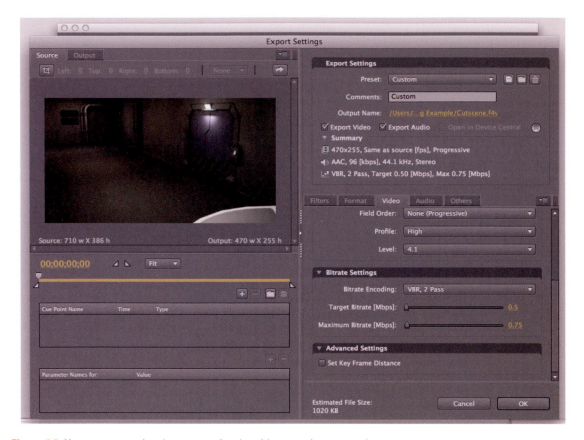

Figure 9.3 You can customize the presets for the video to suit your needs.

of the format is the Preset column. If you were using a standard preset for the video, you could select it from the preset list. In our case, we want to select the very first option in the preset list, "F4V Same as Source." This setting will produce an H.264 Flash video file with the same dimensions and audio settings as the original file (in this case, 710 × 386, 30 fps). Because this cutscene would be used in a Web game, we don't need that level of quality. Click just to the right of the drop-down arrow to customize the settings.

In the lower-right quadrant of the window, you will see a five-tabbed panel for adjusting the settings of the encoder. Select the Video tab and check Resize Video. A good rule of thumb for cutscenes (and video in general) in Flash is that you can very often get away with encoding it between one-half and two-thirds the size of the original and can scale the video in Flash without drastic quality loss. Your tolerance of the compression may vary, but in this case we're going to set the dimensions to 470 × 255. Scroll down in the video panel until you reach the Bitrate Settings. Select VBR, 2 Pass (meaning the encoder will double-check its work to

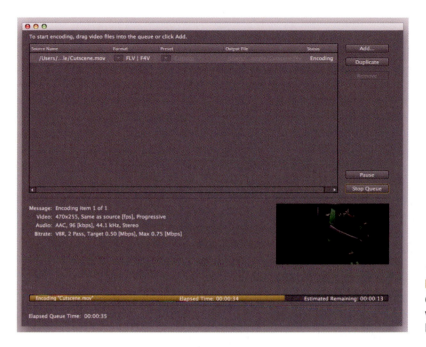

Figure 9.4 Once you've defined the settings for your video, click Start Queue to begin encoding.

deliver the highest possible quality) from the Bitrate Encoding drop-down. Set the Target Bitrate to 0.5 (or 500 kbps) and the Maximum Bitrate to 0.75 (or 750 kbps). Since this clip has a lot of motion in certain parts, we want the encoder to be more generous with those frames but more conservative with others. Next, select the Audio tab. From the Bitrate Settings drop-down, select 96 kbps. This will compress the audio cleanly and still provide ample quality for our needs. At this point the encoder is estimating the file size at right about 1 MB, as you can see to the left of the Cancel button. If you were encoding several videos, you could save these settings as a preset in the upper-right quadrant of the panel. For your purposes, just click OK and return to the main screen. With your video ready to encode, click Start Queue.

Besides the original MOV file, you will end up with an approximately 1-MB F4V file. At approximately 15 seconds in length, this is probably a little large still for people on slower connections, so you'll want to take your audience into account when encoding. Now let's write some code to play what you've just encoded.

CutsceneManager

I typically create a class to manage cutscenes that can sit on top of the gameplay and easily be called to play transition videos, so we'll set one up. There are a couple of reasons for using a custom class, first of which is the fact that just setting up and loading a video in

Flash is many lines of imports and code. Only having to type these lines once by containing them within a flexible wrapper is the essence of sound programming. Another reason to use a custom class is to be able to trigger custom notifications for events. Video playback in Flash generates a *lot* of events, some purely informational and some error-based, and having to filter through all the messages can be cumbersome when all you're trying to do is play a cutscene. By having the class listen for just the pertinent messages and distill them down into a couple of useful events simplifies the process even further.

This class isn't as involved as the SoundEngine we looked at earlier, and it is self-contained in one file.

```
package {

    import flash.display.Sprite;
    import flash.events.AsyncErrorEvent;
    import flash.events.Event;
    import flash.events.KeyboardEvent;
    import flash.events.NetStatusEvent;
    import flash.events.SecurityErrorEvent;
    import flash.media.Video;
    import flash.net.NetConnection;
    import flash.net.NetStream;
    import flash.ui.Keyboard;

    public class CutsceneManager extends Sprite{
    }
}
```

The CutsceneManager extends the Sprite class, so it can easily be added to the Stage like any other DisplayObject. Because it uses video, it needs not only the Video class but also the NetConnection and NetStream classes. Some examples I've seen import the entire events package (import flash.events.*), but for this example I've added each of the necessary events manually. Finally, we'll include the KeyboardEvent and Keyboard classes so that we can bind a key to skip the video—a handy feature that prevents players from having to potentially sit through a video over and over again.

```
public var skipKey:uint = Keyboard.SPACE;
protected var _nc:NetConnection;
protected var _stream:NetStream;
protected var _video:Video;
protected var _activeVideo:String;
```

We only need to keep track of a few variables for this class. The skipKey property is exposed publicly, so you can set it to whatever keystroke you'd like; it defaults to the space bar. The protected properties are all related to keeping track of the video.

```
public function CutsceneManager(width:int, height:int) : void {
      setupConnection();
      _video = new Video(width, height);
      addChild(_video);
}


protected function setupConnection() :void {
      _nc = new NetConnection();
      _nc.addEventListener(NetStatusEvent.NET_STATUS,
        netStatus, false, 0, true);
      _nc.addEventListener(SecurityErrorEvent.SECURITY_ERROR,
        securityError, false, 0, true);
      _nc.connect(null);
}
```

The constructor function creates a new CutsceneManager and sets up both the NetConnection and Video objects and prepares them for use. The NetConnection instance sets up a couple of listeners as well, which we'll look at next.

```
protected function netStatus(e:NetStatusEvent) {
switch (e.info.code) {
            case "NetStream.Play.StreamNotFound":
                  trace("Unable to locate video: " +
                    _activeVideo);
                  break;
            case "NetStream.Play.Start":
                  dispatchEvent(new Event(Event.INIT));
                  break;
            case "NetStream.Play.Stop":
                  stopCutscene(Event.COMPLETE);
                  break;
      }
}


protected function securityError(e:SecurityErrorEvent):void {
      trace(e);
}


protected function asyncError(e:AsyncErrorEvent):void {
      //IGNORE ASYNCHRONOUS ERRORS
}
```

NetStatusEvent messages are used for both NetConnection and NetStream objects. Anytime anything happens to the connection of video stream, messages are broadcast and captured by one event. Using a switch statement, we filter through them for the messages important to us. In this case, we want to know whether the video fails to load, when the video actually starts playing, and when it finishes. There are two other events that we need to set up listeners for, which are error-based. It's not that we should be overly concerned with these errors, but without a listener attached to them, they will throw real run-time errors that can break other parts of your code. Now that we've covered all the "under-the-hood" code, we'll take a look at the main methods used to control the manager.

```
public function playCutscene(url:String) : void {
      _activeVideo = url;
_stream = new NetStream(_nc);
      _stream.addEventListener(NetStatusEvent.NET_STATUS,
        netStatus, false, 0, true);
      _stream.addEventListener(AsyncErrorEvent.ASYNC_ERROR,
        asyncError, false, 0, true);
      _video.attachNetStream(_stream);
      _stream.play(url);
      if (stage) stage.addEventListener(KeyboardEvent.KEY_
        DOWN, skipCutscene, false, 0, true);
}

public function stopCutscene(eventType:String = Event.CANCEL) :
  void {
      _stream.close();
      _video.clear();
      dispatchEvent(new Event(eventType));
      if (stage) stage.removeEventListener(KeyboardEvent.KEY_
        DOWN, skipCutscene);
}

public function get activeVideo():String {
      return _activeVideo;
}

protected function skipCutscene(e:KeyboardEvent) {
      if (e.keyCode == skipKey) stopCutscene();
}
```

The *playCutscene* method is the heart of this class. It accepts a URL string, sets up the stream, and links it to the video. It also adds a listener for keystrokes, so you can define a key that will skip the cutscene. You probably noticed back in the *netStatus* method that on the video finishing it calls *stopCutscene* and passes a parameter of Event.COMPLETE. By default, the *stopCutscene* method will assume that the video is terminated prematurely when it is called. This way you will be able to differentiate from the outside the class whether the video was able to finish playing or it was skipped. In addition to dispatching a message about the status of the video, the *stopCutscene* method performs two other important functions. One is to close out the NetStream object (whether the video is still coming from it) and the other is to clear the video. Without the latter function, the last frame of the video would stay in the Video object, covering up everything behind it.

That completes the CutsceneManager class. Since we reviewed it in pieces, here is the entire script with all the methods in context.

```
package {

    import flash.display.Sprite;
    import flash.events.AsyncErrorEvent;
    import flash.events.Event;
    import flash.events.KeyboardEvent;
    import flash.events.NetStatusEvent;
    import flash.events.SecurityErrorEvent;
    import flash.media.Video;
    import flash.net.NetConnection;
    import flash.net.NetStream;
    import flash.ui.Keyboard;

    public class CutsceneManager extends Sprite{

        public var skipKey:uint = Keyboard.SPACE;

        protected var _nc:NetConnection;
        protected var _stream:NetStream;
        protected var _video:Video;
        protected var _activeVideo:String;

        public function CutsceneManager(width:int, height:
          int) : void {
            setupConnection();
            _video = new Video(width, height);
            addChild(_video);
        }

      public function playCutscene(url:String) : void {
            _activeVideo = url;
            _stream = new NetStream(_nc);
            _stream.addEventListener(NetStatusEvent.
              NET_STATUS, netStatus, false, 0, true);
```

```
                                _stream.addEventListener(AsyncErrorEvent.
                                  ASYNC_ERROR, asyncError, false, 0, true);
                                _video.attachNetStream(_stream);
                                _stream.play(url);
                                if (stage) stage.addEventListener(KeyboardEvent.
                                  KEY_DOWN, skipCutscene, false, 0, true);
        }
        public function stopCutscene(eventType:String = Event.
          CANCEL) : void {
                        _stream.close();
                        _video.clear();
                        dispatchEvent(new Event(eventType));
                        if (stage) stage.removeEventListener(KeyboardEvent.
                          KEY_DOWN, skipCutscene);
        }

        public function get activeVideo():String {
                        return _activeVideo;
        }

        protected function skipCutscene(e:KeyboardEvent) {
                        if (e.keyCode == skipKey) stopCutscene();
        }

        protected function setupConnection() :void {
                        _nc = new NetConnection();
                        _nc.addEventListener(NetStatusEvent.
                          NET_STATUS, netStatus, false, 0, true);
                        _nc.addEventListener(SecurityErrorEvent.
                          SECURITY_ERROR, securityError, false, 0, true);
                        _nc.connect(null);
        }

        protected function netStatus(e:NetStatusEvent) {
                switch (e.info.code) {
                        case "NetStream.Play.StreamNotFound":
                                trace("Unable to locate video: " +
                                  _activeVideo);
                                break;
                        case "NetStream.Play.Start":
                                dispatchEvent(new Event(Event.INIT));
                                break;
                        case "NetStream.Play.Stop":
                                stopCutscene(Event.COMPLETE);
                                break;
                }
        }
```

```
    protected function securityError(e:SecurityErrorEvent):
      void {
          trace(e);
    }

    protected function asyncError(e:AsyncErrorEvent):void {
          //IGNORE ASYNCHRONOUS ERRORS
    }
  }
}
```

Using the CutsceneManager

At this point we've written less than 100 lines of code, and they will allow us to easily call in a video for use as a cutscene in less than five. Open up a new FLA file in Flash and save it next to the Cutscene-Manager class. Set the FLA dimensions to 710 × 386, the original size of the video we're going to load. If you followed the Adobe Media Encoder example mentioned earlier in this chapter, copy the Cuts-cene.f4v file you created next to the FLA. If not, you can find this same file in the Chapter 9 examples folder. Then, on the first frame of the FLA, add the following lines:

```
var cm:CutsceneManager = new CutsceneManager(stage.stageWidth,
  stage.stageHeight);
addChild(cm);
cm.playCutscene("Cutscene.f4v");
```

You should see the video starts to play, filling up the whole Stage. Since we haven't specified another key, press the space bar before the video finishes and you will see it go away quickly and cleanly. If we want to get information about when the video finishes playing, all we need is a few more lines:

```
cm.addEventListener(Event.COMPLETE, cutsceneFinished, false, 0,
  true);
function cutsceneFinished(e:Event) {
      trace(e);
}
```

That's it. This class will work with any format of Flash-compatible video and will save a lot of time when you're in a crunch. This class could also be modified pretty easily to work with a menu background loop as well. Instead of clearing itself when the video reached the end, it would simply need to loop back to the beginning. You would also probably want to remove the skip functionality.

Video on the Timeline

Though an externally loaded file works great for noninteractive videos, it's not the best option for the video that is used in the gameplay or when you need clips with alpha transparency.

Image sequences such as short character animations, particle effects, tend to require a transparent background in order to integrate seamlessly with the background. Conventional thinking in Flash would dictate using a series of PNG images that simply played back in order. Much of the time, however, the best option is actually to import the sequence as a video file directly into your library and use it on the timeline like a MovieClip. If all you have are image sequences to work with (not all animation programs produce video formats directly compatible with Flash), fear not! In the section Setting Up an Internal Video, I'll show you how to use Flash as a video editing tool. There are a few reasons to consider using video instead of a sequence of PNG files.

File Size

Most of the time, an FLV encoded with an alpha channel will be smaller than the equivalent PNG sequence, even with relatively high JPEG compression turned on in Flash, because the On2 codec is designed for handling motion and applies its compression more efficiently than JPEG. When an encoder compresses a video, it makes decisions about what data will change from one frame to the next, stripping out anything it doesn't need to duplicate. Single images only have their image data to work with and cannot benefit from the other images in a sequence. Video can also be encoded in variable bit rate (VBR). Instead of using the same compression across the board for every frame, the encoder determines which frames can benefit from extra compression and which ones need to stay higher quality. For example, if several frames of a video are all one color or have very little details, the encoder will compress them heavily, whereas frames with a lot of motion and color data will receive a lighter compression. While you could manually apply the same principle to all the images in a sequence, it would be much more time-consuming and certainly tedious.

Ease of Use and Library Clutter

Say you have 10 different one-second character animations for a player in a game. At 30 fps, this would equal 300 images. Using a video in place of each of these sequences would result in only 10 library items—much more manageable and easy to update if changes are made. Simply replace one video instead of 30 images. This efficiency also translates to timeline management. Because a video is already treated as a single DisplayObject, sort of like a MovieClip of images, it's much easier to rearrange them on Stage and in the timeline without having to select multiple frames at once.

Performance

Even with the extra performance overhead an alpha-channel video clip brings, it is still more efficient than a series of images, particularly as the dimensions of the clip increase. This is because Adobe has put a lot of effort into making the video playback engine perform well even on modest machines. Also, in the context of Flash's timeline model, a PNG sequence requires the renderer to add and remove images on every frame, which is a more intensive task.

Free Motion Blur

The compression used on video tends to have a slight softening effect, depending on what settings were used in the encoder, and this effect can actually be helpful in creating a sense of motion blur on videos with a lot of movement. Since Flash cannot natively do directional motion blur, this effect would be much harder to produce with a series of images. Obviously, if the encoder is smudging the video *too much*, you might want to change the compression settings.

WHEN PNGs STILL WIN

Say you had an animation sequence of a character crouching. To be as efficient as possible, you would probably use the same animation for the character entering the crouch as that coming out of it, just reversing the latter. This is possible with a sequence of images that you have complete control over but not so with a video. You would have to create the second animation separately, and at that point you will have lost any file size savings from using video in the first place. How you intend to use animation sequences in your game should dictate which format you use.

Setting Up an Internal Video

Let's walk through a practical example of setting up a timeline-based video and test the file size improvement. The support files for this exercise can be found in the Chapter 9 examples folder. In this example, I have a 15-frame running sequence for a character that will need to loop. It currently exists as an image sequence of PNG files. Open a new FLA file and save it as ImageSequence.fla. Set the Stage size to 200 × 200. Import the first image from the sequence into Flash. It will prompt you if you would like to import the whole series; click Yes. You should now have the image sequence on the Stage. Test the SWF, and you will see a running cycle animation that loops. It should be roughly 66 kb. You may be thinking, "66 k is nothing in this broadband age! How much could I possibly gain by using a video instead?" You'd probably be surprised just how much. This is just one video that is less than one second long. The game that employed this particular character had this same animation, as well as about nine others, from three other angles (left, right, and back) in order to make it feel like the character was moving in a three-dimensional space. That is more than 2.5 MB for all those animations, and that's just for one character.

To turn this sequence into a video, select Export → Export Movie from the File menu in Flash. Give the movie the name Image-Sequence and select QuickTime from the Format drop-down. You will be presented with a QuickTime Export Settings window. Check the box to ignore stage color and generate an alpha channel. Tell it to store the temp data on disk, as it is more reliable for most image sequences. Click the QuickTime Settings button to bring up one more dialog. The default settings should be correct, but just make sure the video is set to export at 200 × 200, 24 fps, using the Animation compressor and Millions of Colors+. All this means is that it will create a movie file with an alpha channel that we can then encode as Flash video. Click OK and then click Export. Flash will let you know when it is finished, which should only be a matter of seconds.

At this point you should have a new MOV file ready to encode. Launch Adobe Media Encoder and drag the ImageSequence movie onto it. Select FLV/F4V as the format and select FLV Same as Source (Flash 8) from the preset options. Then, open the settings to customize the preset. Under the Video tab, select the Encode Alpha Channel box. Then, scroll down to the Bitrate Settings and lower the Bitrate to 250 kbps. This may seem small, especially after

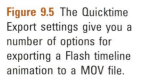

Figure 9.5 The Quicktime Export settings give you a number of options for exporting a Flash timeline animation to a MOV file.

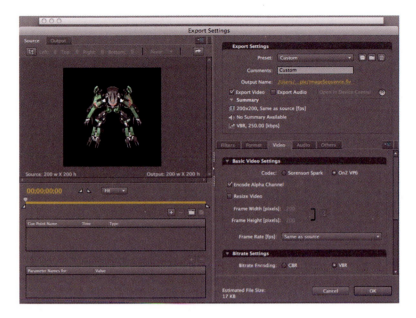

Figure 9.6 When encoding a PNG sequence into an FLV, be sure to check the Encode Alpha Channel box.

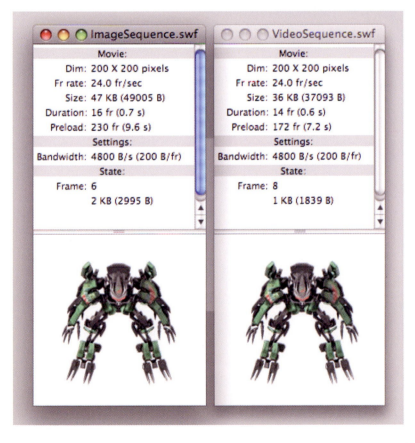

Figure 9.7 A side-by-side comparison of a PNG sequence and a video of the same sequence.

encoding an enormous cutscene file, but for small animations like this it is usually more than enough. This is the one option that I tend to change per project because I haven't found one setting that works across the board for every type of animation. At this point, the encoder should be estimating the FLV at 30–36 k less than the image sequence we created in Flash. Click OK and Start Queue to encode the video.

To do a true comparison of the two resulting SWF files, create a new FLA that is 200 × 200. Save it as VideoSequence. Import the ImageSequence.flv file. It will bring up the Import Video window. Select the option to Embed FLV in SWF and click Continue twice. Click Finish on the summary screen, and the video will be added to your FLA on the Stage. If you test this SWF alongside the Image-Sequence SWF, you'll notice that indeed the video is 30 k smaller and looks almost identical. One could argue that it is possible to lower the JPEG quality of the PNG sequence and that SWF will drop down to around 40 k. However, you still are left managing a bunch of images rather than just one video file, and now the image sequence will (usually) look worse than the video. Remember that even though the savings in this example is small, most games will use far more assets than just a single character; always calculate the savings to the scale of your project to determine if using video is worth the extra few steps.

Summary

In this chapter, we covered the following topics:
- Different formats of video that Flash will accept and when to use them
- How to use the Adobe Media Encoder to create both cutscene-style videos and alpha-channel clips
- How to create a CutsceneManager that handles loading external video files
- How to use video on the timeline in place of image sequences

10

XML AND DYNAMIC CONTENT

Many Flash games are self-contained SWF files. They don't load any additional files in, and they don't send any type of data out. However, this closed architecture prohibits a number of scenarios such as

- Externalized content (such as a puzzle data or even a game copy)
- The ability to save to a public high-score table
- Localization to other languages
- Level editors and user-generated content

In this chapter, we'll explore how features like these can be implemented using a variety of features in ActionScript.

Bringing Data In: Understanding the URLLoader Class

The core component behind sending and loading basic text, XML, and binary data is the URLLoader class. It takes only a few lines of code to load some data and begins working with it. Consider the following example:

```
var loader:URLLoader = new URLLoader(new URLRequest("config.txt"));
    loader.addEventListener(Event.COMPLETE, onTextLoad, false,
    0, true);
```

```
function onTextLoad(e:Event) {
        trace("Text: " + e.target.data);
}
```

All this code does is load a text file and trace what is in it. In and of itself, this is not especially useful until you consider what you could put inside the file. Maybe your game has a lot of text dialogue and you don't want it mixed with your code, or a bunch of legal copy you don't want to mess with pasting inside a text field in Flash. Word-based, trivia, and many other puzzle games are also good candidates for loading in external content, allowing you to add new content without having to republish the game file. We'll look at an example of this type of game shortly, in the form of a crossword puzzle.

XML

By default, a URLLoader simply loads in plain text, which is fine for most applications involving local files. By itself, however, text does not lend a great deal of flexibility. It needs to be organized into a format that has a structure. This is where XML comes in. If you're not already familiar with it, XML is, in brief, a markup language (in format similar to HTML) for organizing data into a structured format. Here is an example of some simple XML defining a quiz:

```
<quiz>
       <problem>
               <question>What does this book cover?</question>
               <answer>Flash Game Development</answer>
               <answer>Java Game Development</answer>
               <answer>C++ Game Development</answer>
       </problem>
       <problem>...etc.</problem>
</quiz>
```

As you can see, XML is incredibly flexible, allowing you to define exactly how you want your data structured. XML structures can become extremely complex, particularly for large-scale applications, but this example also shows how simple it can be. In this case, we've defined that a quiz contains problems. Each problem has a question and three answers, the first of which is correct. By setting up your data with a logical hierarchy, we can access it easily from inside Flash.

E4X

If you had worked with XML in ActionScript 1 or 2, you would know how unwieldy it was to handle. Unless you used a very robust parser, most changes to the structure of the XML would break your code. A new feature in ActionScript 3 is the ability to parse through XML data just like any other object in Flash. This feature is known as E4X (ECMAScript for XML), and it makes XML a native data type in Flash, just like numbers or strings. Because of this, parsing XML is much faster and allows you to move through a structure like you would a set of objects and arrays. The following example uses a URLLoader to load the XML used in the previous example.

```
var quiz:XML;
var loader:URLLoader = new URLLoader(new URLRequest("quiz.xml"));
    loader.addEventListener(Event.COMPLETE, onXMLLoad, false,
      0, true);
function onXMLLoad(e:Event) {
        quiz = XML(e.target.data);
        trace(quiz.problem[0].question); // "What does this book
          cover?"
}
```

To use the data as XML once it is loaded, you simply use the XML conversion function and assign it to a variable. To learn more about the more advanced features of E4X such as filtering and searching, look to the Flash reference documentation on XML. For the purposes of this chapter, our use of XML will be more straight-forward. Let's look at a practical example of how XML can be used to store puzzle data for a game.

Crossword Puzzle

One of the most popular types of word games in print or electronic media is the crossword puzzle. There are many variations of the crossword puzzle, but the traditional American square grid type is the style we will work with (Fig. 10.1). It consists of overlapping horizontal and vertical words with unique numbers denoting the start of a word. Each word has a clue associated with it, which can be another word or an entire phrase.

In the following exercise, we will lay out the structure of a cross-word puzzle in XML and then create a simple crossword engine that will display the puzzle and allow a player to fill it in. Any XML to be used in Flash must have only one *root node*, that is, the node that opens and closes the file. Any additional nodes will be ignored when the XML is parsed. We start with an opening node labeled "crossword," which will encase our entire puzzle. Inside an opening XML tag you can add parameters, called *attributes*, which allow you to add any information pertinent to the node. In this case, we define the width and the height of the puzzle in question. Attribute values should be in quotes and do not need any type of separator between them.

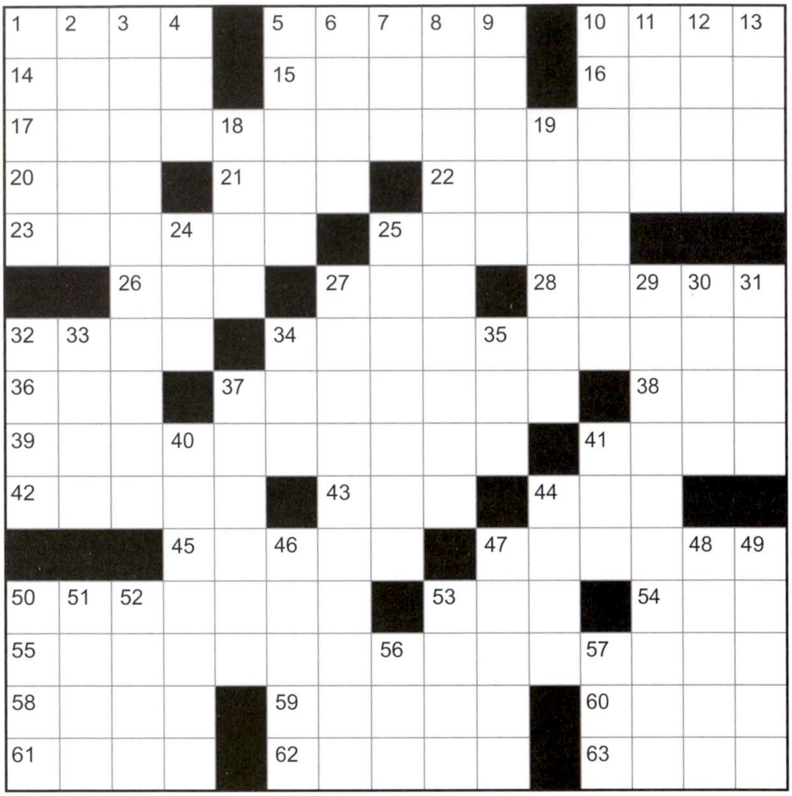

Figure 10.1 An American square grid type crossword puzzle.

```
<crossword width="13" height="13">
</crossword>
```

Now we can begin to break down the crossword into its core components, the grid layout (which we will call the "puzzle" in this case) and the clues. The grid squares can either have letters or be blacked out, so no letters can be entered. We'll break down the puzzle into rows and use a special character to denote the black spaces. For this example, we'll use the underscore ("_"). Each row will spell out one line of the puzzle in a single string.

```
<puzzle>
        <row>ASKS_SON_DOME</row>
        <row>SENT_ONE_EVEN</row>
        <row>HAIR_MOW_FEED</row>
        <row>_STARE_SHIRTS</row>
        <row>___PAWS_IN___</row>
        <row>HAT_WHISPERED</row>
        <row>IRON_ANT_DARE</row>
        <row>DEPARTURE_TAN</row>
        <row>___TO_SEAR___</row>
```

```
    <row>SHRUBS_ARISE_</row>
    <row>TOUR_OAK_DIGS</row>
    <row>ELLA_LIE_EDGE</row>
    <row>PEEL_ODD_REST</row>
</puzzle>
```

As you can see, this structure is very readable and allows us to see basically what the puzzle will look like before it is even in a grid. It is important to remember that while there are many standards in XML, there is no reason to overcomplicate the path to get to your data. Keeping it readable like this will also help us catch mistakes faster.

Next, we need to add the accompanying clues for this puzzle. We will do this by simply adding a clue node with two types of clues in it: down and across.

```
<clues>
    <across>Questions</across>
    <across>Harry Potter to Lily Evans</across>
    <across>Igloo, for example</across>
    <across>Emailed</across>
    <across>Lonely number</across>
    <across>Opposite of 60 Across</across>
    <across>It grows on you</across>
    <across>Cut grass</across>
    <across>Fill a dog's dish</across>
    <across>Look at intently</across>
    <across>They have sleeves</across>
    <across>Animal feet</across>
    <across>With 41 Across, keen on</across>
    <across>Fedora, e.g.</across>
    <across>Spoke quietly</across>
    <across>It's pumped in a gym</across>
    <across>Social insect</across>
    <across>"I __ ya!" (challenge)</across>
    <across>Lounge in an airport</across>
    <across>Lie in the sun</across>
    <across>See 24 Across</across>
    <across>Burn the surface of</across>
    <across>Small trees</across>
    <across>Come up</across>
    <across>Take a trip around</across>
    <across>Mighty tree</across>
    <across>Uses a shovel</across>
    <across>Famous singer Fitzgerald</across>
    <across>Tell a tall tale</across>
    <across>Rim</across>
    <across>Open a banana</across>
```

```
<across>Opposite of 14 Across</across>
<across>Take five</across>
<down>Fire leftover</down>
<down>Oceans</down>
<down>Make a sweater, perhaps</down>
<down>Guitar holder</down>
<down>Sort of</down>
<down>Yoko __</down>
<down>Reporter's offering</down>
<down>Gave the meaning of a word</down>
<down>Above</down>
<down>Get together</down>
<down>Finishes</down>
<down>Not cooked</down>
<down>___-Hop</down>
<down>Cavity in the head</down>
<down>With 50 Down, what one did for Easter, maybe</down>
<down>"___ we there yet?"</down>
<down>Apex</down>
<down>Made like a comet</down>
<down>Remy, the chef, is one</down>
<down>Period in history</down>
<down>Fox's home</down>
<down>Not synthetic</down>
<down>Steal</down>
<down>Hole in the head</down>
<down>Ghost _ (Johnny Blaze)</down>
<down>"__ on it!" (hurry up)</down>
<down>Golfer's target</down>
<down>Be king, say</down>
<down>Alone</down>
<down>Border</down>
<down>See 25 Down</down>
<down>Band-__</down>
<down>Sun__ (day's end)</down>
<clues>
```

Note that we are not interested in which clue is associated with which word in the puzzle, but rather arrange them in ascending order. This is because if we build our crossword engine correctly, there will eventually be a one-to-one association between a word and its clue. Note hard-coding the number allows us to move clues around if a mistake was made or one was left out.

For this example, we'll break down the crossword engine into a few components. At its core, a crossword can be broken down into individual tiles, so we'll create a class to represent a tile. Together they make up the grid, or a puzzle, so the main class driving the engine will be a puzzle class. At this point, one could argue the merits of creating a class to define a word, but in terms of practicality a word is nothing more than an array of tiles, so for our purposes we'll keep it simple. Finally, we need a way to display the clue for a given word, so we'll make a class to handle that.

The CrosswordTile Class

The best way to solve a complex problem is to break it down into smaller, more manageable problems. Such is the case with the CrosswordTile class. This class will keep track of the correct letter for a given tile and whether that tile is active in gameplay. To start, we'll set up our class and package.

```
package {

    import flash.display.MovieClip;
    import flash.events.Event;
    import flash.events.KeyboardEvent;
    import flash.text.TextField;
    import flash.geom.Point;
    import flash.ui.Keyboard;

    public class CrosswordTile extends MovieClip {
    }
}
```

Since this class will handle display as well as the data in the tile, we'll extend it from MovieClip and use frames to store its different states.

Instead of starting with the constructor for the class, let's outline the different properties this tile should keep track of. This will consist of both basic public variables and protected variables with public getters and setters.

```
// PUBLIC DisplayObjects
public var letterField:TextField;
public var wordField:TextField;

// PUBLIC VARIABLES
public var letter:String;
public var acrossIndex:int = -1;
public var downIndex:int = -1;
public var tileIndex:Point;

// PROTECTED VARIABLES
protected var _wordIndex:uint;
protected var _answer:String;
```

```
// GETTER/SETTERS
public function get wordIndex():uint {
       return _wordIndex;
}

public function set wordIndex(value:uint):void {
       _wordIndex = value;
       wordField.text = (_wordIndex) ? _wordIndex.toString() : "";
}
```

First, we declare two TextField objects that will be used to display the letter in the tile when it is entered and the number of the word if it is the first letter. The letter property will be used to store the letter that belongs to this square. Note that this is *not* the letter that will be used to store user input, but rather the correct answer from the XML. The acrossIndex and downIndex variables will store the tile's associations with any horizontal or vertical words. For the tileIndex, or the actual grid position in the puzzle, we use a Point object since it already has *x* and *y* properties.

PUBLIC PROPERTIES ARE OKAY

You don't always have to use getters and setters for every publicly exposed property in your classes. If a variable is purely being stored, the extra overhead of a function to do so is unnecessary. Use getters and setters when some other action needs to take place when a value is set, but you want the simplicity of a simple variable assignment. As long as you keep to a standard convention (protected/private variables always begin with an underscore, for instance), you can easily convert the public variable to a getter/setter property later on and cannot change more than a couple of lines of code. Getters also come in handy when you want a value to be readable but not writeable; simply omit the setter and you're done!

Next, we have two protected variables, one of which has getter/setter methods. The wordIndex property is used to store the word in the puzzle (horizontal or vertical) to which the tile belongs. The _answer property will store a player-inputted answer. We now move on to the publicly exposed methods, which can be called from outside the class.

```
public function setAnswer(e:KeyboardEvent):Boolean {
       if (e.keyCode >= String("A").charCodeAt(0) && e.keyCode
         <= String("Z").charCodeAt(0)) {
               _answer = String.fromCharCode(e.keyCode);
               letterField.text = _answer;
               return true;
       } else if (e.keyCode == Keyboard.BACKSPACE) {
               _answer = "";
               letterField.text = _answer;
       }
```

```
        return false;
}

public function deactivate() {
        gotoAndStop(2);
}

public function activate() {
        gotoAndStop(1);
}
```

When a user enters a keyboard input on a tile, it will call *setAnswer*. This method is a normal public function that another class can call, but it accepts a KeyboardEvent as its parameter like an event handler. This allows another method elsewhere to pass along the received keyboard event for evaluation without having this method attached to a listener. Once it checks to see whether the key pressed is an alphabetic character or backspace, it updates itself accordingly. It does not validate the answer further, but it does return *true* if a letter was entered and *false* if any other key was pressed. The *activate* and *deactivate* methods simply toggle between two different frames to show the tile as a usable square or a blank.

The constructor for the class will build the tile based on the character it is given to display. Remember how we denoted a blanked-out space with an underscore in the XML. We'll define a constant property named EMPTY for this character, so that we can easily reference it (and even change it later if needed).

```
static public const EMPTY:String = "_";

public function CrosswordTile(letter:String = EMPTY) {
        this.letter = letter;
        addEventListener(Event.ADDED_TO_STAGE, init, false, 0,
          true);
        if (letter == EMPTY) {
                deactivate();
        } else {
                activate();
        }
}

protected function init(e:Event) : void {
        if (letterField) {
                letterField.text = "";
                letterField.mouseEnabled = false;
        }
        if (wordField) {
```

```
wordField.text = (_wordIndex) ? _wordIndex.
    toString() : "";
wordField.mouseEnabled = false;
    }
}
```

The constructor stores the letter passed in, sets up a notification for when the tile is added to the display list, and toggles to the normal state or the blacked-out state. The *init* method sets up the text fields and disables mouse interaction with them. To some, these may seem like steps that could simply be accomplished in the constructor, but unfortunately, this is not the case. If you tried to move them into the constructor, Flash would give you a run-time error. This is a point of confusion for many people, but suffice it to say that while we've *declared* that there will be two text fields, we're going to create these objects inside Flash. As long as we give the same name to our text field instances on the Stage, Flash will link the declared variable to the actual object. However, this step does not take place until after the constructor has completed, so the next best time to run these commands is when the tile is added to the Stage and ready to use.

Now that we have the class defining a tile created, we need to see the display object to which it will be linked. Open up the CrosswordPuzzle.fla file from the Chapter 10 examples folder. In the Library, you will find a symbol called CrosswordTile. If you open it, you will see the two text fields (with the names of the variables in the class) and the two frames showing the different states that a tile can use. If you bring up the properties panel for the

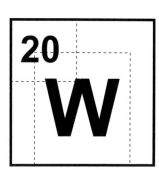

Figure 10.2 The CrosswordTile symbol is made up of a square and two text fields.

Figure 10.3 The CrosswordTile symbol is now linked to its class.

symbol (right-click and choose Properties), you will see that it is set to export with the same name as the class we've just created. Now when a new CrosswordTile is constructed, this library asset will be used as the object to display.

The CrosswordClue Class

Before we delve into building the puzzle itself, let's consider the clue component. It is a relatively simple class—all it needs to do is display the clue for the selected word. With no need for multiple frames, Sprite is a better candidate than MovieClip.

```
package {

    import flash.display.Sprite;
    import flash.text.TextField;

    public class CrosswordClue extends Sprite {

        static public const DEFAULT_VALUE:String = "Clue";

        public var clueText:TextField;

        public function CrosswordClue(){
        }

        public function get text():String {
            return clueText.text;
        }

        public function set text(value:String):void {
            clueText.text = value;
        }

    }
}
```

The class uses a TextField object and a getter/setter combination to assign text to it. You might wonder why we didn't simply use a standard text field instead of a custom class. You very well could for an example as straightforward as this, but there are a couple of reasons to encapsulate it as its own class. First is the ability to define constants, such as what the default value of the text field should be when there is no clue shown. Another reason is expandability and flexibility—by already having a class setup to handle the clue, it will be easier to add animation and other features without adding a lot of code to the puzzle class. One other reason you might not expect is that it is easier to set up a text field inside Flash rather than a code. Custom fonts (basically, anything

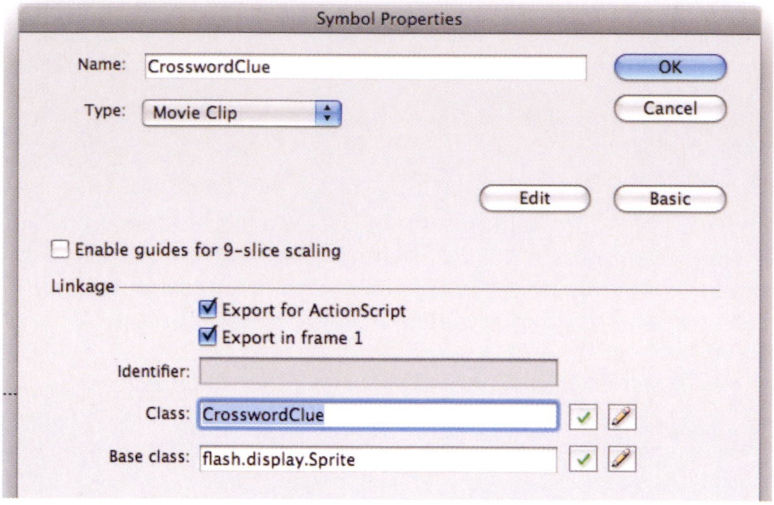

Figure 10.4 The CrosswordClue class extends Sprite, even though it says MovieClip in the symbol properties.

other than system fonts) are clumsily handled through ActionScript and require more hassle than simply creating a symbol with a TextField object inside it and linking it to a class. In fact, spawning a new TextField from scratch in code and assigning it for formatting objects and positioning is as much or more code than the class we just created.

In the CrosswordPuzzle.fla file, you'll find a symbol in the library named CrosswordClue, and it has the single TextField named clueText. It is set to export using the same class name and is extending from the base class Sprite. You may have some cognitive dissonance when you see that the base class field says Sprite, but the type still says MovieClip. This has to do with the way the Flash authoring environment handles timeline-based elements and is a holdover from older versions, presumably for consistency. To help the confusion (or perhaps add to it), Flash now color-codes Sprites in the Library as green instead of the MovieClip blue. Don't dwell too hard on it—it's a quirk of Flash and while annoying does not cause any real problems.

The CrosswordPuzzle Class

With the individual tiles and the clue field ready to be used, it's time to set up the core CrosswordPuzzle engine. Unlike the two previous components, we will not link this class to a symbol in the library. Because crossword puzzles can be any number of sizes, having any type of fixed layout defined in a symbol would make the class too rigid to deal with. Say, for instance, you wanted to support multiple dimensions of puzzles in a single game; if you tied the class to specific symbols, you would need to do so as the base class and have multiple subclasses that extend CrosswordPuzzle, which could get cumbersome quickly. It is easier to set up the puzzle dynamically based on the puzzle data. Like the CrosswordClue, CrosswordPuzzle extends Sprite; since it is being generated dynamically, it will not use frames.

```
package {

    import flash.display.Sprite;
    import flash.geom.ColorTransform;
    import flash.geom.Point;
    import flash.events.Event;
    import flash.events.MouseEvent;
    import flash.events.KeyboardEvent;
    import flash.ui.Keyboard;

    public class CrosswordPuzzle extends Sprite {


    }

}
```

In the basic package definition, we will need to be able to listen for both Keyboard and Mouse events, and we will use the Color-Transform class (the code version of the Color properties drop-down on a timeline-based symbol) to tint tiles that are selected. Next we define the constants and properties of the class, as well as the constructor.

```
// CLASS CONSTANTS
static public const tileSelectedColor:ColorTransform = new
  ColorTransform(0, 1, 1, 1, 0, 0, 0, 0);
static public const wordSelectedColor:ColorTransform = new
  ColorTransform(.7, 1, 1, 1, 0, 0, 0, 0);

// PROTECTED VARIABLES
protected var _content:XML;
protected var _puzzleHeight:int;
protected var _puzzleWidth:int;
protected var _tileList:Array;
protected var _wordListAcross:Array;
protected var _wordListDown:Array;
protected var _selectedWord:Array;
protected var _selectedTile:CrosswordTile;
protected var _crosswordClue:CrosswordClue;

public function CrosswordPuzzle(content:XML){
        _content = content;
        _tileList = new Array();
        _wordListAcross = new Array();
```

```
        _wordListDown = new Array();
        createPuzzle();
}
```

To tint a tile when it is selected, we create two color transforms
(in this case, versions of light blue). One is used for the specific tile
that is selected, and a lighter one will be used for the word associated with that tile. The engine employs a number of variables to
keep track of various pieces of data. The _content XML variable
will store the puzzle data once it is loaded from an external file. It
also keeps track of the width and height of the puzzle, a list of all
the tiles in the play (including blacked-out ones), lists of the horizontal and vertical words, references to the currently selected tile
and the word, and a reference to the CrosswordClue class we created earlier. Finally, the constructor accepts an XML object containing the puzzle content as a parameter. It then initializes the three
lists and calls createPuzzle, which we will look at next.

```
protected function createPuzzle() {
        _puzzleWidth = _content.@width;
        _puzzleHeight = _content.@height;
        var totalWords:int = 1;
        var tile:CrosswordTile;
        //SETUP TILES
        for (var i:int = 0; i < _puzzleHeight; i++) {
                for (var j:int = 0; j < _puzzleWidth; j++) {
                        var letter:String = _content.puzzle.
                          row[i].charAt(j);
                        tile = new CrosswordTile(letter);
                        tile.name = j.toString() + "_" + i.toString();
                        tile.tileIndex = new Point(j, i);
                        if (letter != CrosswordTile.EMPTY) {
                                var startOfWord:Boolean = false;
                                if (j == 0 || _content.puzzle.
                                  row[i].charAt(j-1) == "_") {
                                        tile.acrossIndex =
                                          _wordListAcross.push
                                          (new Array());
                                        _wordListAcross[tile.
                                          acrossIndex-1].push
                                          (tile);
                                        startOfWord = true;
                                }
                                if (i == 0 || _content.puzzle.
                                  row[i-1].charAt(j) == "_") {
                                        tile.downIndex =
                                          _wordListDown.push
                                          (new Array());
```

```
                    _wordListDown[tile.
                       downIndex-1].push(tile);
                    startOfWord = true;
            }
            if (startOfWord) {
                    tile.wordIndex =
                       totalWords++;
            }
            if (tile.acrossIndex < 0) {
                    var previousAcrossTile:
                       CrosswordTile =
                       _tileList[_tileList.
                       length-1];
_wordListAcross[previousAcrossTile.acrossIndex-1].push
  (tile);

                    tile.acrossIndex =
                       previousAcrossTile.
                       acrossIndex;
            }
            if (tile.downIndex < 0) {
                    if (i > 0) {
                            var previousDown
                               Tile:Crossword
                               Tile = _tileList
                               [_tileList.
                               length-
                               _puzzleWidth];
                            if (previousDown
                               Tile.letter !=
                               CrosswordTile.
                               EMPTY) {
_wordListDown[previousDownTile.downIndex-1].push(tile);
                               tile.downIndex=
                                  previousDown
                                  Tile.
                                  downIndex;
                            }
                    }
            }
    }
    _tileList.push(tile);
    tile.x = j*tile.width;
    tile.y = i*tile.height;
    addChild(tile);
    tile.addEventListener(MouseEvent.CLICK,
      selectTile, false, 0, true);
}
```

```
        }
        _crosswordClue = new CrosswordClue();
        _crosswordClue.y = getRect(this).bottom + 20;
        addChild(_crosswordClue);
}
```

There is a lot to the createPuzzle method, so we'll break it down into more manageable chunks.

```
_puzzleWidth = _content.@width;
_puzzleHeight = _content.@height;
var totalWords:int = 1;
var tile:CrosswordTile;
```

The first few lines simply initialize the variables that will be used throughout the rest of the method. Note that the attributes we assigned to the crossword XML earlier are prefixed with the @ symbol. Another great feature of E4X is that it is smart enough to differentiate numbers from strings, so even though the values were in quotes in the XML file, Flash converted them to numbers for us.

```
for (var i:int = 0; i < _puzzleHeight; i++) {
        for (var j:int = 0; j < _puzzleWidth; j++) {
                var letter:String = _content.puzzle.row[i].
                  charAt(j);
                tile = new CrosswordTile(letter);
                tile.name = j.toString() + "_" + i.toString();
                tile.tileIndex = new Point(j, i);
```

Next, we begin two *for* loops that will run through the entire grid of the puzzle, row by row. Each iteration identifies the letter used at that space in the grid and creates a new CrosswordTile object for each one. As you can see, to get down to a specific row in the puzzle node of the XML, we simply use a combination of dot and array syntax. When you have multiple nodes on the same level with the same name, Flash converts it into an XMLList object, like an XML array. To get at a particular item in the XMLList, we use a number from 0 up to the number of items minus 1.

```
if (letter != CrosswordTile.EMPTY) {
        var startOfWord:Boolean = false;
        if (j == 0 || _content.puzzle.row[i].charAt(j-1) ==
          CrosswordTile.EMPTY) {
                tile.acrossIndex = _wordListAcross.push(new
                  Array());
                _wordListAcross[tile.acrossIndex-1].push
                  (tile);
                startOfWord = true;
        }
```

```
if (i == 0 || _content.puzzle.row[i-1].charAt(j) ==
  CrosswordTile.EMPTY) {
        tile.downIndex = _wordListDown.push(new Array());
        _wordListDown[tile.downIndex-1].push(tile);
        startOfWord = true;
}
if (startOfWord) {
        tile.wordIndex = totalWords++;
}
if (tile.acrossIndex < 0) {
        var previousAcrossTile:CrosswordTile = _tile
          List[_tileList.length-1];
        _wordListAcross[previousAcrossTile.
          acrossIndex-1].push(tile);
        tile.acrossIndex = previousAcrossTile.
          acrossIndex;
}
if (tile.downIndex < 0) {
        var previousDownTile:CrosswordTile = _tileList
          [_tileList.length-_puzzleWidth];
        _wordListDown[previousDownTile.downIndex-1].
          push(tile);
        tile.downIndex = previousDownTile.downIndex;
}
}
```

This section of the method performs a series of checks to determine the tile's current state (in-use or blacked-out) and the words with which it is associated. First, we check whether the tile is supposed to be empty. If so, we stop there and don't include it in any word lists. Next, we determine whether the tile is the starting letter of a word, either across or down. We ascertain this by checking if the tile immediately to the left or top of the current tile is a blank. If it is the start of a new word, we add it to the across list and/or the down list. We also increment the total number of words counter and set the tile's wordIndex to this number. If you recall from the CrosswordTile class, when the wordIndex is set, it adds this number to the upper left hand corner TextField. This is the number that will be used to match the tile to its corresponding clue. If the tile is not the start of a word, its acrossIndex and downIndex will still be the default value of -1. We then look up the previous tile to both the left and above the tile to use its same indices and add it to the across list, down list, or both. At this point, the tile shares association with words in the across word list, down word list, and the beginning letter of each word.

```
_tileList.push(tile);
tile.x = j*tile.width;
```

```
                tile.y = i*tile.height;
                addChild(tile);
                tile.addEventListener(MouseEvent.CLICK,
                   selectTile, false, 0, true);
          }
    }
_crosswordClue = new CrosswordClue();
_crosswordClue.y = getRect(this).bottom + 20;
addChild(_crosswordClue);
```

Once the logic has run to determine each tile's link to its neighbors, we add it to the master tile list, position it based on its location in the letter grid, add it to the Stage, and attach a listener for mouse clicks. To end this method after the loop has completed processing all the tiles, we add the previously created CrosswordClue component to the Stage and position it underneath the rest of the puzzle with a little bit of whitespace. A complete crossword puzzle should now exist on the Stage with all the proper blacked-out squares and certain tiles that are assigned clue numbers. You may have noticed that the method attached to the mouse listener for each tile is called *selectTile*. We will discuss it next.

```
protected function selectTile(e:MouseEvent):void {
        var tile:CrosswordTile = e.target as CrosswordTile;
        var acrossWord:Array = _wordListAcross[tile.
          acrossIndex-1];
        var downWord:Array = _wordListDown[tile.downIndex-1];
        clearSelection();
        if (tile.letter == CrosswordTile.EMPTY) {
                _crosswordClue.text = CrosswordClue.
                   DEFAULT_VALUE;
                stage.removeEventListener(KeyboardEvent.KEY_
                   DOWN, keyDown);
                _selectedTile = null;
                return;
        }
        if (!_selectedTile) stage.addEventListener
          (KeyboardEvent.KEY_DOWN, keyDown, false, 0, true);
        if (_selectedWord == acrossWord && _selectedTile == tile)
          _selectedWord = downWord;
                else if (_selectedWord == downWord &&
                   _selectedTile == tile) _selectedWord =
                   acrossWord;
                else if (_selectedWord == acrossWord &&
                   _selectedTile != tile) _selectedWord =
                   acrossWord;
```

```
        else if (_selectedWord == downWord &&
          _selectedTile != tile) _selectedWord =
          downWord;
        else _selectedWord = acrossWord;
    for (var i:int = 0; i < _selectedWord.length; i++) {
        if (_selectedWord[i] == tile) {
            _selectedWord[i].transform.color
              Transform = tileSelectedColor;
        } else {
            _selectedWord[i].transform.color
              Transform = wordSelectedColor;
        }
    }
    _selectedTile = tile;
    var wordNumber:int = _selectedWord[0].wordIndex;
    if (_selectedWord == downWord) {
        _crosswordClue.text = String(wordNumber) +
          " Down: " + (_content.clues.down[tile.
          downIndex-1] || "");
    } else {
        _crosswordClue.text = String(wordNumber) +
          " Across: " + (_content.clues.across[tile.
          acrossIndex-1] || "");
    }
}
```

The *selectTile* method is called when the player clicks a tile. To provide the expected user feedback, this method needs to (1) highlight the selected tile, (2) highlight the word with which the tile is associated, and (3) display the hint associated with the tile. First, we look up the across and down words the tile is associated with and then call *clearSelection*, which we will look at shortly. Suffice it to say now that *clearSelection* will nullify any other currently selected tiles. Next, we check whether the player clicked on a blacked-out tile; if so, we clear the clue text, disable the keyboard input if it is active, and exit the function. If the _selectedTile property is null, meaning no tile was previously selected, we add a listener for the keyboard input so that players can start to type letters once they click a tile. We now need to know whether to use the tile's associated across or down word. By default, if no previous word was selected, we use the tile's across word. We use many conditions to ensure that if a tile is selected as part of a down word, and another tile in that word is clicked, it will keep the same word selected. We also check to see if the same tile was clicked twice; if so, we want to select the opposite type of the word that is currently selected. For instance, if an across word is selected by its first letter, clicking the first letter again will highlight the down word. Once we have determined the proper word to select, we run through a *for* loop that assigns the color transforms we created earlier to each of the tiles in the word. Now all that is left to do is display the clue for the word; to do this, we grab the *wordIndex* of the first tile in the word. Finally, we concatenate a string with the word descriptor ("1 Down," "30 Across," etc.) and the clue itself, pulled from the corresponding XMLList. Now that we have the behavior defined for when the player selects a tile, we need some way of deselecting the tiles and words, like when they click on a blacked-out tile. That's where the *clearSelection* method comes into play.

```
protected function clearSelection():void {
        if (!_selectedWord) return;
        for (var i:int = 0; i < _selectedWord.length; i++) {
                _selectedWord[i].transform.colorTransform = new
                        ColorTransform();
        }
}
```

All this method does is reset the color transforms for the tiles in the currently selected word. If no word is selected when the method is called, it exits. Note that we do not null out the variables *_selectedTile* and *_selectedWord*, because we may need to know the previously selected word. In fact, the *selectTile* method relies on knowing the previously selected word to fulfill all its conditions. Now that we have methods to set up a puzzle and select specific tiles in it and we need one more method to insert letters into the tiles. If you recall in the *selectTile* method, we set up a keyboard event listener when a tile is successfully selected. This method, *keyDown*, is what we'll look at next.

```
protected function keyDown(e:KeyboardEvent):void {
        var selectedIndex:int = (_selectedTile.tileIndex.
          y *_puzzleWidth) + _selectedTile.tileIndex.x;
        var newIndex:int;
        switch (e.keyCode) {
                case Keyboard.UP:
                newIndex = Math.max(0, selectedIndex -
                  _puzzleWidth);
                if (_tileList[newIndex].letter != CrosswordTile.
                  EMPTY) _tileList[newIndex].dispatchEvent(new
                  MouseEvent(MouseEvent.CLICK));
                break;
                case Keyboard.DOWN:
                newIndex = Math.min(_tileList.length-1,
                  selectedIndex + _puzzleWidth);
```

```
    if (_tileList[newIndex].letter != CrosswordTile.
      EMPTY) _tileList[newIndex].dispatchEvent(new
      MouseEvent(MouseEvent.CLICK));
    break;
    case Keyboard.LEFT:
    newIndex = Math.max(selectedIndex - 1, (_selected
      Tile.tileIndex.y * _puzzleWidth));
    if (_tileList[newIndex].letter != CrosswordTile.
      EMPTY) _tileList[newIndex].dispatchEvent(new
      MouseEvent(MouseEvent.CLICK));
    break;
    case Keyboard.RIGHT:
    newIndex = Math.min(selectedIndex + 1,
      ((_selectedTile.tileIndex.y+1) * _puzzleWidth)-1);
    if (_tileList[newIndex].letter != CrosswordTile.
      EMPTY) _tileList[newIndex].dispatchEvent(new
      MouseEvent(MouseEvent.CLICK));
    break;
    case Keyboard.SPACE:
    _selectedTile.dispatchEvent(new MouseEvent
      (MouseEvent.CLICK));
    break;
    default:
    _selectedTile.setAnswer(e);
    break;
  }
}
```

The *keyDown* method is responsible for handling a few different types of keyboard inputs. We employ a *switch* statement to filter through the possible values for the key that was pressed. In addition to responding to alphabetic key presses, we want to give the player the ability to move between different tiles with the arrow keys, as well as the ability to toggle between the across and down words of the selected tile. For the arrow key input, if a tile in the direction the player is attempting to move isn't blacked out, we simulate a mouse click by dispatching a new *MouseEvent* from the tile. The result is that it's as though the tile next to the selected tile was clicked with the mouse and *selectTile* is called to handle it. By simulating already existing functionality, we lessen the possibility for bugs, since the logic on selection of words based on tiles is centralized in one place. The same is true for the space bar; when it is pressed it is as though the selected tile was simply clicked again. For all other keys, we send the event through the *setAnswer* method of the tile. If you recall, that method knows how to filter for proper alphabetic inputs, so we don't have to worry about that here.

All of our classes for the crossword puzzle engine are now defined; let's try it out. If you open the CrosswordPuzzle.fla in the Chapter 9 folder, you will find the following code on the first frame.

```
var loader:URLLoader = new URLLoader(new URLRequest("crossword.
    xml"));
loader.addEventListener(Event.COMPLETE, createCrossword);

var cp:CrosswordPuzzle;

function createCrossword(e:Event) {
        cp = new CrosswordPuzzle(XML(e.target.data));
        cp.x = stage.stageWidth/2 - cp.width/2;
        cp.y = cp.x;
        addChild(cp);
}
```

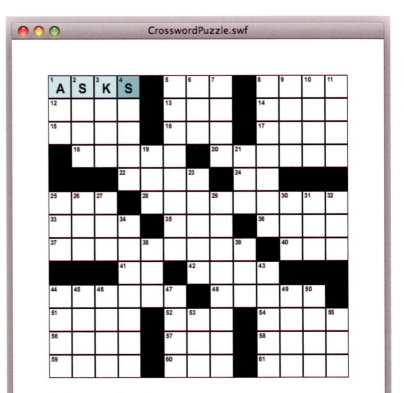

Figure 10.5 The finished crossword puzzle engine, running with the sample puzzle.

This little snippet of code handles loading in the XML file with all the crossword data and creates a new CrosswordPuzzle instance with it. Finally, it centers the puzzle horizontally on the Stage and adds it to the display list. This code could easily be integrated into a larger class that handles, for instance, the loading of multiple puzzles.

The resulting SWF for the whole crossword engine is just less than 15 k, pretty small for a lot of functionality. Using a device, or a system, font for the tiles would bring it down even further, since at least half the file is font data.

Content Is a Two-Way Street: A Crossword Builder

While editing an XML file by hand is certainly not impossible, it would get grueling pretty quickly to have to create entire cross-word puzzles that way. This is where an editor comes into play. Using the same core components, like the tile class and much of the puzzle class, you can take the crossword engine and write its second version that outputs the XML file and even saves it to a local file. While we won't build an entire editor here, a *savePuzzle* method might look like this for such applications.

```
protected function savePuzzle(e:Event = null) {
        _content = new XML(<crossword width={_puzzleWidth}
          height={_puzzleHeight}><puzzle/><clues/></crossword>);
        for (var i:int = 0; i < _tileList.length; i+= _puzzle
          Width) {
                var slice:Array = _tileList.slice(i, i+_puzzle
                  Width-1);
                var str:String = "";
                for (var j:int = 0; j < slice.length; j++) {
                        if (slice[j].letter == "") str += Cross
                          wordTile.EMPTY;
                                else str += slice[j].letter;
                }
                var row:XML = new XML(<row>{str}</row>);
                _content.puzzle.appendChild(row);
        }
        for (i = 0; i < _acrossClues.length; i++) {
                var across:XML = new XML(<across>{_acrossClues
                  [i]}</across>);
                _content.clues.appendChild(across);
        }
        for (i = 0; i < _downClues.length; i++) {
                var down:XML = new XML(<down>{_downClues[i]}
                  </down>);
```

```
                              _content.clues.appendChild(down);
                    }
                    var file:FileReference = new FileReference();
                    file.save(_content,"crosssword.xml");
          }
```

When creating an XML within ActionScript, you don't have to enclose it in "" or convert it from a string. You simply start typing it, hence the one line to create the *_content* container for the XML. To insert ActionScript values in the midst of raw XML, simply use braces ({}) around the expression that needs to be evaluated. In this case, the first line creates the main nodes with the puzzle width and height attributes and two child nodes: puzzle and clues. It then runs through the tile list and builds all the rows for the puzzle. The *appendChild* method is called, which adds each row to the bottom of the puzzle XMLList, like a *push* to an array. Then, the across and down clues are iterated and appended as well. Finally, the FileReference *save* method is called. It brings up a system file dialog window and saves the XML as text data to the file selected. The second parameter is only a suggestion—the end user can select whatever file name they want.

Sending Data Back Out

While the local file saving abilities in the FileReference class are great, the real power comes from saving data to a remote destination, such as a database. Data such as high-score leaderboards, user profiles, and more are all great candidates for XML formatting. To get the information to the database, it must get through some data processing (or *middleware*) layer, such as WebServices, AMF (Remoting), or standard form posts. Here is a quick example of what the latter might look like, simply posting the raw XML to a receiving PHP page.

```
var myXML:XML = <crossword width="10" height="10"><puzzle/>
  <clues/></crossword>;
var request:URLRequest = new URLRequest("myservice.php");
request.contentType = "text/xml";
request.data = myXML.toXMLString();
request.method = URLRequestMethod.POST;
var loader:URLLoader = new URLLoader(request);
```

Just as the URLLoader is the core class for loading remote data into Flash, it is also the sending mechanism when combined with a data-laden URLRequest. In this example, we simply format the request to notify the receiving page that it contains incoming XML content. Of course, sending the XML in its raw form like this is not particularly secure—most any savvy hacker will be able to use any number of HTTP monitoring tools to see the XML being sent (or any being received for that matter). For some data, such as public high-score tables, this won't matter. However, more sensitive data such as user information should be hidden. We'll explore ways to overcome this security deficiency in an online bonus chapter on flashgamebook.com.

One More Example: XML versus Flash Vars

A popular way of getting information into a SWF file from its containing HTML page is through the use of Flash Vars. If you're not familiar with them, Flash Vars are essentially name/value pairs that are passed into the SWF upon loading. Say you had a site in which users could log in and you wanted to display a player's name inside the game. A traditional solution to this problem would be to add the username to the object and embed tags in the HTML page. It would look like as follows:

```
<object classid="clsid:d27cdb6e-ae6d-11cf-96b8-444553540000"
  codebase="http://download.macromedia.com/pub/shockwave/cabs/
  flash/swflash.cab#version=10,0,0,0" width="500" height="600"
  id="CrosswordPuzzle" align="middle">
        <param name="allowScriptAccess" value="sameDomain" />
        <param name="allowFullScreen" value="false" />
        <param name="movie" value="CrosswordPuzzle.swf" />
        <param name="quality" value="high" />
        <param name="bgcolor" value="#ffffff" />
        <param name="flashvars" value="username=Chris" />
<embed src="CrosswordPuzzle.swf" quality="high"
  bgcolor="#ffffff" width="500" height="600" name="Crossword
  Puzzle" align="middle" allowScriptAccess="sameDomain"
  allowFullScreen="false" type="application/x-shockwave-flash"
  pluginspage=http://www.adobe.com/go/getflashplayer
flashvars="username=Chris"/>
</object>
```

If you have multiple pieces of information you need to pass into Flash, they are separated by &'s, just like a URL in a browser. There are a couple of drawbacks to using this system that become very apparent when you start using more than one or two variables. One reason is that you're limited to only single name/value pairs; you can't store any type of complex data in a Flash Var. The other one is that it becomes tricky to manage them in the page, and one typo or error processing could render all of them unavailable. To add to their annoyance during troubleshooting, any special characters must be URL-encoded, increasing their lack of readability.

A better option is to use a single Flash Var, maybe called *config*. The value of this variable is a path to either a static or a dynamic XML file. It would probably look something like the following:

```
<param name="flashvars" value="config=configuration.xml"/>
```

If the information contained within the XML file didn't need to change per user (like the links to various pages or media), it could simply be a file on the server besides your SWF that the SWF loads in on launching. If the information was dynamic (like a username or preferences), it could point to a PHP (or other back-end service) file that returns XML.

```
<param name="flashvars" value="config=configuration.php"/>
```

The URLLoader will load in the data as plain text, regardless of file extension, so as long as the page renders out as XML you're good to go. This keeps your back-end developers (or you if you're a solo operation) from having to wrangle variables within a page of already convoluted HTML. Here is an example of what a config file might look like.

```
<config>
        <mediaPath>http://www.mydomain.com/media/</mediaPath>
        <serviceURL>http://www.mydomain.com/services/
          </serviceURL>
        <userName>Chris</userName>
</config>
```

Remember that you could put whatever information you wanted to in here and in whatever structure. As you can see, this much more readable option is also easier to parse, and due to E4X, your basic data types (such as strings and numbers) come through intact; Flash Vars are *all* strings.

Summary

In this chapter we've explored a few uses of XML in games. There are definitely many more. Some developers I've met are wary of using XML, feeling that doing so forces them to use an elaborate, complex setup or follow some "best practices" guide to formatting they read in a 500-page tome on XML in an Enterprise setting. Nothing could be further from the truth; use XML where it makes sense, keep it simple, and try to follow a structure that lends itself to growth. The great thing about XML is that it is a standard in and of itself, and ActionScript 3 makes working with it a no-brainer.

FOUR-LETTER WORD: M-A-T-H

Few people I know, programmers included, don't groan a little when math and physics are brought up. While not all games utilize them, geometry, trigonometry, and basic physical mechanics are essential parts of game development. Don't worry though; this isn't a physics and math book. There are many of those out in the marketplace already, some of which are even written specifically for games.

In fact, this isn't even going to be an in-depth exploration of those topics because they really aren't necessary for most casual games. In this chapter, we will cover the foundational concepts you'll need to understand to be able to handle a wide variety of challenges involved in game development. We will accomplish this in two parts: Geometry and Trigonometry, and Physics, each with a practical example illustrating the concepts. If when you're done with this chapter, your appetite is whetted for a more in-depth look at these topics, I have provided links to further reading on this book's Web site.

The Math Class

ActionScript includes a core library for performing a lot of the functions we're going to learn about in this chapter. It is the Math class, and it will quickly become invaluable as we get into more complicated problems later on in our code. It doesn't include everything we'll eventually need, but later we'll learn about some companion functions we can write to make it even more useful.

Part One: Geometry and Trigonometry

Geometry, specifically Euclidean geometry, is the branch of mathematics that deals with, among other things, the relationship between points, lines, and shapes in a space. From it, we derive the formulas for finding the distance between two points, as well as the entire *x-y* coordinate system (known as the Cartesian coordinate system) on which Flash's Stage is built. Figure 11.1 illustrates a typical two-dimensional coordinate system.

Flash's coordinate system is slightly different in that it is flipped over the *x-axis*, resulting in *y* values being reversed. The upper-left corner of the Stage is at (0, 0) and expands down and to the right from there, as shown in Fig. 11.2. This is important to note because it is diametrically opposed to the notion that numbers decrease as they move "down" on a graph, and it can cause confusion later when we move into some of the concepts of physics.

Trigonometry (or trig for short) is a related, but more specific, branch that describes the relationships between the sides and angles of triangles, specifically right triangles (triangles with one angle of 90°). All triangles have some fundamental properties:

- A triangle's interior angles always add up to 180°.
- Any triangle (regardless of orientation and type) can be split into two right triangles.
- The relationships between any given side and angle of a triangle are defined by ratios that are known as the *trigonometric functions*.

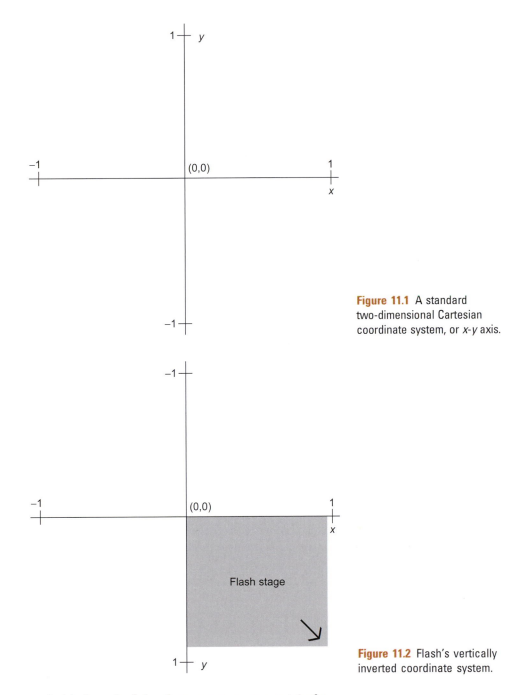

Figure 11.1 A standard two-dimensional Cartesian coordinate system, or *x-y* axis.

Figure 11.2 Flash's vertically inverted coordinate system.

You have probably heard of the three most common trig functions: sine (sin), cosine (cos), and tangent (tan). They each relate to different sides of a triangle. The longest side of the triangle (and in a right triangle, the side opposite the right angle) is the *hypotenuse* (hyp). In Fig. 11.3, we relate to the other two sides of the

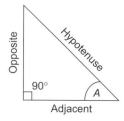

Figure 11.3 The three sides of a right triangle, related to angle *A*.

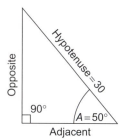

Figure 11.4 Using the information about one angle and one side, we can use the trig functions to find the values of the other two sides.

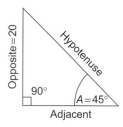

Figure 11.5 A triangle where we know one angle and one side.

triangle based on the angle we're interested in; in this case *A*. The vertical side of the triangle is *opposite* (opp) angle *A*, while the horizontal side is *adjacent* (adj) to it.

The aforementioned trig functions work with these sides as follows:

- The sine of an angle is equal to the opposite side's length divided by the hypotenuse's length: sin *A* = *opp/hyp*
- The cosine of an angle is equal to the adjacent side's length divided by the hypotenuse's length: cos *A* = *adj/hyp*
- The tangent of an angle is equal to the opposite side divided by the adjacent site: tan *A* = *opp/adj*

As you can see, these functions are very helpful if you only know a little bit of information about a triangle and need to determine the other components. Let's look at a few examples. In Fig. 11.4, we know the value of angle *A* is 50° (and by extension, the other missing angle would then be 40°). We also know the length of the hypotenuse is 30.

To find the lengths of the other two sides, we rewrite the sine and cosine equations as follows:

$$adj = \cos A \times hyp, \text{ or } adj = (\cos 50) \times 30$$
$$opp = \sin A \times hyp, \text{ or } opp = (\sin 50) \times 30$$

If you used a calculator with the trig functions on it, you would quickly determine that the value of the adjacent side is ~19.3 and the value of the opposite side is ~23.

In Fig. 11.5, we can see that we now know one angle (45°) and the length of the side opposite that angle (20°).

Once again, we simply manipulate the equations to determine the other two sides, this time using tangent instead of cosine, since cosine has nothing to do with the opposite side:

$$hyp = opp/\sin A, \text{ or } hyp = 20/(\sin 45)$$
$$adj = opp/\tan A, \text{ or } adj = 20/(\tan 45)$$

Using a calculator, this would reveal the hypotenuse to have a length of ~28.3 and the adjacent side to also be 20.

Now let's look at an example (Fig. 11.6) with a triangle where we know the lengths of the two shorter sides, but no angles and no hypotenuse.

Since we know the opposite and adjacent sides, the obvious choice would be to use the tangent equation to determine the value of angle *A* (and flipping the two sides to find out the value of *B*):

$$\tan A = 15/20$$
$$\tan B = 20/15$$

However, now we're stuck. We want the values of *A* and *B*, not the tangent of *A* and *B*. Luckily, there is a way to reverse each trig equation using what are known as the *inverse* trig functions. The names of these functions match their counterparts, but prefixed with the word *arc*. In this case, we need to use *arctangent* to find the value of each of these angles.

$$A = \text{arctan }(15/20)$$
$$B = \text{arctan }(20/15)$$

Based on these equations, angle A would be ~37° and B would be ~53°. If you add these together with the right angle of 90°, you can see that we indeed have a proper triangle of 180°.

For our final theoretical example, look back again to Fig. 11.6. Suppose all you needed was the hypotenuse and you weren't interested in the angles at all. You could do what we did previously, using arctangent to get the values of the angles and then use those angles with either sine or cosine to determine the hypotenuse. However, as this is a multiple-step process, it is inefficient when we have a much quicker way. In addition to the standard trig functions, there is another equation to determine the third side of a triangle when you know the other two, which is known as the Pythagorean theorem. The theorem states that the hypotenuse of a triangle, squared, is equal to the sum of the squares of the other two sides. Let's look at this as an equation, calling the two shorter sides a and b and the hypotenuse c.

$$a^2 + b^2 = c^2$$

Finding any one side when you know the other two is just a simple permutation of this equation as follows:

$$c = \sqrt{(a^2 + b^2)}, \ b = \sqrt{(c^2 - a^2)}, \ a = \sqrt{(c^2 - b^2)}$$

For our purposes, we know sides a and b to be 15 and 20 (or 20 and 15; it doesn't really matter). From these values, the hypotenuse would therefore be equal to $\sqrt{(15^2 + 20^2)}$, or 25.

Now that we have defined these functions and have seen how to use them, let's look at a couple of practical examples in Flash and how to apply the functions there.

A fairly common use of the trig functions is finding the angle of the mouse cursor relative to another point. This angle can then be applied to the rotation of a DisplayObject to make the object "look" at the mouse. If you open the MousePointer.fla file, you'll find just such an example setup. It consists of a triangle MovieClip called "pointer" on the Stage. One of the corners of the triangle is colored differently to differentiate the direction it is pointing. For simplicity, the ActionScript to perform this math is on the timeline; if you were using this code as part of something larger, it would make sense to put it in a class. Let's look at this code now.

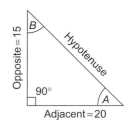

Figure 11.6 A triangle where we know just two of the sides, but no angles and no hypotenuse.

```
addEventListener(Event.ENTER_FRAME, updatePointer, false, 0,
true);

function updatePointer(e:Event) {
        var angle:Number = Math.atan2(mouseY - pointer.y,
          mouseX - pointer.x);
        pointer.rotation = angle * (180 / Math.PI);
}
```

On every frame (30 times per second at our current frame rate), the angle of the pointer relative to the mouse position is updated. There is a fair amount going on in these two lines, so let's look at them one at a time.

```
var angle:Number = Math.atan2(mouseY - pointer.y, mouseX - pointer.x);
```

Remember we learned that if we know two sides of the triangle, we could use that information to find out any of the angles. In this case, we know the difference in *x* and *y* between the mouse cursor and the pointer clip. These constitute the two shorter sides of a right triangle—a straight line drawn between the pointer and mouse would be the hypotenuse of this triangle. This is illustrated in Fig. 11.7.

In the figure, *A* represents the angle we're interested in, as we want the pointer to basically "look down" the imaginary hypotenuse. This makes *x* distance the adjacent side to the angle, and *y* distance the opposite side. Recall the formula for the tangent of an angle: tan *A* = *opp/adj*. To determine *A*, we need to use the arctangent formula: *A* = arctan(*opp/adj*). In ActionScript, there are two ways to implement arctangent—they are the atan() and atan2() methods of the Math class. The first expects to receive one value, assuming you have already divided the opposite side by the adjacent. The second one performs this step for you and is, thus, more commonly used (at least by me); pass it the opposite side first, followed by the adjacent side. In our case, the opposite side is the difference in the *y* value of the mouse cursor and the *y* position of the pointer. Likewise, the adjacent side is the difference in *x* values of the cursor and the pointer. We now have the angle represented by *A* in Fig. 11.7. However, this angle (and all angles returned by the arc functions in ActionScript) is in *radians*, not *degrees*. The rotation property of the pointer is assigned in degrees, so we need to know how to convert one unit to the other.

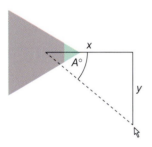

Figure 11.7 The distance between the mouse cursor and the registration point of the pointer clip forms a triangle.

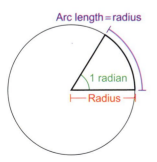

Figure 11.8 When the length of an arc on a circle is equal to the circle's radius, the value of the angle formed is 1 radian.

A Quick Explanation of Radians and Pi

You already know that sum of all angles of a triangle is 180°, and that of a circle is 360°, exactly double. A single radian is the value of the angle created when a slice of the circumference of a circle is equal to the circle's radius; Figure 11.8 illustrates this.

If this explanation is confusing, don't worry—a full understanding of the use of radians is not necessary to perform the math we need. In fact, there is a very handy constant in math that will help us convert between radians and degrees. It is known as Pi (pronounced "pie"), represented by the symbol π, and a nonrepeating decimal number approximately equivalent to 3.141. It represents the number of radians in a triangle, or half the number of radians in a circle. Therefore, 180° is equal to π radians. To convert between radians and degrees, we simply multiply a number of radians by $180/\pi$ or a number of degrees by $\pi/180$. Returning to our ActionScript example from above, the next line of code does just that, using the Math. PI constant.

```
pointer.rotation = angle * (180 / Math.PI);
```

If you test this FLA file, you will see that the pointer consistently points in the direction of your cursor as you move it around the screen. Now that we have this piece of functionality in place, let's add a layer of complexity. Suppose in addition to "looking at" the mouse we wanted the pointer to also move toward the mouse until it reaches the mouse's x and y positions. If you open the example MouseFollower.fla, you'll see how we can accomplish this.

Initially, this example looks very much like the previous one, except for a few extra lines of code. Let's look at this additional ActionScript now.

```
var speed:Number = 5; //PIXELS PER FRAME

addEventListener(Event.ENTER_FRAME, updatePointer, false, 0,
  true);

function updatePointer(e:Event) {
    var angle:Number = Math.atan2(mouseY - pointer.y,
      mouseX - pointer.x);
    pointer.rotation = angle * (180 / Math.PI);
    var xSpeed:Number = Math.cos(angle) * speed;
    var ySpeed:Number = Math.sin(angle) * speed;
    if (Math.abs(mouseX - pointer.x) > Math.abs(xSpeed))
      pointer.x += xSpeed;
    if (Math.abs(mouseY - pointer.y) > Math.abs(ySpeed))
      pointer.y += ySpeed;
}
```

The first line we've added is a speed component. This defines how many pixels the pointer should move per frame, in this case the number of pixels is 5. In the updatePointer function, we've also added a few lines to perform this move. Since the speed is how many pixels we want to move in a straight line, we need to convert it into the amount we need to move in the *x-axis* and *y-axis*.

In order to do this, we need to think of the speed as the hypotenuse of an imaginary triangle. We also already know the angle of the triangle we're interested in, because we just used arctangent to solve it. With this information in hand, we can use the sine and cosine functions to find the adjacent and opposite sides of this triangle, or the *x* and *y* components, respectively.

```
var xSpeed:Number = Math.cos(angle) * speed;
var ySpeed:Number = Math.sin(angle) * speed;
```

Once we have these two speeds, we can simply apply them to the *x* and *y* positions of the pointer to move it. In its simplest form, that code would look like as follows:

```
pointer.x += xSpeed;
pointer.y += ySpeed;
```

However, if you were to leave the code like this, you would find that the pointer would start to move erratically when it got very close to the mouse. This is because while trying to get as close to the cursor as possible, it continues to "jump over" its target and will appear to bounce back and forth endlessly. To circumvent this behavior, we need to check to see if the pointer is close enough to the mouse so that it can stop moving. Doing so will employ another method of the Math class, *abs()*. This method is known in English as the *absolute-value* function. When given a number, either positive or negative, it returns the *unsigned* value of that number; Math.abs(4) = 4, Math.abs(−7) = 7, etc. In our example, we want to know whether the distance between the cursor and the pointer is greater than the distance the pointer is trying to travel. Since we can't know whether difference between the cursor's position and the pointer's position will result in a negative number, we use the absolute value of the number for our calculation to ensure it is always positive. We also apply the function for the *xSpeed* and *ySpeed* variables because there are situations where they could be negative as well.

```
if (Math.abs(mouseX - pointer.x) > Math.abs(xSpeed)) pointer.x
  += xSpeed;
if (Math.abs(mouseY - pointer.y) > Math.abs(ySpeed)) pointer.y
  += ySpeed;
```

If you compile the SWF, you will see that this code causes the pointer to follow the mouse around the screen, always pointing toward it. While this logic is not what most people would consider *intelligence*, it is a form of AI.

Let's look at one more example that will give the pointer a little more "personality." Open MouseFollowDistance.fla to follow along. Continuing on our previous examples, we once again have a clip named pointer and some code in the first frame. However, instead of constantly following the cursor, the pointer will only pursue the mouse when it is within a certain distance.

```
var speed:Number = 5; //PIXELS PER FRAME
var interestDistance:Number = 150; //PIXELS

addEventListener(Event.ENTER_FRAME, updatePointer, false, 0,
  true);

function updatePointer(e:Event) {
      if (getDistance(mouseX, mouseY, pointer.x, pointer.y) >
        interestDistance) return;
      var angle:Number = Math.atan2(mouseY - pointer.y,
        mouseX - pointer.x);
      pointer.rotation = angle * (180 / Math.PI);
      var xSpeed:Number = Math.cos(angle) * speed;
      var ySpeed:Number = Math.sin(angle) * speed;
      if (Math.abs(mouseX - pointer.x) > Math.abs(xSpeed))
        pointer.x += xSpeed;
      if (Math.abs(mouseY - pointer.y) > Math.abs(ySpeed))
        pointer.y += ySpeed;
}

function getDistance(x1:Number, y1:Number, x2:Number,
  y2:Number):Number {
      return Math.sqrt(Math.pow((x2-x1),2) + Math.pow((y2-y1),2));
}
```

The first variable we add is *interestDistance*, or the number of pixels within which the pointer becomes "interested" in the mouse cursor. At the beginning of *updatePointer*, we also add a condition to check if the distance between the two is greater than the amount we specified. We do this by introducing a new function called *getDistance*. If you remember any basic geometry from school, you'll probably recognize this method as the *distance formula*. However, it is also a variation of the Pythagorean theorem. Recall that

$$c^2 = a^2 + b^2$$

where a and b are sides of a triangle. To find c, we rewrite the function as follows:

$$c = \sqrt{(a^2 + b^2)}$$

In our case, a and b represent the differences in x and y, respectively. If we replace these variables with our actual values, it looks like as follows:

$$distance = \sqrt{((x2 - x1)^2 + (y2 - y1)^2)}$$

Written in ActionScript, using the Math class methods for exponents, this same function results in

```
Math.sqrt(Math.pow((x2-x1),2) + Math.pow((y2-y1),2));
```

Upon testing the SWF, you'll see that the pointer will only follow the cursor when the mouse is within 150 pixels of it. We have bestowed the pointer with a basic decision-making ability. So far, these examples have been fairly abstract—they don't really constitute a game. We will use these examples as part of a larger piece of game code, but first we need to understand a little more about Flash's coordinate system.

3D in Flash

A new feature introduced in Flash CS4 is support for "3D" objects. This ability is sometimes misunderstood initially and requires a little clarification. Flash cannot natively use 3D models created in programs such as Autodesk Maya or 3D Studio, though starting in future versions of Flash you will be able to do this through external libraries and hardware acceleration. Rather, the current features manipulate 2D objects in 3D space, allowing for effects such as true perspective skewing and distortion. One way to think about it is to imagine all your objects on the Stage like rigid pieces of paper; they have no perceivable depth, but you can tell their orientation in 3D space. This new ability adds several new properties to DisplayObjects, not the least of which is the introduction of a third, or z, axis. Figure 11.9 illustrates how the z-axis is represented in the two-dimensional environment of

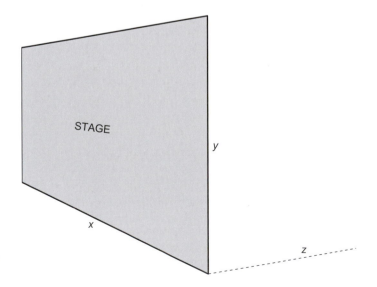

Figure 11.9 The new z-axis in Flash is perpendicular to both the x and y axes.

the Stage; you can think of it as following the invisible line created from your eyes to the screen.

Position

On the z-axis, the value of 0 is at Stage level. Negative values for the z property of a DisplayObject would make the object appear larger and "closer" to the viewer. Positive values for z will increasingly shrink the object, making it "further away." Flash developers who have performed tricks with the x and y scales of objects in the past to achieve the feeling of depth and 3D space will no doubt breathe a sigh of relief at the ease with which this effect can now be achieved with only a line or two of code. It should be noted that the z position of an object only tells Flash how to properly render the object in perspective; it does not affect the display list order. In other words, if you had two objects in a scene (let's say one with a z position of 30, whereas the other had a z position of 10), but the one with the higher z position was added to the Stage later, it would still appear to be on the top in the display list.

Rotation

In addition to 3D positioning, you can also rotate DisplayObjects around any of the three axes. Figures 11.10–11.12 illustrate how a DisplayObject is rendered when its *rotationX*, *rotationY*, and *rotationZ* properties are each set to 45, respectively. You'll notice that the effect of *rotationZ* is not unlike the traditional *rotation* property from previous versions of Flash.

Perspective Projection

At this point it's important to understand how the 3D transformations are computed and are applied to give the illusion of 3D space in a 2D environment. Each DisplayObject in Flash has a vanishing point, that is, the point in 3D space where all parallel lines heading to the point appear to converge. The use of just one vanishing point is known as

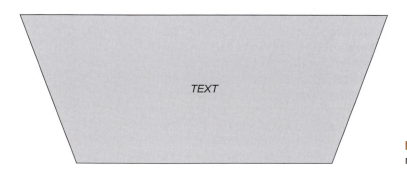

TEXT

Figure 11.10 A DisplayObject rotated 45° on its *x*-axis.

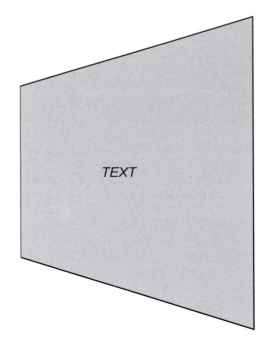

Figure 11.11 A DisplayObject rotated 45° on its *y*-axis.

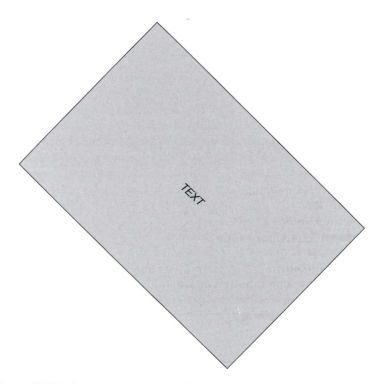

Figure 11.12 A DisplayObject rotated 45° on its *z*-axis.

one-point projection. Figure 11.13 illustrates how four different objects look when using the same vanishing point.

Only being able to use a single vanishing point for all DisplayObjects would be rather limiting, so Flash allows us to assign each DisplayObject its own vanishing point. By default, every new object uses the center of the Stage as its vanishing point. Unfortunately, multiple vanishing points cannot be assigned within the Flash authoring environment. This must be done through ActionScript using the transform property of DisplayObjects. Starting in CS4, Transform objects now have a new property called perspectiveProjection. This object allows us to set the vanishing point for any given DisplayObject. Let's look at a few lines of script, applied to the same clips shown in Fig. 11.13.

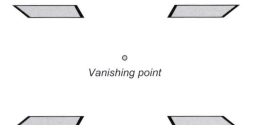

Figure 11.13 Four DisplayObjects rotating toward a single vanishing point.

```
clip1.transform.perspectiveProjection = new
    PerspectiveProjection();
clip2.transform.perspectiveProjection = new
    PerspectiveProjection();
clip1.transform.perspectiveProjection.projectionCenter = new
    Point(0, 200);
clip2.transform.perspectiveProjection.projectionCenter = new
    Point(550, 200);
clip3.transform.perspectiveProjection = clip1.transform.
    perspectiveProjection;
clip4.transform.perspectiveProjection = clip2.transform.
    perspectiveProjection;
```

In this example, we create two new PerspectiveProjection objects, one positioned at the left-hand side of the screen and the other at the right. Figure 11.14 shows the result of this script; the two clips on the left skew to the left, while those on the right skew to the right.

With that basic overview of the 3D abilities of Flash, let's look at a practical example using the math covered earlier in this chapter. It is similar to the premise behind Atari's classic arcade game *Tempest*. The player controls a character at the mouth of a long tunnel that appears to start at the screen in first-person view and diminishes into the distance. We'll use the trig functions and some

○ *Vanishing point 1*   *Vanishing point 2* ○

Figure 11.14 Two pairs of DisplayObjects, each with its own vanishing point.

3D manipulation to construct the game environment and move the various components of gameplay.

The SimpleTunnelShooter Example

The support files for this exercise are in the Chapter 11 folder; the main file is SimpleTunnelShooter.fla. All the class files for it are in the *tunnelshooter* package. This is to eliminate any interference with other examples from this chapter, as well as to demonstrate use of packages for keeping code isolated and organized.

The Basic Mechanics

The game will generate a tunnel in the shape of an octagon through a series of surface *tiles* positioned in 3D space. There need to be enough tiles to create a sense of depth, like the tunnel extends a long distance. The player will move the character around the edges; each side of the tunnel is a "step." Enemies will be generated at the far end of the tunnel and moved toward the player over time.

Classes

There are five classes that we will utilize for this example:
- Game.as: This controls the input and interaction with the other components—the main "engine."
- Tunnel.as: It is a DisplayObject that manages construction of the 3D tunnel and facilitates interaction with the tiles that make up the sides of the tunnel.
- TunnelTile.as: This is a DisplayObject that will be distorted in 3D space and used in conjunction with other tiles to simulate the 3D surface of the tunnel.
- Enemy.as: This is the class defining enemy objects that will be created at one end of the tunnel and moved toward the opening of the tunnel.
- Player.as: This is actually just a *stub* class; it has no code for this example other than to establish a link between a symbol in the library—it would be used later to bestow interactive abilities to the player object.

We'll work with these classes from the "inside out," starting with the Tunnel, TunnelTile, and Enemy classes, and then pulling all of them together in the Game class.

The Tunnel Class

In order to create the illusion of depth, we'll create a 3D surface from multiple flat objects, or tiles. Because it doesn't need access to multiple frames, Tunnel extends the Sprite class.

```
public class Tunnel extends Sprite {

        protected var _radius:Number;
        protected var _sides:int, _depth:int;
        protected var _tileWidth:Number, _tileHeight:Number;
        protected var _tunnelTiles:Array;
        protected var _highlightIndex:int = -1;
```

There are some basic properties we will need to track during and after creation of the tunnel. Even though it is not a circle, the radius will keep track of the distance of each tile from the center of the tunnel. We also need to know the number of sides the tunnel has, as well as how many tiles deep it extends. The *_tunnelTiles* array will keep track of all the tiles so they can be referenced later. Finally, the *_highlightIndex* property will be used later when we want to light up a set of tiles.

```
public function Tunnel(radius:Number, depth:int=10, sides:int=8)
  {
        _radius = radius;
        _sides = sides;
        _depth = depth;
        createTunnel();
}
```

In the constructor, we pass the radius of the tunnel, as well as how many tiles deep and around the tunnel are. After that we call *createTunnel*, which we will look at next.

```
protected function createTunnel():void {
        _tunnelTiles = new Array();
        var tempTile:TunnelTile = new TunnelTile();
        _tileHeight = tempTile.height;
        _tileWidth = (_radius * Math.tan(Math.PI/_sides)) * 2;
        var angle:Number = (Math.PI * 2) / _sides;
        for (var j:int = 0; j < _depth; j++) {
          var tileSet:Array = new Array();
          for (var i:int = 0; i < _sides; i++) {
              tempTile = new TunnelTile();
              tempTile.width = _tileWidth;
              tempTile.x = Math.cos(i*angle) * _radius;
              tempTile.y = Math.sin(i*angle) * _radius;
              tempTile.z = j * _tileHeight;
              tempTile.rotationX = 90;
              tempTile.rotationZ = i * Math.round(radiansToDegrees
                (angle)) + 90;
              var ct:ColorTransform = tempTile.transform.
                colorTransform;
              ct.redMultiplier *= (_depth - j)/_depth;
```

```
        ct.greenMultiplier *= (_depth - j)/_depth;
        ct.blueMultiplier *= (_depth - j)/_depth;
        tempTile.transform.colorTransform = ct;
        tileSet.push(tempTile);
        addChild(tempTile);
      }
    _tunnelTiles.push(tileSet);
    }
  }
```

This method is at the heart of this class. We start by determining the height and width each tile will need to be for the sides to meet all the way around the tunnel. We assume that the artwork for each tile will dictate the height of the tile; in order to maintain the illusion of depth, the pieces will ultimately be taller than they are wide. To determine the width of each tile, we will need to refer back to the trig functions discussed earlier in this chapter. Since we are building our tunnel to have eight sides, we'll use that as our visual reference.

In Fig. 11.15, note the white dashed line represents the virtual circle that touches the center points of all the sides of the octagon. The radius of this imaginary circle is the value passed into the tunnel constructor. In order to find the value of angle A, we divide π (which is half the angle value of a circle) by the number of sides. Since we now know one angle and one side, the best trig function to use is *tangent*. Recall from the earlier discussion in the chapter that

$$\tan A = opp/adj$$

So, it follows that in order to find the value of the opposite side, we rearrange the equation as follows:

$$opp = adj \times \tan A$$

However, this will only give us half the width of a side, so we need to multiply it by 2 as well; thus, the line will be as follows:

```
_tileWidth = (_radius * Math.tan(Math.PI/_sides)) * 2;
```

Before we start the loops that create the tiles, we need to know the angle value of each side, so that we can place the tiles. This is simply the entire angle of the circle (2π) in radians, divided by the number of sides (eight).

```
var angle:Number = (Math.PI * 2)/_sides;
```

Now that we have the information we need to place the tiles around the center of the tunnel, we need to run through two loops to create a multidimensional array. Each layer of eight tiles comprises its own array, stored in a larger array.

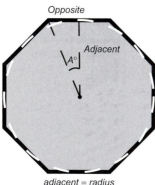

Opposite

Adjacent

$A°$

adjacent = radius
$A = \pi/8$ (number of sides)

Figure 11.15 We can break the shape down into right triangles in order to use trig functions to determine the missing values.

```
for (var j:int = 0; j < _depth; j++) {
        var tileSet:Array = new Array();
        for (var i:int = 0; i < _sides; i++) {


        }

        _tunnelTiles.push(tileSet);
}
```

Each time the outer loop runs, a new tile set is created that the inner loop will fill. That tile set is then added to the larger *tunnelTiles* array.

```
tempTile = new TunnelTile();
tempTile.width = _tileWidth;
```

In the inner loop, we create a new TunnelTile object and set its width to the predetermined value. Next, we need to position it around the center point. We can once again break a side down into right triangles. We know that the hypotenuse to be the value of the radius and the angle is the value between the center points of any two connecting sides, as shown in Fig. 11.16.

```
tempTile.x = Math.cos(i*angle) * _radius;
tempTile.y = Math.sin(i*angle) * _radius;
tempTile.z = j * _tileHeight;
```

The value of *i* is the current side of the tunnel we're dealing with, from 0 to 7. We multiply the *i* value by the angle associated with each side and use the *sine* and *cosine* functions to position *x* and *y* coordinates of the tile. We then use the current depth level, represented by *j* to position the tiles down the *z-axis*. Now the tile is positioned, but it would still appear to be a flat shape on the Stage. We must rotate it in 3D space.

```
tempTile.rotationX = 90;
tempTile.rotationZ = i * Math.round(radiansToDegrees(angle)) + 90;
```

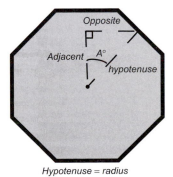

Hypotenuse = radius

We rotate the tile along its *x-axis* to turn it parallel to the tunnel; one end of the tile will now appear closer than the other. Next, we rotate it along the *z-axis* so that each tile faces the center of the tunnel. We convert the angle from radians to degrees (using a function we'll cover momentarily) and add 90. This is to compensate for having rotated the tile along its *x-axis* already; without it, the tiles will align perfectly perpendicular to the Stage and will disappear from view. Now the tile is ready to use.

```
tileSet.push(tempTile);
addChild(tempTile);
```

We add the tile to the tileSet array (which will get added to _tunnelTiles) and then to the display list. If we were to stop here, the tunnel would work just fine, but there's no real sense of depth,

Figure 11.16 We know the value of the hypotenuse and the angle between each side.

since Flash's 3D capabilities do not include any form of lighting. However, we can manually adjust this using a ColorTransform.

```
var ct:ColorTransform = tempTile.transform.colorTransform;
ct.redMultiplier *= (_depth - j)/_depth;
ct.greenMultiplier *= (_depth - j)/_depth;
ct.blueMultiplier *= (_depth - j)/_depth;
tempTile.transform.colorTransform = ct;
```

In order for the tunnel to look like it is truly diminishing from the player's point of view, the mouth of the tunnel should look like the main light source. The light should therefore fall off as the tunnel descends. We can achieve this effect by multiplying the red, green, and blue values of each tile's *colorTransform* object by the depth of the tile. Note that you can't operate directly on an object's color-Transform. You must assign it to a variable, which makes a copy, modify the copy, and assign it back to the object. All transforms in ActionScript work this way. We've now created the tunnel and its entire tile set. Let's look at a few of the other functions the tunnel uses, including one that is mentioned earlier.

```
protected function radiansToDegrees(value:Number):Number {
        return value * (180/Math.PI);
}


protected function degreesToRadians(value:Number):Number {
        return value * (Math.PI/180);
}
```

These two functions simply perform the conversion from radians to degrees and vice versa that we have discussed earlier in this chapter. For simplicity, they're included in this class, but the smartest way to utilize them would be as static methods of a math utilities class.

```
public function get radius():Number {
        return _radius;
}


public function get sides():int {
        return _sides;
}


public function get depth():int {
        return _depth;
}


public function get tunnelTiles():Array {
        return _tunnelTiles;
}
```

Each of these *getter* functions provides easy access to various properties of the tunnel without making them writeable. One could argue that the tunnelTiles getter should return a copy of the tunnel array, not the original, but since you would also have to copy all the arrays inside it as well, it is not a very efficient way to manage the list. It is better to just be mindful that any edits made to the tunnelTiles list could break the tunnel's functionality of appearance.

```
public function highlightSide(angle:Number):void {
    if (angle < 0) angle = Math.PI*2 + angle;
    var index:int = Math.round((angle * _sides)/(Math.PI * 2));
    if (_highlightIndex == index) return;
    for (var i:int = 0; i < _tunnelTiles.length; i++) {
      if (_highlightIndex >= 0) _tunnelTiles[i]
        [_highlightIndex].deactivate();
      _tunnelTiles[i][index].activate();
    }
    _highlightIndex = index;
}
```

The final method in the Tunnel class is one that will be of particular use to the Game class. It allows an entire side (from the top to the bottom) to be highlighted or "lit up." This will be useful if we need to point out which side the player is currently on or if we need to notify the player of an enemy on a particular side. It accepts an angle as a parameter to match with its corresponding side. If the angle is negative, we convert it to its positive equivalent by adding 2π (or 360°). Once we know the correct side, and if it is not already highlighted, we loop through the list from top to bottom to call the *activate* method of each tile and the *deactivate* method of any tiles that are previously highlighted. Afterwards, we set the value of *_highlightIndex* to the currently selected side for reference later. Let's look at the entire class now in context:

```
package tunnelshooter {

    import flash.display.Sprite;
    import flash.events.Event;
    import flash.geom.ColorTransform;

    public class Tunnel extends Sprite {

      protected var _radius:Number;
      protected var _sides:int, _depth:int;
      protected var _tileWidth:Number, _tileHeight:Number;
      protected var _tunnelTiles:Array;
```

```
protected var _highlightIndex:int = -1;

public function Tunnel(radius:Number, depth:int = 10,
  sides:int = 8) {
    _radius = radius;
    _sides = sides;
    _depth = depth;
    createTunnel();
}

protected function createTunnel():void {
    _tunnelTiles = new Array();
    var tempTile:TunnelTile = new TunnelTile();
    _tileHeight = tempTile.height;
    _tileWidth = (_radius * Math.tan(Math.PI/_sides)) * 2;
    var angle:Number = (Math.PI * 2) / _sides;
    for (var j:int = 0; j < _depth; j++) {
        var tileSet:Array = new Array();
        for (var i:int = 0; i < _sides; i++) {
            tempTile = new TunnelTile();
            tempTile.width = _tileWidth;
            tempTile.x = Math.cos(i*angle) * _radius;
            tempTile.y = Math.sin(i*angle) * _radius;
            tempTile.z = j * _tileHeight;
            tempTile.rotationX = 90;
            tempTile.rotationZ = i * Math.round(radians
              ToDegrees(angle)) + 90;
            tileSet.push(tempTile);
            addChild(tempTile);
            var ct:ColorTransform = tempTile.transform.
              colorTransform;
            ct.redMultiplier *= (_depth - j)/_depth;
            ct.greenMultiplier *= (_depth - j)/_depth;
            ct.blueMultiplier *= (_depth - j)/_depth;
            tempTile.transform.colorTransform = ct;
        }
        _tunnelTiles.push(tileSet);
    }
}

protected function radiansToDegrees(value:Number):Number {
    return value * (180/Math.PI);
}

protected function degreesToRadians(value:Number):Number {
    return value * (Math.PI/180);
}
```

```
protected function getRandomColor():ColorTransform {
    var red:Number = Math.random();
    var green:Number = Math.random();
    var blue:Number = Math.random();
    var ct:ColorTransform = new ColorTransform(red,
      green, blue, 1, 0, 0, 0, 0);
    return ct;
}

public function get radius():Number {
    return _radius;
}

public function get sides():int {
    return _sides;
}

public function get depth():int {
    return _depth;
}

public function get tunnelTiles():Array {
    return _tunnelTiles;
}

public function highlightSide(angle:Number):void {
    if (angle < 0) angle = Math.PI*2 + angle;
    var index:int = Math.round((angle * _sides)/(Math.PI * 2));
    if (_highlightIndex == index) return;
    for (var i:int = 0; i < _tunnelTiles.length; i++) {
        if (_highlightIndex >= 0) _tunnelTiles[i]
          [_highlightIndex].deactivate();
        _tunnelTiles[i][index].activate();
    }
    _highlightIndex = index;
}

}

}
```

getRandomColor

You may have noticed that there is one method I didn't discuss. It is the getRandomColor method, and it does exactly the same. It returns a randomly generated colorTransform object that can be applied. I created it as an experiment when writing this class, and though it didn't produce the results I was looking for, it is very interesting and might prove helpful if you want to do something with colored tiles or any other type of color generation.

Next we'll look at the TunnelTile class, which the Tunnel class utilized to build itself. Since the class is pretty short, we'll look at it in its entirety and then explain each method.

```
public class TunnelTile extends MovieClip {

        private var _highlightedTransform:ColorTransform;
        private var _normalTransform:ColorTransform;

        public function TunnelTile() {
        }

        public function activate() {
          if (!_normalTransform) _normalTransform = transform.
            colorTransform;
          if (!_highlightedTransform) createHighlight();
          transform.colorTransform = _highlightedTransform;
        }

        public function deactivate() {
          transform.colorTransform = _normalTransform;
        }

        private function createHighlight() {
          _highlightedTransform = transform.colorTransform;
          _highlightedTransform.redOffset = _highlightedTransform.
            greenOffset = _highlightedTransform.blueOffset = 50;
        }
}
```

The constructor for this class does nothing, as the Tunnel is responsible for placing and manipulating each tile. The methods here mainly deal with activating and deactivating the highlight effect for the tile, as evidenced by their names *activate*, *deactivate*, and *createHighlight*. The first time a tile is activated, it stores its normal color transform (the one given to it by the Tunnel class) in a private variable for future reference. It also creates a highlighted version of that transform, which is done by offsetting all the color values by 50. This creates a tint effect, as thought the tiles were overlaid with white. That way, when *activate* is called, the tint transform is used, and *deactivate* returns the transform to its previous state.

The last class to examine before we begin dissection of the gameplay is the Enemy class. It is also very simple, though further functionality could easily be added.

```
public class Enemy extends MovieClip {

    public var index:int;
    protected var _brightness:Number;

    public function Enemy(index:int) {
      this.index = index;
    }

    public function get brightness ():Number {
      return _brightness;
    }

    public function set brightness (value:Number):void {
      _brightness = value;
      var ct:ColorTransform = transform.colorTransform;
      ct.redMultiplier = ct.greenMultiplier = ct.blue
        Multiplier = _brightness;
      transform.colorTransform = ct;
    }
}
```

Since an enemy in this style of game generally sticks to one side of the tunnel, we keep track of which side through the *index* property, which is passed in when the enemy is created. The other method is a getter/setter combo that set the brightness value of the enemy's colorTransform. This has the opposite effect of the tint we used on the tiles. It will allow us to make the enemy darker the further down the tunnel it is, and make it brighter as it approaches the player.

We are now ready to look at the Game class, and the logic that will control the player and the enemies.

```
public class Game extends Sprite {

        static public var tunnelSize:Number = 175;
        static public var tunnelDepth:int = 8;
        static public var tunnelSides:int = 8;
        static public var enemyFrequency:Number = 3;
        static public var enemyTime:Number = 5;
        protected var _tunnel:Tunnel;
        protected var _player:Player;
        protected var _angleIncrement:Number;
        protected var _enemyFrequency:Number;
        protected var _enemyTime:Number;
```

```
protected var _enemyCreator:Timer;
protected var _enemyList:Dictionary;
```

The class starts out with some static variables; think of these as game settings. We use variables instead of constants because we might want to be able to change these values gradually at runtime. You'll probably recognize the first three as components of the Tunnel class, which the Game will have to create. The next two relate to the creation of enemies. The *enemyFrequency* is the rate in seconds at which enemies are created, and the enemyTime is the amount of time (also in seconds) it takes for an enemy to move from the bottom of the tunnel to the top. We also declare some protected variables we will use later on, such as references to the Tunnel, Player, and list of enemies. You'll notice we also duplicate two of the static variables as protected instance variables. This protects these values from changing in the middle of the game by an outside source. These values will be assigned in the constructor and then are only adjustable from inside the class. We'll look at the constructor next.

```
public function Game(){
    _tunnel = new Tunnel(tunnelSize, tunnelDepth,
      tunnelSides);
    addChild(_tunnel);
    _player = new Player();
    addChild(_player);
    _angleIncrement = 2 * Math.PI / tunnelSides;
    _enemyFrequency = enemyFrequency;
    _enemyTime = enemyTime;
    _enemyCreator = new Timer(_enemyFrequency*1000);
    _enemyCreator.addEventListener(TimerEvent.TIMER,
      addEnemy, false, 0, true);
    _enemyList = new Dictionary(true);
}
```

The constructor sets up a new Tunnel object, a Player object, and the Timer that will release new enemies using the *addEnemy* method. Now we'll look at the methods that start the game and control player movement.

```
public function startGame():void {
    _enemyCreator.start();
    addEventListener(Event.ENTER_FRAME, frameScript, false,
      0, true);
}

protected function frameScript(e:Event):void {
    movePlayer();
}
```

```
protected function movePlayer():void {
    var mouseAngle:Number = Math.atan2(mouseY, mouseX);
    var roundedAngle:Number = _angleIncrement * Math.round
      (mouseAngle/_angleIncrement);
    _player.x = _tunnel.radius * Math.cos(roundedAngle);
    _player.y = _tunnel.radius * Math.sin(roundedAngle);
    var oldRotation:Number = _player.rotation;
    _player.rotation = roundedAngle * (180/Math.PI) + 180;
    if (oldRotation != _player.rotation) _tunnel.highlight
      Side(roundedAngle);
}
```

When *startGame* is called, the Timer object is started to create new enemies, and a frame script is attached to the *enterFrame* event. This *frameScript* method simply calls *movePlayer*, which reads the position of the mouse around the center of the tunnel and adjusts the Player's *x* and *y* positions accordingly to stay along the outside edge. It also rotates the Player so it is always pointing inward toward the tunnel. If the player moves to a new side, that side of the tunnel is highlighted using the methods we looked at earlier.

```
protected function addEnemy(e:TimerEvent):void {
    var index:int = Math.round(Math.random()*(_tunnel.sides-1));
    var enemy:Enemy = new Enemy(index);
    enemy.x = _tunnel.tunnelTiles[0][index].x;
    enemy.y = _tunnel.tunnelTiles[0][index].y;
    enemy.z = _tunnel.tunnelTiles[_tunnel.depth-1][index].z;
    enemy.rotation = index * (360/_tunnel.sides) - 180;
    enemy.brightness = .5;
    addChildAt(enemy, getChildIndex(_player));
    _enemyList[enemy] = enemy;
    var tween:TweenLite = TweenLite.to(enemy, _enemyTime,
      {z:0, brightness:1, ease:Quad.easeIn, onComplete:
      enemyMovementFinished, onCompleteParams:[enemy]});
}


protected function enemyMovementFinished(target:Enemy):void {
    removeChild(target);
    delete _enemyList[target];
}
```

The *addEnemy* function picks a side at random, creates a new enemy object, and positions it on that side, at the bottom of the tunnel. It also sets the enemy to start out at half brightness, so it will be visible, but blend in much more with the tiles. Once the enemy is added, a new tween is created using TweenLite (discussed in Chapter 7), which will animate the enemy from bottom to top over the time we specified earlier. Once the tween is complete, *enemyMovementFinished* is called. At the moment, all it does is remove the enemy from memory, but in a full game it would contain additional logic to cause damage when it hit if the player was not on that side or deduct points from the player's score. The enemy motion could also be handled by a *moveEnemies* method that decrements the enemies' *z* position over time, but this method has two big plusses. First, it is *much* easier to implement—one line of code versus several. Second, and even more importantly, using a tween gives much greater motion control. Notice that the tween uses an *easeIn* function on the animation, which will make the enemy slowly accelerate as it moves. This effect would be much more troublesome to write manually and with very little return. Let's review the Game class in its entirety before we move on to the fun part—linking these classes to an FLA and watching it run!

```
package tunnelshooter {

        import flash.display.Sprite;
        import flash.events.Event;
        import flash.events.TimerEvent;
        import flash.utils.Timer;
        import flash.utils.Dictionary;
        import gs.TweenLite;
        import gs.easing.Quad;

        public class Game extends Sprite {

            static public var tunnelSize:Number = 175;
            static public var tunnelDepth:int = 8;
            static public var tunnelSides:int = 8;
            static public var enemyFrequency:Number = 3;
            static public var enemyTime:Number = 5;

            protected var _tunnel:Tunnel;
            protected var _player:Player;
            protected var _angleIncrement:Number;
            protected var _enemyFrequency:Number;
            protected var _enemyTime:Number;
            protected var _enemyCreator:Timer;
            protected var _enemyList:Dictionary;

            public function Game(){
                _tunnel = new Tunnel(tunnelSize, tunnelDepth,
                  tunnelSides);
                addChild(_tunnel);
                _player = new Player();
                addChild(_player);
```

```
    _angleIncrement = 2 * Math.PI / tunnelSides;
    _enemyFrequency = enemyFrequency;
    _enemyTime = enemyTime;
    _enemyCreator = new Timer(_enemyFrequency*1000);
    _enemyCreator.addEventListener(TimerEvent.TIMER,
      addEnemy, false, 0, true);
    _enemyList = new Dictionary(true);
}

public function startGame():void {
    _enemyCreator.start();
    addEventListener(Event.ENTER_FRAME, frameScript,
      false, 0, true);
}

protected function frameScript(e:Event):void {
    movePlayer();
}

protected function movePlayer():void {
    var mouseAngle:Number = Math.atan2(mouseY, mouseX);
    var roundedAngle:Number = _angleIncrement * Math.
      round(mouseAngle/_angleIncrement);
    _player.x = _tunnel.radius * Math.cos(roundedAngle);
    _player.y = _tunnel.radius * Math.sin(roundedAngle);
    var oldRotation:Number = _player.rotation;
    _player.rotation = roundedAngle * (180/Math.PI) + 180;
    if (oldRotation != _player.rotation) _tunnel.high
      lightSide(roundedAngle);
}

protected function addEnemy(e:TimerEvent):void {
    var index:int = Math.round(Math.random()*(_tunnel.
      sides-1));
    var enemy:Enemy = new Enemy(index);
    enemy.x = _tunnel.tunnelTiles[0][index].x;
    enemy.y = _tunnel.tunnelTiles[0][index].y;
    enemy.z = _tunnel.tunnelTiles[_tunnel.depth-1]
      [index].z;
    enemy.rotation = index * (360/_tunnel.sides) - 180;
    enemy.brightness = .5;
    addChildAt(enemy, getChildIndex(_player));
    _enemyList[enemy] = enemy;
    var tween:TweenLite = TweenLite.to(enemy, _enemy
      Time, {z:0, brightness:1, ease:Quad.easeIn, onComplete:
      enemyMovementFinished, onCompleteParams:[enemy]});
}
```

```
protected function enemyMovementFinished(target:
  Enemy):void {
    removeChild(target);
    delete _enemyList[target];
  }
}
}
```

All the necessary classes for this iteration of the game have been completed. Now, it is time to implement with actual assets. If you open the SimpleTunnelShooter.fla file, you'll find some clips in the library that will be used by the classes. These include the Enemy clip, the Player clip, and the TunnelTile clip. There is also a bitmap used for the tile texture. I chose a brick because it has a nice effect along the seams, but most of the texture would work for the tunnel and some might even stitch together more cleanly.

The only thing on the timeline is the script necessary to instantiate a game and start it. This could also be done with a document class for the FLA, but for simplicity and since this isn't a full game, the timeline suffices just fine.

```
import tunnelshooter.*;

var game:Game = new Game();
game.x = 275;
game.y = 200;
addChild(game);
game.startGame();
```

That's it! We're done with this example. When published, the end result should look something like Fig. 11.17.

While this is by no means a complete game, it contains numerous examples of how the trig functions can be used to manipulate objects in 2D and 3D space. Here are some ideas on functionality that would enhance this game.

- Continually increasing speed of enemy creation
- The ability of the player to either catch enemies or shoot at them
- Subtle rotation or distortion of the entire tunnel over time to create player disorientation
- Multiple types of enemies
- Other shapes of tunnels; eight sides work well for performance reasons, but many more could be used

This concludes Part One of this chapter. We will continue to apply these concepts moving forward into our discussion of physics, as well as in upcoming chapters as we delve into more complex game mechanics.

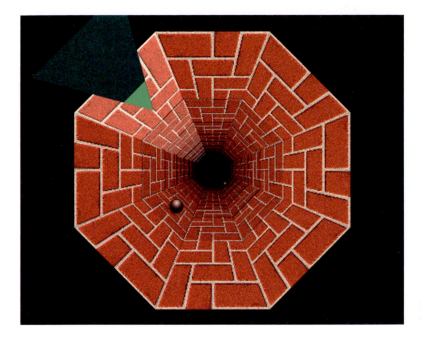

Figure 11.17 The completed tunnel shooter example.

Part Two: Physics

The correct name for this half of the chapter really should be two-dimensional, algebraic physics, since that's all we're going to discuss for our purposes. Physics is, among other definitions, the science of the behavior and interaction of objects in the universe around us. It includes concepts such as forces, mass, and energy. The field of physics is a vast area of study, and this chapter focuses on one specific branch of it, known as *mechanics*. Even more specifically, we will be looking at *classical mechanics*, which, among other things, deals with the interactions between objects in our visible, physical world. In the upcoming section, we will discuss the concepts behind basic mechanics and how to apply them in games. To start out, we need to establish some standardized vocabulary.

Scalar

A scalar is simply a number in traditional mathematical terms. In physics applications, it can represent a magnitude such as speed, four miles per hour (4 mph), for instance. There is no information about the direction or orientation of an object traveling at that speed.

Vector

In contrast to a scalar, a vector contains information about both the magnitude of a physical element and its direction. The direction component is a numeric angle value, but in conversation it is often referred to in looser terminology. For instance, the vector form of the scalar example above could be something like "four miles per hour, heading northwest," though we would not necessarily be able to do any calculation with that information until we assigned it a number.

The Vector3D Class

Among the classes in Flash for handling complex math more efficiently is the Vector3D class. It is the code representation of the *vector* concept we learned about earlier. It contains *x*, *y*, and *z* values to determine its magnitude, and a fourth value, *w*, which stores information about the vector's direction, such as an angle. We will look at an example shortly where we will use the Vector3D class to simplify some vector math.

VECTOR VERSUS VECTOR3D

There is another class in Flash known as Vector, which I mentioned in Chapter 4. It has nothing to do with vectors in physics terms. Rather, it is a special type of Array that stores only one type of value and uses less memory than an Array by doing so. For instance, if you used Arrays of Numbers in previous versions of Flash, you can now use a Vector instead. It has all the same methods and properties of Arrays but is faster to navigate and more efficient. The name Vector comes from the C programming language, but really you can just think of it as a *typed* Array.

Displacement

Displacement is most easily thought of as the distance between any two points in space when connected by a straight line. Though it is technically a vector, we generally think of displacement in terms of a scalar. That is to say, we don't usually consider the direction of one object relative to another when computing their distance apart from each other. It would be odd to refer to the distance from one's self to a nearby table as "4 ft, 30° from my facing direction." We simply say "four feet."

Velocity

Displacement over a period of time results in what we know as *speed*. For instance, if it takes me an hour to walk five miles, my speed is five miles per hour (5 mph). However, as discussed above, this is merely a scalar value as it has no directional information. If we add a direction, such as 90°, we get the vector of *velocity*.

The formula for determining velocity, where d = displacement and t = time, is as follows:

$$v = d/t$$

Acceleration

If we change the velocity of an object over time (whether increasing or decreasing), we create that object's *acceleration*. For sake of clarity, acceleration can be either a positive or negative change, but we usually refer to an acceleration that results in a lower velocity, or slowing down, as a deceleration. The formula for acceleration, where v = velocity and t = time is as follows:

$$a = v/t$$

A naturally occurring example of acceleration that we are all familiar with is that of gravity, the force pulling us downward toward Earth's center. The magnitude of gravity on Earth is approximately 9.8 m/s.

Friction

When two surfaces are in contact with each other, the resistance between the two is known as friction. Each surface has a property unique to it known as the *coefficient of friction*. Simply put, it describes the smoothness or roughness of a surface; the higher the number, the more friction that surface generates. Sandpaper, for example, would have a much higher coefficient of friction than a material like ice. The energy that is lost due to friction is converted to heat, which explains why rubbing your hands together eventually warms them. However, for our purposes, all you really need to understand about friction is its degrading effect on velocity and acceleration. An object's coefficient of friction often has to be determined through trial and error when programming. For instance, the value for the friction of a rolling ball in the real world might not work effectively in a game. The important thing to remember is that none of the values must be set in stone—you can change them as needed to suit gameplay.

Inertia

The counterpart to friction, inertia is an object's resistance to a change that causes it to either want to stay at rest or keep moving. Without friction, static objects would never be able to gain traction, thus remaining still, and moving objects would never be able to come to a stop. You can feel the sensation of inertia when inside an elevator or a vehicle that comes to a sudden stop; your body can feel for a moment like it is still moving.

Simulation versus Illusion

It's important to remember that as fast as ActionScript 3 and the Flash Player are, they still are not powerful enough to run a truly realistic physics simulation. Some open-source implementations of simple physics engines have been written, but most have severe limitations compared to what is possible in software that is written much closer to the hardware level than Flash. However, this is not to say that these engines or even the relatively simple code we will write shortly in this chapter are not effective at conveying the *illusion* of physical reactions. Indeed, we will see that even a bare bones implementation of physics can be effective at suspending disbelief for the purposes of a game.

Reality versus Expectations

Another point that some developers get hung up on when trying to emulate physics in Flash is striving for real-world values and reactions. While this is admirable, it often yields unsatisfactory gameplay. Take, for example, a platform game with multiple levels the player can move between by jumping and dropping. If you were to apply the rather harsh realities of the effects of gravity and friction on moving bodies, the game would become impossibly hard. This is because a realistic simulation factors out human response time. It is hard for people to stop themselves from falling over in real life once the process begins—it would be practically impossible using a keyboard and mouse. Characters in games have often jumped farther, run faster, and controlled themselves in mid-air unlike how real humans would ever be able to do. This is okay; as I mentioned earlier, it only takes so much to suspend a player's disbelief. Part of achieving effective physics in games is knowing what the player will *expect* to happen, rather than simply trying to mimic the world precisely. We will explore this more through the following examples.

Example: A Top–Down Driving Engine

Modern driving games for computers and consoles employ a *lot* of physics. All sorts of aspects such as road conditions, gear ratios, tire materials, and chassis weights factor into the math behind these simulations, and the result (depending on the game) is a fairly accurate representation of real-world physics. For the purposes of most Flash games, however, what we are about to create will suffice for a very satisfactory driving experience. This example is divided into two classes: the Vehicle class, which defines the properties of the car, and the Game class, which handles input and manipulates the car's position and rotation. There is also an additional utility class called Time, which will prove handy both here and elsewhere in later examples. The files for this example are in the Chapter 11 folder: DrivingSim and the drivingsim package. The end result will use the arrow keys to steer, accelerate, and reverse and the space bar to do a hard-brake stop.

The Vehicle Class

This class will define all the basic properties of the car we'll see on screen. It starts with a number of constant and variable declarations:

```
static public const maxAcceleration:Number = 100;
static public const maxSpeed:Number = 350;
static public const maxSteering:Number = Math.PI / 40;
static public const accelerationRate:Number = 50;
static public const handBrakeFriction:Number = .75;
static public const stoppingThreshold:Number = 0.1;
```

The first values set are the maximum acceleration and speed per second, followed by the maximum turning radius. Adjusting these three values yields a very different experience, and you could easily make them instance variables instead of static constants, thereby allowing different cars to have different behavior. We also define the rate of acceleration, meaning how many units we can increase our acceleration per second. Next we set the amount of friction the hand brake applies to the speed of the car. In this case, as long as the hand brake is being held, the car will slow to 75% of its current speed. The last constant is called the *stoppingThreshold*, which is the value below which the game will round the speed down to 0. This is present because when multiplying a number between 0 and 1, the result will gradually get closer to 0, but never reach it.

```
protected var _speed:Number = 0; //PIXELS PER SECOND
protected var _acceleration:Number = 0; //PIXELS PER SECOND
protected var _angle:Number = 0; //ANGLE IN RADIANS
```

Next come three protected variables for speed, acceleration, and the angle of the car, all initially set to 0. Out constructor is empty for this example, so we'll skip it and move on to the three getter/setter function pairs that will complete this class.

```
public function get angle():Number {
        return _angle;
}

public function set angle(value:Number):void {
        _angle = value;
        rotation = _angle * (180 / Math.PI);
}
```

These functions expose the protected _angle variable and also set the visible rotation of the car Sprite on screen.

```
public function get speed():Number {
        return _speed;
}


public function set speed(value:Number):void {
        _speed = Math.max(Math.min(value,maxSpeed),-maxSpeed);
        if (Math.abs(_speed) < stoppingThreshold) _speed = 0;
}
```

For the speed property, since it can be negative or positive, we use the Math min() and max() methods to force restrictions on how high or low the speed can be. This is also where we employ the stoppingThreshold property to truncate the speed if it becomes infinitesimally small.

```
public function get acceleration():Number {
        return _acceleration;
}


public function set acceleration(value:Number):void {
        _acceleration = Math.max(Math.min(value,maxAcceleration),
          -maxAcceleration);
}
```

Much like the speed methods, we use min() and max() again to set the limits for the acceleration property. That is all that is required in the Vehicle class for now. Here, it is in its entirety.

```
package drivingsim {

    import flash.display.Sprite;

    public class Vehicle extends Sprite{

        static public const maxAcceleration:Number = 100;
        static public const maxSpeed:Number = 350;
        static public const maxSteering:Number = Math.PI / 40;
        static public const accelerationRate:Number = 50;
        static public const handBrakeFriction:Number = .75;
        static public const stoppingThreshold:Number = 0.1;

        protected var _speed:Number = 0;
        protected var _acceleration:Number = 0;
        protected var _angle:Number = 0;

        public function Vehicle() {
        }
```

```
public function get angle():Number {
    return _angle;
}

public function set angle(value:Number):void {
    _angle = value;
    rotation = _angle * (180 / Math.PI);
}

public function get speed():Number {
    return _speed;
}

public function set speed(value:Number):void {
    _speed = Math.max(Math.min(value,maxSpeed),-
      maxSpeed);
    if (Math.abs(_speed) < stoppingThreshold) _speed = 0;
}

public function get acceleration():Number {
    return _acceleration;
}

public function set acceleration(value:Number):void {
    _acceleration = Math.max(Math.min(value,
      maxAcceleration),-maxAcceleration);
    }
  }
}
```

The Time Class

Before we move on to the Game class, we should take a quick look at a helpful utility class that will by the game. Since Flash is a frame-based environment, and, therefore, is dependent on the machine it is running on maintaining a consistent frame rate, it's a good idea to have a way to enforce accuracy in our calculations regardless of the number of frames actually being processed. It is also often easier to think of units like speed and acceleration in terms of seconds rather than frames. To gain this accuracy, we need to know how much actual time has transpired between frames. This change in time is often referred to as *delta time*. This value can be obtained within a couple of lines using the *getTimer* method in the flash.utils package. We could have just written these lines into the Game class, but because it has so many applications, it's better to write it once in a class and reference it there from now on.

GETTIMER

This method has been around since Flash 4 and still proves its usefulness to this day. It returns the number of milliseconds that have passed since the Flash Player started running. It is perfect for calculating time spent between frames or any other pair of events. It should be noted that you cannot rely on the method to return a specific number or always start from 0. If multiple instances of the Flash Player are open, they all share the same value, and whichever one opened first started at 0.

We'll look at this class in a single pass, since it is relatively short.

```
package drivingsim {

    import flash.display.Sprite;
    import flash.events.Event;
    import flash.utils.getTimer;

    public class Time extends Sprite {

        static private var _instance:Time = new Time();
        static private var _currentTime:int;
        static private var _previousTime:int;

        public function Time() {
            if (_instance) throw new Error("The Time class cannot
              be instantiated.");
            addEventListener(Event.ENTER_FRAME, updateTime,
              false, 0, true);
            _currentTime = getTimer();
        }

        private function updateTime(e:Event):void {
            _previousTime = _currentTime;
            _currentTime = getTimer();
        }

        static public function get deltaTime():Number {
            return (_currentTime - _previousTime) / 1000;
        }
    }
}
```

This class instantiates a single instance of itself in memory and prevents any other instantiations. The one static, public method it has is a getter for *deltaTime*. Every frame cycle, the class updates the current and previous times so at any moment it is ready to return an accurate delta. Since I like to work in seconds rather than in milliseconds,

I divide the difference by 1000 when I return it. This could easily be modified to return milliseconds instead, if that's what you prefer. It's mainly important to pick a convention and stick with it. We'll now look at how method class is used in the Game class.

The Game Class

Now we've come to the core of the functionality and the math that we'll need to employ. It also functions as the document class for the accompanying FLA. The class starts out with just a few declarations.

```
protected var _leftPressed:Boolean;
protected var _rightPressed:Boolean;
protected var _upPressed:Boolean;
protected var _downPressed:Boolean;
protected var _spacePressed:Boolean;
protected var _friction:Number = .95;
```

There are Boolean values for each key we'll use, so we can know whether that key is being pressed. There is also a value for friction, or rather the coefficient of friction of the surface the vehicle will be driving on. This value will cause the vehicle to slow down when it is not accelerating.

```
public function Game() {
      addEventListener(Event.ADDED_TO_STAGE, addedToStage,
        false, 0, true);
}

private function addedToStage(e:Event):void {
      startGame();
}
public function startGame():void {
      addEventListener(KeyboardEvent.KEY_DOWN, keyDown, false,
        0, true);
      addEventListener(KeyboardEvent.KEY_UP, keyUp, false,
        0, true);
      addEventListener(Event.ENTER_FRAME, gameLoop, false,
        0, true);
}
```

When the game is added to the Stage, it triggers startGame. This method sets up listeners for both keyboard input and the enter-Frame cycle. We'll look at the keyDown and keyUp methods next.

```
protected function keyDown(e:KeyboardEvent):void {
      if (e.keyCode == Keyboard.LEFT) _leftPressed = true;
      if (e.keyCode == Keyboard.RIGHT) _rightPressed = true;
      if (e.keyCode == Keyboard.UP) _upPressed = true;
```

```
        if (e.keyCode == Keyboard.DOWN) _downPressed = true;
        if (e.keyCode == Keyboard.SPACE) _spacePressed = true;
}

protected function keyUp(e:KeyboardEvent):void {
        if (e.keyCode == Keyboard.LEFT) _leftPressed = false;
        if (e.keyCode == Keyboard.RIGHT) _rightPressed = false;
        if (e.keyCode == Keyboard.UP) _upPressed = false;
        if (e.keyCode == Keyboard.DOWN) _downPressed = false;
        if (e.keyCode == Keyboard.SPACE) _spacePressed = false;
}
```

These two functions simply toggle the different Boolean values to either true or false as keyboard input is received.

```
protected function gameLoop(e:Event):void {
        if (stage.focus != this) stage.focus = this;
        readInput();
        moveVehicle();
}
```

Because we're dealing with keyboard input, which automatically focuses on the Stage, on each frame cycle we make sure that the game still has focus, even if the player were to click somewhere else on the screen. It then calls *readInput* and *moveVehicle*, both of which we'll look at next.

```
protected function readInput():void {
        if (_upPressed) vehicle.acceleration += Vehicle.
          accelerationRate * Time.deltaTime;
        if (_downPressed) vehicle.acceleration -= Vehicle.
          accelerationRate * Time.deltaTime;
        if (!_upPressed && !_downPressed) vehicle.acceleration = 0;
        if (_rightPressed) vehicle.angle += (Vehicle.maxSteering *
          (vehicle.speed / Vehicle.maxSpeed));
        if (_leftPressed) vehicle.angle -= (Vehicle.maxSteering *
          (vehicle.speed / Vehicle.maxSpeed));
        if (_spacePressed) {
          vehicle.speed *= Vehicle.handBrakeFriction;
          vehicle.acceleration = 0;
        }
}
```

This method runs through all the key-related Boolean values. If the up or down arrows are pressed, it applies acceleration. If the right and left arrows are pressed, it applies steering based on the speed of the vehicle. Finally, if the space bar is pressed, it applies the hand brake friction to the vehicle's speed and resets any acceleration.

```
protected function moveVehicle():void {
    if (!vehicle.acceleration) vehicle.speed *= _friction;
    vehicle.speed += vehicle.acceleration;
    vehicle.x += Math.cos(vehicle.angle) * (vehicle.speed *
      Time.deltaTime);
    vehicle.y += Math.sin(vehicle.angle) * (vehicle.speed *
      Time.deltaTime);
}
```

While only four lines, this method does a great deal. First, it applies friction to the vehicle's speed if it is not accelerating; not doing so would cause the vehicle to continue moving as though it were one a very slick surface. The vehicle's speed is then increased by its acceleration. The last two lines then compute the vehicle's new *x* and *y* coordinates based on the angle the car is facing and the speed at which it is traveling. Note that both this method and the readInput method use Time.deltaTime property to only apply the speed that is necessary for the amount of time that has passed. By using this method, the framerate of the SWF can now change, either deliberately or accidentally, without consequence to the responsiveness of the simulation. Let's review the Game class in its entirety.

```
package drivingsim {

    import flash.display.Sprite;
    import flash.events.Event;
    import flash.events.KeyboardEvent;
    import flash.ui.Keyboard;

    public class Game extends Sprite {

        protected var _leftPressed:Boolean;
        protected var _rightPressed:Boolean;
        protected var _upPressed:Boolean;
        protected var _downPressed:Boolean;
        protected var _spacePressed:Boolean;
        protected var _friction:Number = .95;

        public var vehicle:Vehicle;

        public function Game() {
            addEventListener(Event.ADDED_TO_STAGE,
              addedToStage, false, 0, true);
        }

        private function addedToStage(e:Event):void {
            startGame();
        }
```

```
public function startGame():void {
    addEventListener(KeyboardEvent.KEY_DOWN, keyDown,
      false, 0, true);
    addEventListener(KeyboardEvent.KEY_UP, keyUp,
      false, 0, true);
    addEventListener(Event.ENTER_FRAME, gameLoop,
      false, 0, true);
}

protected function gameLoop(e:Event):void {
    if (stage.focus != this) stage.focus = this;
    readInput();
    moveVehicle();
}

protected function readInput():void {
    if (_upPressed) vehicle.acceleration += Vehicle.
      accelerationRate * Time.deltaTime;
    if (_downPressed) vehicle.acceleration -= Vehicle.
      accelerationRate * Time.deltaTime;
    if (!_upPressed && !_downPressed) vehicle.
      acceleration = 0;
    if (_rightPressed) vehicle.angle += (Vehicle.max
      Steering * (vehicle.speed / Vehicle.maxSpeed));
    if (_leftPressed) vehicle.angle -= (Vehicle.max
      Steering * (vehicle.speed / Vehicle.maxSpeed));
    if (_spacePressed) {
        vehicle.speed *= Vehicle.handBrakeFriction;
        vehicle.acceleration = 0;
    }
}

protected function moveVehicle():void {
    if (!vehicle.acceleration) vehicle.speed *=
      _friction;
    vehicle.speed += vehicle.acceleration;
    vehicle.x += Math.cos(vehicle.angle) * (vehicle.
      speed * Time.deltaTime);
    vehicle.y += Math.sin(vehicle.angle) * (vehicle.
      speed * Time.deltaTime);
}

protected function keyDown(e:KeyboardEvent):void {
    if (e.keyCode == Keyboard.LEFT) _leftPressed = true;
    if (e.keyCode == Keyboard.RIGHT) _rightPressed = true;
    if (e.keyCode == Keyboard.UP) _upPressed = true;
    if (e.keyCode == Keyboard.DOWN) _downPressed = true;
```

```
        if (e.keyCode == Keyboard.SPACE) _spacePressed = true;
    }

    protected function keyUp(e:KeyboardEvent):void {
        if (e.keyCode == Keyboard.LEFT) _leftPressed = false;
        if (e.keyCode == Keyboard.RIGHT) _rightPressed = false;
        if (e.keyCode == Keyboard.UP) _upPressed = false;
        if (e.keyCode == Keyboard.DOWN) _downPressed = false;
        if (e.keyCode == Keyboard.SPACE) _spacePressed = false;
    }


}
}
```

If you open the FLA file associated with this example and run it, you will see that the vehicle instance on the Stage is now controllable with the arrow keys and space bar. This is just the foundation for a game—it has no collision detection, computer AI, or even goals. One other thing to note about this example is that the car moves like it has the best tires ever made and can turn on a dime. While this is okay and might work perfectly for certain scenarios, the simulation could be a little more realistic with the addition of the ability to "drift" the car, essentially making the motion of the car to continue in the direction it was previously traveling. Let's look at how we could achieve that now.

Example: Top–Down Driving Game with Drift

In the previous example, we applied the acceleration directly to the speed of the car without taking into account the *direction* of the acceleration. Remember how we learned that vectors have both a magnitude and a direction earlier in this chapter. If we set both the acceleration and velocity of the car to vectors, we'll gain more realistic behavior when we combine them. Since this is just a modification of the previous example, I won't cover any sections of the code that haven't changed. The files for this example are in the Chapter 11 folder; the FLA is DrivingSimDrift and the associated package is called drivingsimdrift. Let's start by looking at the changes to the Vehicle class.

```
static public const maxSpeed:Number = 350;
static public const maxSteering:Number = Math.PI / 30;
static public const maxAcceleration:Number = 400;
static public const handBrakeFriction:Number = .75;
static public const stoppingThreshold:Number = 0.1;

protected var _velocity:Vector3D = new Vector3D();
protected var _acceleration:Vector3D = new Vector3D();
protected var _angle:Number = 0;
```

We still have the maxAcceleration, maxSpeed, and maxSteering constants, but the values have changed some. Like the previous example, these values are determined through experimentation and are completely subject to change depending on what kind of handling you want the car to have. The two other major changes are that the speed value has been replaced with velocity and is now of type Vector3D. Acceleration keeps its name but is also a Vector3D. These changes obviously affect their getter/setter functions.

```
public function get velocity():Vector3D {
        return _velocity;
}

public function set velocity(value:Vector3D):void {
        _velocity = value;
        if (_velocity.length > maxSpeed) {
          var overage:Number = (_velocity.length - maxSpeed) /
            maxSpeed;
          _velocity.scaleBy(1 / (1 + overage));
        }
        if (_velocity.length < stoppingThreshold) {
          _velocity.x = _velocity.y = 0;
        }
}

public function get acceleration():Vector3D {
        return _acceleration;
}

public function set acceleration(value:Vector3D):void {
        _acceleration = value;
}
```

While the acceleration functions are not much different from you would expect, the velocity setter has changed significantly. In order to enforce a top speed and the stopping threshold, we must measure the *length* of the vector, which is another term for its magnitude. If the length property is greater than the top speed, we scale the entire vector by the amount of the overage. This will adjust the *x* and *y* properties of the vector in a single line instead of having to do them separately. If the length property is less than the stopping threshold, we also set the *x* and *y* properties to 0. We could have also scaled the vector by 0, but a simple variable assignment is less overhead than performing calculations on all the properties of the vector. Next let's look at the changes to the Game class. Only the readInput and moveVehicle methods have changed, so that's all we'll address here.

```
protected function readInput():void {
      vehicle.acceleration = new Vector3D();
      if (_upPressed) {
        vehicle.acceleration.x += Math.cos(vehicle.angle) *
          Vehicle.maxAcceleration * Time.deltaTime
        vehicle.acceleration.y += Math.sin(vehicle.angle) *
          Vehicle.maxAcceleration * Time.deltaTime;
      }
      if (_downPressed) {
        vehicle.acceleration.x += -Math.cos(vehicle.angle) *
          Vehicle.maxAcceleration * Time.deltaTime
        vehicle.acceleration.y += -Math.sin(vehicle.angle) *
          Vehicle.maxAcceleration * Time.deltaTime;
      }
      if (_rightPressed) vehicle.angle += (Vehicle.maxSteering *
        (vehicle.velocity.length / Vehicle.maxSpeed));
      if (_leftPressed) vehicle.angle -= (Vehicle.maxSteering *
        (vehicle.velocity.length / Vehicle.maxSpeed));
      if (_spacePressed) {
        vehicle.velocity.scaleBy(Vehicle.handBrakeFriction);
      }
}
```

At the onset of the readInput method, we create a new, empty vector object for acceleration. If the up or down arrows are pressed, the vector's *x* and *y* components are adjusted accordingly. If neither is pressed, the acceleration is empty and will have no effect when combined with the velocity. If the space bar is pressed, the velocity is scaled down by the amount of vehicle's hand-brake friction.

```
protected function moveVehicle():void {
      vehicle.velocity.scaleBy(_friction);
      vehicle.velocity = vehicle.velocity.add(vehicle.
        acceleration);
      vehicle.x += vehicle.velocity.x * Time.deltaTime;
      vehicle.y += vehicle.velocity.y * Time.deltaTime;
}
```

When moving the vehicle, we use the friction property to scale the velocity down. We then combine the existing velocity vector with the new acceleration vector. Another way to combine the two would have been the Vector3D incrementBy method. It adds the two relevant vectors without returning a new object. However, in our case, assigning the result back to the velocity property of the vehicle forces it through the maxSpeed check we looked at earlier. If we used incrementBy method, we would have to do that check manually here. Finally, to adjust the *x* and *y* positions of the vehicle, we increment it by the velocity's x and y components and the deltaTime property.

If you export this example and test it, you'll notice immediately the car handles very differently, almost as if it were on ice. When you turn at high speeds, the car continues in its original direction for a time before eventually aligning itself with the new direction. This is because by adding the vectors together with discrete x and y values, it takes a few passes of friction scaling to reduce the effect of previous accelerations. Naturally, most cars don't drift the way this one does. With some additional complexity, you could factor in the weight of the car to determine when the car's velocity overcomes its downward force (essentially, the car's traction) and so get the best of both examples.

Review

We've covered a lot of material in this chapter, so let's run through a high-level reminder of everything we've learned:

- The relationship of triangles to angle and distance problems
- The trigonometric functions (sine, cosine, and tangent) and their uses
- The coordinate system inside Flash, including the 3D transform system
- How to manipulate objects in Flash's 3D space
- How to use perspective projection to create vanishing points
- The difference between scalar and vector values in physics
- The basics of classical mechanics in motion—velocity, acceleration, friction, and inertia
- How to apply simple 2D physics in ActionScript
- How to use the new Vector3D class to simplify the process of combining vectors

There is considerably more material in books and on the Internet to read about physics if you're interested in doing more robust simulations. There are links to a number of resources on this book's Web site.

12

DON'T HIT ME: COLLISION DETECTION TECHNIQUES

If you do much game development, you'll eventually need to determine when two objects on screen are colliding with one another. Although Flash does not automatically notify you of this, there are a number of different methods that can be used to detect it. In this chapter, we'll look at several types of collision detection and in which scenarios they work best. We'll also look at the strategies that can be used with different styles of detection to achieve the desired results.

What You Can Do versus What You Need

A temptation by some developers, particularly those coming from other game-development backgrounds, is to always use the most precise, robust collision detection in all situations. The problem with this approach is the same that we discussed about physics in the last chapter; using more than you need to create an illusion is a waste of effort and computing power that could be used elsewhere. The trick with collision detection is to identify the minimum accuracy that you need to achieve a particular effect, and then implement a system that works for that scenario. One good reason to not try to develop the end-all collision detection system is that there really isn't one that works best in every possible situation. It's rare that I've used the same technique twice in two games that weren't extremely similar. What works well in a driving game might not make sense in a pinball game, and so on. The following sections will outline the different types of detection you can achieve in AS3, with some examples.

HitTestObject—The Most Basic Detection

AS3 provides two methods to developers to detect when DisplayObjects are colliding. The first, and simplest, is *hitTestObject*. You can call it on one DisplayObject and pass it another Display-Object to test against, regardless of location or parental hierarchy. Flash will resolve any differences in coordinate systems. If the two objects are touching, it returns true; otherwise false. Sounds great, right? Unfortunately, there is one big catch. To keep this calculation fast, Flash resolves the two DisplayObjects down to their basic bounding boxes. In other words, even if a shape is very intricate and has large parts that are transparent or void of any data, Flash will see it as a single rectangle. This is shown in Fig. 12.1.

To make matters worse, the bounding box will adjust to what-ever size it needs to be to encompass all the DisplayObject data. If that circle from Fig. 12.1 were a bitmap instead of a shape, it would actually be a square because of the transparent parts of the image. If you were to rotate this circle, the bitmap square is now at an angle. Figure 12.2 shows the larger bounding box that Flash will now use to fit this rotated shape.

As a result of these limitations, *hitTestObject* is generally the least accurate method of determining a collision. That said, it is very fast and definitely has its uses. When all you need to know is whether two Sprites are overlapping into each other's display space, *hitTestObject* is very effective. If your game has DisplayObjects that can change

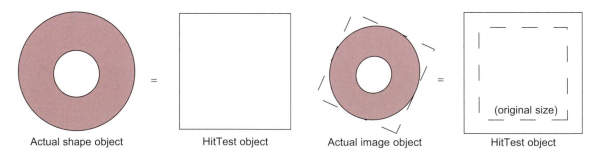

Actual shape object   HitTest object   Actual image object   HitTest object
                                                                            (original size)

Figure 12.1 A shape object like a circle is still seen as a rectangle with its maximum dimensions by Flash's hit detection engine.

Figure 12.2 Once rotated, an image actually takes up a larger space than its actual dimensions, during collision detection.

their "distance" from the player (i.e., move closer or further away from the player's perspective), you're likely going to have to deal with managing the indices of these objects. If you detect that two objects are touching, you have a great opportunity to check their positions and display indices.

HitTestPoint—One Step Up

In earlier versions of Flash, *hitTestObject* and its counterpart, *hitTestPoint*, were both part of the same method *hitTest*. In AS3, Adobe broke the two up into discrete methods, both for speed and for accurate type checking. Unlike the object version of this method, *hitTextPoint* accepts *x* and *y* coordinates to check if the DisplayObject is overlapping a particular pixel. In fact, when testing against objects that have empty space (not transparent image data like an alpha channel, but actually void of data), this method has the option of accurately telling you if the shape is overlapping the point. Obviously, this method is considerably more accurate than *hitTestObject*, but it only does a single point in space. To test a complex shape against another, you'd need to do this test many times at points all around the shape's outer border. This would quickly become taxing for the processor, particularly if there are multiple objects colliding on screen. It is most commonly used when determining whether the mouse coordinates are overlapping a particular shape.

One thing that is important to note about this method is that it expects to receive its coordinates as they would appear on the Stage. If you are testing against a point embedded in several DisplayObjects in the display list and their coordinate systems do not line up with the Stage, then you'll need to convert the coordinates to the Stage's system. Luckily, all DisplayObjects give you a method to do this, called *localToGlobal*. It accepts a point object and converts it numerically to the Stage coordinate system.

```
var clip1:Sprite = new Sprite();
clip1.x = clip1.y = 50;
var testPoint:Point = new Point(0, 0);
testPoint = clip1.localToGlobal(testPoint);
trace(testPoint); //OUTPUTS X = 50, Y = 50
```

In this short snippet, a Sprite is created on the Stage and has its coordinates set to (50, 50). According to the Sprite's coordinate system, its center is at (0, 0). By running *localToGlobal* on the point object, we can see that according to the Stage, the center is actually at (50, 50).

Another good use for this method is when doing hit tests for vehicles against scenery. You can use a pair of points for the two front bumper ends and a pair for the rear.

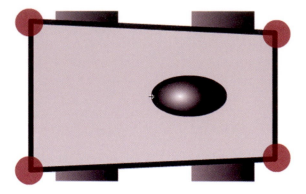

Figure 12.3 This car has two hit points in the front and two in the rear.

As Fig. 12.3 shows, you can use Sprites to visually mark the points on the car, where you want to do a hit test. All you need to do then is to have an identifier, separating the front ones from those in the back. If the car backs into something solid, you want it to be able to drive forward to pull away from it, but not to be able to back up any further.

Let's look at a simple example of how this test can be used in practice. You can follow along in the HitTestPoint.fla file in the Chapter 12 examples folder. When you open up the FLA, you'll find two objects on the Stage: a square and two long rectangles. The square represents our player character (and is named as such) and the rectangles are part of the same clip called "barriers." Note that the square clip has a number of dots along its outer border; these dots represent collision test points. When the SWF is run, the square will move toward the mouse at a given speed but will not be able to move past the barriers. The code for this example is in three different classes: HitTestPoint.as, HitTestCoordinate.as, and Player.as. We'll start with the Player.

```
public class Player extends Sprite {

        private var _speed:int = 50;
        private var _hitPointList:Vector.<HitTestCoordinate>;

        public function Player() {
                addEventListener(Event.ADDED_TO_STAGE, addedToStage,
                    false, 0, true);
        }

        private function addedToStage(e:Event):void {
                _hitPointList = new Vector.<HitTestCoordinate>();
                for (var i:int = 0; i < numChildren; i++) {
                        var child:DisplayObject = getChildAt(i);
                        if (child is HitTestCoordinate)
                                _hitPointList.push(child);
                }
        }
```

```
public function get hitPointList():Vector.
  <HitTestCoordinate> {
        return _hitPointList;
  }


public function get speed():int { return _speed; }
}
```

This class represents the square on the Stage. It has a given speed at which it will move per second (50 pixels), and a vector list of its collision test points. When it is added to the Stage, it enumerates these points in the list. Other than this basic functionality, this class does nothing. Now, we'll look at the class behind the collision points.

```
public class HitTestCoordinate extends Sprite {

      private var _point:Point;

      public function HitTestCoordinate() {
            visible = false;
            _point = new Point(x, y);
      }

      public function get point():Point {
            updatePoint();
            return _point;
      }

      public function get pointGlobal():Point {
            return parent.localToGlobal(point);
      }

      private function updatePoint():void {
            _point.x = x;
            _point.y = y;
      }
}
```

This class is designed to be a visual tool for placing collision points, so that they don't have to be placed manually in code. Any shape could be used to represent them; I chose a circle because it is small and unobtrusive; the shape is, ultimately, irrelevant because the Sprite hides itself on creation. It stores a point within itself representing its position. In addition to providing access to this point, it provides an accessorial method to return the point already converted to the global coordinate space, which is how we'll need to measure the point for the hit test.

CS5.5 FEATURE—VISIBLE PROPERTY

Starting in CS5.5, if you're publishing to Flash Player 10.2 (or any mobile version), you finally have the option to set the initial visible property of a display object on the Stage. This has long been an annoyance in earlier versions, and works as a great alternative to setting the property in the constructor of the class. Figure 12.4 shows where this option resides in the Property Inspector for any Stage object.

Now that we have the player Sprite and its test points, we'll look at the document class driving this example. Note that this class makes use of the Time class we created back in Chapter 11; if you skipped ahead to this chapter, all you need to know is that it has a method to return the time elapsed between the frame cycles.

```
public class HitTestPoint extends Sprite {

    public var barriers:Sprite;
    public var player:Player;

    public function HitTestPoint() {
```

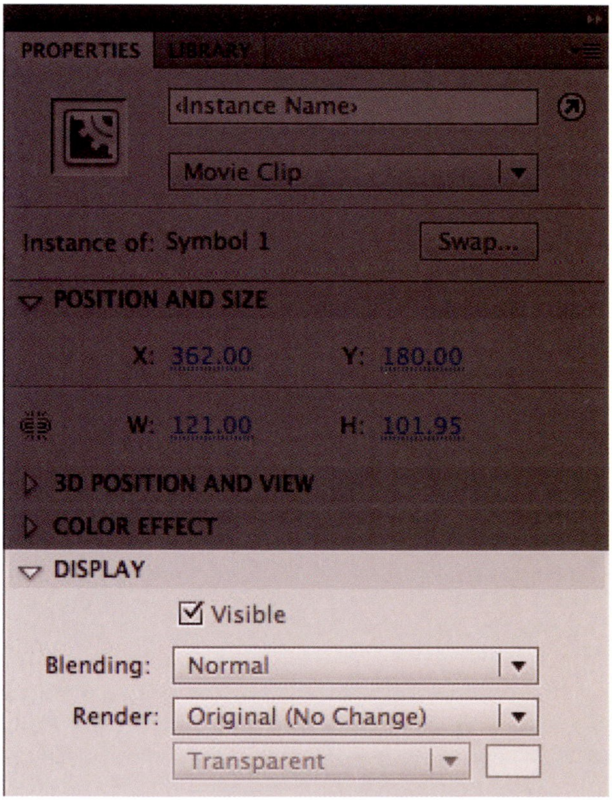

Figure 12.4 The new visibility toggle in the property inspector, under the display category.

```
        addEventListener(Event.ADDED_TO_STAGE, addedToStage,
          false, 0, true);
  }

  private function addedToStage(e:Event):void {
        addEventListener(Event.ENTER_FRAME, enterFrame,
          false, 0, true);
  }

  private function enterFrame(e:Event):void {
        //CHECK DISTANCE AND PERFORM MOVES
        var distance:Number = Math.sqrt(Math.pow(player.x -
          mouseX, 2) + Math.pow(player.y - mouseY, 2));
        var tempPoint:Point = new Point(mouseX, mouseY);
        var dx:Number = 0;
        var dy:Number = 0;
        if (distance > player.speed * Time.deltaTime) {
                var angle:Number = Math.atan2(mouseY -
                  player.y, mouseX - player.x);
                dx = (player.speed * Time.deltaTime) * Math.
                  cos(angle);
                dy = (player.speed * Time.deltaTime) * Math.
                  sin(angle);
                tempPoint.x = player.x + dx;
                tempPoint.y = player.y + dy;
        }
        //DO CHECKS
        for each (var coordinate:HitTestCoordinate in
          player.hitPointList) {
        if (barriers.hitTestPoint(coordinate.pointGlobal.
          x + dx, coordinate.pointGlobal.y + dy, true)) {
           if (barriers.hitTestPoint(coordinate.
             pointGlobal.x + dx, coordinate.pointGlobal.y,
             true)) {
              tempPoint.x = player.x;
           }
           if (barriers.hitTestPoint(coordinate.point
             Global.x, coordinate.pointGlobal.y+dy, true)){
              tempPoint.y = player.y;
           }
        }
      }
      //RE-ASSIGN VALUES
      player.x = tempPoint.x;
      player.y = tempPoint.y;
  }
}
```

Really, the only code happening in this class is in the *enterFrame* method. It measures the distance between the mouse and the player. If it is less than the speed of the player in a single frame, the player attempts to move to the mouse's exact position (this is to prevent the player from eternally jumping back and forth over the mouse). If it is further away, the player will calculate its angle relative to the mouse and then move at its given speed in that direction. However, before the new coordinates are assigned, they are stored in a point object, *tempPoint*. A *for each* loop then iterates through every coordinate in the player's list. It checks these coordinates, adjusted for the change in position, against the barriers clip. If it detects a collision, then it checks the individual x and y values to determine the direction in which the collision is occurring.

If you noticed the position of the test points in the player Sprite, you noted there are a total of eight, one for each side and one for each corner. The distance between them is such that you can actually coerce the square onto the barrier walls, as they are thin enough to fit between the points. Although it looks like a bug, I left this behavior in to make a point (no pun intended). Even if you find a technique that works for you, you will probably have to make some adjustments as you test. In this case, because we're dealing with such thin barriers, we need to position the collision points closer together and probably have more of them. By making these essentially little components, it is very easy to adjust the number and positioning of these points; remember that they only need to be slightly closer together than the smallest object you're testing against. That said, you might have a game where you need to wrap one object around another in which case the current behavior would be ideal.

Radius/Distance Testing—Great for Circles

Although not an actual method of DisplayObjects, a very accurate way of detecting collision between two circular objects (or a circular object and a point) is simply by using the distance formula. If you know the radius of each object you want to test against each other, you can add the two radii together and see if it is greater than the distance between them. In addition to flat, two-dimensional circles, this method works very well for characters on an isometric, or angled, playfield.

In Fig. 12.5, there are two characters with each having a radius of "personal space." A traditional *hitTestObject* would not work here because the objects will visually overlap when one passes in front of another. Instead, we need to measure the distance between the two players and determine if they are close enough to be

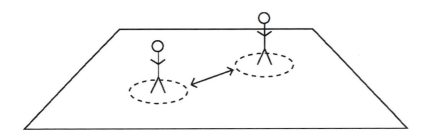

Figure 12.5 These two players each have a radius around them constituting their hit area.

"touching." In this case, we also need to correct for the perspective skew of the field. The best way to make this adjustment would be to have the game engine store their coordinates as though they were being viewed from the top down. Then, the engine can test against traditional circles, but render out the view by applying the perspective correction.

Another nice feature of this type of testing is that it is easy to have multiple testing radii because the only real criterion is a number in pixels. Perhaps when two players get a certain distance from each other, they gain the ability to talk to each other, but only at a closer distance can they fight, exchange inventory, cuddle, and so on.

One more example in which this type of detection is ideal is that of a billiards simulation. In a top–down pool game, for instance, you need to be able to accurately tell when two objects are colliding. The easiest way to do this type of test is a measurement of the distance between their edges. This scenario is shown in Fig. 12.6.

If you recall back to Chapter 10, the distance formula between two points is $\sqrt{(x_2 - x_1) + (y_2 - y_1)}$. As you can see in Fig. 12.6, the value of d is the distance between the two center points of the balls. However, this isn't the value that will tell us when the balls are colliding because by the time the distance between them is 0, they will be on top of each other. To find the distance between their edges, we have to calculate d minus the two radii. If we use the value of r for the radius, and assume the two balls are of the same size (which they would be in billiards), we can then say that the distance between the two edges is

$$d = \sqrt{(x_2 - x_1) + (y_2 - y_1)} - 2r.$$

When the value of d is 0, the two balls are touching. If it is less than 0, they are overlapping and must have their positions corrected.

Rect Testing

Another similar method to the basic *hitTestObject* is what is known as *rect testing*. It involves getting the bounding box rectangle of any two DisplayObjects (using the

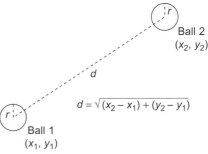

Figure 12.6 A distance collision check applied to two balls on a pool table.

getRect method) and doing comparisons of intersection, overlap, and so on. Although this doesn't seem like it would be any better than the *hitTestObject* method, it has a number of advantages. The first is what I like to call *predictive* testing; basically, once you have the rect of an object, you can move it around, scale it, and perform point tests against it without any effect on the original object. In order to test whether two objects are *about* to hit with the *hitTestObject* method, you must actually move the objects around, which can occasionally cause glitches in the renderer. This is because when you update the position, scale, or rotation of a DisplayObject on the Stage, Flash will put it in the queue to redraw. By extracting the rectangle first, you can do tests on it that don't involve the display list at all and save the performance.

Another reason rect tests are a generally superior method of detection is their greater flexibility. You can easily have multiple hit areas on an object or determine how much two rectangles are overlapping to determine the force of a collision. Let's say you have a vehicle that has multiple places in which it can take damage. You could place Sprites (that would make themselves invisible at runtime) to act as hit "sensors," so to speak. When you needed to perform collision tests, you would iterate through these sensors to get their rects. Once you have a set of rectangles, you can test them individually or test them in combinations, using the *union* method.

This next example will demonstrate rect testing by expanding on a lesson from Chapter 7. Remember the SimpleShooter scolling example? We'll take that base code and add enemies and collision detection using rects. You can follow the example in the SimpleShooterCollisions.fla file and associated classes. There are two main additions that have been made to the file since we last looked at it: the new Enemy class and some method additions to the SimpleShooterCollisions class.

The Enemy Class

```
public class Enemy extends MovieClip {

    static public const FRAME_DESTROY:String = "destroy";

    protected var _speed:Number;
    protected var _alive:Boolean = true;

    public function Enemy(speed:Number = 0) {
        this.speed = speed;
        stop();
    }
```

```
public function destroy() {
        _alive = false;
        gotoAndStop(FRAME_DESTROY);
}

public function get speed():Number {
        return _speed;
}

public function set speed(value:Number):void {
        _speed = value;
}

public function get alive():Boolean {
        return _alive;
}
}
```

Like the Projectile class, Enemy objects have a speed parameter assigned to them on creation. They also have a Boolean value, specifying whether they are alive or dead. Finally, they have a *destroy* method, which toggles the *alive* value and plays a destruction animation. In the FLA file, you can see an item in the library named Enemy that is linked to this class. It is a MovieClip with two frames: the static flying position and the destruction animation. Next, we'll look at the additional methods that are now a part of the main game class.

The SimpleShooterCollisions Class Additions

In the code below, the sections in bold are new to this iteration of the game. Refer to Chapter 7 for explanations on the other methods.

```
protected var _enemyList:Vector.<Enemy>;
protected var _enemySpeed:Number = -10;
protected var _enemyGenerator:Timer;
protected var _enemyFrequency:int = 2000;

public function SimpleShooterCollisions() {
    addEventListener(Event.ADDED_TO_STAGE, addedToStage,
      false, 0, true);
    addEventListener(Event.ENTER_FRAME, frameScript, false, 0,
      true);
    _projectileList = new Vector.<Projectile>();
    _enemyList = new Vector.<Enemy>();
    _enemyGenerator = new Timer(_enemyFrequency);
```

```
        _enemyGenerator.addEventListener(TimerEvent.TIMER,
          createEnemy, false, 0, true);
    }

    protected function addedToStage(e:Event):void {
        _stageWidth = stage.stageWidth;
        _stageHeight = stage.stageHeight;
        addEventListener(MouseEvent.MOUSE_DOWN, createProjectile,
          false, 0, true);
        _enemyGenerator.start();
    }

    protected function frameScript(e:Event):void {
        movePlayer();
        moveProjectiles();
        moveEnemies();
        checkCollisions();
        moveForeground();
        moveBackground();
    }
```

In the initialization functions, there are now variables for how frequently enemies are generated, how fast they move, and a Timer object to create them. In the frame loop, there are also two new methods called which we will look at next.

```
    protected function moveEnemies():void {
        for each (var enemy:Enemy in _enemyList) {
            enemy.x += enemy.speed;
            if (enemy.x + enemy.width < 0) {
                removeEnemy(enemy);
            }
        }
    }

    protected function createEnemy(e:TimerEvent = null):void {
        var enemy:Enemy = new Enemy(_enemySpeed);
        enemy.x = _stageWidth + enemy.width;
        enemy.y = Math.random() * (_stageHeight - enemy.height) +
          (enemy.height/2);
        addChild(enemy);
        _enemyList.push(enemy);
    }

    protected function removeEnemy(enemy:Enemy):void {
        if (enemy.parent == this) removeChild(enemy);
        _enemyList.splice(_enemyList.indexOf(enemy),1);
    }
```

```
protected function checkCollisions():void {
    var enemyRect:Rectangle;
    var projectileRect:Rectangle;
    for each (var enemy:Enemy in _enemyList) {
        if (!enemy.alive) continue;
        enemyRect = enemy.getRect(this);
        for each (var projectile:Projectile in _projectileList) {
            projectileRect = projectile.getRect(this);
            if (enemyRect.intersects(projectileRect)) {
                removeProjectile(projectile);
                enemy.destroy();
            }
        }
    }
}
```

You'll likely notice some similarities between how the projectiles and enemies are each moved. The *createEnemy* method, called by the Timer, places new Enemy objects at the right side of the Stage and they gradually travel across to the opposite side in the *moveEnemies* function. Once everything has been moved, the *checkCollisions* method runs. It loops through the two lists of projectiles and enemies and tests rects against each other. If a projectile hits an enemy that is still alive, the enemy will be destroyed. Note that, at this point, we don't remove the enemy. We rely on the *destroy* method of the Enemy class to display the destruction, and the object will get removed, once it reaches the left side of the Stage. When you test this SWF, you will see that when a projectile from the player hits an enemy, it explodes. Add a scoring mechanism to the number of ships destroyed and a way for the player to be hurt, and you've got yourself a really simple but complete game!

Weaknesses of This Method

Even though this type of checking is overall pretty thorough, it will also break down in certain scenarios. If you were to increase the speed of the ships and the projectiles enough, they would eventually reach a point where they would "jump over" each other. In a single frame, they would go from facing each other to passing each other without a collision being recorded. Granted, they would have to be traveling *very* fast—faster than would probably be practical for this type of game—but that doesn't keep the underlying detection from being fundamentally flawed on some level. Because the detection is tied to the game's frame cycle, it also means that lowering the frame rate will lower the frequency of detection, effectively creating the same problem I had just mentioned.

Luckily, there is a solution to this problem: iterative testing. Essentially, we want to test the space between a Sprite's new position and its previous position to see if a collision had occurred "between frames." In our shooter example, if the distance traveled between the frame cycles is less than the width of either the projectile or enemy rects, then our current test is sufficient. However, once their speed exceeds their width, both Sprites need to iterate over their traveled distance to determine if they collided with anything in the dead space. This is where using rectangles for the tests are particularly helpful because you can use a loop to move them at a certain interval and perform checks each time. Here's an example of how you could perform this loop.

```
for each (var enemy:Enemy in _enemyList) {
        if (!enemy.alive) continue;
        enemyRect = enemy.getRect(this);
        if (enemyRect.width <= Math.abs(enemy.speed)) {
                //"LITE" CHECK SUFFICIENT
                for each (var projectile:Projectile in _projectileList) {
                        projectileRect = projectile.getRect(this);
                        if (enemyRect.intersects(projectileRect)) {
                                removeProjectile(projectile);
                                enemy.destroy();
                        }
                }
        } else {
                var numberOfChecks:int = Math.ceil(Math.abs(enemy.
                  speed)/enemyRect.width);
                for (var i:Number = 0; i <= numberOfChecks; i++) {
                        var newRect:Rectangle = enemyRect.clone();
                        newRect.x -= enemyRect.width*i;
                                for each (var projectile:Projectile in
                                  _projectileList) {
                                projectileRect = projectile.getRect(this);
                                if (newRect.intersects(projectileRect)) {
                                        removeProjectile(projectile);
                                        enemy.destroy();
                                }
                        }
                }
        }
}
```

In this modified example of the shooter collision check, if the width of the enemyRect is less than the speed it moved in a single frame, then the check is performed as usual. However, if the speed exceeds the width of the rectangle, then we determine how many checks we need to perform by dividing the speed by the width and rounding up. We add another *for* loop, this time counting the number of checks we need to perform and creating a new rectangle with a new position to test against. If this seems like a lot of looping, remember that the number of checks you're likely to have to perform is still pretty low unless the rectangle you're checking against is very small. Even then, AS3 should be able to handle it just fine. To be even more accurate, it would be wise to add the same iterative checking for the projectiles as well, but I'll leave this to you as an exercise to complete.

Pixel-Perfect Collision Detection and Physics

Although for many applications, the methods I've discussed so far are very effective (and the most efficient for mobile platforms), there are some instances where you simply will need pixel-perfect detection of two arbitrary shapes. There are ways to do this using BitmapData drawing and comparisons, but I'm not going to discuss that here. Instead, I'm going to recommend the excellent Collision Detection Kit developed by Corey O'Neil. I've included the latest version (as of this writing) with the chapter files that can be downloaded from www. flashgamebook.com. On the site you will also find direct links to Corey's site and his Google Code repository for the source. It's a pretty great library and takes very little time to implement.

Sometimes, even pixel-accurate detection is less important than the way objects react when they collide. In these cases, you may need a full rigidbody collision engine with its own physics simulation. For scenarios where you'll have a lot of objects colliding at once and needing to react to each other, writing your own physics engine from scratch can be daunting. Luckily, there's an open source library that has been ported to just about every language under the sun called Box2D. It has been used in a number of award-winning games and is very full-featured for doing 2D physics and collisions. However, because it is so full-featured, it can be daunting to approach. The physics simulation runs independently of any visuals, so you must bind DisplayObjects to the colliders in the engine. This increased flexibility also makes it more involved to implement. To compound this, because it was ported from the C programming language, there are some conventions in naming that can seem off-putting at first. Those "warnings" aside, it is an excellent piece of software and performs extremely well, even with many objects in the simulation at once. On www.flashgamebook. com, you can find links to tutorials and examples that people in the community have written to get started, as well as links to the latest source code. The example in Chapter 16 also makes use of this library and discusses some of the basics.

When All Else Fails, Mix 'N Match

Sometimes, any one approach to collision detection is not enough to get the job done, effectively. That's when a combination of approaches can work, depending on the scenario. For instance, in the earlier example, we saw how the distance detection method served well to determine collisions between the two players. However, that method doesn't work well to determine the overlap of the player Sprites on screen. In addition to using distance for interaction, we can do a basic *hitTestObject* test to determine when they are overlapping and to adjust their indices in the display list. In that perspective skewed instance, when one player has a lower *y* value, it should appear behind the other player.

The most important thing to keep in mind when applying collision detection techniques is to keep an open mind to different options. Like in the case of physics simulation, pixel-perfect precision is rarely necessary and will end up costing you too much in performance. It is a balance of accuracy, speed, and flexibility that ultimately yields the best detection. We'll look at more practical examples of collision detection in Chapters 14–16.

13

MIXUP—A SIMPLE ENGINE

Up to this point, we've gone through many examples of different aspects of game development. Now, let's pull them together to create a simple game from start to finish. In this chapter, we will discuss how to create a basic image scramble game that we'll call MixUp. This is a popular type of puzzle game, in which an image is broken into rectangles on a grid and reshuffled. Players must click on these "pieces" to interchange their positions and, ultimately, restore the original image. The difficulty of these puzzles is a combination of the number and size of the rectangles the image is broken into and the amount of detail in the imagery. We'll create an engine that will use and support any resolution of source image (within reason and memory restrictions) and divide it, dynamically, into any number of grid rectangles. We'll then see how this basic engine can be easily extended to support other source images like video or a live camera feed. Let's get started!

When defining the parameters for a game such as this, it's important to lay out a set of basic rules before starting to program. We won't do a full-design document, as this is a simple game and that's not the point of this exercise. Instead, we'll just do a bullet-point list of the feature set and components, so that we know what we're dealing with.

Real-World Flash Game Development, Second Edition.
© 2012 Elsevier Inc. All rights reserved.

Game screens and interface elements:

- Title Screen
  - Game logo
  - Play button
  - How To Play button
- How To Play Popup
  - Rules textfield
  - Close button
- In-game Screen
  - Game status displays
  - Quit button
- Results Screen
  - Game results textfields
  - Play Again button
  - Back to Title Screen button

In-game Functionality and Rules

- Game will shuffle pieces on grid, with no piece in its original position
- Game will include timer, which will count up from 0
- Game will dispatch events, when certain things happen, including the following:
  - Player completing puzzle
  - Player moving two pieces
  - Player moving at least one piece to its correct position
- Game will be played with the mouse
  - Players will click on a piece to select it
  - If they click on the same piece again, they will deselect it
  - If they click on another piece that is not locked down, then the two selected pieces will trade positions, and the game will check to see if either are now in the right place
  - Players will not be able to move pieces that are correctly positioned

We could go into even more detail, but this should be enough to get us started. Game design is an iterative process, meaning it grows and changes as it progresses. It is totally reasonable to change mechanics that don't make sense or prove to not work once in practice, but this initial layout allows us to try predicting potential problems and saving time in the long run by anticipating trouble down the road.

Now that we have the basic guidelines for the game down, we can look at the file and class structure. In this case, we're going to work with one main FLA file that will house the game assets, and we'll use a number of classes and interfaces to control different aspects of the game functionality. Here's a quick breakdown of the classes we'll use and what each one is responsible for:

- MixUp: Document class, manages game state/screens, retains static game history, and handles display of rules
- Title: Title/menu screen

- RulesPanel: Handles display and closure of the How To Play Popup
- Game: Shows GameBoard, timer, and UI elements
- GameBoard: Creates puzzle from source image, shuffles pieces, and handles game logic
- IGamePiece: An interface that defines the methods for what constitutes a game piece
  - GamePiece: Implements IGamePiece and defines specific behavior for pieces (with regard to animation, mouse interaction, and so on)
- ISourceImage: Base interface for plugging in different image sets or video for use with the GameBoard
  - SourceImageEmbedded: Uses images embedded in the SWF
  - SourceImageCamera: Uses camera feed
- GameHistory: Simple data class containing static properties for the player's performance each time they play a round
- Results: Screen displaying game results when the game is over

We'll work through each of these classes and the basic setup of the FLA one by one. So that we have some context for the code we'll be working with, we'll start with the structure of the MixUp.fla file. You can open it from the Chapter 13 Examples folder that you downloaded (or should download) from www.flashgamebook.com.

The Main Document

When you open up MixUp.fla and look at the library and timeline, you'll notice a couple of things. First, they are very simple. The timeline has three labels and three matching pieces of content for each one: the title screen, the game screen, and the results screen. They are given their own discrete space on the timeline for organizational purposes and to simplify screen management. In the library, there are only a handful of items. Each screen is contained within its respective clip; there are a couple of different buttons; and there is an image to be used as the source for the puzzle. Each of the screens is linked to a class with the same name. If you look at the document properties panel, you'll also see that the document is pointing to a class called MixUp. We'll start here first and work our way inward through the structure of the game.

The MixUp Class

This document class file controls the main logic for navigating between the screens in the game and displaying the rules panel. As the top-level in our game, it is the one class that persists through-out the entire experience and is in the unique position of storing useful data such as the current session's game history (for showing best scores, average scores, and so on).

```
public class MixUp extends MovieClip {

        static public const FRAME_TITLE:String = "title";
        static public const FRAME_GAME:String = "game";
        static public const FRAME_RESULTS:String = "results";

        static public var gameHistory:Array = new Array();

        protected var _imageNameList:Array = ["goldengate.jpg"];
        protected var _imageList:Vector.<ISourceImage>;

        public var title:Title;
        public var game:Game;
        public var results:Results;

        public function MixUp() {
            enumerateFrameLabels();
            addEventListener(FRAME_TITLE, setupTitle, false,
              0, true);
            addEventListener(FRAME_GAME, setupGame, false, 0,
              true);
            addEventListener(FRAME_RESULTS, setupResults,
              false, 0, true);
            createImagePool();
    }

    protected function createImagePool():void {
            _imageList = new Vector.<ISourceImage>();
            for each (var imageName:String in _imageNameList)
                _imageList.push(new SourceImageEmbedded
                    (imageName));
    }
```

There are only a few variables in this class: one for each of the main screens, an Array for the game history, and a constant defining each of the frame labels. In addition to these public properties are two lists. One will store the list of available images to use for the puzzle (in this case, the one that is embedded in the library), and the other will store the list of image objects that will be used by the game. In the constructor for the class, *enumerateFrameLabels* is called and listeners are added to each of the frame names. It also calls *createImagePool*, which runs through the list of image names and creates new SourceImageEmbedded objects for each of them. More information will be provided on this later when we get to the in-game classes.

```
private function dispatchFrameEvent():void {
        dispatchEvent(new Event(currentLabel));
}

private function enumerateFrameLabels():void {
        for each (var label:FrameLabel in currentLabels)
                addFrameScript(label.frame-1, dispatchFrameEvent);
}
```

These two functions use the addFrameScript method to dispatch events, whenever a frame label is hit. Combined with the listeners in the constructor, events will be fired when the title screen, game screen, and results screen are reached.

```
protected function setupTitle(e:Event):void {
        stop();
        title.addEventListener(Title.PLAY_GAME, playGame, false,
          0, true);
        title.addEventListener(Title.SHOW_RULES, showRules,
          false, 0, true);
}

protected function showRules(e:Event):void {
        var rules:RulesPanel = new RulesPanel();
        rules.x = stage.stageWidth/2;
        rules.y = stage.stageHeight/2;
        addChild(rules);
}

protected function playGame(e:Event):void {
        gotoAndStop(FRAME_GAME);
}

protected function mainMenu(e:Event):void {
        gotoAndStop(FRAME_TITLE);
}
```

When the title screen is reached, we attach listeners to it for two events that are defined in the Title class: PLAY_GAME and SHOW_RULES. When showRules is called, it creates a new RulesPanel instance, positions it, and adds it to the Stage. The playGame method does exactly what you'd expect it to do—go to the frame with the game in it. The *mainMenu* method will be used later to return to the title screen, but it is included here for consistency.

```
protected function setupGame(e:Event):void {
        stop();
        game.init(_imageList[0], 3, 4);
        setTimeout(game.startGame, 1500);
```

```
        game.addEventListener(Game.GAME_OVER, gameOver, false,
            0, true);
    }

protected function gameOver(e:Event):void {
        var history:GameHistory = new GameHistory(true, e.target.
            timeElapsed, e.target.movesMade);
        history.formattedTime = e.target.timeElapsedText.text;
        gameHistory.unshift(history);
        gotoAndStop(FRAME_RESULTS);
    }

protected function setupResults(e:Event):void {
        results.addEventListener(Results.PLAY_AGAIN, playGame,
            false, 0, true);
        results.addEventListener(Results.MAIN_MENU, mainMenu,
            false, 0, true);
    }
```

These three methods follow much the same pattern of doing initialization, when a frame label is reached. The *setupGame* method runs functions on the game object and adds a listener for the GAME_OVER event. We'll return to the *gameOver* method, later, once we've progressed through the game logic that will get us there. Suffice it to say that we'll store stats about the player's most recent game in the history array. Now that the document class is defined, we're ready to delve into each of the individual screens.

The Title Class

Most games have some sort of main menu of options; few drop you directly into the action without explanation or pause. In this example, we have only two options on the title screen, which keeps it simple for explanation. A player can choose to start a game or first view the rules.

```
public class Title extends MovieClip {

        static public const PLAY_GAME:String = "playGame";
        static public const SHOW_RULES:String = "showRules";

        public var playButton:SimpleButton;
        public var rulesButton:SimpleButton;

        public function Title() {
                addEventListener(Event.ADDED_TO_STAGE, addedToStage,
                    false, 0, true);
        }
```

```
    private function addedToStage(e:Event):void {
            playButton.addEventListener(MouseEvent.CLICK,
              playButtonClick, false, 0, true);
            rulesButton.addEventListener(MouseEvent.CLICK,
              rulesButtonClick, false, 0, true);
    }

    private function playButtonClick(e:MouseEvent):void {
            dispatchEvent(new Event(PLAY_GAME));
    }

    private function rulesButtonClick(e:MouseEvent):void {
            dispatchEvent(new Event(SHOW_RULES));
    }
}
```

As you can see, the logic behind this screen is very simple.
When either of the two buttons on the Title screen are clicked,
events are dispatched with names corresponding to the listeners
we saw in the MixUp class. Adding buttons to this screen is as simple as adding a constant for the event it generates a variable for
the DisplayObject and a listener for button click.

The RulesPanel Class

From the Title screen, the player can choose to view the rules panel.
In the MixUp class, we saw how this panel is instantiated and added
to the Stage. Now, we'll look at the internal logic behind it.

```
public class RulesPanel extends Sprite {

    public var closeButton:SimpleButton;

    public function RulesPanel() {
            addEventListener(Event.ADDED_TO_STAGE, addedToStage,
              false, 0, true);
    }

    private function addedToStage(e:Event):void {
            TweenLite.from(this, .4, { y : -height } );
            closeButton.addEventListener(MouseEvent.CLICK,
              closeButtonClick, false, 0, true);
    }

    private function closeButtonClick(e:MouseEvent):void {
            closeButton.removeEventListener(MouseEvent.
              CLICK, closeButtonClick);
```

```
                              TweenLite.to(this, .4, { y : -height, onComplete:
                                parent.removeChild, onCompleteParams:[this] } );
                }
        }
```

When the rules panel becomes part of the display list, it animates itself in from the top of the screen. It also adds a listener to the close button that reverses this animation and on completion removes the panel from the Stage. Because there are no other references to the panel than the display list, once it is removed from the Stage, Flash will garbage-collect it. Now, we're ready to dive into the Game class and see the logic going on behind the scenes.

The Game Class

We've now reached the meat of the code is, so to speak. The Game class is a composite of a few different components. The first and most important is the GameBoard class, which we will review shortly. The GameBoard controls the actual logic that keeps track of each of the images, shuffles them, and determines whether or not the puzzle has been completed. In addition, the Game class stores an instance of whatever the source image is—in this case, a still image from the library. Finally, this class manages all of the UI relevant to the game, like the quit button and text fields. We'll start breaking it down with the variable declarations.

```
public class Game extends MovieClip {

        static public const GAME_OVER:String = "gameOver";

        public var piecesLeftText:TextField;
        public var movesMadeText:TextField;
        public var timeElapsedText:TextField;
        public var quitButton:SimpleButton;

        private var _sourceImage:ISourceImage;
        private var _gameBoard:GameBoard;
        private var _totalPieces:int;
        private var _piecesLeft:int;
        private var _movesMade:int;
        private var _timeElapsed:int;
        private var _timer:Timer;

        public function Game() {
                addEventListener(Event.ADDED_TO_STAGE, addedToStage,
                  false, 0, true);
```

```
        _timer = new Timer(1000);
        _timer.addEventListener(TimerEvent.TIMER,
          timerUpdate, false, 0, true);
    }

    private function addedToStage(e:Event):void {
        quitButton.addEventListener(MouseEvent.CLICK,
          gameOver, false, 0, true);
    }
```

There are three TextField objects that display the remaining number of pieces, number of moves that have been made, and the time that has elapsed, as well as a button the player can use to quit the game. Each of the private variables stores some piece of information related to gameplay, including the source image in the form of an interface (rather than a class). Along with the Game-Board, we'll discuss this interface in a subsequent section. The constructor sets up the quit button and also creates a Timer object. The timer will fire every second (or 1000 ms) once started, creating a very basic clock. Whenever a second passes, the Timer will call *timerUpdate*.

```
public function get movesMade():int { return _movesMade; }
public function set movesMade(value:int):void {
    _movesMade = value;
    movesMadeText.text = String(_movesMade);
}

public function get piecesLeft():int { return _piecesLeft; }
public function set piecesLeft(value:int):void {
    _piecesLeft = value;
    piecesLeftText.text = String(_piecesLeft);
}

public function get timeElapsed():int { return _timeElapsed; }
public function set timeElapsed(value:int):void {
    _timeElapsed = value;
    var timeString:String;
    if (_timeElapsed < 60) {
        timeString = "0:";
    } else {
        timeString = String(Math.floor(_timeElapsed /
          60)) + ":";
    }
    var seconds:int = _timeElapsed % 60;
    if (seconds < 10) {
        timeString += "0" + String(seconds);
    } else {
```

```
                    timeString += String(seconds);
            }
            timeElapsedText.text = timeString;
    }
```

This set of six methods comprises the accessor, or getter/setter, methods that we'll use for this class. The get function simply returns the value of the private variable. The set function sets the private variable and also updates the corresponding TextField object. In the case of the timeElapsed property, in particular, the time must be updated from just a number of seconds to a standard formatting of "mm:ss."

```
public function init(sourceImage:ISourceImage,
                            rows:int,
                            columns:int,
                            imageWidth:int = 0,
                            imageHeight:int = 0,
                            boardPosition:Point = null):void {
        _totalPieces = piecesLeft = rows * columns;
        movesMade = 0;
        _sourceImage = sourceImage;
        _gameBoard = new GameBoard(_sourceImage, GamePiece, rows,
          columns, imageWidth, imageHeight);
        if (!boardPosition) boardPosition = new Point();
        _gameBoard.x = boardPosition.x;
        _gameBoard.y = boardPosition.y;
        _gameBoard.createBoard();
        addChildAt(_gameBoard, 0);
        _gameBoard.shuffleBoard();
    }

public function startGame():void {
        _gameBoard.activate();
        _gameBoard.addEventListener(GameBoard.GAME_OVER,
          pauseBeforeGameOver, false, 0, true);
        _gameBoard.addEventListener(GameBoard.PIECE_SWAP,
          pieceSwap, false, 0, true);
        _gameBoard.addEventListener(GameBoard.PIECE_LOCK,
          pieceLock, false, 0, true);
        timeElapsed = 0;
        _timer.start();
    }
```

You may have noticed that these two public methods are the same two called by the MixUp class earlier. The *init* function sets up the game for play, and *startGame* activates the GameBoard for mouse input and starts the Timer. There are a number of parameters for *init*, which include the source image object to be used for the puzzle, the number of rows and columns the grid should be divided into, the width and height in pixels of the image that will be displayed, and the physical position of the GameBoard object in the form of a point. Only the source image, rows, and columns are required. By default, we will use the native width and height of the image we're slicing up and set the board at 0,0. The total number of pieces for the puzzle is calculated as the number of rows multiplied by the number of columns. The *init* function is also where the GameBoard object is actually created. Most of the same parameters that were passed into the function are similarly passed along to the GameBoard constructor, and it is subsequently added to the Stage. The GameBoard will dispatch a number of events as things occur in the game, so in *startGame*, we add listeners for these events. We'll look at these listeners next.

```
private function pauseBeforeGameOver(e:Event):void {
        _timer.stop();
        setTimeout(gameOver, 2000, null);
}

private function pieceSwap(e:Event):void {
        movesMade++;
}

private function pieceLock(e:Event):void {
        piecesLeft--;
}

private function gameOver(e:Event):void {
        _timer.stop();
        _gameBoard.deactivate();
        _gameBoard.cleanUp();
        dispatchEvent(new Event(GAME_OVER));
}

private function timerUpdate(e:TimerEvent):void {
        timeElapsed = _timer.currentCount;
}
```

The method *pauseBeforeGameOver* merely stops gameplay and inserts a two-second pause before calling the *gameOver* method, so that the player has a moment to see the image they completed. When a piece swap is made, the number of moves is incremented, and when a piece is locked into its correct position, the number of pieces is decremented. Finally, after the post-game pause is complete, *gameOver* deactivates the GameBoard, performs clean up, and dispatches the GAME_OVER event back up to the MixUp class.

The Interfaces

Before we proceed any further into the GameBoard engine, we need to look at the two interfaces that will be used in it, and which we've already seen glimpses of in the MixUp and Game classes. As you'll recall from Chapter 4, an interface simply defines the names and parameters of public methods that will be used in a class. There is no actual logic performed in an interface. They are used to supply a common *interface* through which classes of disparate types can be used in the same context. The first is *ISourceImage*. It is this interface that must be implemented by any source of imagery the game will use for its puzzle, regardless of whether it is still embedded photos, external photos, video, and so on.

```
package {

        import flash.display.BitmapData;

        public interface ISourceImage {

                function getImages(rows:int, columns:int, width:
                  int = 0, height:int = 0):Vector.<BitmapData>;
                function cleanUp():void;
                function destroy():void;

        }
}
```

Classes that implement this interface only need to have three methods defined in them. The first method, *getImages*, is arguably the most important. It needs to return a vector list of BitmapData objects representing the sliced up original image, based on the number of rows and columns. The next two, *cleanUp* and *destroy*, do pretty much what you would expect based on their names. The *cleanUp* method will be called when the GameBoard wants to dispose of the sliced up images used to create the puzzle. The *destroy* method takes it one step further and also is intended to dispose of the original source image as well. Because BitmapData takes up a lot of space in memory, it is important to provide easy ways of freeing up that space.

The other interface used with the GameBoard class is one called *IGamePiece*. It defines the methods that will be used by the clickable game pieces that will make up the game board. Each game piece will have a BitmapData object from the vector list returned by *ISourceImage.getImages()*.

```
package {

        import flash.display.BitmapData;
        import flash.events.IEventDispatcher;
```

```
public interface IGamePiece extends IEventDispatcher {

        //DisplayObject Properties
        function get x():Number;
        function set x(value:Number):void;
        function get y():Number;
        function set y(value:Number):void;
        function get width():Number;
        function set width(value:Number):void;
        function get height():Number;
        function set height(value:Number):void;

        //GamePiece-specific Methods
        function select():void;
        function deselect():void;
        function activate():void;
        function deactivate():void;
        function movePiece(x:Number, y:Number):void;
        function lock():void;

        //GamePiece-specific Accessors
        function get image():BitmapData;
        function set image(value:BitmapData):void;
        function get index():int;
        function set index(value:int):void;
        function get currentIndex():int;
        function set currentIndex(value:int):void;

    }
}
```

This interface has considerably more definitions in it because unlike the source images, these game pieces will also need to be DisplayObjects. Because there is no common interface for DisplayObject classes to extend from, we'll need to define some of the basic properties that a game piece will need to have. These include *x* and *y* position, as well as width and height. For convenience, because the pieces will also need to dispatch events, we can extend IEventDispatcher to keep us from having to retype all those methods. For the game logic, every piece must have a way to be selected, deselected, activated, deactivated, moved, and locked. They must also have properties that define the Bitmap-Data displayed inside them, and their original and current positions on the game board. We'll look at the classes that implement these interfaces shortly, but now that we at least know how these objects will be defined, we'll move on to the GameBoard class.

The GameBoard Class

This class is the engine at the heart of this entire game, and where all the major logic happens. In order to be as flexible and reusable as possible, it refers to objects by their interfaces rather than by their specific class.

```
public class GameBoard extends Sprite {

        static public var GAME_READY:String = "gameReady";
        static public var GAME_OVER:String = "gameOver";
        static public var PIECE_SWAP:String = "pieceSwap";
        static public var PIECE_LOCK:String = "pieceLock";

        protected var _pieces:Vector.<IGamePiece>;
        protected var _rows:int, _columns:int;
        protected var _imageWidth:int, _imageHeight:int;
        protected var _boardImage:ISourceImage;
        protected var _selectedPiece:IGamePiece;
        protected var _pieceClass:Class;

        public function GameBoard(boardImage:ISourceImage,
          pieceClass:Class, rows:int, columns:int, imageWidth:int = 0,
          imageHeight:int = 0) {
                _rows = rows;
                _columns = columns;
                _imageWidth = imageWidth;
                _imageHeight = imageHeight;
                _boardImage = boardImage;
                _pieceClass = pieceClass;
        }
```

When a new GameBoard object is created, it looks for an image object to slice, the number of rows and columns, to use the width and height of the puzzle, and which class to use for the game piece (because it will be generically referred to as IGamePiece for the rest of the code). In addition to these properties, the class defines four different events that it will dispatch, and a list object, _pieces_, which will store a list of the game pieces in play.

```
public function createBoard():void {
        _pieces = new Vector.<IGamePiece>();
        var numPieces:int = _rows * _columns;
        var imageData:Vector.<BitmapData> = _boardImage.
          getImages(_rows, _columns);
        for (var i:int = 0; i < numPieces; i++) {
                var piece:IGamePiece = new _pieceClass();
                piece.index = i;
```

```
            piece.image = imageData[i];
            piece.x = piece.width * (i % _columns);
            piece.y = piece.height * Math.floor(i / _columns);
            _pieces.push(piece);
            addChild(piece as DisplayObject);
        }
    }


public function shuffleBoard():void {
        randomize(_pieces);
        for (var i:int = 0; i < _pieces.length; i++) {
            movePiece(_pieces[i], i);
        }
    }
```

The *createBoard* function is the process by which the image data is pulled from its source and inserted into game pieces. For every piece of image data, a new game piece is created and added to the Stage. The result of *createBoard* is a reproduction of the original image, but in adjacent pieces rather than a single bitmap. The *shuffleBoard* method is used to mix up the images and move them from their original places. We'll, shortly, review the *randomize* and *movePiece* methods it calls. The two methods above are separated in order to allow the game to display the original image for a period, if needed, before rearranging the board.

```
public function activate():void {
        for each (var piece:IGamePiece in _pieces) {
            piece.activate();
            piece.addEventListener(MouseEvent.CLICK,
              pieceClicked, false, 0, true);
        }
    }


public function deactivate():void {
        for each (var piece:IGamePiece in _pieces) {
            piece.deactivate();
            piece.removeEventListener(MouseEvent.CLICK,
              pieceClicked);
        }
    }


public function cleanUp():void {
        _boardImage.cleanUp();
        _pieces = null;
    }
```

These methods are what are used on beginning and completion of a game. Calling *activate* will enable each piece and make it clickable. The *deactivate* method reverses this action, and the *cleanUp* function calls the same method on the source image that we looked at earlier in the interface.

```
protected function pieceClicked(e:MouseEvent):void {
        var piece:IGamePiece = e.target as IGamePiece;
        if (!_selectedPiece) {
                _selectedPiece = piece;
        } else if (_selectedPiece == piece) {
                _selectedPiece.deselect();
                _selectedPiece = null;
        } else {
                var index:int = _selectedPiece.currentIndex;
                dispatchEvent(new Event(PIECE_SWAP));
                piece.deselect();
                _selectedPiece.deselect();
                movePiece(_selectedPiece, piece.currentIndex);
                checkPiece(_selectedPiece);
                movePiece(piece, index);
                checkPiece(piece);
                _selectedPiece = null;
                checkWin();
        }
}

protected function checkPiece(piece:IGamePiece):Boolean {
        if (piece.currentIndex == piece.index) {
                piece.removeEventListener(MouseEvent.CLICK,
                  pieceClicked);
                piece.lock();
                dispatchEvent(new Event(PIECE_LOCK));
                return true;
        }
        return false;
}

protected function checkWin():void {
        var won:Boolean = true;
        for each (var piece:IGamePiece in _pieces) {
                if (piece.currentIndex != piece.index) won = false;
        }
        if (won) {
                deactivate();
                dispatchEvent(new Event(GAME_OVER));
        }
}
```

```
protected function movePiece(piece:IGamePiece, newIndex:int):
  void {
      piece.movePiece(piece.width * (newIndex % _columns),
        piece.height * Math.floor(newIndex / _columns));
      piece.currentIndex = newIndex;
}
```

I have grouped these methods together because they are all interrelated and easier to look at in the context of each other. The *pieceClicked* method is called when—you guessed it—a piece is clicked. It checks if another piece has already been selected. If not, this piece becomes the currently selected piece. If this piece is already selected, it will be deselected. If a different piece has already been selected, the game dispatches a PIECE_SWAP event and proceeds to exchange the two pieces' positions. The *movePiece* function calls the same method on the corresponding piece and updates its *currentIndex* property. Once moved, the position of the piece is evaluated by the *checkPiece* method. If the piece's *currentIndex* matches its original *index*, the piece is in place and is locked. Finally, once the two pieces have been moved and checked, *checkWin* is called to determine if all the pieces are now in their correct positions. If they are, the game deactivates itself and dispatches the GAME_OVER event.

```
protected function randomize(vector:Vector.<IGamePiece>):
  Vector.<IGamePiece> {
      for (var i:int = 0; i < vector.length-1; i++) {
              var randomIndex:int = Math.round(Math.random()*
                (vector.length − 1 − i)) + i;
              swapElements(vector, i, randomIndex);
      }
      return vector;
}

protected function swapElements(vector:Vector.<IGamePiece>,
  index1:int,index2:int):void {
      var temp:IGamePiece =vector[index1];
      vector[index1]=vector[index2];
      vector[index2]=temp;
      temp=null;
}
```

These two final methods of the GameBoard class are not specific to the game logic but are actually generic utility functions that I wrote originally to manipulate Arrays. Here, they have been modified to do the same with vectors of a specific type. The randomize method shuffles the vector so that all of the elements are in new positions. By swapping each index with a random one after it, we ensure that we get a unique order every time. This method makes direct use of the *swapElements* function to move the elements in the list. Now, we'll look at the GamePiece class that is used for the implementation of the IGamePiece interface. Remember how the GameBoard class only referenced pieces through the IGamePiece interface? Because of this, the GamePiece class has the luxury to have whatever internal mechanisms we want, as long as it correctly implements all the methods of the interface. As a result, this class has a fair amount of "hard-coded" values, such as the color, size, and speed of animations. To make a different type of game piece, you could use this class as a starting point and then modify any of the functionality inside it or start from scratch. Ultimately, all that matters in this case is that the interface methods are defined and that the game piece in some way extends from DisplayObject, or preferably InteractiveObject. This is because in the GameBoard class, pieces are added to the Stage and a non-DisplayObject descendant will display an error.

```
public class GamePiece extends Sprite implements IGamePiece {

        protected var _image:Bitmap;
        protected var _index:int;
        protected var _currentIndex:int;
        protected var _rolloverHighlight:Shape;
        protected var _clickHighlight:Shape;

        public function GamePiece() {
        }
```

For this implementation, GamePiece will extend Sprite and contains a Bitmap variable to store its image slice, two int variables to store its current and original index, and two Shape variables that will be used for rollover and click states.

```
protected function createRolloverHighlight():void {
        _rolloverHighlight = new Shape();
        _rolloverHighlight.graphics.lineStyle(1, 0xFFFFFF, 1);
        _rolloverHighlight.graphics.beginFill(0xFFFFFF, .3);
        _rolloverHighlight.graphics.drawRect(.5, .5, _image.
          width-1, _image.height-1);
        _rolloverHighlight.graphics.endFill();
        addChild(_rolloverHighlight);
        _rolloverHighlight.visible = false;
}

protected function createClickHighlight():void {
        _clickHighlight = new Shape();
        _clickHighlight.graphics.lineStyle(2, 0, 1);
```

```
        _clickHighlight.graphics.beginFill(0xFFFFFF, .2);
        _clickHighlight.graphics.drawRect(1, 1, _image.width-2,
          _image.height-2);
        _clickHighlight.graphics.endFill();
        addChild(_clickHighlight);
        _clickHighlight.visible = false;
}
```

These two methods create the aforementioned Shape instances that will constitute the piece's alternate states. Both of them are arbitrarily defined and could be styled any number of ways or even make reference to clips in the FLA library.

```
public function get index():int { return _index; }

public function set index(value:int):void {
        _index = value;
}


public function get currentIndex():int { return _currentIndex; }

public function set currentIndex(value:int):void {
        _currentIndex = value;
}


public function get image():BitmapData { return _image.
  bitmapData; }

public function set image(value:BitmapData):void {
        if (!_image) {
                _image = new Bitmap(value);
                addChild(_image);
                createRolloverHighlight();
                createClickHighlight();
        }
        else _image.bitmapData = value;
}
```

These accessor methods are implementations from the interface. The only one that requires a little extra explanation is the set function for the *image* property. If the image already exists, it is assigned directly to the Bitmap instance. If not, it creates the Bitmap and the highlighted states.

```
protected function onClick(e:MouseEvent):void {
        select();
}


protected function onRollOver(e:MouseEvent):void {
```

```
        _rolloverHighlight.visible = true;
}

protected function onRollOut(e:MouseEvent):void {
        _rolloverHighlight.visible = false;
}

public function select():void {
        _clickHighlight.visible = true;
}

public function deselect():void {
        _clickHighlight.visible = false;
}

public function activate():void {
        addEventListener(MouseEvent.CLICK, onClick, false, 1,
            true);
        addEventListener(MouseEvent.ROLL_OVER, onRollOver,
            false, 0, true);
        addEventListener(MouseEvent.ROLL_OUT, onRollOut, false,
            0, true);
        buttonMode = true;
}

public function deactivate():void {
        removeEventListener(MouseEvent.CLICK, onClick);
        removeEventListener(MouseEvent.ROLL_OVER, onRollOver);
        removeEventListener(MouseEvent.ROLL_OUT, onRollOut);
        buttonMode = false;
        _rolloverHighlight.visible = false;
        deselect();
}
```

The first three methods are triggered by mouse events and toggle the rollover state and select method. The next four are more implementations from the interface, all of which affect the different states and mouse input.

```
public function lock():void {
        deactivate();
        setTimeout(pieceLockAnimation, 500);
}

public function movePiece(newX:Number, newY:Number):void {
        TweenLite.to(this, .5, { x:newX, y:newY, ease:Expo.
            easeOut} );
}
```

```
protected function pieceLockAnimation():void {
    var shape:Shape = new Shape();
    shape.graphics.beginFill(0x00CC00, .5);
    shape.graphics.drawCircle(0, 0, Math.max(width, height)/2);
    shape.graphics.endFill();
    shape.x = width / 2;
    shape.y = height / 2;
    addChild(shape);
    TweenLite.to(shape, 1, { scaleX:2, scaleY:2, alpha:0,
      onComplete:removeChild, onCompleteParams:[shape]} );
    parent.setChildIndex(this, parent.numChildren - 1);
}


override public function toString():String {
    return "GamePiece: index = " + index + " , currentIndex = " +
    currentIndex;
}
```

Finally, wrapping up the class are the methods to lock the piece in place and also to move it. The *pieceLockAnimation* method is another custom animation function, which could be substituted for just about any other treatment. In this case, when a piece is locked, it flashes a green (usually the color associated with a positive move) square over the piece and fades it out.

SHAPES

Shape objects are a low-impact form of DisplayObject that are great to use when all you need is something to draw in using the Graphics API or to use as an overlay. Because they don't extend InteractiveObject, you don't have to worry about them receiving or blocking mouse or keyboard events that you need your container to get. Because they're so simple they also consume fewer resources, so if you did a puzzle with 100+ pieces, you wouldn't be consuming nearly as much in memory or rendering power.

The SourceImageEmbedded Class

Now that we have all the logic for the game itself and functional pieces, the last component to this puzzle is the image itself. We've seen the *ISourceImage* interface that is used by the GameBoard class to pull in a list of BitmapData objects. But how does the original BitmapData get pulled in and then sliced? The answer is "depends." It depends on the source of the image. If the images are embedded in the FLA library, as in our example, the BitmapData is just waiting there for us to instantiate. But for other sources, like external image files or a camera feed, it's a little more complicated. We'll start out by seeing how to use an embedded image. You may have noticed an image in the MixUp.fla library that was set to export as "goldengate." This image of the Golden Gate Bridge in San Francisco (taken by yours truly circa 2003) will be available to us as raw BitmapData when the SWF is exported. Back in the MixUp.as document class, we also defined a list of image names (in this case, just one image) that would be used to load in the data. Those names were then used to create instances of a class called SourceImageEmbedded. We'll look at that class now.

```
public class SourceImageEmbedded implements ISourceImage {

        private var _imageClass:Class;
        private var _sourceBitmap:BitmapData;
        private var _pieceList:Vector.<BitmapData>;

        public function SourceImageEmbedded(linkageName:String)
          {
                _imageClass = getDefinitionByName(linkageName) as
                  Class;
        }
```

When a new SourceImageEmbedded object is created, the linkage name in the library for the image we want to use is passed into the constructor. That name is then used to look up and retrieve the actual class that name is associated with. If you recall, there were three required methods of the ISourceImage interface. We'll now look at this class's implementation of those functions.

```
public function getImages(rows:int,
                          columns:int,
                          width:int = 0,
                          height:int = 0):Vector.<BitmapData> {
        if (_pieceList) return _pieceList;
        _sourceBitmap = new _imageClass(width, height);
        var pieceBitmap:BitmapData;
        var pieceWidth:int = Math.floor(_sourceBitmap.width /
          columns);
        var pieceHeight:int = Math.floor(_sourceBitmap.height / rows);
        _pieceList = new Vector.<BitmapData>();
        for (var j:int = 0; j < rows; j++) {
                for (var i:int = 0; i < columns; i++) {
                        pieceBitmap = new BitmapData(pieceWidth,
                          pieceHeight);
                        var rect:Rectangle = new Rectangle(i * piece
                          Width, j * pieceHeight, pieceWidth,
                          pieceHeight);
                        pieceBitmap.copyPixels(_sourceBitmap,
                          rect, new Point());
```

```
                       _pieceList.push(pieceBitmap);
               }
       }
       return _pieceList;
}

public function cleanUp():void {
       for each (var bmd:BitmapData in _pieceList) {
               bmd.dispose();
       }
       _pieceList = null;
}

public function destroy():void {
       cleanUp();
       _sourceBitmap.dispose();
       _imageClass = null;
}
```

The *getImages* method is, definitely, the heavy-lifter of this class. If the list of BitmapData objects already exists (in other words, the image has already been cut up), the function simply returns that list again. This is to prevent destruction of still usable objects and creation of unnecessary new objects, as BitmapData can be costly to create and destroy repeatedly. For each rectangle on the grid, a new BitmapData object is created in fixed dimensions and has the pixel data from the original image copied to it. The cleanUp and destroy functions, as mentioned earlier in the section on the interface, are there to properly dispose of the references to BitmapData, when the game is through with them. Although not particularly crucial with only one image, if you had a game with 10, 50, or 100 images, then you would not want to keep all of them in memory at once—just the one you're working with at any given moment. Now, we have all the classes we need to make the game work, but we have no measure of skill or statistics to associate with the player's performance. From here, we switch gears to what happens when the game is over.

The GameHistory and Results Classes

Although it sounds like a cool course that you'd take at a college, this class contains a few pieces of data about how the player did in a particular round of MixUp.

```
public class GameHistory {

       public var won:Boolean;
       public var time:int;
```

```
public var formattedTime:String;
public var movesMade:int;

public function GameHistory(won:Boolean, time:int, moves
  Made:int) {
        this.won = won;
        this.time = time;
        this.movesMade = movesMade;
    }

}
```

That's it. As you can see, there's not much to this class. This is just the most basic set of data. You could feasibly store all sorts of information about how the player performed, but for this example, we're limiting it to whether or not they won (as opposed to quitting prematurely), how much time it took them, and the number of moves they made. This information is stored in the MixUp *game-History* Array and used by the Results Class.

```
public class Results extends MovieClip {

        static public const PLAY_AGAIN:String = "playAgain";
        static public const MAIN_MENU:String = "mainMenu";

        public var movesMadeText:TextField;
        public var finalTimeText:TextField;
        public var playAgainButton:SimpleButton;
        public var mainMenuButton:SimpleButton;

        public function Results() {
                addEventListener(Event.ADDED_TO_STAGE, addedTo
                    Stage, false, 0, true);
        }

        private function addedToStage(e:Event):void {
                var history:GameHistory = MixUp.gameHistory[0];
                movesMadeText.text = String(history.movesMade);
                finalTimeText.text = history.formattedTime;
                playAgainButton.addEventListener(MouseEvent.
                    CLICK, playAgain, false, 0, true);
                mainMenuButton.addEventListener(MouseEvent.
                    CLICK, mainMenu, false, 0, true);
        }

        private function playAgain(e:MouseEvent):void {
                dispatchEvent(new Event(PLAY_AGAIN));
        }
```

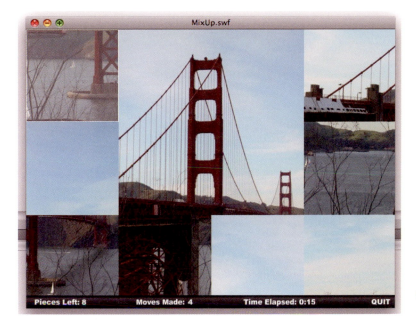

Pieces Left: 8   Moves Made: 4   Time Elapsed: 0:15   QUIT

Figure 13.1 The MixUp game in action.

```
private function mainMenu(e:MouseEvent):void {
        dispatchEvent(new Event(MAIN_MENU));
    }
}
```

Like the Title class, this screen is pretty minimal in its current form, but it could support many other pieces of information or options. Because GameHistory objects are added to the beginning of the Array in the MixUp class, to get the latest object, the Results class simply looks at the first element.

At this point, we at last have a game that can be played start to finish and has multiple screens. If you publish the SWF and test it, you will see how the game works, as in Figure 13.1.

Before we end this chapter, however, we have one more class to look at. It is an alternative class to use for the ISourceImage implementation. It is called SourceImageCamera, and it will use a live feed for the grid instead. If you don't have any kind of webcam, then you can either skip to the next chapter or you can read on for enlightenment.

The SourceImageCamera Class

Our previous implementation, the SourceImageEmbedded class, was simply a generic object. It only ran code when it was requested and was silent the rest of the time. For this next example, we'll need to be able to continually update the BitmapData in the pieces after they're cut up in order for a camera feed to be worthwhile.

```
public class SourceImageCamera extends Sprite implements
  ISourceImage {

        protected var _rows:int, _columns:int;
        protected var _video:Video;
        protected var _camera:Camera;
        protected var _sourceBitmap:BitmapData;
        protected var _pieceList:Vector.<BitmapData>;

        public function SourceImageCamera(width:int, height:int,
          fps:int = 15) {
                _camera = Camera.getCamera();
                _video = new Video(width, height);
                _camera.setMode(width, height, fps);
                _video.attachCamera(_camera);
        }
```

You'll notice a number of similarities between this class and the one for embedded images. In this version, we create variables to store the number of rows and columns for later use, as well as references to use with the Video and Camera classes. For more information on using the Camera class, refer to Appendix A, which can be found at flashgamebook.com. When this class is constructed, new Camera and Video objects are created to match the desired dimensions and frame rate.

```
public function getImages(rows:int, columns:int, width:int = 0,
  height:int = 0):Vector.<BitmapData> {
        if (_pieceList) return _pieceList;
        if (width == 0) width = _video.width;
        if (height == 0) height = _video.height;
        _rows = rows;
        _columns = columns;
        _sourceBitmap = new BitmapData(width, height);
        _sourceBitmap.draw(_video, new Matrix());
        var pieceBitmap:BitmapData;
        var pieceWidth:int = Math.floor(_sourceBitmap.width /
          _columns);
        var pieceHeight:int = Math.floor(_sourceBitmap.height /
          _rows);
        _pieceList = new Vector.<BitmapData>();
        for (var j:int = 0; j < _rows; j++) {
                for (var i:int = 0; i < _columns; i++) {
                        pieceBitmap = new BitmapData(pieceWidth,
                          pieceHeight);
```

```
                var rect:Rectangle = new Rectangle(i *
                    pieceWidth, j * pieceHeight, pieceWidth,
                    pieceHeight);
                pieceBitmap.copyPixels(_sourceBitmap,
                    rect, new Point());
                _pieceList.push(pieceBitmap);
            }
        }
        addEventListener(Event.ENTER_FRAME, updateImages, false,
            0, true);
        return _pieceList;
    }
```

Once again, you probably notice a number of similarities to the image version of this class, except for two main differences. The first is that instead of simply instantiating a new BitmapData image from a class, we have to create an empty one and draw the video into it. The second is that once the list is done being created, an ENTER_FRAME listener is added to call a method called *update-Images*, which we'll look at next.

```
protected function updateImages(e:Event):void {
    _sourceBitmap.dispose();
    _sourceBitmap = new BitmapData(_video.width, _video.
        height);
    _sourceBitmap.draw(_video);
    var pieceBitmap:BitmapData;
    var pieceWidth:int = Math.floor(_sourceBitmap.width /
        _columns);
    var pieceHeight:int = Math.floor(_sourceBitmap.height /
        _rows);
    for (var j:int = 0; j < _rows; j++) {
        for (var i:int = 0; i < _columns; i++) {
            pieceBitmap = _pieceList[i + (j *
                _columns)];
            var rect:Rectangle = new Rectangle(i *
                pieceWidth, j * pieceHeight, pieceWidth,
                pieceHeight);
            pieceBitmap.copyPixels(_sourceBitmap,
                rect, new Point());
        }
    }
}
```

Most of this function mirrors the same process we did in *get-Images*, except that we now dispose of the original source image and draw a new one on every frame loop (to keep up with the changing camera image). Also, instead of creating a new list of

BitmapData objects, we simply update the images we've already created. Because these objects are associated with the Bitmaps inside of the game pieces, those Bitmaps will automatically be updated when the pixel data inside their BitmapData changes.

```
public function cleanUp():void {
        for each (var bmd:BitmapData in _pieceList) {
                bmd.dispose();
        }
        removeEventListener(Event.ENTER_FRAME, updateImages);
        _pieceList = null;
}


public function destroy():void {
        cleanUp();
        _sourceBitmap.dispose();
        _video = null;
        _camera = null;
}
```

Finally, only minor changes are needed to the *cleanUp* and *destroy* methods. The frame loop must be removed, and the video and camera objects nulled. Back in the MixUp class, you only need to change one line to change the game from using a static image to using this new source. On the game.init line in the *setupGame* method, change the line to look like this:

```
game.init(new SourceImageCamera(640, 480, 24), 3, 4);
```

The game will now use a live feed in all the rectangles, which makes the game even more interesting if there is much motion in the background behind you. You can apply these same techniques to create new SourceImage classes that pull in imagery.

Review

In this chapter, we took a simple game from basic concept and rule set to completion using interfaces to keep it modular. In the next chapter, we will apply these concepts further on a much larger, more complicated game.

14

BRINGING IT ALL TOGETHER: A PLATFORMER

Real-World Flash Game Development, Second Edition.
© 2012 Elsevier Inc. All rights reserved.

In the process of deciding what game I should walk through the creation of in this chapter, I asked a lot of my developer friends what they would find most useful. I even posted a public survey for people to cast votes on a variety of game types. I was impressed that by a huge margin (the runner-up had about half as many votes), the winner was a platformer-style game. When I asked other developers why they thought this was the case; the answer was simple, albeit daunting: the platformer is an example of many different game design and development principles all working together at once: level design, animation, keyboard input, physics, collision detection, and basic AI. So, in the name of democracy, that's the type of game we will create in this chapter.

The Platformer Genre

If you've played very many games in your life, particularly on a console, odds are you've probably played a platformer game at one point. In fact, if you've played almost any of Nintendo's popular line of *Mario* games, you've played a platformer. Although that famous Italian plumber tends to be the iconic representation of platformer games, this subgenre of action/adventure games is actually much broader than squashing enemies from above and collecting oversized mushrooms. Some might take place in a single screen, whereas others scroll horizontally and/or vertically. Some might focus on solving a puzzle by moving objects around, collecting keys, or manipulating the game environment to allow the player to escape.

Despite all the variations and possible styles of platformer games, they all tend to follow a few core tenets:

- The user controls some kind of protagonist, generally, just referred to as a player.
- The player can move left and right and can almost always jump or use ladders.
- Some basic rules of physics, such as gravity and basic collisions with solid objects, usually apply; some games use other forces like wind, buoyancy, or rubbery surfaces that cause the player to bounce.
- Gameplay is level-based; each level has a start and an endpoint, or ends based on accomplishing a particular objective (collecting certain items, destroying all enemies, and so on).
- There is a backstory, however brief, explaining what the player is doing and why.

Next, we'll define the rule set for our game based on these fundamental ideas.

Data Flow

It's important to outline the responsibilities of the different components of the game before going any further.

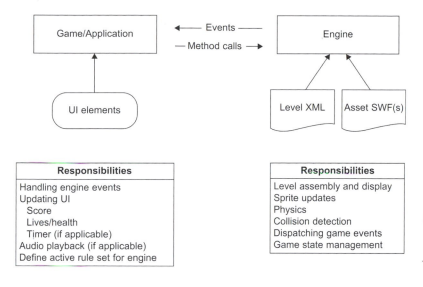

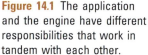

Figure 14.1 The application and the engine have different responsibilities that work in tandem with each other.

In Fig. 14.1, I've outlined what each component of our game is responsible for controlling. When I talk about the "engine," I'm referring to the set of classes that make up the core mechanics of a platformer game. This engine is game-agnostic—it is the code that is meant to be reused later. When I talk about the game or application-level code, I'm referring to the current *implementation* of the engine. Let's say I wanted to build two different platformer games with different art sets and basic behaviors (modified physics, for example). The engine code should remain unchanged from one game to the next (other than to add/fix features that affects all games), while the game code and art are unique to each implementation.

We applied a similar process with MixUp in Chapter 13, just not as explicitly outlined; the GameBoard class and the accompanying interfaces were the engine and the other classes were the implementation. It is important to delineate each component's "jurisdiction" ahead of time; it is easier than separating the code, later, into different classes. When we look at the code for this game later on in the chapter, it will be split into these two categories.

The Game Flow and Features

As a platformer is more complicated than the simple puzzler in Chapter 13, it requires even better definition of scope and mechanics. This rule applies to game development across the board—an increase in complexity necessitates an increase in documentation. There are so many possible feature sets that can be included in a platformer, and it is important to narrow them down to just what we will implement in this version of the engine; otherwise, this chapter would engulf an entire book and take you weeks to build it. It is important to remember that most well-written applications start out with a basic feature set and are modular enough to add feature sets over time. Take any given professional level app, even Flash itself; we are now on version 10, and it *still* does not have all the features we might want it to have. Instead, Adobe has chosen to focus on certain feature sets and fine tune them so that they work reliably and consistently. We must remember to give ourselves this same breathing room. No one developer is going to create the next *World of Warcraft* by himself/herself; it takes hundreds of people and thousands of hours of work.

The Setting

For the purposes of this book and learning the mechanics of a platformer, we don't really need a backstory. Suffice it to say that for this game, the player will be exploring dungeon-like mazes, avoiding enemies, and collecting treasure for points. Although this may sound simple and familiar, that is intentional. Ultimately, we want to create a generic engine that can be reused for any number of implementations and environments.

The Level Design and Walls

The levels for this platformer will be based around a grid design of squares. This helps to simplify level creation and enforces a standard for asset artwork. Any given grid square can be either solid or empty, either blocking the player or allowing them to pass through it. Going forward, we will refer to solid grid squares as walls. We will examine how a sample level layout will look on paper, momentarily. If there are no walls along the bottom of the level, it will be possible for the player to fall off the map. This would cause the level to end and the player to lose a life.

Portals

Every level will have an exit point that will signify completion of the level, when the player passes through it. We'll call this exit a portal, as it transports the player somewhere else. You may be wondering why we're not simply calling it an exit. While this implementation of the game and engine may only ever have one exit, future iterations might span a level over a series of screens and these portals would actually be a means of moving between them.

The Player Character

In this game, the arrow keys will control the player. The Left and Right arrow keys will move him or her in those directions, respectively. The Up arrow will make the player jump, and the Down arrow will be used to enter portals. The player's jump height is equal to 1.5 times the height of a grid square. This allows for the player to clear gaps one grid space in width and to easily jump onto grid squares one unit above. Additionally, the player has the ability to carry items in an inventory. In our iteration, these items will primarily consist of treasure and keys for unlocking doors, but could include other pickups like health in the future.

Items

Both keys for unlocking portals and treasure are classified as *items*. They share a similar relationship in that they both disappear and are added to the player's inventory when the player moves over them. The game will define certain special types of items (such as keys), which will be used by the game engine in a particular way. Items not predefined by the engine will simply accumulate in the inventory, and it will be up to the particular implementation of the game as to how to handle them when they are picked up.

Enemies

An enemy in this game will be defined as any entity that is toxic to the player. Coming into contact with an enemy will damage the player, either by taking a life or eating away at the player's health. By using this more general definition, an enemy could be a sharp inanimate object or a moving creature with basic AI. As such, enemies can either process physics such as gravity or choose to ignore them (imagine stalactites in a cave).

In Fig. 14.2, you'll see a level design for the platformer based around a 10 × 10 grid. As the key below shows, black squares represent walls and white squares are movable areas for the player. The dollar signs are treasure that can be picked up for points, and the key icon represents the key required to exit through the portal at the top of the level. There is also one enemy along the bottom of the level that will move back and forth. The player must jump over the enemy to avoid it. The player will start the level at the top, in the one notch cut out of the border wall surrounding the level. All of the levels for the game can (and probably should) be mapped out this way. This type of system is also very handy because it can translate into a standardized format like XML (which we will look at momentarily), and it is relatively straightforward to create an editor app for building levels.

The Level File Format and Asset Structure

It is a good idea to keep all of the data for each level in external files. This allows you to load new levels at runtime, as well as create your own in a standardized format, either by hand or

Sample platformer level layout

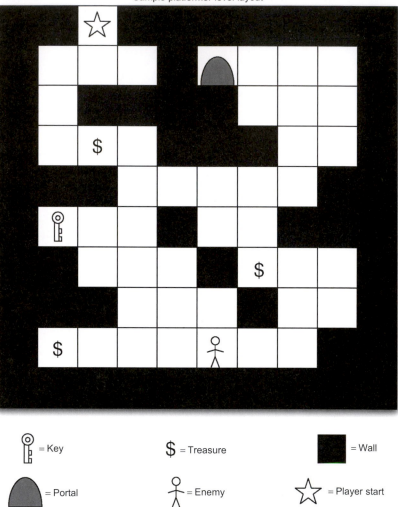

= Key $ = Treasure   = Wall

= Portal   = Enemy   = Player start

Figure 14.2 Because of the grid design of the levels, it is easy to map out a potential level design on "paper" first.

(preferably) using a custom editor. Much like in Chapter 10, we'll store this level data in XML. This keeps the data modular and flexible, making it easy to add/remove elements from a level. It also enforces a level of organization on the data, keeping it readable if you needed to make edits by hand.

In addition to the level data living outside the final game SWF, it's a good idea with a game like this to externalize as many assets as possible. As such, we'll look at maintaining separate SWF files for the different art assets used in the game. Each level XML file will include the asset SWFs it uses, and the engine will handle loading those files before assembling the level. Keeping these assets in separate SWFs also allows for other developers or artists to work on different aspects of the game without stepping on each other's toes. When we get to the code behind the engine, we'll define the rules that asset files must follow in order to work properly with the engine.

The Level XML

Here is what Fig. 14.2 looks like represented as XML. Note that to make the wall nodes more readable, I have inserted carriage returns between each column. In the final format, there is no reason to have these and it is a nonstandard XML practice.

```
<level width="10" height="10" gridSquareSize="50">
    <assets>
        <asset file="player.swf"/>
        <asset file="enemies.swf"/>
        <asset file="items.swf"/>
        <asset file="environment.swf"/>
    </assets>
    <player spriteClass="Player" x="2" y="0" />
    <enemies>
        <enemy spriteClass="Enemy1" name="enemy1" x="5" y="8" />
    </enemies>
    <items>
        <item spriteClass="Key" type="key" name="key1"
          x="1" y="5" points="0"/>
        <item spriteClass="Treasure" type="treasure"
          name="treasure1" x="2" y="3" points="100"/>
        <item spriteClass="Treasure" type="treasure"
          name="treasure2" x="1" y="8" points="100"/>
        <item spriteClass="Treasure" type="treasure"
          name="treasure3" x="6" y="6" points="100"/>
    </items>
    <portals>
        <portal spriteClass="LevelEndDoor" destination=
          "nextLevel" x="5" y="1">
                <requirement type="inventory" name="key1"/>
        </portal>
    </portals>
    <walls>
        <wall spriteClass="StandardWall" x="0" y="0"/>
        <wall spriteClass="StandardWall" x="0" y="1"/>
        <wall spriteClass="StandardWall" x="0" y="2"/>
        <wall spriteClass="StandardWall" x="0" y="3"/>
        <wall spriteClass="StandardWall" x="0" y="4"/>
        <wall spriteClass="StandardWall" x="0" y="5"/>
        <wall spriteClass="StandardWall" x="0" y="6"/>
```

```
<wall spriteClass="StandardWall" x="0" y="7"/>
<wall spriteClass="StandardWall" x="0" y="8"/>
<wall spriteClass="StandardWall" x="0" y="9"/>

<wall spriteClass="StandardWall" x="1" y="0"/>
<wall spriteClass="StandardWall" x="1" y="4"/>
<wall spriteClass="StandardWall" x="1" y="6"/>
<wall spriteClass="StandardWall" x="1" y="7"/>
<wall spriteClass="StandardWall" x="1" y="9"/>

<wall spriteClass="StandardWall" x="2" y="2"/>
<wall spriteClass="StandardWall" x="2" y="4"/>
<wall spriteClass="StandardWall" x="2" y="7"/>
<wall spriteClass="StandardWall" x="2" y="9"/>

<wall spriteClass="StandardWall" x="3" y="0"/>
<wall spriteClass="StandardWall" x="3" y="2"/>
<wall spriteClass="StandardWall" x="3" y="9"/>

<wall spriteClass="StandardWall" x="4" y="0"/>
<wall spriteClass="StandardWall" x="4" y="1"/>
<wall spriteClass="StandardWall" x="4" y="2"/>
<wall spriteClass="StandardWall" x="4" y="3"/>
<wall spriteClass="StandardWall" x="4" y="5"/>
<wall spriteClass="StandardWall" x="4" y="9"/>

<wall spriteClass="StandardWall" x="5" y="0"/>
<wall spriteClass="StandardWall" x="5" y="2"/>
<wall spriteClass="StandardWall" x="5" y="3"/>
<wall spriteClass="StandardWall" x="5" y="6"/>
<wall spriteClass="StandardWall" x="5" y="9"/>

<wall spriteClass="StandardWall" x="6" y="0"/>
<wall spriteClass="StandardWall" x="6" y="3"/>
<wall spriteClass="StandardWall" x="6" y="7"/>
<wall spriteClass="StandardWall" x="6" y="9"/>

<wall spriteClass="StandardWall" x="7" y="0"/>
<wall spriteClass="StandardWall" x="7" y="5"/>
<wall spriteClass="StandardWall" x="7" y="9"/>

<wall spriteClass="StandardWall" x="8" y="0"/>
<wall spriteClass="StandardWall" x="8" y="4"/>
<wall spriteClass="StandardWall" x="8" y="5"/>
<wall spriteClass="StandardWall" x="8" y="8"/>
<wall spriteClass="StandardWall" x="8" y="9"/>
```

```
        <wall spriteClass="StandardWall" x="9" y="0"/>
        <wall spriteClass="StandardWall" x="9" y="1"/>
        <wall spriteClass="StandardWall" x="9" y="2"/>
        <wall spriteClass="StandardWall" x="9" y="3"/>
        <wall spriteClass="StandardWall" x="9" y="4"/>
        <wall spriteClass="StandardWall" x="9" y="5"/>
        <wall spriteClass="StandardWall" x="9" y="6"/>
        <wall spriteClass="StandardWall" x="9" y="7"/>
        <wall spriteClass="StandardWall" x="9" y="8"/>
        <wall spriteClass="StandardWall" x="9" y="9"/>
    </walls>
</level>
```

In the opening tag of the XML, the width and height of the level and the pixel size of each grid square are set. In this case, the level is 10 × 10, with a square size of 50 pixels. This GameBoard will ultimately be 500 × 500 pixels. In the first set of nodes, I define which asset SWFs the level will use. The engine will load these files before parsing the rest of the level. Whenever a node makes reference to a class, it will be defined and contained within one of the asset SWFs. I'll shortly outline the creation of these asset SWFs.

The next individual node defines the player class and start position. Note this *x* and *y* will not translate directly to an *x* and *y* on the Stage, but rather the corresponding grid reference in the level. To match the arrays that will eventually exist to house the grid, the *x* and *y* coordinates are 0-based. Thus, the player's start position of (2, 0) will actually be in the third column at the top. The next two sets of nodes follow the same pattern, just with enemies and items. Items have a couple of extra attributes, including the type (so the engine knows how to use the item), a unique name (so that the item can be tied to functionality in the game), and a point value. Note that the key is not worth any points, but will be a requirement to exit the level.

Next in the file are any portal nodes. This level has only one, and its destination attribute designates that it will go to the next level. Portals also have optional requirement nodes; these are things that must be done for the portal to be active. In this case, the item tagged with the name "key1" is required to have been picked up in order for the portal to be used. With this structure, you could theoretically have multiple requirements, such as destroying all enemies on a level or gathering all the treasure.

Finally, the file ends with the wall definitions. Each of these nodes defines a grid square that holds a wall. The player will not be able to move into these squares. Every one of these wall squares will look the same, but you could, in fact, define a different asset class for each of them. This would allow you to create grid squares that seam together to form larger images.

Asset SWFs

To keep the game as modular as possible, and load times low, the various art assets for the game will be stored in external SWFs and loaded in at runtime. This will provide a few benefits:

- Assets will only be loaded when needed, meaning the main game SWF will not be weighted down with a ton of art in its initial load, should an implementation of this game have many levels.
- Multiple developers and artists are capable of working on specific assets in tandem without needing access to the core FLA file.
- Adding new character and scenery art will be as simple as dropping in new SWFs and referencing them in the level XML.

This structure is similar to how many commercial games work; the EXE or main application file is the "engine" and is accompanied by one or more resource files (pak, was, and rsc are some common extensions).

The asset files will have no active timeline. Each will consist merely of library items with class linkages. Once the assets are loaded into the game, they will be stored in memory and then accessed by instantiating new copies the assets. When a level is complete, the assets will be purged from memory, but if they need to be loaded again they should already be cached in the user's browser, preventing a repeat download.

The Game Outline

Before we dig into the code behind this game, I'll outline all the classes that will come into play. The classes are divided into three categories, each with a specific purpose:

- Engine code: These files are at the heart of the game mechanic and are where the core feature set of the engine is implemented; in addition to classes, this code also contains interfaces for creating the different game components. These files are all within the *com.flashgamebook.engines.platformer* package.
- Game code: These classes control how this specific instance of the engine looks and behaves, and other logic like switching between levels and creation of all the engine instances.
- Asset classes: For each of the asset SWFs in use, we'll specify unique class names for each individual asset, but we won't actually create AS files for any of them—more on this will be discussed, shortly.

We'll now look at all the classes involved, in the aforementioned order. It's important to note that unlike the MixUp game in Chapter 13, this example does not include multiple screens with navigation—we will focus on the game only. There is already enough code at work here and I did not want to bog you down with information not directly pertinent to the tasks at hand. I'm nice like that!

The Engine Classes

In this section, I will outline each of the classes involved in the core engine of this platformer and walk through the code of each. This is where the bulk of the code for this game resides, and it's important to understand all the components at play.

- PlatformerEngine.as: This is the big one; all the core functionality of the game is run here; all the other classes in the package act as support for the engine.
- CollisionGrid.as: To efficiently store information about the game grid, we will use this custom data structure, which relies on multidimensional arrays and vectors to keep track of everything going on in the game.
- GridReference.as: Each grid square has an accompanying GridReference object, which stores which enemies, items, walls, and portals are in a given slot on the grid.
- PlatformerConfig.as: This is a data class that allows for easy configuration of different aspects of the engine, and makes it easier to change the behavior of the engine properties from level to level by storing preconfigured instances of this class.
- PortalRequirement.as: Each portal instance has an array of these objects, which define what requirements must be met in order to finish a level.
- PortalDestination.as: An enumeration class, this file simply contains preapproved destinations for portals (which map to those mentioned earlier in the XML) and makes it easy to add new ones.
- PlatformerEvent.as: Tucked inside the *events* subpackage, this class extends a normal DataEvent that the PlatformerEngine can dispatch when certain things happen inside the game; it also stores enumerations for all the different game events.
- ISprite.as, IPlayer.as, IEnemy.as, IItem.as, IPortal.as, IWall.as: This set of interfaces in the *Sprites* subpackage all define the necessary methods required for Sprites, which wish to act as the player, enemies, and so on in the game.

We'll work through these classes in reverse order, so that the main engine class will make more sense in context.

The ISprite Interface

This interface is the foundation for all of the other types of Sprites, except walls. It extends IEventDispatcher, so that if, at some point, we need the Sprites to be able to easily dispatch events, there will be no interface conflicts.

```
package com.flashgamebook.engines.platformer.sprites {

    import flash.display.Sprite;
    import flash.display.DisplayObject;
```

```
import flash.events.IEventDispatcher;
import flash.geom.Rectangle;

public interface ISprite extends IEventDispatcher {

        function get x():Number;
        function set x(value:Number):void;
        function get y():Number;
        function set y(value:Number):void;
        function get width():Number;
        function set width(value:Number):void;
        function get height():Number;
        function set height(value:Number):void;
        function get rotation():Number;
        function set rotation(value:Number):void;
        function get hitArea():Sprite;
        function getRect(coordinateSpace:DisplayObject):
          Rectangle;
        function get name():String;
        function set name(value:String):void;

    }
}
```

You probably noted that all of these methods and accessors are included in DisplayObjects, specifically Sprites. Implementing this interface on a Sprite-based class will require no extra functionality, but makes it more flexible in the engine by referring to this interface rather than any particular DisplayObject type.

The IPlayer Interface

Wherever the engine refers to the character the user controls in the game, it is done through the IPlayer interface, which extends ISprite.

```
package com.flashgamebook.engines.platformer.sprites {

    import flash.geom.Vector3D;

    public interface IPlayer extends ISprite {

            function get netForce():Vector3D;
            function set netForce(value:Vector3D):void;
            function get isJumping():Boolean;
            function set isJumping(value:Boolean):void;
            function get isFalling():Boolean;
            function set isFalling(value:Boolean):void;
            function update():void;
```

```
function get tempX():Number;
function set tempX(value:Number):void;
function get tempY():Number;
function set tempY(value:Number):void;


    }
}
```

Note the use of Vector3D objects, much like in the examples of Chapter 11.

The IEnemy Interface

Similar to the IPlayer interface, IEnemy also extends ISprite. In fact, it repeats a couple of the accessors from IPlayer, but it didn't make sense to make them part of ISprite just so they would be inherited.

```
package com.flashgamebook.engines.platformer.sprites {

    import flash.geom.Vector3D;
    import com.flashgamebook.engines.platformer.
      GridReference;

    public interface IEnemy extends ISprite {

        function update():void;
        function get tempX():Number;
        function set tempX(value:Number):void;
        function get tempY():Number;
        function set tempY(value:Number):void;
        function get receivesForces():Boolean;
        function get motion():Vector3D;
        function get gridReference():GridReference;
        function set gridReference(value:GridReference):
          void;


    }
}
```

One unique aspect of this interface is that enemies must keep track of where they currently are on the collision grid because they are the only type of entity besides the player that can move. As such, implementors of this interface have an accessor for a GridReference object, which we'll look at soon.

The IItem Interface

Although admittedly an awkward name for an interface, IItem is used for any items the player can pick up.

```
package com.flashgamebook.engines.platformer.sprites {

    public interface IItem extends ISprite {

            function get points():Number;
            function set points(value:Number):void;
            function get type():String;
            function set type(value:String):void;
            function pickUp():void;

    }
}
```

The IPortal Interface

As I mentioned earlier in the chapter, portals are the devices that players use to move between levels.

```
package com.flashgamebook.engines.platformer.sprites {

    public interface IPortal extends ISprite {

            function get requirements():Array;
            function set requirements(value:Array):void;
            function get destination():String;
            function set destination(value:String):void;

    }
}
```

The IWall Interface

The final interface, and the only one that doesn't extend from something else, is the one used for instances of walls. Although all of these functions are defined in ISprite, IWall intentionally has a smaller subset to keep it separate from that hierarchy. Collision detection with walls is handled differently than with other objects, so this gives us an opportunity to expand this interface without ramifications to other parts of the engine.

```
package com.flashgamebook.engines.platformer.sprites {

    import flash.display.DisplayObject;
    import flash.geom.Rectangle;

    public interface IWall {
            //DISPLAY OBJECT PROPERTIES AND METHODS
            function get x():Number;
```

```
function set x(value:Number):void;
function get y():Number;
function set y(value:Number):void;
function get width():Number;
function set width(value:Number):void;
function get height():Number;
function set height(value:Number):void;
function getRect(targetCoordinateSpace:
  DisplayObject):Rectangle;


    }
}
```

The PlatformerEvent Class

All the messages dispatched by the PlatformerEngine, with the exception of progress messages during loading, are in the form of a PlatformerEvent object.

```
package com.flashgamebook.engines.platformer.events {

    import flash.events.DataEvent;

    public class PlatformerEvent extends DataEvent {

            public static const LEVEL_LOAD_COMPLETE:String =
              "levelLoadComplete";
            public static const ASSET_LOAD_COMPLETE:String =
              "assetLoadComplete";
            public static const GAME_START:String = "gameStart";
            public static const PLAYER_DIE:String = "playerDie";
            public static const INVENTORY_UPDATE:String =
              "inventoryUpdate";
            public static const ENTER_PORTAL:String =
              "enterPortal";

            public function PlatformerEvent(type:String, data:
              String = null, bubbles:Boolean = false,
              cancelable:Boolean = false) {
                    super(type, bubbles, cancelable, data);
            }

        }
}
```

As it becomes necessary to dispatch events about additional functionality, those event enumerations will easily be added here.

The PortalDestinations and PortalRequirement Classes

Because they're both very short, we'll now look at the two classes related to portal behavior.

```
package com.flashgamebook.engines.platformer {

    public class PortalDestinations {

            public static const NEXT_LEVEL:String = "nextLevel";
            public static const PREV_LEVEL:String = "prevLevel";


        }
}
```

While these two enumerations could have potentially been tucked away into the PlatformerEngine class, it makes more sense for them to be singled out. This is because there may be more functionality to add to portal behavior, such as the ability to move between two different portals on in a single map. This framework allows for that extensibility.

```
package com.flashgamebook.engines.platformer {

    public class PortalRequirement {

            public static const INVENTORY:String = "inventory";
            public static const ENEMY_KILLED:String =
              "enemyKilled";

            public var type:String;
            public var name:String;

            public function PortalRequirement(type:String,
              name:String) {
                    this.type = type;
                    this.name = name;
            }


        }
}
```

PortalRequirement objects are also very simple and could have had their limited functionality handled by a generic object, but it's a better practice to statically type it and create a space for future functionality.

The PlatformerConfig Class

This class exposes certain properties of the engine by allowing you to preconfigure the behavior of the engine before even creating it.

It is prepopulated with values that work well for our purposes, but these are all easily changed later.

```
package com.flashgamebook.engines.platformer {

    import flash.geom.Rectangle;
    import flash.geom.Vector3D;
    import flash.ui.Keyboard;

    public class PlatformerConfig {

        public var gravity:Vector3D = new Vector3D(0,25);
        public var friction:Number = .75;
        public var drag:Number = .92;

        //INPUT
        public var keyJump:int = Keyboard.UP;
        public var keyUse:int = Keyboard.DOWN;
        public var keyLeft:int = Keyboard.LEFT;
        public var keyRight:int = Keyboard.RIGHT;

        //PLAYER PROPERTIES
        public var playerMovement:Vector3D = new Vector3D(30);
        public var playerJump:Vector3D = new Vector3D(0,-10);

    }
}
```

Notice this is a good way of creating and assigning input schemes, as well as defining things like the effects of gravity and friction.

The GridReference Class

As stated earlier, every square on the game grid has an associated GridReference object. It stores which walls, enemies, items, and portals are in a given square.

```
package com.flashgamebook.engines.platformer {

    import com.flashgamebook.engines.platformer.sprites.*;

    public class GridReference {

        public var walls:Vector.<IWall> = new Vector.
          <IWall>();
        public var items:Vector.<IItem> = new Vector.
          <IItem>();
        public var enemies:Vector.<IEnemy> = new Vector.
          <IEnemy>();
```

```
public var portals:Vector.<IPortal> = new Vector.
  <IPortal>();

public function hasEnemy(sprite:IEnemy):Boolean {
        return (enemies.indexOf(sprite) > -1);
}

public function removeEnemy(sprite:IEnemy):void {
        if (enemies.indexOf(sprite) > -1) {
                enemies.splice(enemies.indexOf
                    (sprite),1);
        }
}

public function hasItem(sprite:IItem):Boolean {
        return (items.indexOf(sprite) > -1);
}

public function removeItem(sprite:IItem):void {
        if (items.indexOf(sprite) > -1) {
                items.splice(items.indexOf
                    (sprite),1);
        }
}

public function concat(gridReference:
  GridReference): void {
        if (!gridReference) return;
        walls = walls.concat(gridReference.walls);
        items = items.concat(gridReference.items);
        enemies = enemies.concat(gridReference.enemies);
        portals = portals.concat(gridReference.portals);
}

public function toString():String {
        var str:String = "GRID REFERENCE:\n";
        str +=" WALLS:" + walls +"\n";
        str +=" ITEMS:" + items +"\n";
        str +=" ENEMIES:" + enemies +"\n";
        str +=" PORTALS:" + portals;
        return str;
}

public function clear():void {
        walls = null;
        items = null;
        enemies = null;
```

```
            portals = null;
        }
    }
}
```

Every type of object a grid reference can store has a vector created just for it. Many of these vectors may stay empty, but they consume very little memory by themselves, so it is a small price to pay for such flexibility. Similar to an array, grid reference objects have a *concat* method, which allows you to merge one grid reference with another. With this functionality, it is possible to combine multiple grid references into one for easy checking.

There are also convenient methods for removing enemies and items from a grid reference, and a custom *toString* method that allows you to easily see what's in a grid reference with a simple trace statement. Finally, there is also a *clear* method that can be called during engine cleanup.

The CollisionGrid Class

In order to store all the grid references in a cohesive structure, we need a container. We could use a simple array or vector to keep track of all of them, but in our case, it makes more sense to create a custom data structure: enter the CollisionGrid. This class uses both an array and multiple vectors to create a multidimensional grid.

```
package com.flashgamebook.engines.platformer {

    import flash.geom.Point;

    public class CollisionGrid {

        private var _width:int;
        private var _height:int;
        private var _grid:Array;

        public function CollisionGrid(width:int, height:int) {
            _width = width;
            _height = height;
            _grid = new Array(_width, true);
            for (var i:int = 0; i < _width; i++) {
                _grid[i] = new Vector.<GridReference>
                  (_height, true);
                for (var j:int = 0; j < _height; j++) {
                    _grid[i][j] = new GridReference();
                }
            }
        }
    }
```

```
public function getGridReference(x:int, y:int):
  GridReference {
        if (x < 0 || y < 0) return null;
        if (x >= _width || y >= _height) return null;
        return _grid[x][y];
    }

public function clear():void {
        for (var i:int = 0; i < _grid.length; i++) {
            for each (var gridReference:
              GridReference in _grid[i]) {
                gridReference.clear();
            }
            _grid[i] = null;
        }
        _grid = null;
    }

  }
}
```

When a new CollisionGrid object is created, it needs a width and height. It constructs all the necessary containers and fills them with empty GridReference objects. Because the structure and dimensions of a level can't change on the fly, the vector containers have a fixed length. This improves speed and memory usage.

Getting at a specific GridReference object is as simple as calling the *getGridReference* method and passing it *x* and *y* values. If a grid square outside the range of the grid is requested, the method returns null. Like a GridReference object, the grid also has a *clear* method, which performs cleanup and disposal of all the objects.

The PlatformerEngine Class

Now, we've reached the heart of the entire game. This class is very large (500+ lines), so I will break it up into discrete pieces. The class is divided logically into different sets of tasks, so it's easier to find what you're looking for. These tasks are as follows:

- Level XML load handling
- Asset load handling
- Level creation
- Game loop functionality (what's run every frame)
- Helper methods
- Input handlers

This largely maps to the order of events that occur when using the engine as well, so it is straightforward to follow. This class also uses a ton of imports, which I'll skip here in the text, but you can find in the source files for this chapter. We'll start by looking at all the properties defined in the class.

```
public class PlatformerEngine extends Sprite {

    protected var _gravity:Vector3D;
    protected var _friction:Number;
    protected var _config:PlatformerConfig;
    protected var _currentLevel:XML;
    protected var _previousTime:int;
    protected var _deltaTime:Number;
    protected var _keyLeftPressed:Boolean;
    protected var _keyRightPressed:Boolean;
    protected var _walls:Array;
    protected var _items:Array;
    protected var _enemies:Array;
    protected var _portals:Array;
    protected var _player:IPlayer;
    protected var _collisionGrid:CollisionGrid;
    protected var _gameRunning:Boolean = false;
    protected var _inventory:Vector.<IItem>;
    protected var _assetDomain:ApplicationDomain;
    protected var _assetPath:String = "";
    protected var _assetQueue:Vector.<String> = new Vector.
      <String>();
    protected var _assets:Vector.<Loader> = new Vector.<Loader>();

    public function PlatformEngine() {
    }
```

The properties listed here mostly consist of containers for different types of objects. A couple of important things to note are the container for the player's inventory and the *_assetDomain* property. The latter is used to store all the class definitions for the assets the engine will load. This will keep those definitions from overriding any that might exist in the engine but will keep them from being separated from each other. Note that the constructor does nothing—it is there merely as an acknowledgment. Initialization is handled through the *init* method, which we will look at next.

```
public function init(config:PlatformerConfig):void {
    _config = config;
    _gravity = _config.gravity;
    _friction = _config.friction;
    _assetDomain = new ApplicationDomain(ApplicationDomain.
      currentDomain);
    _inventory = new Vector.<IItem>();
}
```

This method handles creation of a number of basic engine properties. It is the first of a handful of public-facing methods.

The majority of the functionality of this engine is protected and inaccessible from the outside.

```
public function startGame():void {
        if (!stage) throw new Error("PlatformEngine instance must
           be added to stage before startGame() is called.");
        stage.addEventListener(KeyboardEvent.KEY_DOWN, onKeyDown,
           false, 0, true);
        stage.addEventListener(KeyboardEvent.KEY_UP, onKeyUp,
           false, 0, true);
        addEventListener(Event.ENTER_FRAME, update, false, 0, true);
        _previousTime = getTimer();
        _gameRunning = true;
}

public function stopGame():void {
        if (!stage) throw new Error("PlatformEngine instance must
           be added to stage before stopGame() is called.");
        stage.removeEventListener(KeyboardEvent.KEY_DOWN,
           onKeyDown);
        stage.removeEventListener(KeyboardEvent.KEY_UP, onKeyUp);
        removeEventListener(Event.ENTER_FRAME, update);
        _gameRunning = false;
}
```

Once the game is added to the Stage and has had all of its data loaded, the *startGame* and *stopGame* methods can be called. They handle the enterFrame and keyboard listener attachment, and also toggle a Boolean value called *_gameRunning*. This will be used, later, in case the game is stopped and disposed of before all the game loop code has finished running.

```
public function get inventory():Vector.<IItem> {
        return _inventory.slice();
}
```

One of the facets the game does expose is a copy of the inventory vector. This allows the UI to display information about what is in the player's inventory. Storing everything the player picks up allows us to tie portal requirements to specific items later on.

```
public function get inventoryWorth():Number {
        var worth:Number = 0;
        for each (var item:IItem in _inventory) {
                worth += item.points;
        }
        return worth;
}
```

In addition to the list of inventory items, there's a helpful method for retrieving the total worth of the inventory in points. If you recall from the level XML, every item has a point attribute; in some cases, that value is 0, but all of them have it.

```
public function destroy():void {
        clearReferences();
        for (var i:int = numChildren-1; i >= 0; i--) {
                removeChildAt(i);
        }
}


protected function clearReferences():void {
        _collisionGrid.clear();
        _inventory = null;
        _walls = null;
        _items = null;
        _enemies = null;
        _portals = null;
        _player = null;
        for each(var loader:Loader in _assets) {
                loader.unload();
        }
        _assets = null;
        _assetQueue = null;
}
```

Both of these methods are used to perform cleanup on the engine. Because there are so many pieces of data in so many containers, it is important to null them all out. Note also that each of the Loader objects in the asset list call the *unload* method on themselves. We'll discuss the level and asset loading next.

```
//LEVEL MANAGEMENT
public function loadLevel(uri:String):void {
        var request:URLRequest = new URLRequest(uri);
        var levelLoader:URLLoader = new URLLoader(request);
        levelLoader.addEventListener(Event.COMPLETE,
          levelLoaded, false, 0, true);
        levelLoader.addEventListener(IOErrorEvent.IO_ERROR,
          levelError, false, 0, true);
        levelLoader.addEventListener(SecurityErrorEvent.
          SECURITY_ERROR, securityError, false, 0, true);
}


protected function levelLoaded(e:Event):void {
        _currentLevel = XML(e.target.data);
```

```
        _collisionGrid = new CollisionGrid(Number(_currentLevel.
          @width), Number(_currentLevel.@height));
        var assets:XMLList = _currentLevel.assets.children();
        for (var i:int = 0; i < assets.length(); i++) {
                _assetQueue.push(assets[i].@file);
        }
        var pe:PlatformerEvent = new PlatformerEvent(Platformer
          Event.LEVEL_LOAD_COMPLETE);
        dispatchEvent(pe);
        loadNextAsset();
}


protected function levelError(e:IOErrorEvent):void {
        trace("PlatformEngine: Error Loading Level:",e.text);
}


protected function securityError(e:SecurityErrorEvent):void {
        trace("SecurityError:",e.text);
}
//END LEVEL MANAGEMENT
```

Once the engine is created and initialized, it is ready to load a level XML file. As such, there is a public method called *loadLevel* that does just this. Once the level data is loaded and converted to an XML object, a new CollisionGrid object is created, as well as a list of all the necessary assets needed to play the level. Once this list is complete, asset loading begins.

```
//ASSET MANAGEMENT
protected function loadNextAsset(e:Event = null):void {
        var loader:Loader = new Loader();
        var nextAsset:String = _assetQueue[_assets.length];
        var context:LoaderContext = new LoaderContext(false,
          _assetDomain);
        loader.load(new URLRequest(_assetPath + nextAsset), context);
        loader.contentLoaderInfo.addEventListener(Event.
          COMPLETE, assetsLoaded, false, 0, true);
        loader.contentLoaderInfo.addEventListener(Progress
          Event.PROGRESS, assetLoadProgress, false, 0, true);
        loader.contentLoaderInfo.addEventListener(IOErrorEvent.
          IO_ERROR, assetLoadError, false, 0, true);
        loader.contentLoaderInfo.addEventListener(Security
          ErrorEvent.SECURITY_ERROR, securityError, false, 0, true);
        _assets.push(loader);
}
```

The *loadNextAsset* method is called each time one asset finishes loading, until the entire manifest has been pulled into the engine.

Note that the Loader has a specific LoaderContext object created for it, which directs it to place the Loader's class definitions in a common ApplicationDomain. Each Loader also has a progress event linked to it, which we will discuss next.

```
protected function assetLoadProgress(e:ProgressEvent):void {
      var baseCompletion:Number = 100 * (_assets.length-1)/
        _assetQueue.length;
      var currentProgress:Number = (100/_assetQueue.length) *
        (e.bytesLoaded/e.bytesTotal);
      var bytesLoaded:int = Math.round(baseCompletion +
        currentProgress);
      var pe:ProgressEvent = new ProgressEvent(ProgressEvent.
        PROGRESS, false, false, bytesLoaded, 100);
      dispatchEvent(pe);
}
```

To create an accurate percentage of how much of the level assets have loaded (without knowing the file size of each one), we have to create a custom ProgressEvent. It takes into account the number of items to load and the individual progress of each asset to create an event with somewhere between 0 and 100 bytes loaded, which represents the percent loaded. Naturally, if the asset files are dramatically different in size, this means of measuring completion will seem a little erratic, but it will be as accurate as we can get without loading all of the files at once (which can choke on some Internet connections).

```
protected function assetsLoaded(e:Event):void {
      if (_assets.length < _assetQueue.length) {
            loadNextAsset();
            return;
      }
      var pe:PlatformerEvent = new PlatformerEvent(Platformer
        Event.ASSET_LOAD_COMPLETE);
      dispatchEvent(pe);
      createLevel();
}

protected function assetLoadError(e:IOErrorEvent):void {
      trace("PlatformEngine: Error Loading Asset:",_assetQueue
        [_assets.length-1]);
}

protected function getAssetClass(assetName:String):Class {
      if (_assetDomain.hasDefinition(assetName)) {
            return _assetDomain.getDefinition(assetName) as
              Class;
      }
```

```
        throw new ArgumentError("Asset Class"+assetName+" cannot
          be found in loaded asset files.");
    }
//END ASSET MANAGEMENT
```

Once all the assets are loaded successfully, the level is ready to be created through *createLevel*. To link up the classes referenced in the XML, there is one helper function called *getAssetClass* that accepts a class name as a string. It looks up the class definition in the common asset ApplicationDomain and either returns it as a Class object or displays an error if the asset does not exist.

```
//BEGIN LEVEL CREATION
protected function createLevel():void {
    createWalls();
    createPortals();
    createEnemies();
    createItems();
    //CREATE PLAYER
    var playerClass:Class = getAssetClass(_currentLevel.
      player.@spriteClass);
    _player = new playerClass();
    _player.x = Number(_currentLevel.player.@x) * Number
      (_currentLevel.@gridSquareSize);
    _player.y = Number(_currentLevel.player.@y) * Number
      (_currentLevel.@gridSquareSize);
    addChild(_player as DisplayObject);
}
```

There is a lot going on in this method; it calls individual methods for creating each type of core object, and then creates the player Sprite. I'll show all of the creation methods back to back, as they are largely similar in structure.

```
protected function createWalls():void {
    _walls = new Array();
    var walls:XMLList = _currentLevel.walls.children();
    for (var i:int = 0; i < walls.length(); i++) {
        var wallClass:Class = getAssetClass(walls[i].
          @spriteClass);
        var wallSprite:IWall = new wallClass();
        wallSprite.x = Number(walls[i].@x) * Number
          (_currentLevel.@gridSquareSize);
        wallSprite.y = Number(walls[i].@y) * Number
          (_currentLevel.@gridSquareSize);
        _walls.push(wallSprite);
        var gridReference:GridReference = _collisionGrid.
          getGridReference(Number(walls[i].@x),
          Number(walls[i].@y));
        gridReference.walls.push(wallSprite);
```

```
                        addChild(wallSprite as DisplayObject);
                }
        }

protected function createEnemies():void {
        _enemies = new Array();
        var enemies:XMLList = _currentLevel.enemies.children();
        for (var i:int = 0; i < enemies.length(); i++) {
                var enemyClass:Class = getAssetClass(enemies[i].
                  @spriteClass);
                var enemySprite:IEnemy = new enemyClass();
                enemySprite.x = Number(enemies[i].@x) * Number
                  (_currentLevel.@gridSquareSize);
                enemySprite.y = Number(enemies[i].@y) * Number
                  (_currentLevel.@gridSquareSize);
                enemySprite.name = enemies[i].@name;
                _enemies.push(enemySprite);
                var gridReference:GridReference = _collisionGrid.
                  getGridReference(Number(enemies[i].@x),
                  Number(enemies[i].@y));
                gridReference.enemies.push(enemySprite);
                enemySprite.gridReference = gridReference;
                addChild(enemySprite as DisplayObject);
        }
}

protected function createItems():void {
        _items = new Array();
        var items:XMLList = _currentLevel.items.children();
        for (var i:int = 0; i < items.length(); i++) {
                var itemClass:Class = getAssetClass(items[i].
                  @spriteClass);
                var itemSprite:IItem = new itemClass();
                itemSprite.x = Number(items[i].@x) * Number
                  (_currentLevel.@gridSquareSize);
                itemSprite.y = Number(items[i].@y) * Number
                  (_currentLevel.@gridSquareSize);
                itemSprite.points = Number(items[i].@points);
                itemSprite.name = items[i].@name;
                itemSprite.type = items[i].@type;
                _items.push(itemSprite);
                var gridReference:GridReference = _collisionGrid.
                  getGridReference(Number(items[i].@x),
                  Number(items[i].@y));
                gridReference.items.push(itemSprite);
                addChild(itemSprite as DisplayObject);
        }
}
```

```
protected function createPortals():void {
        _portals = new Array();
        var portals:XMLList = _currentLevel.portals.children();
        for (var i:int = 0; i < portals.length(); i++) {
                var portalClass:Class = getAssetClass(portals[i].
                  @spriteClass);
                var portalSprite:IPortal = new portalClass();
                portalSprite.x = Number(portals[i].@x) * Number
                  (_currentLevel.@gridSquareSize);
                portalSprite.y = Number(portals[i].@y) * Number
                  (_currentLevel.@gridSquareSize);
                portalSprite.destination = portals[i].
                  @destination;
                for each (var requirement:XML in portals[i].
                  requirement) {
                        portalSprite.require,ments.push(new
                          PortalRequirement(requirement.@type,
                          requirement.@name));
                }
                _portals.push(portalSprite);
                var gridReference:GridReference = _collisionGrid.
                  getGridReference(Number(portals[i].@x),
                  Number(portals[i].@y));
                gridReference.portals.push(portalSprite);
                addChild(portalSprite as DisplayObject);
        }
}
//END LEVEL CREATION
```

Because there is so much code to digest here, I've bolded the most significant areas. Each of the types of Sprites adds itself to the appropriate GridReference object, and each enemy Sprite stores a reference to its respective GridReference. In *createPortals*, each portal defines a new PortalRequirement object for every requirement necessary to use that portal. Every type of Sprite is added both to an engine-level list, as well as a grid reference, and then added to the Stage at its specified position from the XML.

The level has now been created and is in the display list. From this point forward, *startGame* and *stopGame* can be called on the engine, and the player Sprite is ready to receive input. However, we're going to jump slightly out of order in the file for a moment to outline the helper methods before we dive into the main game loop. Then, we'll examine the keyboard input handlers the game uses as well.

```
//BEGIN UTILITY
protected function getGridPosition(sprite:ISprite):Point {
        var spriteRect:Rectangle = sprite.getRect(this);
        var centerX:Number = spriteRect.x + (spriteRect.width/2);
```

```
        var xPos:int = Math.floor(centerX / Number(_currentLevel.
          @gridSquareSize));
        var centerY:Number = spriteRect.y + (spriteRect.height/2);
        var yPos:int = Math.floor(centerY / Number(_currentLevel.
          @gridSquareSize));
        return new Point(xPos, yPos);
}


protected function updateGridReference(sprite:IEnemy):void {
        var position:Point = getGridPosition(sprite);
        var newGridReference = _collisionGrid.getGridReference
          (position.x, position.y);
        if (newGridReference == sprite.gridReference) return;
        sprite.gridReference.removeEnemy(sprite);
        sprite.gridReference = newGridReference;
        newGridReference.enemies.push(sprite);
}


protected function getCollisionReference(sprite:ISprite):
  GridReference {
        var testPoint:Point = getGridPosition(sprite);
        var testReference:GridReference = new GridReference();
        //CHECK THE CURRENT GRID REFERENCE, AND THE EIGHT
          SURROUNDING
        testReference.concat(_collisionGrid.getGridReference
          (testPoint.x-1, testPoint.y-1));
        testReference.concat(_collisionGrid.getGridReference
          (testPoint.x, testPoint.y-1));
        testReference.concat(_collisionGrid.getGridReference
          (testPoint.x+1, testPoint.y-1));
        testReference.concat(_collisionGrid.getGridReference
          (testPoint.x-1, testPoint.y));
        testReference.concat(_collisionGrid.getGridReference
          (testPoint.x, testPoint.y));
        testReference.concat(_collisionGrid.getGridReference
          (testPoint.x+1, testPoint.y));
        testReference.concat(_collisionGrid.getGridReference
          (testPoint.x-1, testPoint.y+1));
        testReference.concat(_collisionGrid.getGridReference
          (testPoint.x, testPoint.y+1));
        testReference.concat(_collisionGrid.getGridReference
          (testPoint.x+1, testPoint.y+1));
        return testReference;
}
//END UTILITY
```

To make it easy to determine the grid space for any given Sprite in the game, there is a single method, which returns a Point object.

Any given Sprite is measured from the centerpoint of its Stage Rectangle to determine the grid space in which is resides.

As I mentioned earlier, enemies are capable of moving between grid squares, so they need the ability to update the Grid-Reference objects to which they are linked. This is where the *updateGridReference* method comes in handy—it handles removing an enemy from one reference and into another with a single command.

The final, and perhaps most important, helper method is *getCollisionReference*. This method assembles an entirely new GridReference object concatenated from the eight grid squares surrounding a Sprite, plus the square in which the Sprite currently exists. This is important because it ensures that we only test for collisions in *nearby* grid references. There is no need to test the player against another Sprite on the other side of the level. This ensures that there will be no more and no less than nine checks per cycle, which means that the level size can scale almost indefinitely without a performance drop. This method will be called at the onset of every collision detection check.

```
//BEGIN INPUT MANAGEMENT
protected function onKeyDown(e:KeyboardEvent):void {
    switch (e.keyCode) {
        case _config.keyLeft: _keyLeftPressed = true;
        break;
        case _config.keyRight: _keyRightPressed = true;
        break;
        case _config.keyJump: playerJump();
        break;
        case _config.keyUse: checkPortals();
        break;
    }
}


protected function onKeyUp(e:KeyboardEvent):void {
    switch (e.keyCode) {
        case _config.keyLeft: _keyLeftPressed = false;
        break;
        case _config.keyRight: _keyRightPressed = false;
        break;
    }
}
//END INPUT MANAGEMENT
```

The key input for this platformer is very simple. The left and right keys (regardless of the actual key they're assigned to in the Config class) act as toggles, while the jump and use keys (Up and Down arrows, by default), perform one-time actions.

On every frame update, the game will call the *update* method. This function determines the amount of time that has elapsed since it was last called, and then this function calls a number of other methods.

```
//BEGIN GAME LOOP LOGIC
protected function update(e:Event):void {
        _deltaTime = (getTimer() - _previousTime)/1000;
        _previousTime = getTimer();
        readKeyInput();
        applyForces();
        movePlayer();
        moveEnemies();
        checkPlayerCollisions();
        render();
}
```

As a top-level summary, before we dig into each method individually, here is the process that takes place in the course of an *update*.

- The game checks to see which keys are pressed, so that it can apply player forces if necessary.
- Physics forces are applied to the player.
- The player's cumulative forces are used to update the player's position in the form of temporary properties (*tempX* and *tempY*).
- All of the enemies in the game are moved according to their motion parameter; they are also checked for collisions against walls.
- The player is collision-checked against different kinds of Sprites, depending on the player's position in the grid; portals are not checked, until the "use" key is pressed.
- If the player is colliding with a wall, the player's temp position is updated to adjust for the wall.
- If the player is colliding with an enemy, a death event is dispatched.
- If the player is colliding with an item, the item is added to the inventory, and an inventory update event is dispatched.
- The player's and enemies' temporary positions are assigned to their respective *x* and *y* values, having been correctly adjusted for collisions.

```
protected function readKeyInput():void {
        var movement:Vector3D = _config.playerMovement.clone();
        movement.scaleBy(_deltaTime);
        if (_keyLeftPressed) {
                _player.netForce.decrementBy(movement);
        }
```

```
if (_keyRightPressed) {
        _player.netForce.incrementBy(movement);
}
}
```

In *readKeyInput*, the player's horizontal movement is applied as a force (scaled by the amount of time that has passed) to the player's physics object.

```
protected function playerJump():void {
        if (_player.isJumping || _player.isFalling) return;
        _player.isJumping = true;
        var jump:Vector3D = _config.playerJump.clone();
        _player.netForce.incrementBy(jump);
}
```

When the user presses the jump key, it triggers the *playerJump* method. If the player is already jumping or is falling through the air, the jump command is ignored. The jump is applied directly one time, rather than being scaled over time; gravity will, eventually, overcome the force of the jump.

```
protected function applyForces():void {
        var gravity:Vector3D = _config.gravity.clone();
        gravity.scaleBy(_deltaTime);
        _player.netForce.incrementBy(gravity);
        if (_player.isJumping) {
                _player.netForce.x *= _config.drag;
        } else {
                _player.netForce.x *= _config.friction;
        }
}

protected function movePlayer():void {
        _player.tempX = _player.x + _player.netForce.x;
        _player.tempY = _player.y + _player.netForce.y;
}
```

Next, the forces of gravity, drag, and friction are all applied to the player's force object. Then the player's position is updated to its *tempX* and *tempY* properties based on the current amount of force being applied. Before checking for collisions, however, we need to update the positions of all enemies in the game.

```
protected function moveEnemies():void {
        for each (var enemy:IEnemy in _enemies) {
                var motion:Vector3D = enemy.motion.clone();
                motion.scaleBy(_deltaTime);
                enemy.tempX = enemy.x + motion.x;
                enemy.tempY = enemy.y + motion.y;
```

```
//CHECK WALL COLLISIONS
var testReference:GridReference = getCollision
  Reference(enemy);
var enemyRect:Rectangle = enemy.hitArea.getRect
  (this);
var oldRect:Rectangle = enemyRect.clone();
enemyRect.offset(enemy.tempX - enemy.x, enemy.
  tempY - enemy.y);
for each (var wall:IWall in testReference.walls) {
        var wallRect:Rectangle = wall.getRect
          (this);
        var intersection:Rectangle = wallRect.
          intersection(enemyRect);
        if (!intersection.width || !intersection.
          height) continue;
        if (wallRect.right <= oldRect.left) {
          //WALL IS TO THE LEFT
                enemyRect.x += intersection.width;
                enemy.motion.x *= -1;
        }
        if (wallRect.left >= oldRect.right) {
          //WALL IS TO THE RIGHT
                enemyRect.x -= intersection.width;
                enemy.motion.x *= -1;
        }
}
enemy.tempX = enemy.x + enemyRect.x - oldRect.x;
enemy.tempY = enemy.y + enemyRect.y - oldRect.y;
        }
}
```

Each enemy has its own motion force, individually defined, and each one is applied separately. In the same process, because we're already looping through the list of enemies, we test for wall collisions using the *getCollisionReference* method we discussed earlier. If an enemy is hitting a wall, its direction is reversed. For this example, there is no accounting for physics on enemies, so gravity would not affect them. However, it would not be terribly difficult to add support for forces to be applied to enemies, as well as the player.

```
protected function checkPlayerCollisions():void {
      var testReference:GridReference = getCollisionReference
        (_player);
      //CHECK INDIVIDUAL SPRITES
      checkWalls(testReference);
      checkItems(testReference);
      checkEnemies(testReference);
}
```

The *checkPlayerCollisions* method actually consists of several methods that test against individual kinds of Sprites. The tests for each are very similar, but the results are handled differently in each case.

```
protected function checkWalls(testReference:GridReference):
  void {
      var testRect:Rectangle = _player.hitArea.getRect(this);
      var oldRect:Rectangle = testRect.clone();
      testRect.x += _player.tempX - _player.x;
      testRect.y += _player.tempY - _player.y;
      for each (var wall:IWall in testReference.walls) {

          var wallRect:Rectangle = wall.getRect(this);

          var intersection:Rectangle = wallRect.
            intersection(testRect);
          if (!intersection.width || !intersection.height)
            continue;

          if (wallRect.top >= oldRect.bottom) { //WALL IS
            BELOW
                  testRect.y -= intersection.height;
                    //OFFSET BY INTERSECTION HEIGHT
                  _player.netForce.y = 0;
          }

          intersection = wallRect.intersection(testRect);
          if (wallRect.right <= oldRect.left) { //WALL IS TO
            THE LEFT
                  testRect.x += intersection.width;
                  if (intersection.width) _player.netForce.
                    x = 0;
          }

          intersection = wallRect.intersection(testRect);
          if (wallRect.left >= oldRect.right) { //WALL IS TO
            THE RIGHT
                  testRect.x -= intersection.width;
                  if (intersection.width) _player.netForce.
                    x = 0;
          }

          intersection = wallRect.intersection(testRect);
          if (wallRect.bottom <= oldRect.top) { //WALL IS
            ABOVE
                  testRect.y += intersection.height;
                    //OFFSET BY INTERSECTION HEIGHT
```

```
                if (intersection.height) _player.
                    netForce.y = 0;
            }

            //ADJUST VALUES TO MATCH NEW RECT
            _player.tempX = _player.x + (testRect.x - oldRect.x);
            _player.tempY = _player.y + (testRect.y - oldRect.y);
        }
}
```

The wall collision check is the most involved, as it requires the most calculation and action on the engine's part. If the player is overlapping into a wall, then the player's position must be corrected relative to the wall. If no overlap occurs, the full check and adjustment is skipped to minimize calculations.

```
protected function checkItems(testReference:GridReference):
  void {
        var testRect:Rectangle = _player.hitArea.getRect(this);
        for each (var item:IItem in testReference.items) {
                var itemRect:Rectangle = item.hitArea.getRect(this);
                if (testRect.intersects(itemRect)) {
                        var itemPoint:Point = getGridPosition(item);
                        var gridReference:GridReference =
                          _collisionGrid.getGridReference
                          (itemPoint.x, itemPoint.y);
                        gridReference.removeItem(item);
                        _inventory.push(item);
                        _items.splice(_items.indexOf(item),1);
                        removeChild(item as DisplayObject);
                        var pe:PlatformerEvent = new Platformer
                          Event(PlatformerEvent.INVENTORY_
                          UPDATE,item.name);
                        dispatchEvent(pe);
                }
        }
}
```

The next type of Sprite to check against is items. A similar rectangle intersection test is performed, but no position adjustments are needed. If the player collides with an item, it should simply be removed from the screen and all collision lists, and added to the player's inventory.

```
protected function checkEnemies(testReference:GridReference):void {
        var testRect:Rectangle = _player.hitArea.getRect(this);
        for each (var enemy:IEnemy in testReference.enemies) {
                var enemyRect:Rectangle = enemy.hitArea.getRect
                  (this);
```

```
                    if (testRect.intersects(enemyRect)) {
                            var enemyPoint:Point = getGridPosition
                              (enemy);
                            var gridReference:GridReference =
                              _collisionGrid.getGridReference
                              (enemyPoint.x, enemyPoint.y);
                            gridReference.removeEnemy(enemy);
                            _enemies.splice(_enemies.indexOf(enemy),1);
                            removeChild(enemy as DisplayObject);
                            var pe:PlatformerEvent = new Platformer
                              Event(PlatformerEvent.PLAYER_DIE,
                              enemy.name);
                            dispatchEvent(pe);
                    }
            }
    }
```

The *checkEnemies* method is very similar to the item check, except that a different outcome occurs in the form of a PLAYER_ DIE event. The enemy is also removed from all lists.

```
protected function checkPortals():void {
        var testPoint:Point = getGridPosition(_player);
        var testReference:GridReference = _collisionGrid.
          getGridReference(testPoint.x, testPoint.y);
        if (testReference.portals.length) {
                var portal:IPortal = testReference.portals[0];
                var portalRect:Rectangle = portal.hitArea.getRect
                  (this);
                if (_player.hitArea.getRect(this).intersects
                  (portalRect)) {
                        var metRequirements:Boolean = true;
                        for each (var requirement:PortalRequirement
                          in portal.requirements) {
                                if (requirement.type ==
                                    PortalRequirement.INVENTORY) {
                        if (!checkInventory(requirement.name)) {
                            metRequirements = false;
                            break;
                        }
                                }
                        }
                        if (metRequirements) {
                                var pe:PlatformerEvent = new
                                    PlatformerEvent(PlatformerEvent.
                                    ENTER_PORTAL, portal.destination);
                                dispatchEvent(pe);
```

```
                    }
              }
        }
}

protected function checkInventory(name:String):Boolean {
        var found:Boolean = false;
        for (var i:int = 0; i < _inventory.length; i++) {
                if (_inventory[i].name == name) {
                        found = true;
                        break;
                }
        }
        return found;
}
```

When the use key is pressed, the engine runs the *checkPortals* method. This not only tests to see if the player is colliding with a portal, but it checks the portal's requirement list to make sure the player has completed the requirements for passing through the portal. The one type of requirement the engine currently accounts for is an inventory item. The *checkInventory* method is called to see if an item with the specified name is in the player's inventory. If it is, the requirement is met and the player is allowed access to the portal.

```
protected function render():void {
        if (!_gameRunning) return;
        _player.x = _player.tempX;
        _player.y = _player.tempY;
        _player.update();
        for each (var enemy:IEnemy in _enemies) {
                enemy.x = enemy.tempX;
                enemy.y = enemy.tempY;
                updateGridReference(enemy);
                enemy.update();
        }
}
//END GAME LOOP LOGIC
```

The final method of the engine class updates the player's and all enemies' *x* and *y* positions to their corrected temp values. It also calls the update method on both of these types of objects. This allows animation/graphic updates in those types of Sprites to occur regularly and without having to call any specific code. Now, we've discussed the entire engine package—next, we'll review the game classes that put this engine into action.

The Game Class

For this example, all of the classes associated with game code are in the "example" package, differentiating itself from the main engine. One of these classes is tied to the PlatformerExample.fla file, found with the Chapter 14 support files. The other classes are related to the assets, which we will examine shortly.

The PlatformerExample Class

The document class used for this example handles creation of the engine instances, as well as notification and progress messaging.

```
package example {

        import flash.display.Sprite;
        import flash.events.ProgressEvent;
        import flash.text.TextField;

        import com.flashgamebook.engines.platformer.*;
        import com.flashgamebook.engines.platformer.events.
          PlatformerEvent;

    public class PlatformerExample extends Sprite{

            public var pointsText:TextField;
            public var loadingText:TextField;
            public var percentText:TextField;
            public var gameOverText:TextField;

            private var _platformer:PlatformerEngine;
            private var _config:PlatformerConfig;
            private var _level:int = 0;
            private var _score:Number = 0;
            private var _previousScore:Number = 0;

            public function PlatformerExample() {
                    nextLevel();
            }

            public function nextLevel() {
                    _level++;
                    loadingText.visible = true;
                    percentText.text = "0%";
                    percentText.visible = true;
                    gameOverText.visible = false;
                    _platformer = new PlatformerEngine();
                    _config = new PlatformerConfig();
```

```
        _platformer.init(_config);
        _platformer.loadLevel("level"+_level+".
          xml");
        _platformer.addEventListener(Progress
          Event.PROGRESS, loadProgress, false, 0,
          true);
        _platformer.addEventListener(Platformer
          Event.ASSET_LOAD_COMPLETE, loadComplete,
          false, 0, true);
        _platformer.addEventListener(Platformer
          Event.ENTER_PORTAL, levelComplete,
          false, 0, true);
        _platformer.addEventListener(Platformer
          Event.PLAYER_DIE, playerDied, false, 0,
          true);
        _platformer.addEventListener(Platformer
          Event.INVENTORY_UPDATE, inventoryUpdate,
          false, 0, true);
}

private function loadProgress(e:ProgressEvent):
  void {
        percentText.text = Math.round(100 *
          (e.bytesLoaded/e.bytesTotal)) +"%";
}

private function loadComplete(e:PlatformerEvent):
  void {
        loadingText.visible = false;
        percentText.visible = false;
        addChild(_platformer);
        _platformer.startGame();
}

private function levelComplete(e:PlatformerEvent) {
        if (e.data = PortalDestinations.
          NEXT_LEVEL) {
              _platformer.stopGame();
              trace("GAME OVER:",_platformer.
                inventoryWorth,"points");
              _previousScore = _platformer.
                inventoryWorth;
              _platformer.destroy();
              removeChild(_platformer);
              nextLevel();
        }
}
```

```
private function playerDied(e:PlatformerEvent) {
        _platformer.stopGame();
        trace("GAME OVER: Player killed by",
          e.data);
        _platformer.destroy();
        removeChild(_platformer);
        gameOverText.visible = true;
}


private function inventoryUpdate(e:Platformer
  Event) {
        _score = _previousScore + _platformer.
          inventoryWorth;
        pointsText.text = _score.toString();
}
    }
}
```

The primary method behind this class is *nextLevel*. It creates the objects necessary to instantiate the game engine and start the loading process. If you test this SWF using the bandwidth profiler inside of Flash, you'll see that it accurately moves from 0 to 100% over the course of loading all the assets. The method also sets up listeners for the major game events, like the player dying, picking up items, and going through the end portal. Overall, this class is pretty bare bones—this is only slightly more than the bare minimum code required to get an instance of the PlatformerEngine up and running. Next, we'll look at the different asset classes, and how each one is tied to specific game assets.

The Asset Classes

The PlatformerEngine only makes use of interfaces to manipulate the Sprites used in the game. In order for us to build assets for the game, we must create classes that implement those interfaces for each type of object. If you look in the example package, you'll notice that each of the classes besides the main document file map to one of the five types of interfaces in the engine: player, enemy, item, wall, and portal. Let's examine how each of these classes implements the appropriate interface. Because we're going for a minimalist implementation here, these classes are pretty simple and only include the bare essentials to meet the requirements of the interfaces.

The Player Class

This class will be used to implement the IPlayer interface.

```actionscript
package example {

    import com.flashgamebook.engines.platformer.sprites.
      IPlayer;
    import flash.display.Sprite;
    import flash.geom.Vector3D;

    public class Player extends Sprite implements IPlayer {

        private var _netForce:Vector3D = new Vector3D();
        private var _tempX:Number = 0;
        private var _tempY:Number = 0;

        public function get netForce():Vector3D {
            return _netForce;
        }

        public function set netForce(value:Vector3D):void {
            _netForce = value;
        }

        public function get isJumping():Boolean {
            if (_netForce.y < 0) return true;
            return false;
        }

        public function set isJumping(value:Boolean):void {
        }

        public function get isFalling():Boolean {
            if (_netForce.y > 0) return true;
            return false;
        }

        public function set isFalling(value:Boolean):void {
        }

        public function get tempX():Number {
            return _tempX;
        }

        public function set tempX(value:Number):void {
            _tempX = value;
        }

        public function get tempY():Number {
            return _tempY;
```

```
                }

                public function set tempY(value:Number):void {
                        _tempY = value;
                }

                public function update():void {

                }

                override public function get hitArea():Sprite {
                        return this;
                }
        }
}
```

Note that the hitArea accessor can be overridden to return any Sprite you wanted to use as the rectangle for collision testing. In this case, we're just using the bounding box of the Sprite itself.

The Enemy Class

This class implements the IEnemy interface.

```
package example {

        import com.flashgamebook.engines.platformer.sprites.
          IEnemy;
        import com.flashgamebook.engines.platformer.
          GridReference;
        import flash.display.Sprite;
        import flash.geom.Vector3D;

        public class Enemy extends Sprite implements IEnemy {

                private var _motion:Vector3D = new Vector3D(-20);
                private var _tempX:Number;
                private var _tempY:Number;
                private var _gridReference:GridReference;

                public function get tempX():Number {
                        return _tempX;
                }

                public function set tempX(value:Number):void {
                        _tempX = value;
                }
```

```
public function get tempY():Number {
        return _tempY;
}

public function set tempY(value:Number):void {
        _tempY = value;
}

public function get motion():Vector3D {
        return _motion;
}

public function get receivesForces():Boolean {
        return false;
}

public function get gridReference():GridReference {
        return _gridReference;
}

public function set gridReference(value:Grid
  Reference):void {
        _gridReference = value;
}

public function update():void {

}

override public function get hitArea():Sprite {
        return this;
}
    }
}
```

There is one aspect of note in this implementation; the motion vector is entirely arbitrary. Because this does not affect the engine code, we can set the enemy's speed to any value we want.

The Item Class

This class implements the IItem interface.

```
package example {

    import com.flashgamebook.engines.platformer.sprites.
      IItem;
```

```
import flash.display.Sprite;

public class Item extends Sprite implements IItem {

        private var _points:Number;
        private var _type:String;

        public function get points():Number {
                return _points;
        }

        public function set points(value:Number):void {
                _points = value;
        }

        public function get type():String {
                return _type;
        }

        public function set type(value:String):void {
                _type = value;
        }

        public function pickUp():void {

        }

        override public function get hitArea():Sprite {
                return this;
        }
    }
}
```

In another implementation of this engine, the *pickUp* method could be used to play some type of animation or play a sound.

The Portal Class and Wall Class

These classes implement the IPortal and IWall interfaces.

```
package example {

        import com.flashgamebook.engines.platformer.sprites.
          IPortal;
        import flash.display.Sprite;

        public class Portal extends Sprite implements IPortal {

                private var _requirements:Array = new Array();
                private var _destination:String;
```

```
public function get requirements():Array {
        if (!_requirements) _requirements = new
          Array();
        return _requirements;
}

public function set requirements(value:Array):
  void {
        requirements = value;
}

public function get destination():String {
        return _destination;
}

public function set destination(value:String):
  void {
        _destination = value;
}

override public function get hitArea():Sprite {
        return this;
}
    }
}

package example {

    import com.flashgamebook.engines.platformer.sprites.
      IWall;
    import flash.display.Sprite;

    public class Wall extends Sprite implements IWall {

        public function Wall() {
        }
    }
}
```

Even though it does nothing, the Wall class exists to fulfill the requirement of an IWall implementation. Without it, we could not substitute this class for instances in which an IWall is required.

The Assets

We've now discussed every class in play throughout this game. Whew! Give yourself a pat on the back for having slogged through it all. Now, crack open the player.fla file in the main

Chapter 14 examples folder. We'll see how these classes are implemented.

Once you open the FLA file (and any of the other asset FLAs, for that matter), you'll notice one thing right off the bat: there is nothing on the Stage. All of these assets are being exported directly from the library with linkages. If you right-click on the Player Sprite in the library and select properties, then you'll see a dialog like Fig. 14.3.

This Player Sprite is nothing more than a green square, and it uses the Player class file in the example package as its *base* class from which it derives a new class, simply called "Player" (with no package association). The reason for this structure is so the level XML does not have to directly associate itself with a particular package implementation. If you open any of the other asset files—environment.fla, for example—you'll see that each asset is set up in a similar fashion. Figure 14.4 reflects this.

Once each of these individual SWFs is compiled, they can be loaded into the engine and have all their class definitions recognized. Running the main PlatformerExample SWF should look like Fig. 14.5. Doesn't it bring back that classic NES nostalgia?

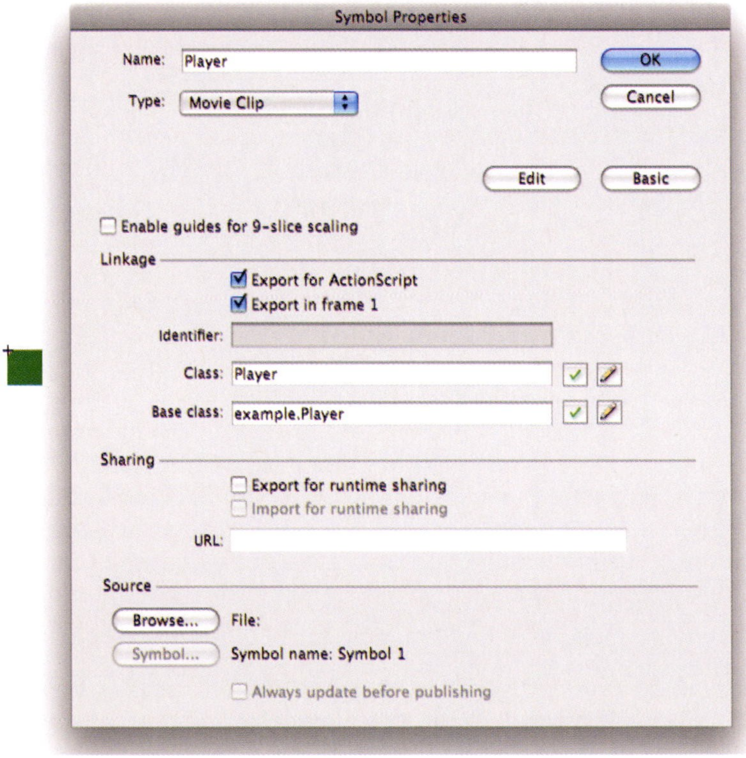

Figure 14.3 For each asset, the base class points to the actual code implementation, and the class field points to a unique, unpackaged name that matches the level XML.

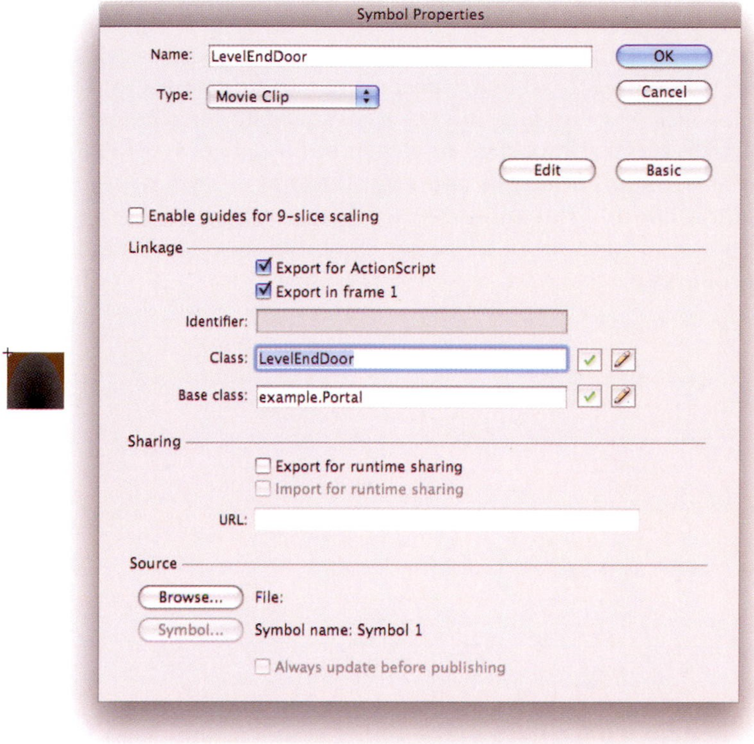

Figure 14.4 The level-end portal has the name LevelEndDoor, but is an instance of the Portal class.

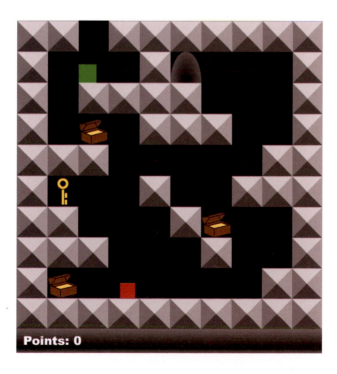

Figure 14.5 The completed engine implementation, running level1.xml.

Taking It Further

There is a lot more that is possible with this game engine, from making it scroll to adding a second player to creating more types of enemies and items. Platformers can have an obscene number of features, and it's important to remember that high-end platformers like Little Big Planet for the Playstation 3 or any of the recent Mario games by Nintendo have set the bar very high. If you build a platformer in Flash, make sure it differentiates itself in some way from the pack.

15

MARBLE RUNNER: OUR FIRST MOBILE GAME

Up to this point in this book, almost all the examples I've shown are geared toward Flash running in a browser on a desktop PC. Shortly after the release of the first edition of this book, Adobe announced that Flash CS5 would be able to export native iOS applications and, later, Android applications using a forthcoming version of AIR (Adobe's runtime for desktop deployment). Although between that announcement and the present, there has been a great deal of drama surrounding Flash on mobile devices, as of this writing both of those plans have come to pass. Using Flash CS5 (and CS5.5), you can now deploy mobile applications for iOS (iPhone, iPod Touch, and iPad) and Android devices. In this chapter and in Chapter 16, I'll explore building games for both platforms, including best practices, resource management, and deployment. If you need a primer on how to set up the necessary developer accounts and SDKs associated with these platforms, check out the online bonus chapter "Introduction to Mobile Development" on www.flashgamebook.com.

This chapter will be split into two parts. In the first part, we'll look at creating a simple demo application and some of the best practices associated with mobile development for iOS. In the second part, we'll build our first mobile game for the iPhone based around the accelerometer. In Chapter 16, we'll explore Android development and the differences in development for that platform, which is far less restrictive.

Part 1: Best Practices for iOS Games

Mobile development has and will probably always require a different approach from desktop development. In addition, to have a smaller screen, the computing resources are simply much more limited. In the case of iPhone or iPod Touch, you can expect it to have about one-tenth the processing power of the average desktop computer. Memory is also limited and must be utilized carefully. Fear not, however; in this chapter, we'll examine how best to work within these limitations and how some of these practices will help enforce more disciplined programming when you switch back to desktop applications. We'll start by looking at features of Flash you should use sparingly or just avoid altogether when creating games for iOS, as well as those APIs that simply do not exist on that platform. Notice that I said "games"—some of these features might make sense in a non-performance-driven productivity application, but that's not what we're covering in this book. Also remember that few of these rules are hard and fast—they're all just factors to consider and weigh when making game design decisions. After covering the "gray" functionality areas, we'll look at some general guidelines and techniques to follow while coding, which will help get the absolute best performance out of your iOS device. Adobe has done a great job of making sure almost all of the features of the Flash Player are available in iOS applications produced by Flash CS5. However, despite this, there are some features that are left untouched, particularly for game development. This is mainly due to the fact that many of the APIs in Flash are memory and CPU intensive, at least by mobile standards. In this section, we'll cover what you should avoid while developing games.

Filters (and PixelBender)

Ever since they were added in Flash Player 8, the various real-time filter effects such as blurs, glows, and drop shadows have saved a lot of time for designers and developers on faking or pre-applying these effects to images in external applications such as Photoshop. To a less common extent, features such as the DisplacementMap and Convolution filters allowed for distortion effects completely controllable by code. Filters are a great feature of Flash and very easy to implement. However, they are also very costly in terms of system resources. In a desktop application on a computer, this cost is pretty minimal in the grand scheme of all the other running processes, particularly on computers that have advanced video cards. On iOS, it is another story. Processing these filters and keeping them updated in real time is very taxing rendering and brings performance down very quickly with only a couple of filters running at a time. Adobe has even recommended against their use for any type of application in which performance is vital.

This is not to say that a savvy developer couldn't still make use of a filter or two when judiciously applied. The most important factor to consider is *when* you apply the filter. One way to use a filter is on Bitmap objects, or more specifically, on the BitmapData inside them. If you were using Bitmaps for objects within a game, and you needed a filter applied that would persist until the object was removed (such as, say, a drop shadow), you could call the *applyFilter* method on the BitmapData to render the filter effect into the image itself (and thus eliminating the repeat cost of rendering the effect over and over again). This could potentially save file size on the images used and would provide some level of runtime flexibility to be able to change the values of the filter prior to applying it. Once again, it's important to emphasize that this is a costly process on iOS, so if this was a feature you planned to implement, you would want to perform these operations at the onset of a level or gameplay session to avoid noticeable stuttering in your game.

On a related note, filters created with PixelBender (or ShaderFilters) are not supported in iOS-exported Flash applications. This has to do with the way that the Shaders are applied, but even if they were supported, they would come with even stronger performance caveats and warnings. This is important to consider if you're attempting to port an existing Flash game to iOS; if your game mechanic relies heavily on Shaders, you'll need to either find a way to recreate the effect another way or change the functionality completely.

Vector Shapes (and Shape Tweens)

The ability to create file-size efficient and clean vector graphics has been a hallmark of Flash since the very beginning. Like filters, they are another core feature of the Flash Player that designers and developers make use of frequently. Unfortunately, like filters, they come with fairly substantial overhead cost when the renderer has to redraw the screen, particularly when dealing with complex shapes. This cost is further multiplied when performing shape tweens (known as MorphShapes in ActionScript), so these should be avoided altogether.

In general, it's a good idea to stick with bitmaps as much as possible when creating games for iOS devices. They are the fastest type of display object for the rendered to process, and with proper compression the artwork for a game should not get out of hand very quickly in terms of file size. Thanks to the new CS5.5 Export as Bitmap option we looked at in Chapter 6, you can now set some of your vector instances to rasterize on compile. That said, there are times when it is okay to use vector graphics without incurring too great a resource load. When determining whether to use vector art for an element in your game, consider the following questions:

- Will the art remain static?
- Can I group multiple vector elements together inside a single DisplayObject?
- Is the art complex (a square or circle vs. a custom-drawn character)?

If the answer to these questions is yes, then you can probably use the vector elements without consequence by simply exporting them as bitmaps or caching them to the GPU first. Bitmap/GPU caching is the process of storing a "snapshot" of a graphical element in memory on the video card of the device, thereby not requiring the CPU to render it every frame. If the art is for an animation sequence (and therefore not static), such as a character running or an explosion, it is not going to be a good candidate to keep in vector graphics. It is better for this type of art be imported as a bitmap sequence because caching relies on the content of a DisplayObject not changing over time to recognize a savings in resources. We'll look at a couple of examples of bitmap caching a little later in this chapter.

Text

Text in Flash on iOS falls along similar lines as vector shapes. This is because static text (text that is baked into the SWF rather than editable or changeable at runtime) is actually converted to vector shapes by the Flash compiler when creating a SWF file. All the same rules therefore apply to static text as to vector shapes. If you need the flexibility of editable text in the Flash IDE (and really, who doesn't?), try to find a way to group the text into DisplayObjects that can then be cached to the GPU. If the text is heavily treated/processed in some way (with multiple filters, for instance), or uses a very complex, detailed font, it can still be advisable to first flatten the text into a bitmap in a program like Fireworks or Photoshop.

Dynamic text (or in fringe cases, Input text) is a somewhat different beast. Unless you're treating every element in your game iconically or graphically, at some point you'll need some kind of text, so it's important that you use it as carefully as possible. If you're using a text field to display some type of changing, in-game information, like a score or number of lives, there is really nothing to be gained by caching it. In this case, it's best to pick a font that has a relatively simple character set or a system font such as Arial or Verdana. Sometimes fonts such as these (which are often the bane of designers with typography experience) are not stylistically appropriate for the task at hand, so this is an area for aesthetic and functional compromise. In some scenarios, there might be a limited number of values a text field can have, such as when using words instead of numbers to display a particular aspect of a game. For instance, if you had a text field in your interface that had the optional values of High, Medium, and Low, you could "bake" this text either as cached static text or as a pre-rendered bitmap and simply swap out the appropriate DisplayObject at a given moment. This limits the number of characters that must be embedded from a font and improves performance, but this technique really has to be applied on a case-by-case basis. Sometimes, such as when dealing with numeric values that have far too many possible combinations, it is simply not feasible to use anything other than a standard text field. However, if your approach is to use as few of these as possible, you should find a good balance between flexibility and optimization.

Motion Tweens

Although Adobe does not recommend against it, I have found through tests that the new Motion Tweens introduced in Flash CS4 and Flash Player 10 are not especially efficient for use on iOS devices. Unlike the classic tweens of previous versions, which were ultimately converted to keyframe animations on export, the new Motion Tweens are converted into code, utilizing a number of classes in the fl.motion package. As of this writing, they appear to use enough overhead to make the very animations they are created to execute choppy. At some point in a future version, the collective efforts of Apple to improve the iPhone and Adobe to improve their export process from Flash may yield a Motion Tween that will run fine in that environment. It is best to stick with either a keyframed animation or a basic script-based tweening package such as TweenLite.

The Drawing API, Masks, and Blends

Although it does not come up often in game development, Adobe recommends avoiding the entire drawing API for runtime creation of vector shapes. Slightly more prevalent in games are masks and use of blend modes for certain graphical effects. It is best to avoid using them altogether. If they are absolutely necessary to achieve a visual effect, they should be handled the same way as filters; place them inside a DisplayObject, cache them to the GPU, and then leave them alone.

Runtime Loaded SWFs

A common technique in Flash development is to spread content out over a number of SWFs, so as to not incur the entire load of a site or game up front when streaming over the Internet. It is less common in smaller games, where it makes sense to bundle everything together, but in larger games that have a lot of artwork and audio, it is a better practice to deploy across multiple files. Not only does this mean that content is only downloaded when needed, but it makes multideveloper projects easier by clearly demarcating one code base from another. Unfortunately, this ability is not available in Flash applications created for iOS. This is because, as mentioned in online chapter Introduction to Mobile Development, all of the ActionScript code inside an iOS application is precompiled rather than interpreted at runtime. Because there is, in fact, no runtime interpreter or compiler, any code loaded in from an external SWF is ignored. This means larger games that work on the Web in multiple pieces will need to be rearchitected to work as a single file. Let me be clear though; this does not preclude loading individual assets such as sounds, images, or text data from external sources; this still works fine and in the same manner as the standard Flash Player. It simply means that any and all classes that need to be available to a game must be compiled up front into the single SWF.

The GPU Is Here to Help

Now that we've covered what to avoid or limit when doing iOS development, let's look at one huge improvement Adobe has made to the display list to increase performance. When running on the device, all DisplayObjects now have a new property called *cacheAsBitmapMatrix*. It is meant to work in conjunction with the *cacheAsBitmap* option that has been available since Flash 8. The matrix of a DisplayObject is a single-object representation of all the visual transformations that are being applied to it, such as translation (*x* and *y* coordinates), rotation, and scaling. You can learn more about the matrix property of DisplayObjects in Adobe's ActionScript reference. By assigning a matrix object to the *cacheAsBitmapMatrix* property of a DisplayObject, Flash will use this information to store a bitmap version of the object on the device's graphics card. In essence, this is how OpenGL works in the traditional iOS development workflow using XCode and Objective-C. This means that all of the energy spent compositing that DisplayObject into the scene and rendering it is offloaded from the CPU to the GPU, freeing up memory and horsepower to be used on other things such as code execution.

The most advantageous new behavior is that unlike just using *cacheAsBitmap*, the cached image data is not limited to just *x* and *y* translations. You can rotate, scale, and skew any object with this matrix, and Flash will simply tell the GPU to perform those transformations. This feature is specifically for use with objects you only intend to work with in 2D space. For the 3D transformations that we looked at in Chapter 7, Flash will automatically perform this GPU caching if it is enabled in the Publish Settings. This feature is especially important for game development, where it is often necessary to have several objects on screen at once, many of them in motion. The initial comparison simulations Adobe released showed huge performance gains by using this new feature, and it will likely be the best antidote available to bottlenecks on iOS devices (and even Android ones as well).

Not Without Its Limits

Before you close this book and think bitmap caching has solved all of the performance challenges, let's examine its limitations. The resources on the GPU are also limited, so you shouldn't exceed a total of roughly four million pixels of cached data, which is roughly 26 full, third-generation iPhone screens worth of data. This should be more than enough space for your average single-screen puzzle or strategy game, but it can definitely become an issue if you've got scrolling backgrounds or many animated Sprites. Adobe also recommends limiting the size of any individually cached element to 1020 × 1020 pixels or less—a little over one million pixels or ¼ of the total cache. This is due to actual hardware limitations on iOS devices.

The memory limitation means you'll have to be shrewd about those elements you choose to cache, but your approach should either make extensive use of the feature or not at all. When exporting your application, you will have to select whether it will use CPU or GPU compositing of display objects. Using the GPU option and caching only an image or two in your entire application will actually *slow down* the performance. This is because the CPU has to send all of the noncached objects up to the GPU to be rendered every frame—*lots* of data. If your game is very simple and it only makes sense to cache a handful of elements, you very well might be better off letting the CPU do all the works. As always, once you are done with a DisplayObject, be sure it is properly set for garbage collection so that memory will get freed up for something else. This means deleting all references to it and purging it from the Stage. We'll look in depth at a practical example of caching data to the GPU shortly.

Code Matters, Too

In desktop/web-targeted Flash development, the overhead generated by ActionScript code is not typically a concern. Graphical considerations (size of elements on Stage, rendering performance, etc.) will almost always be the key bottlenecks to overcome or circumvent. This is largely due to the very fast virtual machine that interprets and compiles AS3 at runtime and the substantial processors in most modern computers. Although there are certainly optimizations all programmers can make to get extra performance out of their code, it is not a high priority except in extremely complex applications.

The same cannot be said for ActionScript running on iOS devices. This is because the code is not compiled or interpreted at runtime like in the Flash Player. As I mentioned earlier, it is compiled ahead-of-time (AOT) into iOS machine code along with the standard Flash libraries. In this entirely different process, certain elements of ActionScript are slower and performance of code becomes essential to maintaining responsiveness and a decent frame rate in your games. We'll now look at the best practices to follow when coding games for the iPhone.

Declare Your Types

This first and most basic practice should be familiar to anyone who has read any programming books (or Chapter 4 of this book), but the importance of it is magnified in Flash on the iPhone. When you declare a variable to be of a specific type, you are allocating a specific amount of memory for that object, as well as keeping the runtime code from having to look up the variable in a table in memory.

```
var myString:String = "something"; //CORRECT
var myUnknown = 5; //INCORRECT, AND YOU SHOULD BE ASHAMED
```

This also applies to method signatures—always be sure to specify the types of parameters a method accepts, as well as a return type. Avoid this use of dynamic arguments except when critically necessary.

```
//GOOD PRACTICE
private function doSomething(arg1:int, arg2:String):void
//BAD PRACTICE
private function doSomething(...args)
```

While this seems elementary, it makes a huge difference to both the compiler and the application at runtime. Frankly, if you aren't already typing your variables in AS3, you really should be ashamed anyway.

Use Static Properties and Functions

When a member variable or function of a class is *static*, only one instance of it is ever created for the class. Many of the variables and methods used by a class will only make sense within the context of a specific instance of that class, but any values that are constant across all instances should become static. Here are a couple of examples:

```
private static const MAX_SPEED:int = 10;
private static const MAX_AMMO:int = 20;
private var _health:int = 100;
```

Assume the three lines above were part of an Enemy class for a game. The first two, MAX_SPEED and MAX_AMMO, are not going to change per Enemy instance; they are universal across all Enemies, so they should be marked as *static*. The third value, health, is specific to each Enemy, so it should be remain instance based. The same applies to methods as well. Consider these two methods:

```
public function getScore():int;
public static function getHighScore():int;
```

If you create a new instance of a game class for each session of play, it might have individual values, such as the player's score. In this case, it makes sense to have a method for retrieving that specific score from a specific game instance. However, in the case of the highest score achieved over multiple sessions of a game, it makes more sense to store this value in a static variable and retrieve it from a static method.

Make Final Your Answer

Another seemingly trivial optimization that can be made to your classes and methods is to mark them with the *final* keyword. When a method or class is *final*, it cannot be extended through a subclass, and the compiled code that is generated requires less lookups in memory to execute the method. In fact, the compiler is smart enough to make decisions about how to generate the final method code based on how many times the method is called and its size. If you were using a base game engine that is extended for multiple applications, it wouldn't be practical to declare it as final. However, all of the *application-specific* classes (those that are not generic and are only related to the application at hand) for a game should easily be marked as final. Even when a class might need to be extended and you don't want to mark it final, there are often individual methods that would make sense to "finalize"—every little bit helps.

Recycle, Both In Your Code and In Your Home

The process of creating and destroying objects in memory is taxing for the iPhone (or any limited-resource mobile device). Some types of games, such as modern-day Asteroids™ knockoffs, create numerous objects on the Stage and then proceed to destroy them and create new ones. This technique is very common in game development, and as long as guidelines for proper garbage collection are followed, it is not a noticeable performance hit until the number of objects being created and destroyed gets into the thousands at a time. iOS devices have a much lower tolerance for that much creation and destruction, so we want to limit these processes in our code as much as possible. We can't really do so much about the initial creation step—the objects have got to get there somehow. However, an alternative to deletion (and thus the creation of new objects) is to re-use or "recycle" them.

Returning to the example of Asteroids, imagine that there are never more than 10 of the aforementioned space rocks on screen at any given time. According to the rules of that game, every time you shoot a full-size asteroid, two to four smaller ones are created. Using the standard creation or deletion process, this will mean that if the player destroys all of the asteroids successfully, the game will have generated and garbage collected 40 objects (or more if the smaller asteroids also split apart). While this may not seem like much in the grand scheme, keep in mind that we are working in a constrained mobile environment and this example scales to much larger projects as well. If you used a recycling process, once an asteroid was "destroyed" by the player, it would have some sort of *reset* method called on it that would kill any processes and return it to the state it was in just after creation. This prevents the object from garbage collecting, thereby foregoing the deletion phase. In the example later in this chapter, we'll use object recycling to increase performance and decrease memory usage.

Avoid Extremely Large Frameworks and Libraries

There are numerous open- and closed-source frameworks and code libraries for helping Flash developers to write their code faster. These can range from text formatting utilities to encryption libraries to design pattern frameworks (such as pureMVC, for example). Some developers rely on these resources regularly for speeding up their jobs. Many of these libraries are large and contain many thousands of lines of code and potentially hundreds of methods. In the standard Flash Player, only methods that are called are compiled into machine code (using the JIT compiler). This means any methods that are not used are never allocated memory beyond the tiny bytecode that is compiled into the SWF. In the AOT compilation process for the iPhone, Flash must assume that every function may potentially be called during the course of an application, so it has to compile *all* of them into machine code. This means there is a considerable increase in file size of the final application, as well as a moderate increase in the amount of memory needed to store all of the code (that might not even be called at runtime).

Whenever possible, avoid using libraries from which you call only a handful of methods. A good example of this might be any number of the utility packages for formatting strings and text for display. Say you use it for a convenient method to properly insert commas into large numbers (meaning 1000 becomes 1,000) for readability. If the class has, say, nine other methods for performing different operations and you are only using the one method, consider copying and pasting that method into your own code. That will result in machine code one-tenth the size it could have been and more memory for essential code that is used. This is not a hard-and-fast rule—some libraries are efficient about componentizing themselves so that only the classes that you need active for your application are included; the TweenLite/TweenMax animation platform by Jack Doyle is a great example of this architecture. In general, however, be mindful of how much code ends up in your final SWF—it *does* matter.

TOO BIG WILL FAIL TO BE DOWNLOADED

As of this writing, Apple has a 20-MB limit on the size of the application that can be downloaded to an iOS device over a carrier's 3G network. This means applications and games larger than 20 MB must be downloaded either through iTunes or over a Wi-Fi connection. While this probably isn't a deal breaker for most of the people, if you're right at or just over this threshold with your app, cleaning up unused code means you'll get that much more exposure from customers who can download it from anywhere.

Keep Your Display List Shallow

While this doesn't come up too often in game development, another way to increase performance of the renderer is to keep your display list from branching too deeply. Depending on the type of game you are creating, this might have extensive implications or none at all. Just keep in mind that every layer deeper you go into the display list increases rendering and processing time.

Don't Use Events Where You Can Easily Use Functions

Function calls require less memory than using the event model hierarchy, especially when using bubble or capture events that must traverse the display list. This is not to suggest that the event model should be thrown out altogether—events are still required for listening for input and for any number of other common ActionScript tasks such as ENTER_FRAME loops, and individual events used wisely help maintain flexibility for re-purposing code. However, there are some cases in which a method would work just as well and will decrease overhead. This is particularly helpful for events that would otherwise get dispatched over and over again in a game loop. Perhaps the enemy Sprites in a game broadcast information about themselves repeatedly throughout gameplay. Rather than dispatching an event every time, a method could be passed to each enemy Sprite to call on their recipients. Consider the following two examples:

```
//EXAMPLE #1
//DISPATCHES AN EVENT EVERY FRAME
```

```
private function onEnterFrame(e:Event):void
{
        dispatchEvent(new CustomEvent(CustomEvent.UPDATE));
}


//EXAMPLE #2
//CALLBACK GETS SET THROUGH A PUBLIC ACCESSOR
private var _updateCallback:Function;
public function set updateCallback(value:Function):void
{
        _updateCallback = value;
}
//ENTER FRAME HANDLER CALLS METHOD INSTEAD OF DISPATCHING EVENT
private function onEnterFrame(e:Event):void
{
        _updateCallback(someData);
}
```

The first example makes use of an event dispatched every single frame, which is taxing. Instead, if there is only one recipient for the update event, it is more efficient to simply call a method. As mentioned earlier regarding the depth of display list, this is not likely to be a huge issue for games, but it is an area you can look to for optimization if you find the performance of your application a little lacking.

A Question of Balance: Inheritance versus Interfaces

As you've no doubt seen throughout this book, one of the key elements to writing modular, re-usable code is to make use of interfaces. The heavy usage of these interfaces can be seen in examples in Chapters 13 and 14. Because of the AOT compiler for iOS and how it allocates memory for each method, interfaces perform more slowly than directly referring to an instance of a class. In other words, see the below example:

```
protected var _boardImage:ISourceImage;
var imageData:Vector.<BitmapData> = _boardImage.getImages
  (_rows, _columns);
```

would perform more slowly than this:

```
protected var _boardImage:SourceImage;
var imageData:Vector.<BitmapData> = _boardImage.getImages
  (_rows, _columns);
```

This is because an interface just represents how something works rather than the thing by itself, Flash always has to look up what object is representing the interface and where the actual method is in memory. This is actually true of the regular desktop Flash Player as well, but its impact is barely felt in that environment, if at all. However, on an iOS device, frequent memory lookups during the course of a performance-intensive application like a game can result in degradation. In the case of the previous examples, because the methods in question are called pretty infrequently over the course of the application, it would not have a noticeable impact on performance. However, the other interface mentioned, IGamePiece, has methods that are called quite often during the game, so it might eventually become necessary to reference those classes directly. Ultimately, like with so many elements of Flash, it comes down to striking a balance between performance and practicality. Sometimes the performance of your game has to come before following every best practice to a tee.

A Real-World Example

We'll now look at a very simple program example that could feasibly be used in a game and see how it performs when utilizing bitmap caching. In the spirit of the classic example I've referenced a number of times in this chapter, it will consist of several "space rocks" floating across a slowly tiling background. It will also demonstrate the use of object recycling to keep the memory footprint as low as possible, as well as a utility to measure frame rate performance without any tricky debugging.

The XFL Document

You can find the XFL file for this application in the Chapter 15 examples folder. If you open the document, you'll find a library with just five items in it: two images, two Sprite symbols, and a component. The main timeline does not have any object placed on it other than an instance of the FrameRate Profiler component (for ease of setting the component parameters). We'll return to this component shortly—for now let's jump into the code. I'll start with the classes for the two Sprites as the document class references them later and it will be helpful to know how it works.

Space.as

This class is extremely simple as it just contains the code needed to update its position based on a constant value. This code could arguably exist in the main document class instead, but this would provide the flexibility to add more functionality later and keep the main class from getting cluttered.

```
public class Space extends Sprite
{

        private static const SCROLL_SPEED:Number = 20;
        //PIXELS PER SECOND

        private var _previousTime:int = 0;
        private var _deltaTime:Number = 0;

        public function Space()
        {
                cacheAsBitmap = true;
        }

        public function update():void
        {
                if (_previousTime)
                {
                        _deltaTime = (getTimer() - _previousTime)/1000;
                        x -= SCROLL_SPEED * _deltaTime;
                }
                _previousTime = getTimer();
        }

}
```

Since this Sprite is actually the same smaller image tiled three times (so that it can appears to seamlessly stretch on forever), the constructor caches the whole object as a bitmap so that the GPU can render it more quickly. Since we won't be doing anything but *translation* (*x* and *y* movements), there's no need to use *cacheAs-BitmapMatrix* just yet. The update method simply detects the amount of time that has passed since it was last called and moves itself the appropriate distance based on the constant scrolling speed of 20 pixels per second. In a more robust application, it would be wise to store separate values for *x* and *y* movements so as to be able to tile the image in any direction. For now, this will suffice.

Rock.as

The Rock class will handle creation of our floating debris and the randomization of size and speed, which will give this example a dynamic feel. Here, we will see the use of *cacheAsBitmapMatrix* and object recycling.

```
public class Rock extends Sprite
{
```

```
private static const MOVEMENT_SPEED_MAX:Number = 100;
//PIXELS PER SECOND
private static const MOVEMENT_SPEED_MIN:Number = 50;
//PIXELS PER SECOND
private static const ROTATION_SPEED_MAX:Number = 30;
//DEGREES PER SECOND
private static const ROTATION_SPEED_MIN:Number = -20;
//DEGREES PER SECOND

private static var _availableRocks:Vector.<Rock> = new
    Vector.<Rock>();

private var _movementSpeed:Number = 0;
private var _rotationSpeed:Number = 0;
private var _previousTime:int = 0;
private var _deltaTime:Number = 0;

public function Rock()
{
        init();
}

private function init():void
{

        var scaleRand:Number = Math.random();
        scaleX = scaleY = scaleRand;
        transform.colorTransform = new ColorTransform
          (scaleRand, scaleRand, scaleRand);
        _movementSpeed = (MOVEMENT_SPEED_MAX - MOVEMENT_
          SPEED_MIN) * Math.random() + MOVEMENT_SPEED_MIN;
        _rotationSpeed = (ROTATION_SPEED_MAX - ROTATION_
          SPEED_MIN) * Math.random() + ROTATION_SPEED_MIN;
        cacheAsBitmapMatrix = new Matrix();

}
```

The rocks will move and rotate at different random values, so
we define constants for the lower and upper limits of those ranges.
There is also a static Vector that we will keep track of every
instance of the Rock class that is created. The constructor does
nothing more than call the *init* method. This is one of the key components to designing objects to be recycled; since you can't call the
constructor on an object more than once, you need a way to dele-
gate any initialization to a method you can call whenever you
need. In the *init* function, a random value for the scale of the rock
is generated and also applied in a ColorTransform object. This will
create the appearance that smaller rocks are further away by tinting

them darker than larger ones. Values for movement speed and rotation speed are then calculated based on the minimum and maximum settings we observed earlier. Finally, the rock is cached to the GPU as the last step in the process—we do this finally so that the GPU doesn't have to draw it multiple times due to the changes we've made to its scale and color transform. Now, whenever this Rock is manipulated on the Stage, its rendering will be handled solely by the graphics processor on the device.

```
public function reset():void
{
        scaleX = scaleY = 1;
        transform.colorTransform = new ColorTransform();
        _movementSpeed = 0;
        _rotationSpeed = 0;
        _previousTime = 0;
        _availableRocks.push(this);
        cacheAsBitmapMatrix = null;
}
```

Acting as a counter to the *init* method, the class also has a *reset* method that can be called to restore all of the key values of the class to their default states. When other classes (specifically the document class) are done using this instance, they will call this method to tag it for recycling. Note that the Rock adds itself to the static Vector list *_avaialbleRocks*. This will become important in the next method we examine.

```
public static function getRock():Rock
{
        if (_availableRocks.length)
        {
                var rock:Rock = _availableRocks.pop();
                rock.init();
                return rock;
        }
        else
        {
                return new Rock();
        }
}
```

The static *getRock* method acts as the crux of the recycling process. Instead of having Rocks get created by calling the constructor (which will ultimately result in an untracked number of rock instances), this method will check to see if there are any dormant rock instances available which could be re-used. Once a rock has become inactive using the *reset* method, it is added to the pool of available instances. If there are any items in this list, *getRock* plucks the object off the end of the Vector, reinitializes it (since it's not being constructed again), and returns it. If the list is empty (like at the start of the application), a new rock is created and returned instead. In a moment, we'll see how this works in practice to eliminate unnecessary garbage collection.

```
public function update():void
{
        if (_previousTime)
        {
                _deltaTime = (getTimer() - _previousTime)/1000;
                rotation += _deltaTime * _rotationSpeed;
                x += _deltaTime * _movementSpeed;
        }
        _previousTime = getTimer();
}
```

The final method in the class is an *update* method, which will look very similar to the one in the Space class. It has the additional *rotation* property set, which will make the rocks spin as they move.

SpaceRocks.as: The Document Class

The main document class will drive this example since it is more of a technical demonstration than anything else. It will be responsible for placing all of the objects on screen, sending them update events, and removing those that are no longer needed.

```
public class SpaceRocks extends Sprite
{
        public static const ROCK_CREATION_INTERVAL:Number = 800;
        //MILLISECONDS
        private var _rockList:Dictionary = new Dictionary(true);
        private var _rockTimer:Timer;
        private var _space:Space;

        public function SpaceRocks()
        {
                //SETUP EVENT LISTENER
                addEventListener(Event.ENTER_FRAME, onEnterFrame,
                  false, 0, true);
                //CREATE SPACE
                _space = new Space();
                addChildAt(_space, 0);
                //SETUP ROCK CREATION TIMER
                _rockTimer = new Timer(ROCK_CREATION_INTERVAL);
                _rockTimer.addEventListener(TimerEvent.TIMER,
                  onRockTimer, false, 0, true);
                _rockTimer.start();
        }
```

The class starts by defining the constant value for how often to create new rocks. There is also a Dictionary object for keeping track of all the rocks in use. Inside the constructor, an enterFrame listener is attached, which will drive all of the updates. It also creates a new instance of the Space Sprite and sets up the timer for generating new Rocks.

```
private function onRockTimer(e:TimerEvent):void
{
        var rock:Rock = Rock.getRock();
        addChild(rock);
        rock.x = -rock.width * 2;
        rock.y = Math.random() * loaderInfo.height;
        _rockList[rock] = rock;
}
```

Whenever the timer for creating new rocks is called, you can see that the static *Rock.getRock* method is used. This will allow us to use either new or recycled instances of the class as it sees fit and does not complicate our implementation. Once a "new" rock is retrieved, it is placed just offscreen at a random *y* value and added to the Dictionary object.

```
private function onEnterFrame(e:Event):void
{
        //UPDATE ROCKS
        for each (var rock:Rock in _rockList)
        {
                rock.update();
                if (rock.x > loaderInfo.width + rock.width)
                {
                        removeChild(rock);
                        delete _rockList[rock];
                        rock.reset();
                }
        }
        //UPDATE SPACE
        _space.update();
        if (_space.x <= -_space.width/3)
        {
                _space.x = _space.x + (_space.width/3);
        }
}
```

On every frame, the class iterates over all of the rocks in the Dictionary object, calling their *update* methods. Once a rock is out-of-bounds (has left the other side of the screen), it is removed from the list of active rocks and reset. The Space instance is also updated, repositioning itself once it gets to the point where it can loop back to create a seamless texture.

There are two lines I commented out in the source code for this example, which can be found in the Rock class. They consist of two trace commands: one is called when a new rock is created and the other when a rock is "recycled." If you uncomment these lines and export this SWF to run in the AIR player, you'll see that in practice, the application creates a whole slew of rocks from scratch at the beginning and then begins to transition to using existing rocks instead. This change is not immediate since the speed of the rocks is variable, and it will take a little while for enough rocks to have been created to account for this latency.

The FrameRateProfiler Class

The final piece of this application, which we'll examine, is not directly related to SpaceRocks at all. Instead, it is a utility class that will prove useful going forward for measuring the performance of Flash applications on iOS. It is based on a class I created (discussed in the online bonus chapter on debugging and performance issues, found at www.flashgamebook.com), which displays the actual frame redraw rate (as opposed to the *intended* rate) of a SWF. The previous version used a text field to simply display the frame rate as a number. When I initially dropped it into Space-Rocks to use, I saw immediate performance degradation. This is because I was placing a live-updating text field (which cannot be cached to the GPU) directly over objects that the GPU was trying to render. The net result was that the CPU still had to composite everything, so I lost all intended performance gain from using *cachAsBitmapMatrix* to begin with.

This new version of the profiler takes a graphical approach. It creates two simple vector boxes (one white, one green), caches them to the GPU (so that they can sit on top of everything else and be properly composited), and then adjusts the *scaleX* value of the one on top to reflect the percentage of the intended frame rate. Figure 15.1 shows how this looks in practice. As it is not pertinent to the current example, I won't step through all of the code for the profiler here, but feel free to peruse it in the Chapter 15 examples folder. Now, let's look at a full game example for iOS.

Part 2: Marble Runner

One of the reasons the new mobile devices such as the iOS and the Android families are garnering such appeal from a broad range of users is their simple yet sophisticated approach to user input. Most devices (aside from those with a slide-out keyboard) have anywhere from one to four buttons. All other inputs are handled by one of two ways: either by touch interaction with the screen or through the use of the built-in accelerometer. This mechanism

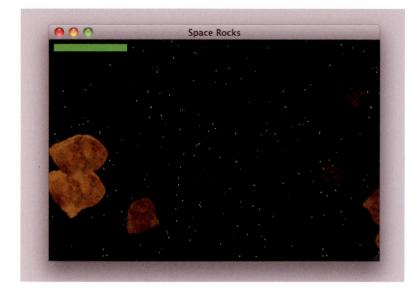

Figure 15.1 The FrameRate Profiler, used in SpaceRocks, currently reflects 100% of the intended frame rate. As performance lessened, the green bar would shrink, revealing a white bar underneath.

allows you to know the orientation of the device in 3D space and respond to movement. In this example, we'll create a game that uses the accelerometer as the primary means of input. It's also worth noting that this game will be intended for the iPhone in particular, so it will make use of a fixed screen aspect ratio and resolution. In Chapter 16, when we create an Android game, we'll make sure that the game supports multiple screen sizes.

The Accelerometer Class

Flash CS5 has an extremely simple class for interfacing with a mobile device's accelerometer. If you want to read values from the device, you simply instantiate a new Accelerometer object and listen for its UPDATE event.

```
import flash.events.AccelerometerEvent;
import flash.sensors.Accelerometer;

var accelerometer:Accelerometer = new Accelerometer();
accelerometer.addEventListener(AccelerometerEvent.UPDATE,
  onAccelerometerUpdate, false, 0, true);

function onAccelerometerUpdate(e:AccelerometerEvent):void
{
}
```

In this case, the *onAccelerometerUpdate* method will be called on creating the listener (to establish the initial orientation of the device), and then afterwards at a fixed interval. You can define this interval in milliseconds by calling *setRequestedUpdateInterval* on the Accelerometer instance and passing it a value. In general, however, you probably won't want to use anything faster than the default interval, and more frequently you start using up extra battery life—something users of your games won't appreciate. In fact, if you find you can, it's not a bad idea to *reduce* the frequency of intervals as it mean that you're polling the device even less and in fact *saving* battery power.

When you receive an AccelerometerEvent, you'll find that it has four distinct values inside. The first three are the *x*, *y*, and *z* values for the acceleration along each of those respective axes. Each of these properties ranges from around −1 G to +1 G (a "G" is approximately 9.8 m/s^2), cumulatively representing the orientation of the device and the forces of acceleration due to gravity. When the device is moved or rotated, these values fluctuate, reflecting the acceleration applied to the device at given angles. We'll look at a visual representation of this concept momentarily. The fourth value is a *timestamp* identifying the number of milliseconds since the application started when the event was created. You can think of it as though *getTimer* was called when the event occurred. This data might be useful if you wanted to delay or ignore reaction to an AccelerometerEvent without messing with the update interval.

How Accelerometer Values Are Computed

When an iPhone or other mobile device is stationary, the values from AccelerometerEvents are consistent as they represent the force of gravity acting downwards on it. Figure 15.2 shows the three axes that are used to determine the orientation of an iPhone's accelerometer.

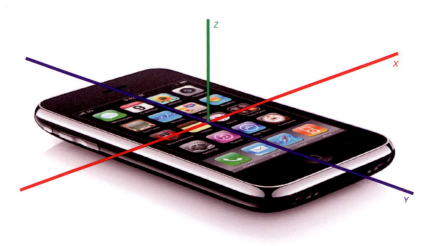

Figure 15.2 The three axes of the iPhone's accelerometer.

When the device is moved along its x axis (shown in red in Fig. 15.2), which runs across the front of the display from left to right, it registers negative or positive forces. If you were to hold the device in a horizontal orientation in front of you with the menu button on the right, as shown in the top half of Fig. 15.3, it would show y and z values of 0 and an x value of −1. This represents the force of gravity moving down the x-axis. Conversely, if you rotated the device 180 degrees around the z-axis, as shown in the bottom of Fig. 15.3, this value would reverse to +1.

Similarly, when the device is held upright with the menu button on the bottom—the most common orientation when using an iPhone, shown in Fig. 15.4—the y value is affected. In this position, the force of gravity is traveling straight down the face of the iPhone and is thus −1. To get a y value of +1, turn the device so that the menu button is on top.

Finally, when laid facing up on a flat surface, the device registers x and y values of 0, while the z value is approximately −1. Flipping the iPhone upside down onto its face will change this z value

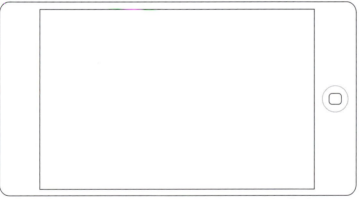

accelerationX = −1, accelerationY = 0, accelerationZ = 0

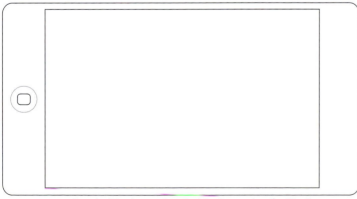

accelerationX = 1, accelerationY = 0, accelerationZ = 0

Figure 15.3 The accelerometer values for the iPhone when it is facing you and on its side.

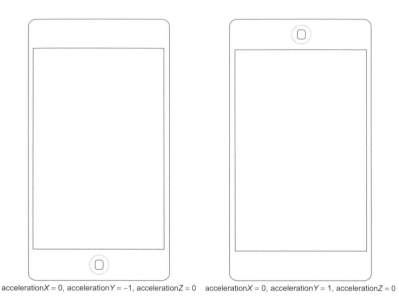

Figure 15.4 The accelerometer values for the iPhone when it is fully upright and facing you.

accelerationX = 0, accelerationY = –1, accelerationZ = 0   accelerationX = 0, accelerationY = 1, accelerationZ = 0

to 1. This shows that the force of gravity is traveling straight down through the face of the device, as shown in Fig. 15.2. It is important to understand these orientation relationships, particularly *x* and *y*, as they will make up the core input mechanism in the game we are about to create.

The Game: Marble Runner

In the following game example, we will create an experience similar to the wooden marble labyrinths that have existed for many years. Such a game is shown in Fig. 15.5, where the player would turn the two knobs to navigate the marble safely through the maze without falling down a hole.

In our version, rather than having knobs that adjust the angle of the game board, we will move the surface of the phone itself to simulate the very same effect. Each level of the game will require the player to navigate more complicated mazes with more hazards. To make it more interesting, we'll also incorporate a timer element; finish with time left and your score will be higher, run out of time and you must replay the level.

In addition to the use of the accelerometer, this game will require us to cover a number of concepts, including the following:

1. Technical
   a. Collision detection
   b. Timers
   c. Simulated 3D effects

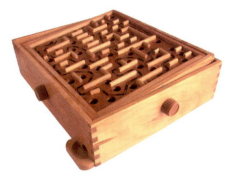

Figure 15.5 A tabletop marble maze game—the inspiration for an example of this chapter.

    d. Storing save game data for return play
    e. Loading and saving data using remoting services
2. Game design
    a. Hazards and risk/reward scenarios
    b. Score calculation
    c. Laying out a level in the Flash IDE
So, without further ado, let's dig in!

The XFL File

From the Chapter 15 examples folder, open the MarbleRunner.xfl file in the directory of the same name. There are some immediate things to note about this file:

- The document frame rate is set to 24 fps. For a game such as this with some heavier collision detection calculations going on this strikes a good balance of visual smoothness and load on the CPU.
- The main timeline consists of a set of labels and clips, representing the different screens of the application. We'll look into these classes in depth shortly.
- The library assets are sorted into folders based on the screen to which they belong, except for fonts (which are shared by all the screens).

The Classes

The classes for this game are split into two categories: the core game logic that is extensible and agnostic for a labyrinth-style game (the "engine" classes) and the custom functionality that is specific to this Marble Runner implementation (the "application" classes). As such, they are logically located in two different packages. The engine set of files can be found in

`com.flashgamebook.iphone.engines.labyrinth`

The application classes are located in

`com.flashgamebook.iphone.examples.chapter15.marblerunner`

    We'll start with the core engine and work our way outwards. The concepts may seem somewhat abstract at first but will take shape once you see how they are implemented. These files consist of the following:

- *LabyrinthEngine.as*: This class is pretty self-explanatory—it is the center of all the logic handling collision detection, ball movement, and level completion.
- *LabyrinthLevel.as*: The base class for any levels built in the Flash IDE—we use an inheritance model rather than an interface because levels are more rigidly controlled and we want to be able to do some validation on them.

- *IBall.as*: An interface that will be implemented by the player ball.
- *IHazard.as*: The interface required by any object acting as a hazard in the engine.
- *IWall.as*: Any object that will be treated as a wall by the engine will need to implement this interface.

LabyrinthEngine

```
final public class LabyrinthEngine extends Sprite
{
        static public var MAX_BALL_SPEED:Number = 150;
        static public var ACCELERATION_MULTIPLIER:Number = 80;

        static private const DISTANCE_TO_ENDPOINT:Number = 10;

        private var _currentLevel:LabyrinthLevel;
        private var _ball:IBall;
        private var _ballDO:DisplayObject;
        private var _levelEndCallback:Function;
        private var _accelerometer:Accelerometer;
        private var _ax:Number = 0;
        private var _ay:Number = 0;
        private var _previousTime:int;
```

There are relatively few member variables in this class: one to store the current level, two for the ball (one that uses IBall and the other that casts it as a DisplayObject for convenience later), a callback for when the level is complete (meaning the player successfully moved the ball to a designated endpoint), and a few to store the Accelerometer instance and its acceleration values. Also included are a couple of static variables that can be used to alter general properties of the engine.

```
public function LabyrinthEngine(ballClass:Class,levelClass:
  Class)
{
        _ball = new ballClass();
        _ballDO = DisplayObject(_ball);
        _currentLevel = new levelClass();

        var validationError:Error = _currentLevel.validate();
        if (validationError) throw validationError;

        addChild(_currentLevel);
        _currentLevel.addChild(_ballDO);
        resetBall();
}
```

The constructor for the engine accepts two classes that it will be responsible for instantiating. The first is the class used for the ball; in theory, this could be any class that implements IBall, but in practice it will be some kind of DisplayObject. As such, we cast it and store the second reference to prevent casting it again when we need it later. The level class is also instantiated, validated (through a method we'll look at shortly), and then added to the engine's display list. The ball is then added to the level and has its position reset.

This class has three public methods that can be called from other classes. We'll look at these next.

```
public function startLevel(callback:Function):void
{
        _levelEndCallback = callback;
        _accelerometer = new Accelerometer();
        _accelerometer.setRequestedUpdateInterval(100);
        _accelerometer.addEventListener(AccelerometerEvent.
          UPDATE, onAccelerometerUpdate, false, 0, true);
        _previousTime = getTimer();
        addEventListener(Event.ENTER_FRAME, onEnterFrame,
          false, 0, true);
}


public function endLevel(callback:Boolean = true):void
{
        removeEventListener(Event.ENTER_FRAME, onEnterFrame);
        _accelerometer.removeEventListener(AccelerometerEvent.
          UPDATE, onAccelerometerUpdate)
        if (callback && _levelEndCallback != null) _levelEndCallback();
}


public function dispose():void
{
        removeEventListener(Event.ENTER_FRAME, onEnterFrame);
        removeChild(_currentLevel);
        _currentLevel = null;
        _ball = null;
        _ballDO = null;
        _accelerometer = null;
}
```

In *startLevel*, the engine creates an accelerometer instance, sets it to update every tenth of a second, and starts the game loop. It also accepts a function that will later be called when the level ends. As you might expect, *endLevel* undoes pretty much everything *startLevel* does, with the option to trigger the callback function if it exists. Finally, *dispose* can be called when the engine is being discarded to help with quicker garbage collection. Next, we'll look at the two event handlers for the Accelerometer and game loop.

```
private function onAccelerometerUpdate(e:AccelerometerEvent):void
{
        _ax = (_ax + e.accelerationX)/2;
        _ay = (_ay - e.accelerationY)/2;
}


private function onEnterFrame(e:Event):void
{
        var currentTime:Number = getTimer();
        var deltaTime:Number = (currentTime - _previousTime)/1000;
        _previousTime = currentTime;
        moveBall(deltaTime);
        checkCollisions();
        checkHazards();
        checkWin();
}
```

Whenever an Accelerometer update occurs, the x and y values are pulled from the resulting event and averaged with the values stored in the engine. This will help with the sometimes erratic jumps and spikes in the numbers returned by the device. You may also notice that we add the value to the x acceleration but subtract it from the y. This is because Flash's coordinate system is inverted from a typical Cartesian coordinate plane. In traditional geometry, x values increase as you move from left to right and y values increase as you move *up*, as shown in Fig. 15.6. In Flash, y values increase as you move *down*, so the values for acceleration along that axis must also be inverted.

The *onEnterFrame* game loop basically acts as the catalyst for several other methods that are called. We'll look at each of these in order they appear here, but here's a quick summary of what takes place every frame:

1. The ball is moved based on how much time has passed since the last frame.
2. The engine detects all collisions with walls and adjusts positions accordingly.
3. The engine detects any collisions with hazards in the level.
4. The engine checks to see if the player has reached their destination.

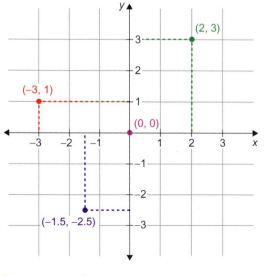

Figure 15.6 The Cartesian coordinate system.

```
private function moveBall(deltaTime:Number):void
{
        var maxDelta:Number = MAX_BALL_SPEED * deltaTime;

        _ball.vx += _ax * deltaTime * ACCELERATION_MULTIPLIER;
        if (_ball.vx > maxDelta)
        {
                _ball.vx = maxDelta;
        }
        else if (_ball.vx < -maxDelta)
        {
                _ball.vx = -maxDelta;
        }

        _ball.vy += _ay * deltaTime * ACCELERATION_MULTIPLIER;
        if (_ball.vy > maxDelta)
        {
                _ball.vy = maxDelta;
        }
        else if (_ball.vy < -maxDelta)
        {
                _ball.vy = -maxDelta;
        }

        _ball.x += _ball.vx;
        _ball.y += _ball.vy;
}
```

When *moveBall* is called, the ball's current velocity is incremented based on the current acceleration from the Accelerometer and the time that has elapsed. If the ball's velocity exceeds the set maximum value, it is clamped to prevent an infinite increase. This resultant velocity is then applied to the ball's position. You may notice that I'm multiplying the acceleration by a static value, in this case 80. The reason for doing this was something I learned through playtesting. When using the raw values from the accelerometer, they were so small that you had to tilt very dramatically the iPhone to get enough response to move the ball. This doesn't lead to a very fun experience as I had to move the phone in a very unnatural fashion to get the ball to respond. By multiplying it by a much larger number, you get a fairly sensitive response time from much smaller movements of the device. After testing a few different values, I settled on this one for having the best *feel*.

```
private function checkCollisions():void
{
        for each (var wall:IWall in _currentLevel.walls)
        {
```

```
var hitting:Boolean = wall.hitTestObject(_ballDO);
if (hitting)
{
        var ballRect:Rectangle = _ball.getRect
          (_currentLevel);
        var wallRect:Rectangle = wall.getRect
          (_currentLevel);
        var intersection:Rectangle = ballRect.
          intersection(wallRect);

        if (!intersection.width && !intersection.
          height) continue;

        var rectCenter:Point = new Point
          (intersection.x + intersection.width/2,
          intersection.y + intersection.height/2);
        var angle:Number = Math.atan2(rectCenter.
          y - _ball.y, rectCenter.x - _ball.x);
        angle = Math.round(angle/(Math.PI/2));
        angle *= Math.PI/2;

        var angleSin:Number = Math.sin(angle);
        var angleCos:Number = Math.cos(angle);

        var offsetX:Number = angleCos * intersection.
          width;
        var offsetY:Number = angleSin * intersection.
          height;

        _ball.x -= offsetX;
        _ball.y -= offsetY;


    }
  }
}
```

The *checkCollisions* method is the one in which the heaviest math in the engine occurs. Every one of the individual wall segments is tested against the ball to see if they overlap. First, every comparison starts with the rather blunt but fast *hitTestObject* check. If there is a collision, a more informative test is performed. This is done by getting the bounding box rectangles of both objects and by determining their rectangle of overlap (or intersection). The angle of the collision is then determined by measuring the angle between the middle of the ball and middle of the collision rectangle. This is illustrated in Fig. 15.7. The gray area represents the collision rectangle. The dashed line connecting the center point of the ball and the center of the collision is used to determine the angle of the collision.

Once the angle of collision has been determined, it is rounded to the nearest 90 degrees. This is so that the appropriate offset can be calculated to "push" the ball and the wall apart. This offset is then applied to the *x* and *y* coordinates of the ball since the walls in this example not to move in response to being hit.

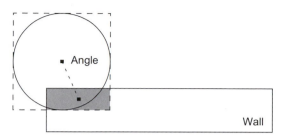

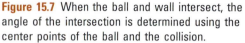

Figure 15.7 When the ball and wall intersect, the angle of the intersection is determined using the center points of the ball and the collision.

```
private function checkHazards():void
{
        var ballRect:Rectangle = _ball.getRect
          (_currentLevel);
        for each (var hazard:IHazard in _currentLevel.hazards)
        {
                if (hazard.getRect(_currentLevel).intersects
                  (ballRect))
                {
                        resetBall();
                        break;
                }
        }
}

private function resetBall():void
{
        _ball.x = _currentLevel.startPoint.x;
        _ball.y = _currentLevel.startPoint.y;
        _ball.vx = 0;
        _ball.vy = 0;
}
```

Once the wall collisions have been resolved, the engine iterates through all of the hazards in a level and determines if they intersect. If the ball collides with any hazard, it is reset to initial starting point with its velocity dropped to zero.

```
private function checkWin():void
{
        var testPoint:Point = new Point(_ball.x, _ball.y);
        if (Point.distance(testPoint, _currentLevel.endPoint) <
          DISTANCE_TO_ENDPOINT)
        {
                endLevel();
        }
}
```

The final method of the class, *checkWin*, simply measures the distance between the ball and the endpoint specified by the level.

In this case, when the ball is within 10 pixels of the endpoint, it is considered a win and *endLevel* is called, which we looked previously. In just under 200 lines of code, we've laid out the core functionality behind this game. While we're far from done, most of the heavy lifting is out of the way.

LabyrinthLevel

This class is never meant to be used directly. It is the base for every level that will be created in the IDE. It establishes all of the necessary criteria for a level and provides the ability to validate itself. As I mentioned before, this differs from the other components of the engine in that all of the levels inherit from it instead of implementing an interface. This is because we need more rigidity in how the levels are built, whereas we need not be so particular about the ball, walls, or hazards.

```
public class LabyrinthLevel extends Sprite
{
        static public const ERROR_NO_START_POINT:String = "Level
          Invalid: No start point specified - place a DisplayObject
          named \"startPointClip\" in the level.";
        static public const ERROR_NO_END_POINT:String = "Level
          Invalid: No end point specified - place a DisplayObject
          named \"endPointClip\" in the level.";
        static public const ERROR_NO_WALLS:String = "Level Invalid:
          Level requires at least one DisplayObject that implements
          IWall.";

        private var _hazards:Vector.<IHazard>;
        private var _endPoint:Point;
        private var _startPoint:Point;
        private var _walls:Vector.<IWall>;
```

A level in Marble Runner is defined as a set of walls and hazards, as well as a starting point and endpoint. When the level validates itself, it may throw errors stating which required components are missing. There are constants provided for missing starting and ending points, as well as when the level cannot find any walls.

```
public function LabyrinthLevel()
{
        _hazards = new Vector.<IHazard>();
        _walls = new Vector.<IWall>();
        for (var i:int = 0; i < numChildren; i++)
        {
                var child:DisplayObject = getChildAt(i);
                if (child is IHazard)
                {
                        _hazards.push(child);
```

```
          }
          else if (child.name == "startPointClip")
          {
                  _startPoint = new Point(child.x, child.y);
                  child.visible = false;
          }
          else if (child.name == "endPointClip")
          {
                  _endPoint = new Point(child.x, child.y);
                  child.visible = false;
          }
          else if (child is IWall)
          {
                  _walls.push(child);
          }
          else if (child is Shape)
          {
                  child.cacheAsBitmap = true;
          }
      }
}
```

When the level initializes in the constructor, it walks through its entire display list, identifying each component and storing it in the appropriate variable or Vector. This type of "scan" allows the level to be fairly loosely designed in the IDE, with no requirements for layering order of any of the components.

```
public function validate():Error
{
      var err:Error;
      if (!_startPoint)
      {
            err = new Error(ERROR_NO_START_POINT);
      }
      else if (!_endPoint)
      {
            err = new Error(ERROR_NO_END_POINT);
      }
      else if (!_walls.length)
      {
            err = new Error(ERROR_NO_WALLS);
      }
      return err;
}
```

As we saw in the engine class, the *validate* method returns one of three different errors, depending on elements that are missing from the level. If nothing is missing, the error is null and will be ignored by the engine.

```
public function get startPoint():Point
{
        return _startPoint;
}


public function get endPoint():Point
{
        return _endPoint;
}


public function get hazards():Vector.<IHazard>
{
        return _hazards;
}


public function get walls():Vector.<IWall>
{
        return _walls;
}
```

Finally, every level provides read-only accessors for each of its private member variables. These were used in multiple places by the engine, particularly with respect to collision detection. Since we're already on the topic, we'll also take a quick look in the XFL file at how a level is composed. If you opened the Game folder in the library and selected the symbol named Level 1, and then opened its properties panel, you would see as that in Fig. 15.8. The base class is listed as the file we just looked at, and the symbol class name is simply "Level1." If you select the two black dots in the level, you'll see that they are simply markers for the starting and end points. All of the blue walls are made up of one symbol in the library whose class we'll look at shortly.

IBall, IHazard, IWall

These three interfaces are all very simple, so we'll look at them altogether in one pass.

```
public interface IBall extends IEventDispatcher
{
        function get x():Number;
        function set x(value:Number):void;
        function get y():Number;
        function set y(value:Number):void;
        function get width():Number;
        function set width(value:Number):void;
```

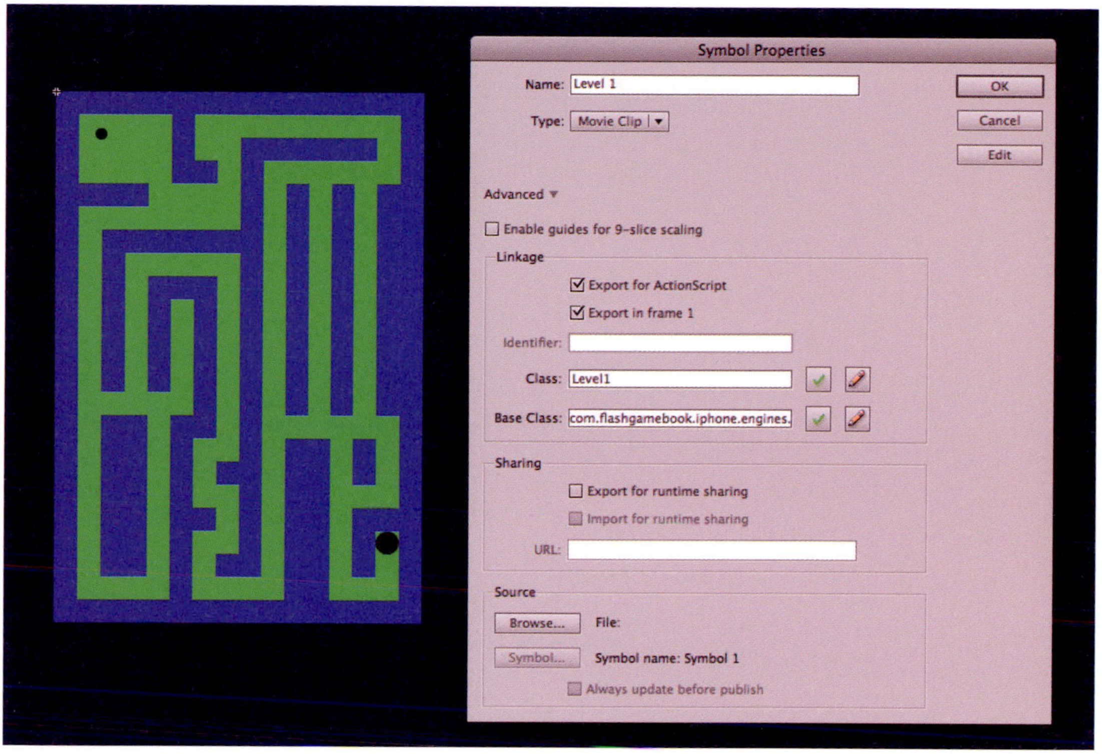

Figure 15.8 The properties panel and layout for the first level of Marble Runner.

```
        function get height():Number;
        function set height(value:Number):void;
        function getRect(coordinateSpace:DisplayObject):Rectangle;
        function hitTestObject(obj:DisplayObject):Boolean;

        function get vx():Number;
        function set vx(value:Number):void;
        function get vy():Number;
        function set vy(value:Number):void;
}

public interface IHazard
{
        function get x():Number;
        function set x(value:Number):void;
        function get y():Number;
        function set y(value:Number):void;
        function getRect(coordinateSpace:DisplayObject):Rectangle;
        function hitTestObject(obj:DisplayObject):Boolean;
}
```

```
public interface IWall
{
        function get x():Number;
        function set x(value:Number):void;
        function get y():Number;
        function set y(value:Number):void;
        function getRect(coordinateSpace:DisplayObject):Rectangle;
        function hitTestObject(obj:DisplayObject):Boolean;
}
```

As you can see, the three interfaces share a great deal of functionality and almost all methods that are native to DisplayObjects. In fact, IHazard and IWall have identical method signatures. However, they must both exist so that the engine can differentiate between one type of object and another. However, you could create an interface based on all the common traits of these (called, say, *IDisplayObject*) and simply extend it to add specific functionality. I did not do that in this case, however, because using interfaces on the iPhone is already slightly slower at runtime, and because there were only three of them, I opted to not abstract them one layer further. If you had a version of this game with several other components such as pickups or transporters, it would begin to make sense to try to consolidate functionality into shared interfaces.

That sums up the engine components of Marble Runner. Next, we'll take a look at the application-specific classes for this implementation. These classes consist of the following:

- *MarbleRunner.as*—the base document class for the game
- *Title.as*—the title screen
- *HowToPlay.as*—the rules screen
- *Leaderboard.as*—the screen displaying the top scores, and the class that handles all communication with the back-end services
- *GameClip.as*—the screen that instantiates the game engine and displays UI elements like the score and timer
- *Marble.as*—the class that implements *IBall* for the game
- *StandardWall.as*—the sole class we'll use to implement *IWall*
- *HazardPit.as*—the hazard used in the second level—implements *IHazard*
- *Results.as*—the screen displayed at the end of a level

The only one of these classes we won't examine is How To Play. It's so simple that it is not worth breaking down; suffice it to say that it has a "back" button that returns to the title screen.

MarbleRunner: The Document Class

```
final public class MarbleRunner extends MovieClip
{
        static public const EVENT_NAVIGATE:String = "navigate";
```

```actionscript
static public const FRAME_TITLE:String = "title";
static public const FRAME_HOW_TO_PLAY:String = "howtoplay";
static public const FRAME_GAME:String = "game";
static public const FRAME_LEADERBOARD:String = "leaderboard";
static public const FRAME_RESULTS:String = "results";

static private var _gameData:SharedObject;

public function MarbleRunner()
{
      stop();
      addEventListener(Event.ADDED_TO_STAGE, onAdded
        ToStage, false, 0, true);
      addEventListener(EVENT_NAVIGATE, onNavigate,
        false, 0, true);
}

private function onAddedToStage(e:Event):void
{
      loadGameData();
      gotoAndStop(FRAME_TITLE);
}

private function onNavigate(e:DataEvent):void
{
      gotoAndStop(e.data);
}

static public function get gameData():SharedObject
{
      return _gameData;
}

static public function loadGameData():void
{
      if (_gameData)
            return;
      _gameData = SharedObject.getLocal("MarbleRunner");
}

static public function saveGameData(level:int, score:int):
  void
{
      if (!_gameData)
            loadGameData();

      _gameData.data.level = level;
```

```
            _gameData.data.score = score;
            _gameData.flush();
        }
}
```

The main document serves two primary functions for Marble Runner. It is used to change screens, which is done when a screen dispatches a *DataEvent* of the type "navigate." Although bubbling an event up to the root level clip like this is not at all advisable in performance-sensitive areas like playing the actual game, it's totally fine when navigating between static menu screens. The other purpose of the document class is to save the user's progress, so if they have to take a call or otherwise unexpectedly quit from the game, they can return to it later. This is done through the use of a *Shared-Object*, which you may be familiar with if you've ever used it in the desktop version of Flash to save small pieces of data to use later. In this case, we store the current level the player is on and their score at the time. Next, we'll look at the title screen where this is first used.

Title

The title screen simply consists of some buttons and the game logo. Players have the option to start a new game, continue their previous game, see how to play the game, or view the leaderboard (see Fig. 15.9).

```
final public class Title extends Sprite
{

        public var btnNewGame:SimpleButton;
        public var btnContinueGame:SimpleButton;
        public var btnHowToPlay:SimpleButton;
        public var btnLeaderboard:SimpleButton;

        public function Title()
        {
                addEventListener(Event.ADDED_TO_STAGE,
                    onAddedToStage, false, 0, true);
        }

        private function onAddedToStage(e:Event):void
        {
                btnNewGame.addEventListener(MouseEvent.CLICK,
                    onNewGame, false, 0, true);
                btnContinueGame.addEventListener(MouseEvent.
                    CLICK, onContinueGame, false, 0, true);
                btnHowToPlay.addEventListener(MouseEvent.CLICK,
                    onHowToPlay, false, 0, true);
```

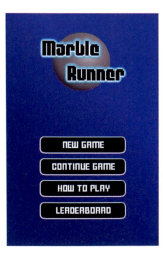

Figure 15.9 The title screen of Marble Runner.

```
        btnLeaderboard.addEventListener(MouseEvent.
          CLICK, onLeaderboard, false, 0, true);

        if (!MarbleRunner.gameData.data.level)
        {
                btnContinueGame.alpha = .5;
                btnContinueGame.mouseEnabled = false;
        }
}

private function onNewGame(e:MouseEvent):void
{
        MarbleRunner.saveGameData(1, 0);
        onContinueGame(null);
}

private function onContinueGame(e:MouseEvent):void
{
        dispatchEvent(new DataEvent(MarbleRunner.EVENT_
          NAVIGATE, true, false, MarbleRunner.FRAME_GAME));
}

private function onHowToPlay(e:MouseEvent):void
{
        dispatchEvent(new DataEvent(MarbleRunner.EVENT_
          NAVIGATE, true, false, MarbleRunner.
          FRAME_HOW_TO_PLAY));
}

private function onLeaderboard(e:MouseEvent):void
{
        dispatchEvent(new DataEvent(MarbleRunner.EVENT_
          NAVIGATE, true, false, MarbleRunner.
          FRAME_LEADERBOARD));
}
}
```

If there is no save data option, the Continue button is faded out and disabled. When a new game is started, it saves initial data that can later be used to continue from where they left off. All of the other buttons simply dispatch navigation events that the document class will use to move between screens—pretty straightforward stuff.

Leaderboard

In creating a global leaderboard for a game, Flash developers have a staggering number of options for communicating storing the data. For this example (and all others in this book), the leaderboard connects to a database via the AMF (Action Message Format) protocol, sometimes referred to as Flash remoting. On the back end, it is connected to this book's Web site, which is running AMFPHP middleware. I prefer AMF to other alternatives for a few different reasons:

- The data sent out and received by the game is binary and therefore very small; if you have bandwidth restrictions (such as the iPhone's 3G network) or will be sending lots of data back and forth over the course of a game, the savings in data size over something like XML will become noticeable very quickly.
- Types and data structures remain intact when they finally get to the ActionScript code: strings are strings, numbers are numbers, and even Arrays work as you would expect them to do without any conversion or parsing; as long as you know the format of the data being returned by the service, you can start using it immediately.
- The setup for AMF is extremely quick in AS3; in just a few lines of code, you can connect to a service, call a remote method, and receive a response.
- Most AMF back-end software (like AMFPHP) is free and very easy to set up, and there are flavors for any number of other platforms from .NET to Java.

In the following code snippets, I will only be explaining the client-side (Flash) code. You can find a full explanation of the PHP code in Appendix D on www.flashgamebook.com. If you are a solo developer and will need to know how to build these types of services yourself, I hope it is extremely useful to you. However, if like me you work with a team of dedicated back-end developers, this information isn't as relevant, and PHP is a different enough language that I don't want to create confusion here in the text.

The leaderboard class serves two purposes. Its static methods and properties provide a globally accessible way of pulling in and saving out data to the database. Its instance methods are used to display the high-score list screen. As I dissect the code over the next few pages, I'll split it into these two categories to help clarify this distinction. Note that while it uses many others, the only import I've reprinted here is a custom one from the included *utils* package: an MD5 hashing algorithm.

```
import com.flashgamebook.iphone.utils.MD5;

final public class Leaderboard extends Sprite
{
        static public const GATEWAY_URL:String = "http://www.
          flashgamebook.com/services/gateway.php";
        static public const GAME_ID:String = "MarbleRunner";
        static public const SECRET_KEY:String = "fandango";
        static public const NUMBER_OF_RESULTS:int = 10;
```

```
static public const STATUS_MESSAGE_ERROR:String = "An error
    occurred when retrieving scores.\nPlease try again later.";

static private var _netConnection:NetConnection;
```

The static constants for the leaderboard are the URL of the AMF gateway to which the game will connect, the game name (ID), a secret key value that will be used for security purposes, the number of results to pull from the database, and the text to display in the event of an error (like the lack of an Internet connection). A reference to a NetConnection object is also created, as this will be how the AMF communication is handled.

```
static public function createConnection():void
{
        if (!_netConnection)
        {
                _netConnection = new NetConnection();
                _netConnection.connect(GATEWAY_URL);
        }
}


static public function saveScore(score:int, initials:String)
{
        createConnection();
        var responder:Responder = new Responder(onScoreSaved,
          onScoreSaveError);
        var date:Date = new Date();
        var hash:String = MD5.hash(MD5.hash(SECRET_KEY + score +
          initials + date.toString()));
        _netConnection.call("games.HighScores.saveScore",
          responder, GAME_ID, score, initials, date.toString(), hash);
}


static private function onScoreSaved(result:Object):void


{
        trace("Score Saved:",result);
}


static private function onScoreSaveError(result:Object):void
{
        //ERROR OCCURRED
}
```

Any time a call to the AMF service is made; *createConnection* is called to make sure the NetConnection has been established. When a score is saved to the database, which can be done from any other class, a Responder object is created for handling the returned data. To make sure that the data being saved is valid and the service is not being hacked, the method creates a date stamp and combines it with the other pieces of data (including the secret key). This value is then *hashed* twice using MD5. If you're not familiar with hashing, you can refer to the bonus online chapter on securing your games, On Your Guard. Briefly, it is the process of taking a chunk of data and reducing it algorithmically to a fixed length string of numbers and letters. The goal is that it should be impossible or nearly impossible for someone to be able to determine the original data. MD5 is just one of many other algorithms, including a number of them that are far more secure, such as SHA256. I chose MD5 because it is very fast to process and is a native part of PHP, a back-end software that will perform a comparison hash to validate the data.

Once this hash value is created, a remote method is called via the NetConnection, *saveScore*, which is part of the *HighScores* class in the *games* package in the PHP code. This method accepts the game ID, score, and the various pieces of validation data. Note that we do not send the secret key—it will be up to the author of the back-end service (in this case, me) to make sure I have the same key in use there. Next, we will look at the code that executes when loading the leaderboard screen.

```
public var btnBack:SimpleButton;
public var tfRank:TextField;
public var tfInitials:TextField;
public var tfScores:TextField;
public var tfStatusMessage:TextField;

public function Leaderboard()
{
        addEventListener(Event.ADDED_TO_STAGE, onAddedToStage,
          false, 0, true);
}


private function onAddedToStage(e:Event):void
{
        btnBack.addEventListener(MouseEvent.CLICK, onBack,
          false, 0, true);
        createConnection();
        loadScores();
}


private function loadScores():void
{
        var responder:Responder = new Responder(onScoresLoaded,
          onScoresLoadedError);
```

```
        _netConnection.call("games.HighScores.getScores",
          responder, GAME_ID, NUMBER_OF_RESULTS);
}


private function onScoresLoaded(result:Object):void
{
        if (result is Array)
        {
                var scores:Array = result as Array;
                tfRank.text = "";
                tfInitials.text = "";
                tfScores.text = "";
                tfStatusMessage.text = "";
                for (var i:int = 0; i < scores.length; i++)
                {
                    tfRank.appendText(String(i+1) + "\n");
                    tfInitials.appendText(scores[i].initials + "\n");
                    tfScores.appendText(scores[i].score+"\n");
                }
        }
}


private function onScoresLoadedError(result:Object):void
{
        tfStatusMessage.text = STATUS_MESSAGE_ERROR;
}


private function onBack(e:MouseEvent):void
{
        dispatchEvent(new DataEvent(MarbleRunner.EVENT_NAVIGATE,
          true, false, MarbleRunner.FRAME_TITLE));
}
```

As you can see, when a leaderboard screen is instantiated and added to the Stage, it calls the same *createConnection* method we looked at earlier. It then proceeds to load the scores from the database. Note how the call is similarly formed to the *saveScore* method. Once the scores are loaded in, the data is appended to the different text columns as shown in Fig. 15.10. If the scores fail to load for some reason, the generic error message is displayed in lieu of the data.

GameClip

Once a new game is started, the GameClip class is instantiated. It creates an instance of the LabyrinthEngine we looked at earlier and keeps track of the timer and the player's current level (based on the data stored in the shared object).

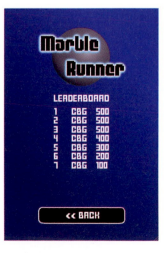

Figure 15.10 The Leaderboard screen of Marble Runner.

```
import com.flashgamebook.iphone.engines.labyrinth.LabyrinthEngine;

final public class GameClip extends Sprite
{
        static public const LEVEL_LENGTH:int = 75; //IN SECONDS
        static public const SCORE_MULTIPLIER:int = 150;

        public var tfLevel:TextField;
        public var tfTime:TextField;
        public var tfScore:TextField;

        private var _engine:LabyrinthEngine;
        private var _level:int = 1;
        private var _score:int = 0;
        private var _timer:Timer;
```

Because the engine does all of the heavy lifting, our *implementation* of a labyrinth game is pretty simple. There's a Timer and a few TextFields to display important information, and then a handful of methods we'll look at next.

```
public function GameClip()
{
        addEventListener(Event.ADDED_TO_STAGE, onAddedToStage,
          false, 0, true);
}

private function onAddedToStage(e:Event):void
{
        _level = MarbleRunner.gameData.data.level;
        _score = MarbleRunner.gameData.data.score;
        tfLevel.text = _level.toString();
        tfScore.text = _score.toString();
        nextLevel();
}

private function nextLevel():void
{
        _timer = new Timer(1000, LEVEL_LENGTH);
        _timer.addEventListener(TimerEvent.TIMER, onTimer,
          false, 0, true);
        _timer.addEventListener(TimerEvent.TIMER_COMPLETE,
          onTimerComplete, false, 0, true);
        _timer.start();
        var levelClass:Class = getDefinitionByName("Level" +
          _level) as Class;
        _engine = new LabyrinthEngine(Marble, levelClass);
        _engine.y = 20;
```

```
        addChild(_engine);
        _engine.startLevel(levelComplete);
}

private function levelComplete():void
{
        _timer.stop();
        _score += (LEVEL_LENGTH - _timer.currentCount) *
          SCORE_MULTIPLIER;
        tfScore.text = _score.toString();
        _level++;
        MarbleRunner.saveGameData(_level,_score);
        dispatchEvent(new DataEvent(MarbleRunner.EVENT_NAVIGATE,
          true, false, MarbleRunner.FRAME_RESULTS));
}

private function onTimer(e:TimerEvent):void
{
        var currentTime:int = LEVEL_LENGTH - Timer(e.target).
          currentCount;
        tfTime.text = timeToString(currentTime);
}

private function onTimerComplete(e:TimerEvent):void
{
        _engine.endLevel(false);
}

private function timeToString(time:int):String
{
        var timeStr:String = Math.floor(time / 60).toString();
        timeStr += ":";
        var seconds:String = "0" + (time % 60);
        seconds = seconds.substr(-2);
        timeStr += seconds;
        return timeStr;
}
```

Every level clip is a class that extends LabyrinthLevel, which we examined earlier. In the XFL document library, you can find each of these levels, exported as Level1, Level2, etc. Since we're not adding any custom functionality, these classes will be generated automatically by Flash on export. When *nextLevel* is called in the GameClip, it concatenates "Level" with the current level number and looks up the class definition. This and the Marble class we'll look at shortly are then passed to a new instance of the LabyrinthEngine class. The engine instance is offset 20 pixels down from the top of the screen to make room for the UI elements like the score, current level, and timer indicators.

The timer is also started at this point; when the timer runs out, the game engine's *endLevel* method is triggered to end the game. However, if the level is completed before the timer runs out, the *levelComplete* method that was passed into *startLevel* will be called. This method calculates the player's score based on how much time they had left, increments the level counter, and saves their progress. After that it redirects them to the results screen that we'll look at shortly. First, we'll take a quick look at three other classes used in the game: the Marble, the HazardPit, and the StandardWall.

Marble

The IBall interface we examined earlier requires very little more than a simple DisplayObject in order to serve the purposes of the game engine. However, as this is the player "character," it makes sense to put a little more effort into its implementation. Our ball will have a texture applied to it and appear to be three dimensional as the texture will move in accordance with the ball's movement. This is accomplished by clever use of a mask and radial gradient. If you open the Marble symbol from the XFL library, you'll see several layers. Figure 15.11A illustrates how the first two layers are made up of a texture and a circular mask. Figure 15.11B shows the gradient effect that will be laid over the masked texture to give it lighting and a three-dimensional look. Finally, Fig. 15.11C represents the final composited effect.

In reality, the texture would bend around the edges of the ball a little, an effect that could be created with a DisplacementMapFilter or a PixelBender Shader. However, because it is so small, this effect is entirely convincing for a moving ball and much less costly on the CPU. Next, we'll look at how we should use code to move the texture underneath the mask.

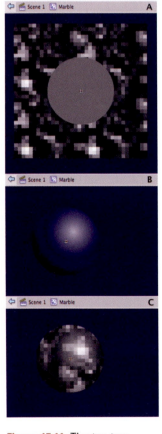

Figure 15.11 The top two components blended together (A, B) result in the convincing marble ball in the bottom image (C).

■ CREATING SCROLLABLE TEXTURES

The texture we're using for the marble actually started out ¼ of its current size. It is a seamless texture that is tiled into four quadrants, as shown in Fig. 15.12. The reason we quadruple the image data is so that as the texture moves it will need to be repositioned to maintain the illusion of an infinitely wrapping surface. If we were using higher resolution textures, or many more than lone image in question, the quadrupling could be done inside Flash by making multiple instances of the single tile.

```
import com.flashgamebook.iphone.engines.labyrinth.IBall;

final public class Marble extends Sprite implements IBall
```

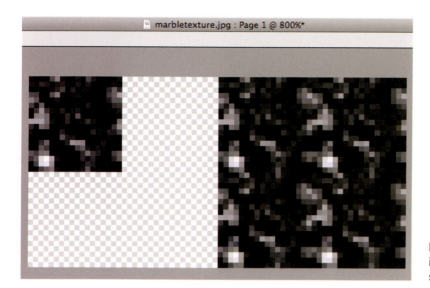

Figure 15.12 The texture used is actually four copies of the same texture in quadrants.

```
{
    public var shine:Sprite;
    public var texture:Sprite;

    private var _vx:Number = 0;
    private var _vy:Number = 0;
    private var _textureOffsetX:Number;
    private var _textureOffsetY:Number;

    public function Marble()
    {
        _textureOffsetX = shine.width/2;
        _textureOffsetY = shine.height/2;
    }
```

Both the texture and the three-dimensional effect (or "shine") are inside Sprites on the Stage. The shine also has cacheAsBitmap turned on inside Flash though it could have just as easily been enabled here in the code. The two-texture offset values represent the coordinates at which the texture Sprite needs to have its position reset. We'll use these in a moment.

```
override public function getRect(coordinateSpace:DisplayObject):
    Rectangle
{
    return shine.getRect(coordinateSpace);
}
```

One quirk of DisplayObjects in Flash is that even areas outside of a mask count toward the calculated dimensions of an object.

In other words, even though the ball itself is 18 × 18 pixels, the rectangle returned by *getRect* is 36 × 36 because those are the dimensions of the texture. Since this rectangle will be crucial in performing hit detection in the engine, we employ a work-around here; we override the *getRect* method to instead return the rectangle for the shine Sprite. It reflects the correct dimensions and will provide the desired data.

```
override public function set x(value:Number):void
{
        var difference:Number = value - x;
        texture.x += difference;
        if (texture.x > _textureOffsetX)
                texture.x -= shine.width;
        else if (texture.x < -_textureOffsetX)
                texture.x += shine.width;
        super.x = value;
}


override public function set y(value:Number):void
{
        var difference:Number = value - y;
        texture.y += difference;
        if (texture.y > _textureOffsetY)
                texture.y -= shine.height;
        else if (texture.y < -_textureOffsetY)
                texture.y += shine.height;
        super.y = value;
}
```

In addition to the override for *getRect*, we need to alter the default behavior of the *x* and *y* accessors. Whenever the *x* and *y* are set, we need to also update the position of the texture. This will ensure that whenever the ball is moved, it will appear to roll in that direction. The first step is to determine the distance the ball is being moved and also move the texture by that amount. Then, we test to see if the texture has moved outside of its "safe zone" and reposition as necessary.

```
public function get vx():Number
{
        return _vx;
}


public function set vx(value:Number):void
{
        _vx = value;
}
```

```
public function get vy():Number
{
        return _vy;
}

public function set vy(value:Number):void
{
        _vy = value;
}
```

The last methods in the class are just the accessors required by the IBall interface. The *x* and *y* velocity values are simply stored as member variables. We don't do anything with these values since they are set and read by the engine. The final result from this class is a ball that looks and reacts like a real ball would as it moves around the labyrinth.

HazardPit and StandardWall

These last two game classes exist simply to fulfill the interface requirements for the game engine. As such, they implement their respective interfaces, cache themselves as bitmaps, and that's it. Here both of them are back to back since they're almost identical.

```
import com.flashgamebook.iphone.engines.labyrinth.IHazard;

final public class HazardPit extends Sprite implements IHazard
{
        public function HazardPit()
        {
                cacheAsBitmap = true;
        }
}
import com.flashgamebook.iphone.engines.labyrinth.IWall;

final public class StandardWall extends Sprite implements IWall
{
        public function StandardWall()
        {
                cacheAsBitmap = true;
        }
}
```

If we wanted to have a hazard that consisted of a spinning blade or a wall that animated in some kind of nonstandard way, we would create new classes similar to these and add the required functionality. This is where the extra effort of programming to interfaces bears fruit. Although both of these classes are Sprites, there's no reason we couldn't use a MovieClip instead or extend them from some other type of DisplayObject. For that matter, they could even be Shape objects that draw their contents dynamically; the engine doesn't care as long as the interface is implemented properly.

Results

The final screen in Marble Runner is the results screen, where the player's score is totaled and can be submitted to the high-score table. Figure 15.13 shows how this screen looks in practice.

```
final public class Results extends Sprite
{
        public var btnPostScore:SimpleButton;
        public var btnContinue:SimpleButton;
        public var btnQuit:SimpleButton;
        public var tfScore:TextField;
        public var tfName:TextField;

        public function Results()
        {
                addEventListener(Event.ADDED_TO_STAGE,
                  onAddedToStage, false, 0, true);
        }

        private function onAddedToStage(e:Event):void
        {
                tfScore.text = String(MarbleRunner.gameData.data.
                  score);
                tfName.restrict = "A-Z";
                btnPostScore.addEventListener(MouseEvent.CLICK,
                  onPostScore, false, 0, true);
                btnContinue.addEventListener(MouseEvent.CLICK,
                  onContinue, false, 0, true);
                btnQuit.addEventListener(MouseEvent.CLICK,
                  onQuit, false, 0, true);
        }

        private function onPostScore(e:MouseEvent):void
        {
                if (tfName.length < 3)
                {
                        return;
                }
                Leaderboard.saveScore(MarbleRunner.gameData.
                  data.score, tfName.text.toUpperCase());
                btnPostScore.removeEventListener(MouseEvent.
                  CLICK, onPostScore);
```

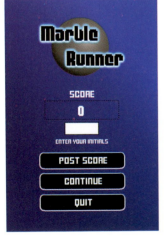

Figure 15.13 The results screen of Marble Runner.

```
        btnPostScore.mouseEnabled = false;
        btnPostScore.alpha = .5;
    }

    private function onContinue(e:MouseEvent):void
    {
        dispatchEvent(new DataEvent(MarbleRunner.EVENT_
            NAVIGATE, true, false, MarbleRunner.FRAME_GAME));
    }

    private function onQuit(e:MouseEvent):void
    {
        dispatchEvent(new DataEvent(MarbleRunner.EVENT_
            NAVIGATE, true, false, MarbleRunner.FRAME_TITLE));
    }
}
```

This screen uses an input TextField that allows a player to enter his or her initials and submit them to the database. When the player selects this input box, the iPhone's virtual keyboard will appear for them to type. Once they click Post Score, the *saveScore* method of the Leaderboard class is called, which we dissected earlier. To keep a player from submitting the score repeatedly, we disable the button after it has been tapped once.

Design Considerations

Now that we've taken an in-depth look at all of the codes behind Marble Runner, let's take a moment to consider the elements of game design that come into play in this example.

Level Design

If you open one of the Level clips inside the library, you'll see that it is composed of a bunch of wall Sprites and some positioning clips. By building the engine and level classes to use this framework, any developer could open this file and build new levels for the game without having to touch any code, assuming they used only the existing assets. This is an extremely important and intentional decision to make when architecting a game engine. If you're a solo developer, you will have built yourself a powerful toolset for making level design less tedious. If you are part of a team, someone else (maybe not even a developer) can be responsible for laying out levels and testing them without modifying the code base. This is actually similar to how larger scale commercial games are produced.

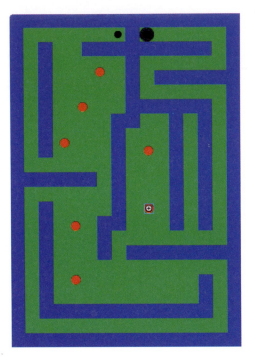

Figure 15.14 The second level of Marble Runner, where hazards are introduced.

Risk and Reward Scenarios

In the second level, I introduce the first hazards (red dots), as shown in Fig. 15.14. These red dots will reset the player to the start of the level if they collide. The most direct path for the player to take through the level involves navigating around these red dots in very close proximity. However, you'll also notice that there is also a secondary path along the left and bottom of the level. This path has no hazards but is much more out of the way and will take longer to navigate, assuming the player doesn't hit a hazard on the more direct path. This is known as a risk/reward scenario; a player is presented with the option to take a calculated risk in order to reap a benefit. In this case, the reward for navigating the hazards successfully is more time left on the clock and a higher score. It is important to think about scenarios like this in level design because it provides a much richer experience for a broader range of players. More conservative gamers who are more interested in getting to the end might take the safe path, whereas the user interested only in leaderboard rank will always want to risk being reset to achieve the highest possible score.

Where to Take It

This engine provides a solid base on which many hundreds of levels could be built with variety of artworks. However, there are a number of enhancements that should be considered before you could consider this a *great* game. Here are a few to ponder.

Scoring

This example features extremely basic scoring principles. For every second left on the clock, 150 points are awarded. It doesn't get much more straightforward than that. To make it more interesting for players, though, it would be a good idea to introduce other ways to earn points. Maybe every level has a base score value that you receive automatically for completing it. Maybe there is an additional bonus that can be earned for completing a level without restarting it because of a hazard.

Pickups

Although it would require modifying the base engine, a feature that would be very welcome would be the idea of pickups. These would be treated programmatically similarly to hazards, except that the player would *want* to collide with them. Maybe they're worth points. Maybe they're power-ups that make the ball temporarily invulnerable to hazards. Maybe they're required to exit the level. How ever they're implemented, this would bring a whole new dimension to Marble Runner's gameplay.

Scrolling Levels

In an early version of Marble Runner, I actually had this feature implemented. Levels could be designed larger than the iPhone's screen size and the whole engine clip would reposition itself to keep the ball centered in the frame as much as possible. While this was not technically challenging to include, I removed it when running into performance problems on the iPhone. All of the redrawing that occurred was very tasking on the iPhone and I felt it was in the best interest of the example to remove it. There are other alternatives for drawing the level to the screen that would be more complicated, but I'll leave that up to your ingenuity.

That concludes our look at Marble Runner. If you decide to make a full-fledged game with this engine, please let me know. I'd love to feature such a game on www.flashgamebook.com. In Chapter 16 the final chapter, we'll look at a two-player game intended for use on Android devices, which will cover a handful of new topics.

16

AIR HOCKEY: A MULTITOUCH, MULTIPLAYER TABLET GAME

While the iPhone and iPad have been hogging the attention of device users lately, Google's Android platform has been the fastest in terms of growth. This is because just about everything about the platform is open source—people can feasibly make their own versions of the Android OS customized for their needs. This also means all the basic tools to develop Android applications are free as well, and there are few to no restrictions about putting applications on phones or tablets. This also means that devices made by manufacturers can have a pretty wide variance in specifications (screen size, processor and video speed, memory, storage, media devices like cameras, and keyboards—virtual and slideout), leading to hardware fragmentation. On top of that, in many cases the carriers of a handset (such as AT&T, Sprint, Verizon, and so on) control when users are allowed to upgrade to a new version of the OS. Google releases new updates a couple of times a year, so devices can quickly fall behind, leading to software fragmentation. These types of fragmentation are arguably the biggest criticisms of the platform, as on paper everything else about Android is pretty awesome. One of the best things about it is that starting with version 2.1 (and 2.2 more solidly), the Android OS allows for the use of Flash in two flavors:

- As a plug-in to the Android OS Web browser, so you can view Web sites just as you would on a desktop
- In the form of AIR, Adobe's integrated package for desktop applications built using HTML and Flash

In this chapter, we'll be looking at the second of these two options, using AIR for Android to publish a game directly to the device. To use this example, you'll need an Android phone or tablet supporting v2.2 of the OS, like many newer devices by HTC, Motorola, Samsung, and Google. If you have such a device, you'll need to visit the Android marketplace and download Adobe AIR for it. Also, while in the name of the chapter, I call it out as a tablet game; Android tablets are, as of this writing, still very expensive. I actually developed this example on a Google Nexus One, so it *is* playable on a phone. I simply imagined that the experience would be better on a much larger screen with more room to move around.

A Trio of Topics

In each of the examples in this book, I've tried to introduce new aspects of game development along the way, even if they are only indirectly related to the example. This chapter will cover three topics I have mentioned only in passing up until now:

- Multitouch input (with an Android device, though the same API works with iOS)
- A finite-state machine for controlling game flow and logic (referenced in Chapter 1)
- A full rigid-body physics engine that is open-source, fast, and used in many popular Flash games

This may seem like a lot, but don't worry—I'm not diving terribly deep into any of these topics, just what we need to get the job done. By the time you finish with this chapter, you should feel totally comfortable building games that use all three of the above elements, as well as beginning to dig deeper into each of them. We'll pull all of these pieces together to create a simple, two-player air hockey game like the one you may have played in an arcade or even at someone's house.

Multitouch Input for Devices

In Chapter 15, we explored using the accelerometer in a device to control movement in a game. The other primary means of input on a modern mobile device is a touch screen. All iOS or Android devices support varying degrees of multitouch input, meaning they support a variable number of points being touched on the screen simultaneously. This is a very different model that we're used to in Flash, having relied on a single mouse or keyboard input. It's also very powerful, allowing a whole new level of control. Adobe has done a particularly good job of implementing touch input inside of Flash. There are three different modes in which Flash operates when reading input from the touch display. These modes are defined by the MultitouchInputMode class and are as follows:

- NONE: Any touches detected by the device are translated as mouse events. This is the default mode in which all Flash applications start, making it very easy to translate existing content into mobile applications without any change in the input scheme—this is also the mode we used in Chapter 15.
- TOUCH_POINT: Touches are translated into a series of new events, defined by the TouchEvent class. Every touch has a unique ID (integer) so as to distinguish them when they happen simultaneously. This is needed when you need to be able to capture more than one touch at once or to write handlers to recognize custom gestures. This mode will be used in gameplay later on in this chapter.
- GESTURE: Certain predefined gestures commonly supported by touch devices (such as swipes, press-and-hold touches, rotations, and so on) are read in this mode. Any touches that don't fall into a predefined gesture are treated like mouse events, not unlike "NONE" mode. This mode is less relevant in most games, unless they make specific use of the gestures. We'll use it briefly in this chapter just to show how it is implemented.

Flash can only operate in a single touch mode at a time, so you need to plan for which kind makes the most sense for each part of your application. Changing modes is as simple as setting the Multi-touch.inputMode property to one of those three enumerations.

The Finite-State Machine

Up to this point, we've not looked at an example with complicated enough behavior to warrant a full-state machine implementation, but I would be doing a disservice to not demonstrate it at least once. The version I'll make use of in this chapter is essentially the same model I use on a daily basis at Blockdot. It was written by Jim Montgomery, one of my teammates, and was simple, straight-forward, and very flexible. I won't dig into the code under the hood (though it is included as part of the source files), but I will take a moment to describe *how* it works, which is ultimately more important. In games in which you need to handle switching between different logic during gameplay (which is most of them), a state machine will become the backbone of your application. Here are the steps you go through to set up the state machine we'll be using in this chapter:

1. Define all the states your game will need to use, each with a unique integer identifier (in the case of the air hockey game, I'll make use of four discrete states).
2. Create event handlers for the logic that needs to happen in each state. There are three components to every state:
   a. ENTER: This event occurs once when a state is switched to from another state.
   b. UPDATE: This event occurs repetitively (usually on a frame cycle) as long as the machine stays in this state.
   c. EXIT: This event occurs when a call is made to the machine to switch to a new state; this is usually reserved for doing cleanup from the state being left.
3. Create a new instance of the state manager class and add each of the states to it.
4. On an ENTER_FRAME loop or similarly timed event, call the *update* method of the state machine.

Some of this will make more sense when we look at how it is actually implemented in the game, which we'll get to shortly. In the meantime, suffice it to say that in practice, it is very simple to set up and provides the most flexibility for adding new states or changing the flow between states throughout development. There's a reason we use it on a daily basis!

Physics Simulation with Box2D

In Chapter 11, we took a look at some elementary physics principles that we will use commonly in games. In Chapters 14 and 15, we implemented some very basic physics using simple collision detection and gravity. However, in this example, a little more is required. If you've ever played air hockey, you'll know that the puck ricochets off the two-player paddles, as well as the walls. Gravity and friction are abated by the presence of upward blowing air. We could write our own physics simulation to recreate all this, but I'm not going to, favoring instead to use the very popular, open-source Box2D library that has been ported to just about every platform imaginable. I'm doing this for two reasons:

- Don't re-invent the wheel. There are some cases in which rolling your own physics is the best way to go because it will have the lightest memory or processor overhead. We used a custom system in Marble Runner in Chapter 15 because on the iPhone, every single cycle was counted and it was more important to be efficient than robust. On the Android, we've got more speed available to us, so using a vetted, powerful physics package makes the most sense.

- Box2D is widely used for Flash game development. It is popular because it works well, is free, and is open source. It is continually improved by the community, and because it is supported on so many different platforms, it allows you to switch between Flash and, say, native iOS development, and maintain almost identical syntax.

There are a couple of things to note about Box2D. First is that I will only be scratching the surface of its capabilities in this chapter. I encourage you to explore it further on your own; it has a very active community around it. The second is that the library has its roots in the C language, so some of the ways in which you interact with it are decidedly less "ActionScript like." Everything about it is engineered to run as fast and efficiently as possible. Luckily, it is pretty well documented, so it is relatively easy to figure out how to perform a specific task with it. The final note is that, like any robust physics solution, Box2D operates abstracted away from the elements of the display list. What this means is that most of the work we'll be doing will be to bind the objects in the physics simulation with DisplayObjects on the Stage to achieve the look we want. We'll dig into this further when we explore the air hockey engine.

The Game: Two-Player Air Hockey

The concept of air hockey, if you're unfamiliar with it, is extremely simple. The game is played on a table, usually designed to look like a traditional hockey rink, with two openings on either end acting as the goals. Two players are each given a round plastic instrument, usually called a paddle (shown on the right in Fig. 16.1), with which they must hit the puck (the disc shown on the left) into their opponent's goal. For the record, if you haven't played this game and my description just now was your first exposure to it, put down this book right now and go find a place to play it. It's very fun!

For the virtual simulation of this game, we'll define some quick rules.

- In real air hockey, the puck and the paddles are not too different in size from each other, radius wise. In this version, the paddles will be enlarged somewhat in proportion to the puck so as to provide a usable target to hit with one's finger.
- In the live game, players can feasibly reach across the table to their opponent's side to hit the puck (though that is usually against the rules). This will be very rigidly disallowed here

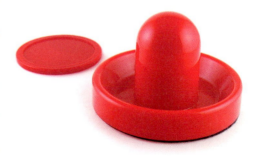

Figure 16.1 The puck (left) and paddle (right) used in a typical air hockey game.

because we need to be able to assign touch events to either one side or the other. If both players were tapping on the same side of the screen, we wouldn't be able to distinguish the difference between them.

- This game will enforce a score limit of three goals to end a session.

That should be about all the setup we need—let's dig into some code!

The XFL File

From the Chapter 16 examples folder, open the AirHockey.xfl file in the AirHockey directory. Note the differences and similarities to the file we created for Marble Runner:

- The document frame rate is set to 30 fps. Since we're on an Android device (and, ideally, on a more powerful tablet rather than just a phone), we can bump up the frame rate to a smoother setting.
- The main timeline follows the same structure as before, utilizing frame labels to denote the three main parts of the application.
- The library is also laid out in much the same way.
- Under the Publish Settings, the file is set to export as AIR for Android.

The Classes

There are fewer classes we'll be working with than the two previous examples, primarily because we're using Box2D for all the physics (which consists of a *lot* of classes) and the game itself doesn't need the logic broken up into a bunch of components. We'll still follow the engine/application division of labor, where the engine should behave as agnostically as possible to the application in which it resides. However, the engine itself is mostly just there to provide a communication layer between the application and the physics simulation. We'll look at this in depth shortly.

Because this example makes use of the Box2D library, as well as a generic state machine and the Greensock Tweening library, the game classes will live parallel to a lot of other code. The components we'll be looking at will be found at:

```
com.flashgamebook.android.airhockey
```

and

```
com.flashgamebook.android.airhockey.engine
```

Below are the classes we'll examine and their responsibilities:

- *AirHockeyEngine.as*: As the engine, this manages the physics simulation and updates the positions of the puck and two-player paddles in reaction to the physics.

- *AirHockeyEngineConfig.as*: This is simply a basic structure, consisting of parameters you need to define for the engine to work. This is more practical than setting values directly on the engine itself or passing in a horde of parameters to an initialization function. Doing it in this way also lends itself better to validation, like we performed on levels in Marble Runner; however, I don't implement any validation here.
- *Main.as*: The document class for the whole application. There will be very little here, which is new from previous examples.
- *Title.as*: The class wrapper for the title screen—as basic as it gets.
- *Rules.as*: The class wrapper for the rules screen, where I'll briefly demonstrate gesture events.
- *Game.as*: The heart of the application, which creates and controls the state machine, routes input information, and instantiates the engine.
- *GameTouchController.as*: The wrapper for touch input in the game since we need it to behave in a specific way to avoid twitchiness or hiccups.

We'll start with the relatively superficial bits of application functionality and then move to the game itself.

Main.as

As with other examples, the main document class just handles navigation between sections of the game, which number three in this application.

```
public class Main extends MovieClip
{
        static public const FRAME_TITLE:String = "title";
        static public const FRAME_RULES:String = "rules";
        static public const FRAME_GAME:String = "game";

        static private var mInstance:Main;

        public function Main()
        {
                mInstance = this;
                enumerateFrameLabels();
                addEventListener( FRAME_TITLE, onFrameTitle,
                  false, 0, true);
                addEventListener( FRAME_RULES, onFrameRules,
                  false, 0, true);
                addEventListener( FRAME_GAME, onFrameGame, false,
                  0, true);
                gotoAndStop(FRAME_TITLE);
        }
```

```
static public function getInstance():Main
{
        return mInstance;
}

private function onFrameTitle( _evt:Event ):void
{
        Multitouch.inputMode = MultitouchInputMode.NONE;
}

private function onFrameRules( _evt:Event ):void
{
        Multitouch.inputMode = MultitouchInputMode.GESTURE;
}

private function onFrameGame( _evt:Event ):void
{
        Multitouch.inputMode = MultitouchInputMode.
          TOUCH_POINT;
}

private function dispatchFrameEvent():void
{
        dispatchEvent(new Event(currentLabel));
}

private function enumerateFrameLabels():void
{
        for each (var label:FrameLabel in currentLabels)
        {
                addFrameScript(label.frame-1,
                  dispatchFrameEvent);
        }
}
}
```

The most notable element of this class is that each of the three different application states uses a different form of multitouch input. The title screen will use mouse events, the rules screen will rely on gestures, and the game itself will use raw touch point data. There's also a static pointer (through *getInstance*) to the class so that sections can easily navigate to other sections.

Title.as

On the heels of such a simple document class, an even simpler title screen component can be obtained. Note that it uses standard mouse events, so it will function in the same manner when being run on a desktop machine.

```
public class Title extends Sprite
{
        public var btnPlay:SimpleButton;
        public var btnRules:SimpleButton;

        public function Title()
        {
                addEventListener(Event.ADDED_TO_STAGE,
                  onAddedToStage, false, 0, true);
        }

        private function onAddedToStage( _evt:Event ):void
        {
                btnPlay.addEventListener(MouseEvent.CLICK,
                  onPlayClick, false, 0, true);
                btnRules.addEventListener(MouseEvent.CLICK,
                  onRulesClick, false, 0, true);
        }

        private function onPlayClick( _evt:MouseEvent ):void
        {
                Main.getInstance().gotoAndStop(Main.FRAME_GAME);
        }

        private function onRulesClick( _evt:MouseEvent ):void
        {
                Main.getInstance().gotoAndStop(Main.FRAME_RULES);
        }
}
```

Rules.as

This class is a little more involved. If you refer to the XFL document and open the Rules clip from the library, you'll see that there are two screens of instructions, but only one is visible on stage. The other is off to the right, but they are both contained in a single display object called *clipRulesText*. We'll use a combination of gestures and TweenNano (the superlight version of TweenLite) to simulate the popular swiping effect used in many iOS and Android applications. There are other ways to have organized this content, but for the sake of this example, this was the most straightforward.

```
import flash.events.TransformGestureEvent;
import com.greensock.TweenNano;
import com.greensock.easing.Quad;
```

```
public class Rules extends Sprite
{
        static private const NUMBER_OF_PAGES:int = 2;

        public var clipRulesText:Sprite;
        public var btnBack:SimpleButton;

        private var mCurrentPage:int = 1;

        public function Rules()
        {
                addEventListener( Event.ADDED_TO_STAGE,
                   onAddedToStage, false, 0, true );
        }

        private function onAddedToStage( _evt:Event ):void
        {
                addEventListener( TransformGestureEvent.GESTURE_
                   SWIPE, onGestureSwipe, false, 0, true );
                btnBack.addEventListener( MouseEvent.CLICK,
                   onBackButtonClick, false, 0, true );
                clipRulesText.cacheAsBitmap = true;
        }
```

Note that in setting up the input for this screen, we use the predefined GESTURE_SWIPE event. Also worth noting is that we attached a normal mouse listener to the back button since that is how any nongesture input will be treated by Flash in this mode. We also cache the text box as a bitmap for the best performance when animating it with TweenNano.

```
private function onGestureSwipe( _evt:TransformGestureEvent ):
  void
{
        if ( _evt.offsetX < 0 )
        {
                changePage( 1 );
        }
        else if ( _evt.offsetX > 0 )
        {
                changePage( -1 );
        }
}
private function onBackButtonClick( _evt:MouseEvent ):void

{
        Main.getInstance().gotoAndStop( Main.FRAME_TITLE );
}
```

```
private function changePage( _direction:int ):void
{
      mCurrentPage += _direction;
      mCurrentPage = ( mCurrentPage < 1 ) ? 1 : mCurrentPage;
      mCurrentPage = ( mCurrentPage > NUMBER_OF_PAGES ) ?
        NUMBER_OF_PAGES: mCurrentPage;
      var targetX:int = ( mCurrentPage - 1 ) * -loaderInfo.width;
      TweenNano.to( clipRulesText, .25, { x: targetX, ease:
        Quad.easeInOut } );
}
```

In the *onGestureSwipe* event handler, we simply use the offset property of the event to determine if they swiped from left to right (positive) or right to left (negative). However, the behavior we're expecting is the inverse. When swiping from right to left, the user wants to advance to the content on the right and vice versa for going from left to right. This is handled by the *changePage* method, which determines the new page to display and uses TweenNano to slide the text clip around on stage. The net result is very natural, similar to the native swiping used for menus in the Android OS.

Now that we're done with the ancillary components to our game, let's dig into the gameplay itself. We'll start with the touch controller, so you'll have context for what it does in the game. Then, we'll look at the application end of the game and how it manages states. We'll finish out the game with the engine and how it drives the physics.

GameTouchController.as

As you saw in the *main* document class, when we enter the game state of the application, we changed to the touch point form of multitouch input. This will give us the flexibility we need for two active players. The *GameTouchController* class is linked directly to a display object on stage. In this case, there are two of them, one for each side of the game board. They are on the layer input zones in the XFL file, inside of the game clip. They are simply shapes filled with a transparent color, so they will receive input events but not be visible. Now let's take a look at the code.

```
public class GameTouchController extends Sprite
{

      private var mPosition:Point;
      private var mCoordinateSpace:DisplayObjectContainer;
      private var mDistanceThreshold:Number;
      private var mTouching:Boolean = false;

      public function GameTouchController()
```

```
        {
                mPosition = new Point();
                addEventListener( TouchEvent.TOUCH_BEGIN,
                  onTouchBegin, false, 0, true );
                addEventListener( TouchEvent.TOUCH_MOVE,
                  onTouchMove, false, 0, true );
                addEventListener( TouchEvent.TOUCH_END, onTouchEnd,
                  false, 0, true );

                addEventListener( MouseEvent.MOUSE_DOWN,
                  onMouseDown, false, 0, true );
                addEventListener( MouseEvent.MOUSE_MOVE,
                  onMouseMove, false, 0, true );
                addEventListener( MouseEvent.MOUSE_UP, onMouseUp,
                  false, 0, true );
        }

    public function init( _coordinateSpace:DisplayObject
      Container, _initialPosition:Point, _distanceThreshold:
      Number ):void
    {
                mCoordinateSpace = _coordinateSpace;
                mPosition = _initialPosition;
                mDistanceThreshold = _distanceThreshold;
                mTouching = false;
    }
```

This class needs to keep track of a few things. One is the touch position of the user's finger, stored in *mPosition*. It also keeps track of the coordinate space to translate the touch position, as having the position relative to the touch controller itself isn't likely to be useful. There is a distance threshold variable, which is used to validate whether the placement of a touch event is close enough to the point stored in *mPosition* to update. This will prevent someone from simply using two fingers to tap opposite sides of the game board and have their paddle "snap" across the table. When a touch occurs, if it is outside this distance threshold, it is ignored. The last property the class stores is a flag to find whether a touch is occurring. This will prevent updates unless someone starts touching within the distance threshold. These values are all set in the *init* function, which we will see later is called by the *Game* class. You'll also notice that in the constructor, we add listeners for both touch events and mouse events. This is done for the purposes of debugging. Since touch events only work on a device, if you want to test simple functionality without publishing to that device every time, you can just export a SWF in the Flash player and the behavior will be mimicked using the mouse. In practice, it would be a good idea when deploying the game to comment out the last three lines of the constructor, so these methods are not called.

```
public function get position():Point
{
        return mPosition.clone();
}


public function dispose():void
{
        removeEventListener(TouchEvent.TOUCH_BEGIN, onTouchBegin );
        removeEventListener(TouchEvent.TOUCH_MOVE, onTouchMove );
        removeEventListener(TouchEvent.TOUCH_END, onTouchEnd );
        removeEventListener(MouseEvent.MOUSE_DOWN, onMouseDown );
        removeEventListener(MouseEvent.MOUSE_MOVE, onMouseMove );
        removeEventListener(MouseEvent.MOUSE_UP, onMouseUp );
}
```

There is an accessor for getting the current finger position, which simply returns a copy of the internally stored position. We return a copy, so this value can't be accidentally modified and mess up the internal mechanics of the controller. The *dispose* function should be self-explanatory by now. It does cleanup of listeners to free up memory.

```
private function onTouchBegin( _evt:TouchEvent ):void
{
        var newPosition:Point = new Point( _evt.stageX, _evt.stageY
)

        newPosition = mCoordinateSpace.globalToLocal(newPosition);

        if (Point.distance( mPosition, newPosition ) <= mDistance
          Threshold )
        {
                mTouching = true;
                onTouchMove( _evt );
        }
}


private function onTouchMove( _evt:TouchEvent ):void
{
        if (mTouching)
        {
                mPosition.x = _evt.stageX;
                mPosition.y = _evt.stageY;
                mPosition = mCoordinateSpace.globalToLocal(mPosition);
        }
}
```

```
private function onTouchEnd( _evt:TouchEvent ):void
{
        mTouching = false;
}
```

When a new touch is detected, *onTouchBegin* is called. It translates the position of the touch into the coordinate space defined in the *init* function and then compares it to the internally stored position. If it falls within the threshold, the touching flag is set to true and *onTouchMove* is called manually to force an update of the position. *onTouchMove* is called automatically whenever movement occurs on the touch display. When the touch is no longer detected, *onTouchEnd* is called, setting the flag back to false.

```
// For Desktop debugging
private function onMouseDown( _evt:MouseEvent ):void
{
        var newPosition:Point = new Point( _evt.stageX, _evt.stageY
)

        newPosition = mCoordinateSpace.globalToLocal(newPosition);

        if (Point.distance( mPosition, newPosition ) <= mDistance
          Threshold )
        {
                mTouching = true;
                onMouseMove( _evt );
        }
}

private function onMouseMove( _evt:MouseEvent ):void
{
        if (mTouching)
        {
                mPosition.x = _evt.stageX;
                mPosition.y = _evt.stageY;
                mPosition = mCoordinateSpace.globalToLocal
                  (mPosition);
        }
}

private function onMouseUp( _evt:MouseEvent ):void
{
        mTouching = false;
}
```

These three methods are the mouse versions of the touch handlers we just examined. You'll notice that they're practically identical because the events are so similar. This was a very wise move on

Adobe's part when creating the touch event API—it's very easy to swap out mouse events for touch ones. Now, we'll look at how this class is used in the game.

Game.as

Before we dig heavily into the code for the *Game* class, let's look at what is inside the game clip in the XFL document. I've grouped the different types of components into layers for easy access, per Figure 16.2.

In the bottom-most layer is the basic line art for the rink, encapsulated in a Sprite and set for bitmap caching. The second layer contains the score display objects. They resemble text fields, but they are actually MovieClips with the four possible score values advancing over each frame. This would not be practical for a game with an uncapped score, but for our purposes, it will work fine.

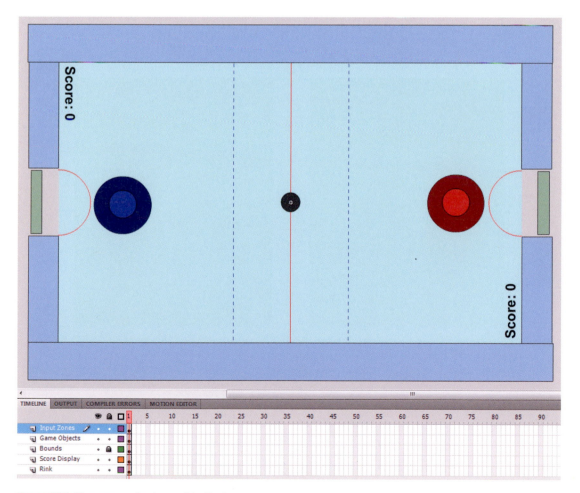

Figure 16.2 The game clip, layered in Flash.

Alternatively, you could place dynamic text fields inside the clips and update them with the score. They are also cached as bitmaps because they will live underneath other cached elements. Text in particular has rendering performance lag when layered between GPU-cached elements. You're probably thinking "but wait, the contents of the clip will change whenever the player scores, causing Flash to redraw it." You'd be right; however, this re-caching process will take place when the game is not active, so there will be no noticeable hiccup. The alternative would be to not cache it and have it slow down the whole game considerably—not the best option.

The third layer, "Bounds," contains box clips I've created to act as the borders of the table. The physics system will translate these boxes (with the help of our engine) into mathematical constructs. This allows us to fine-tune the layout of elements visually without adjusting numbers in code. Note that each of these clips is named. Since there are a limited number of them, I simply reference them later on in the *Game* class. If the number of clips grew or had no limit, I would apply the same method of crawling the display list that I used in Marble Runner. However, because that involves the creation of unnecessary stub classes, I've omitted that process here. The "Game Objects" layer contains the puck and both paddles. Finally, the top-most layer holds the *GameTouchController* objects we looked at earlier. Now we're ready to dive into the code for this sucker. We'll start by examining the member variables and constants.

```
public class Game extends Sprite
{

        static public const STATE_PRE_GAME:int = 1;
        static public const STATE_GAME_ACTIVE:int = 2;
        static public const STATE_GAME_SCORE:int = 3;
        static public const STATE_POST_GAME:int = 4;

        static public const MAX_SCORE:int = 3;

        static private const OVERLAY_PRE_GAME_COUNTDOWN:String =
          "PreGameCountdown";
        static private const OVERLAY_PLAYER_1_SCORE:String =
          "Player1Score";
        static private const OVERLAY_PLAYER_2_SCORE:String =
          "Player2Score";
        static private const OVERLAY_PLAYER_1_WON:String =
          "Player1Won";
        static private const OVERLAY_PLAYER_2_WON:String =
          "Player2Won";
```

```
public var clipPaddle1:Sprite, clipPaddle2:Sprite,
  clipPuck:Sprite;
public var clipGoal1:Sprite, clipGoal2:Sprite;
public var clipWall1:Sprite, clipWall2:Sprite, clipWall3:
  Sprite, clipWall4:Sprite, clipWall5:Sprite, clipWall6:
  Sprite;
public var clipTouchController1:GameTouchController,
  clipTouchController2:GameTouchController;
public var clipScoreDisplay1:MovieClip, clipScoreDisplay2:
  MovieClip;

private var mStateMachine:FSMManager;
private var mEngine:AirHockeyEngine;
private var mPlayer1Score:int = 0, mPlayer2Score:int = 0;
private var mOverlayClip:MovieClip;
```

The first four constants defined here represent the four different states in which the game can function. Our state machine requires a unique "int" identifier for every state registered with it, so this is an easy way to enumerate them. The PRE_GAME state will consist of the countdown prior to gameplay. GAME_ACTIVE will represent the game in a state of play, where both players can give input and the physics will be active. The GAME_SCORE state will take over when a player scores, displaying who scored and resetting the game board. Finally, when the game is finished, it will go to the POST_GAME state.

The second set of constant values contains the names of overlays that will be displayed in the game at different points. These name values correspond to MovieClips in the XFL library, as shown in Fig. 16.3.

All of the public variables map to various display objects, all pre-fixed with the word "clip." This will allow us to easily pass these objects into the engine, so it can bind them to the physics simulation. Finally, there are member variables storing an instance of the finite-state manager (more on that in a moment), an instance of the *AirHockeyEngine*, the scores of the two players, and a reference that will be used to store which overlay clip is currently active. When none is displayed, this property should be null.

Game - Player 1 Score	Player1Score
Game - Player 1 Won	Player1Won
Game - Player 2 Score	Player2Score
Game - Player 2 Won	Player2Won
Game - Pre Game Countd...	PreGameCountdown

Figure 16.3 The overlay MovieClips used in the game—their class names match the constant values in the *Game* class.

```
public function Game()
{
        addEventListener( Event.ADDED_TO_STAGE, onAddedToStage,
          false, 0, true );
}

private function onAddedToStage( _evt:Event ):void
{
        // Create engine configuration and link it to stage display
          objects
        var config:AirHockeyEngineConfig = new AirHockeyEngineConfig();
        config.mClipReference = this;
        config.mPlayer1 = clipPaddle1;
        config.mPlayer2 = clipPaddle2;
        config.mPlayer1Goal = clipGoal1;
        config.mPlayer2Goal = clipGoal2;
        config.mPuck = clipPuck;
        config.mPlayer1ScoreCallback = onPlayer1Score;
        config.mPlayer2ScoreCallback = onPlayer2Score;
        var boundaries:Vector.<DisplayObject> = new Vector.
          <DisplayObject>();
        boundaries.push( clipWall1, clipWall2, clipWall3,
          clipWall4, clipWall5, clipWall6 );
        config.mBoundaryList = boundaries;
        mEngine = new AirHockeyEngine( config );

        // Set up state manager
        mStateMachine = new FSMManager();
        mStateMachine.addState( STATE_PRE_GAME, "AirHockeyState::
          PreGame", onPreGameEnter, onPreGameUpdate, null );
        mStateMachine.addState( STATE_GAME_ACTIVE, "AirHockeyState::
          GameActive", onGameActiveEnter, onGameActiveUpdate, null );
        mStateMachine.addState( STATE_GAME_SCORE, "AirHockeyState::
          GameScore", onGameScoreEnter, onGameScoreUpdate, null );
        mStateMachine.addState( STATE_POST_GAME, "AirHockeyState::
          PostGame", onPostGameEnter, onPostGameUpdate, null );
        mStateMachine.gotoState( STATE_PRE_GAME );

        // Start the game loop
        clipScoreDisplay1.gotoAndStop(1);
        clipScoreDisplay2.gotoAndStop(1);
        addEventListener( Event.ENTER_FRAME, onEnterFrame, false,
          0, true );
}

private function onEnterFrame( _evt:Event ):void
{
        mStateMachine.update( Time.deltaTime );
}
```

```
public function dispose():void
{
        removeEventListener( Event.ENTER_FRAME, onEnterFrame );
        clipTouchController1.dispose();
        clipTouchController2.dispose();
        mStateMachine.dispose();
        mEngine.dispose();
}
```

The first chunk of functionality in the class is all about initialization and disposal. When the clip is added to the stage, it performs three main tasks. It creates an *AirHockeyEngineConfig* instance, which as I mentioned earlier is just a structure for passing relevant data to the engine. Although it is taking things a bit out of order, here is the main content of that configuration class, for context.

```
public var mClipReference:Sprite;
public var mBoundaryList:Vector.<DisplayObject>;
public var mPlayer1:Sprite;
public var mPlayer2:Sprite;
public var mPlayer1Goal:DisplayObject;
public var mPlayer2Goal:DisplayObject;
public var mPuck:DisplayObject
public var mPlayer1ScoreCallback:Function;
public var mPlayer2ScoreCallback:Function;
```

Most of these should be self-explanatory, but I will call out a couple of them for clarity. The clip reference member exists so the engine has a context for the game that is using it. The boundary list Vector is an easy way of pre-encapsulating all of the walls for processing later since we don't need to know about them individually. The two callback variables are for tying functionality from the engine back to the *Game* class, by allowing the engine to trigger events without knowing their context. We could use events for this same purpose, but in the spirit of being efficient for mobile, callbacks will work just fine.

Getting back to the initialization of the *Game* class, once all the values for the config object have been assigned, a new instance of an engine is created and passed this object. Next, the state manager is created. For each of the four states we've already defined, we must add that state to the manager. The FSM *addState* method expects a numeric ID (the values we defined first in the class), a string description, and then up to three methods to call for that state. In the case of this game, we're not really interested in when a state is exited in favor of another one. Instead, we want to know when a state is entered and an update method to call every frame. We'll look at all of these methods shortly. Once the states are added, we tell the machine to go to the PRE_GAME state, which will automatically start the game.

The last task performed in the initialization is resetting the score displays to their initial state (of 0) and attaching a listener to the ENTER_FRAME event. In turn, the *onEnterFrame* handler simply calls the state machine's update method, passing it the delta time. The machine will handle all of the other processing. Compared to similar ENTER_FRAME loops we've looked at up to this point, this is remarkably simple and will keep the logic for the game well separated. You'll notice that we don't compute a value for the delta time like we have in previous examples. Instead, we make use of a class called *Time* with a *deltaTime* property. This is a custom utility class that handles calculating these values for us. We'll look at how it works shortly, but for now suffice it to say that it is simply returning a number that represents the change in time from the previous frame in seconds.

The last method in the chunk of code we're examining is the *dispose* function. It performs cleanup across the board, calling the *dispose* method of all of the game components and removing the frame loop. When we leave the game, this will be called to free up memory before moving to another section.

```
private function onPlayer1Score():void
{
    mPlayer1Score++;
    clipScoreDisplay1.nextFrame();
    var overlayClass:Class = Class( getDefinitionByName(
      OVERLAY_PLAYER_1_SCORE ) );
    mOverlayClip = new overlayClass() as MovieClip;
    mOverlayClip.cacheAsBitmap = true;
    addChild(mOverlayClip);
    mStateMachine.gotoState( STATE_GAME_SCORE );
}

private function onPlayer2Score():void
{
    mPlayer2Score++;
    clipScoreDisplay2.nextFrame();
    var overlayClass:Class = Class( getDefinitionByName(
      OVERLAY_PLAYER_2_SCORE ) );
    mOverlayClip = new overlayClass() as MovieClip;
    mOverlayClip.cacheAsBitmap = true;
    addChild(mOverlayClip);
    mStateMachine.gotoState( STATE_GAME_SCORE );
}
```

These two methods are almost identical; they are the callbacks used for when the engine registers either player scoring a goal. They display the correct overlay clip, increment that player's score, and change the state manager to the GAME_SCORE state.

We'll now look at the methods we've defined for each state of the game, breaking them into pairs.

```
private function onPreGameEnter():void
{
      var overlayClass:Class = Class( getDefinitionByName(
        OVERLAY_PRE_GAME_COUNTDOWN ) );
      mOverlayClip = new overlayClass() as MovieClip;
      addChild(mOverlayClip);
}


private function onPreGameUpdate( _dt:Number ):void
{
      if (mOverlayClip.currentFrame == mOverlayClip.totalFrames)
      {
            removeChild( mOverlayClip );
            mOverlayClip = null;
            mStateMachine.gotoState( STATE_GAME_ACTIVE );
      }
}
```

When the PRE_GAME state is entered, it creates an overlay for the countdown clip, which has a simple animation play to its completion. In the update loop for this state, we simply check to see if the animation is done playing. If it is, we remove the animation and then head directly into the GAME_ACTIVE state.

```
private function onGameActiveEnter():void
{
      clipTouchController1.init( this, new Point( clipPaddle1.x,
        clipPaddle1.y ), clipPaddle1.height * 0.75 );
      clipTouchController2.init( this, new Point( clipPaddle2.x,
        clipPaddle2.y ), clipPaddle2.height * 0.75 );
}


private function onGameActiveUpdate( _dt:Number ):void
{
      clipPaddle1.x = clipTouchController1.position.x;
      clipPaddle1.y = clipTouchController1.position.y;
      clipPaddle2.x = clipTouchController2.position.x;
      clipPaddle2.y = clipTouchController2.position.y;
      mEngine.setPlayer1Position( clipTouchController1.position.
        x, clipTouchController1.position.y );
      mEngine.setPlayer2Position( clipTouchController2.position.
        x, clipTouchController2.position.y );
      mEngine.update( _dt );
      mEngine.checkForCollisions();
}
```

When the game becomes active, we initialize the two controllers with the current position of each paddle and set the distance threshold to include a small amount of area outside the circumference of each paddle. This "buffer" area will allow for the inherent imprecision of touch displays and give a margin of error, so the player doesn't have to have their finger directly on the center of a paddle in order to move it. In the update loop, we adjust each paddle's position to match that of the position stored in the controller. We also update the player positions inside of the engine and call two additional methods. We'll explore these in depth later in this chapter, but for now, all you need to really know is that the *update* function of the engine advances the physics simulation and the *checkForCollisions* method sees if the puck has come into contact with either player's goal. If it has, the callbacks we looked at earlier are called and the game changes state to GAME_SCORE.

```
private function onGameScoreEnter():void
{
        trace( "::Entering Score State :: Player 1 -", mPlayer1Score,
          ", Player 2 -", mPlayer2Score );
}


private function onGameScoreUpdate( _dt:Number ):void
{
        mEngine.update( _dt );
        if (mOverlayClip.currentFrame == mOverlayClip.totalFrames )
        {
                removeChild( mOverlayClip );
                mOverlayClip = null;
                if ( mPlayer1Score == MAX_SCORE || mPlayer2Score ==
                  MAX_SCORE )
                {
                        mStateMachine.gotoState( STATE_POST_GAME );
                }
                else
                {
                        mEngine.reset();
                        mStateMachine.gotoState( STATE_GAME_ACTIVE );
                }
        }
}
```

The entrance function to this state doesn't really have anything to do since the score callbacks handled all of the immediate logic. I included it for posterity and with a trace for debugging purposes so that you can see when the game changes state. Like the PRE_GAME state, the update loop here checks to see if the score animation has finished. When it does finish, the game checks to see if either player has reached the maximum score for the game, defined at the beginning as a constant value of 3. If neither player has reached the maximum score, the engine is reset and the game goes back to the active state. If a player has won, the game goes to its final state of POST_GAME.

```
private function onPostGameEnter():void
{
        var overlayClass:Class;
        if ( mPlayer1Score > mPlayer2Score )
        {
                overlayClass = Class( getDefinitionByName( OVERLAY_
                   PLAYER_1_WON ) );
        }
        else
        {
                overlayClass = Class( getDefinitionByName( OVERLAY_
                   PLAYER_2_WON ) );
        }
        mOverlayClip = new overlayClass() as MovieClip;
        mOverlayClip.cacheAsBitmap = true;
        addChild(mOverlayClip);
}


private function onPostGameUpdate( _dt:Number ):void
{
        if (mOverlayClip.currentFrame == mOverlayClip.totalFrames )
        {
                removeChild( mOverlayClip );
                mOverlayClip = null;
                dispose();
                Main.getInstance().gotoAndStop( Main.FRAME_TITLE );
        }
}
```

All of this should look familiar at this point—an overlay is displayed showing the winner, and after that animation has finished playing, the game disposes of itself and returns to the title screen. That's the extent of the *Game* class. Before diving into the engine class, where we'll roll up our sleeves with physics, let's take a quick look at the *Time* class I created earlier. It is generic enough that you can use it in any project.

```
public class Time extends Sprite
{
        static public const FPS24:Number = 1/24;
        static public const FPS30:Number = 1/30;
```

```
static private var mInstance:Time = new Time();
static private var mCurrentTime:int;
static private var mPreviousTime:int;
static private var mFixedDelta:Number = -1;

public function Time()
{
        if (mInstance) throw new Error("The Time class cannot
            be instantiated.");
        addEventListener(Event.ENTER_FRAME, onUpdateTime,
            false, 0, true);
        mCurrentTime = getTimer();
}


private function onUpdateTime(_evt:Event):void
{
        mPreviousTime = mCurrentTime;
        mCurrentTime = getTimer();
}


static public function fixDelta(_value:Number = -1):void
{
        mFixedDelta = _value;
}


static public function get deltaTime():Number
{
        if (mFixedDelta > 0)
        {
                return mFixedDelta;
        }
        return (mCurrentTime - mPreviousTime) / 1000;
}
}
```

All of the values stored inside the class are static, but it creates an internal instance of itself in order to create its own ENTER_FRAME loop. As you can see, it stores values for the current time and the time in the previous frame so that when the accessor for *deltaTime* is called, it can compute it on the fly. There's also an additional function called *fixDelta*. In certain cases, like with a physics simulation, you might want the delta time to always be a consistent value so as to maintain the fidelity of things like collision checking. This method allows you to set the desired value that *deltaTime* will return every time you call it. Although we won't use it in this game, there are times when it might well come in handy—there are even preset constants defined for 24 and 30 fps deltas. To use this method, you'd simply call

```
Time.fixDelta( Time.FPS30 );
```

From then on, you'd get a consistent value for the *deltaTime*, no matter how much time had actually passed. To undo this action, simply pass in a value of 0 or less:

```
Time.fixDelta( 0 );
```

You're welcome. Now to get back to the game at hand.

AirHockeyEngine.as

The engine for this game, as I've already mentioned, utilizes Box2D for its physics simulation. However, before we get started in the engine, here is a quick look at Box2D's core principles. I'll be staying very much on the surface of this library, but if you want to dig further, you can find a link to a fantastic series of tutorials at www.flashgamebook.com.

- Box2D works in meters as its basic unit of measurement; one of the first things to do when using the library is to establish your conversion rate of pixels to meters. 30 pixels per meter is the unofficial standard, because of how the simulation internally handles its calculations.
- Every element inside a Box2D simulation is a mathematical construct. It knows nothing about display objects, so our engine will be responsible for mapping the simulation objects to visuals on-screen.
- The coordinate space in which Box2D runs its simulation is known as "the world" and is represented by an instance of the b2World class. Objects in the world that take up physical space are called "bodies," represented by the b2Body class.
- Bodies can be static, dynamic, or kinematic. Static bodies do not respond to forces and do not move, like concrete walls. Dynamic objects move freely and respond to forces in the world (like gravity and impacts with other objects). Kinematic objects (which we won't use in our game) are ones that move but don't respond to force—a good example might be gears that rotate by themselves and move other bodies.
- Bodies are represented by *shapes* (such as squares, circles, and triangles), and these shapes determine how they react in collisions. However, shape objects do not have any knowledge of the physical properties of the body, such as friction, density, and so on. There is a separate kind of object, called a *fixture*, which is used to define these properties for a body and bind it to a shape.
- No objects in Box2D are created directly. Rather, definition or "def" objects are created, which are then passed to the world to create the actual objects. Think of def objects such as blueprints for the actual object to be created. You can use a def over and over again, once the world uses it to create an object, it retains

no knowledge of the def. You'll notice throughout the code below that class names in Box2D consistently end with "Def" when they refer to this construct.

Let's now look at how these principles work in the context of our engine.

```
public class AirHockeyEngine
{
        public static const DISTANCE_RATIO:Number = 30;

        private var mPhysicsEngine:b2World;
        private var mConfig:AirHockeyEngineConfig;
        private var mPlayer1:b2Body, mPlayer2:b2Body;
        private var mPuck:b2Body, mGoal1:b2Body, mGoal2:b2Body;
        private var mCollisionBodies:Vector.<b2Body>;
        private var mPlayer1Joint:b2MouseJoint, mPlayer2Joint:
          b2MouseJoint;
        // Origin positions
        private var mPlayer1Origin:b2Vec2, mPlayer2Origin:
          b2Vec2, mPuckOrigin:b2Vec2;
```

The first thing we define as a constant is the pixels per meter ratio I mentioned a moment ago. We then define member variables for the different Box2D components we'll want to keep track of: the world and bodies for the paddles, puck, goals, and walls. There's a member variable to keep track of the engine config object we created earlier in the *Game* class. We also define a new kind of object called a b2MouseJoint. Joints are used in Box2D to connect two objects to each other with some kind of physical constraints. In the case of a b2MouseJoint, we'll use it to connect the paddle bodies to the world object so that we can use the mouse (or in our situation, touch input) to apply forces to it. We'll see how this works shortly. The last thing we define are origin positions for the two paddles and the puck. These b2Vec2 objects, which you can sort of think of like a cross between the Point and Vector3D objects in ActionScript, will keep the original positions of the objects so that we can restore the state of the game board at a moment's notice.

```
public function AirHockeyEngine( _config:AirHockeyEngineConfig )
{
        if ( !_config )
        {
                throw new ArgumentError( "The AirHockeyEngine
                  requires a AirHockeyEngineConfig struct to
                  instantiate." );
        }

        mConfig = _config;
```

```
        // Set up Box2D World
        setupPhysics();
}


public function dispose():void
{
        mPhysicsEngine = null;
        mConfig = null;
        mPlayer1 = null;
        mPlayer2 = null;
        mPuck = null;
        mGoal1 = null;
        mGoal2 = null;
        mPlayer1Joint = null;
        mPlayer2Joint = null;
        mCollisionBodies = null;
}
```

In the constructor, we simply pass and store the *AirHockey-EngineConfig* object and then call *setupPhysics*, which we'll examine next. The dispose function, which the *Game* class calls, simply nulls out every member variable.

```
private function setupPhysics():void
{
        mPhysicsEngine = new b2World(new b2Vec2(), false);
        // Create paddle bodies
        mPlayer1 = displayObjectToCircle( mConfig.mPlayer1,
          mPhysicsEngine );
        mPlayer1Origin = mPlayer1.GetPosition().Copy();
        mPlayer2 = displayObjectToCircle( mConfig.mPlayer2,
          mPhysicsEngine );
        mPlayer2Origin = mPlayer2.GetPosition().Copy();
        // Create paddle reaction joints
        var jointDef:b2MouseJointDef = new b2MouseJointDef();
        jointDef.bodyA = mPhysicsEngine.GetGroundBody();
        jointDef.bodyB = mPlayer1;
        jointDef.target = mPlayer1.GetPosition();
        jointDef.maxForce = 300.0 * mPlayer1.GetMass();
        mPlayer1Joint = mPhysicsEngine.CreateJoint( jointDef ) as
          b2MouseJoint;
        jointDef.bodyB = mPlayer2;
        jointDef.target = mPlayer2.GetPosition();
        jointDef.maxForce = 300.0 * mPlayer2.GetMass();
        mPlayer2Joint = mPhysicsEngine.CreateJoint( jointDef ) as
          b2MouseJoint;

        // Create puck and goals
```

```
mPuck = displayObjectToCircle( mConfig.mPuck,
  mPhysicsEngine );
mPuck.SetLinearDamping( .8 );
mPuckOrigin = mPuck.GetPosition().Copy();
mGoal1 = displayObjectToBox( mConfig.mPlayer1Goal,
  mPhysicsEngine );
mGoal2 = displayObjectToBox( mConfig.mPlayer2Goal,
  mPhysicsEngine );

for each (var boundary:DisplayObject in mConfig.
  mBoundaryList)
{
    displayObjectToBox( boundary, mPhysicsEngine );
}

mCollisionBodies = new Vector.<b2Body>(2, true);
}
```

When setting up a b2World object, you can define certain properties of it, such as gravity and whether objects are allowed to sleep (that is, be removed from the calculations of the simulation if they're not moving). In our case, since the gravity of our game is downward through the *z*-axis of the board, we don't want the physics engine to apply gravity. Passing an empty b2Vec2 gives us a gravity of 0. The next few lines create the body objects for the paddles and copy their original position for the origin objects. You'll notice that this process uses a method called *displayObjectToCircle*. This is a static function we'll look at shortly. It takes a display object and the corresponding b2World object and performs all the processes of "converting" the visual representation into a mathematical circle. For the walls, we'll use a very similar function, *displayObjectToBox*, which works for rectangular objects.

After defining the bodies for the paddles, we need joints to attach them to the world, so they have a reaction to input. This is done by creating a new joint definition of the type b2MouseJointDef. Joints have to have two bodies to work, so the first body we supply is the world's "body" and the second is the paddle to which it will attach. The target of a joint is the position to which it wants to move. When reading input later on, we'll change this target vector to reflect the position of the player's finger. This change in target will cause the joint to react, exerting a force on the paddle body. The last thing we do before creating the joint in the world is to specify a *maxForce* property, which, according to the Box2D manual, is "used to prevent violent reactions when multiple dynamic bodies interact." Think of it as a throttle on the force you can exert. I wish I could say the value of 300 times the mass of the paddle was a value I calculated carefully. Unfortunately, like so much of working with physics in games, it was a value that after some testing "felt right." Often, real-world accuracy is not what is desired in a physics simulation, so elements like this will require some futzing with values to get the desired feel. After creating the joints for the paddles, we simply convert the other display objects passed into the config. We'll now look at these two conversion functions and how they work. They're very similar overall, so we'll start with the *displayObjectToBox* and then look at the differences when we need a circle instead.

```
private static function displayObjectToBox( _displayObject:
  DisplayObject, _world:b2World ):b2Body
{
      // Create body def
      var bodyDef:b2BodyDef = new b2BodyDef();
      bodyDef.type = b2Body.b2_staticBody;
      var rect:Rectangle = _displayObject.getRect(_displayObject.
        parent);
      bodyDef.position.Set( (rect.left + rect.width/2) /
        DISTANCE_RATIO, (rect.top + rect.height/2) / DISTANCE_
        RATIO );
      // Create shape and fixture
      var boxShape:b2PolygonShape = new b2PolygonShape();
      boxShape.SetAsBox( ( rect.width / 2 ) / DISTANCE_RATIO,
        ( rect.height / 2 ) / DISTANCE_RATIO );
      var fixtureDef:b2FixtureDef = new b2FixtureDef();
      fixtureDef.shape = boxShape;
      fixtureDef.density = .5;
      fixtureDef.friction = 1;
      fixtureDef.restitution = 0.1;
      // Create body
      var body:b2Body = _world.CreateBody( bodyDef );
      body.CreateFixture( fixtureDef );
      return body;
}
```

For all of the boxes in this engine, we just need them to provide fixed boundaries, so we can conveniently define all of the box body types as static. We use the *getRect* method of the DisplayObject we've used in previous chapters to get the dimensions of the box. We then use this rectangular object to set the position and shape of the body. The shape object we use, which is a generic b2Polygon-Shape, has a convenient *SetAsBox* method that is used to quickly define a rectangular shape. You may notice that we pass the *SetAsBox* method half the width and height of the rectangle. This is because the box will be centered on its position and the method wants to know how far out from the center to travel. Next, we create a fixture object that defines the physical properties of the walls. As these objects are static, the only real value we're concerned with is restitution, which is how much bounce occurs when things hit the walls. A value of 0 would mean that no bounce occurred. A value of 1 would mean that a bounce of exactly the same magnitude of its incoming force would occur. We'll see how this applies for the paddle and puck objects in a moment. The final step is to create a body in the world using the definition object, and then attach its fixture.

```
private static function displayObjectToCircle( _displayObject:
  DisplayObject, _world:b2World ):b2Body
{
        // Create body def
        var bodyDef:b2BodyDef = new b2BodyDef();
        bodyDef.type = b2Body.b2_dynamicBody;
        bodyDef.position.Set( _displayObject.x / DISTANCE_RATIO,
          _displayObject.y / DISTANCE_RATIO );
        // Create shape and fixture
        var circleShape:b2CircleShape = new b2CircleShape(
          (_displayObject.height / 2) / DISTANCE_RATIO );
        var fixtureDef:b2FixtureDef = new b2FixtureDef();
        fixtureDef.shape = circleShape;
        fixtureDef.density = .5;
        fixtureDef.friction = .5;
        fixtureDef.restitution = 1;
        // Create body
        var body:b2Body = _world.CreateBody( bodyDef );
        body.CreateFixture( fixtureDef );
        return body;
}
```

For circle objects like the puck and paddles, we do almost the same process, except that we use a b2CircleShape instead of a polygon. We also apply a restitution of 1, so there will be a nice bounce when the paddles impact the puck. Now that we've got all of the setup in order, we'll look at what happens with the engine updated every frame.

```
public function update( _dt:Number ):void
{
        mPhysicsEngine.Step( 1/30, 10, 10 );
        mPhysicsEngine.ClearForces();

        mConfig.mPlayer1.x = mPlayer1.GetPosition().x *
          DISTANCE_RATIO;
        mConfig.mPlayer1.y = mPlayer1.GetPosition().y *
          DISTANCE_RATIO;
        mConfig.mPlayer2.x = mPlayer2.GetPosition().x *
          DISTANCE_RATIO;
        mConfig.mPlayer2.y = mPlayer2.GetPosition().y *
          DISTANCE_RATIO;
```

```
mConfig.mPuck.x = mPuck.GetPosition().x * DISTANCE_RATIO;
mConfig.mPuck.y = mPuck.GetPosition().y * DISTANCE_RATIO;

}
```

Surprisingly simple, you say? This is where the beauty of Box2D really shines. Once the simulation has been configured correctly, you simply tell the world to advance or *Step*, passing it the delta time (in this case, a fixed 1/30th of a second), and the number of collision iterations to perform. The values I'm using for both types of collisions, 10 and 10, are fairly standard in the Box2D community for most uses. Basically, the more iterations it performs, the more accurate the simulation and the lower the risk of missed collisions. However, every iteration adds computation cycles that eat processing power. You generally want to keep this as efficient as possible, especially on a mobile device. The *ClearForces* method is then called to "clear any forces you applied to bodies," according to the Box2D manual. In earlier versions, this was done automatically by the stepping process, but it is now done manually so that you can perform multiple steps before resetting forces. After the two commands of the physics simulation are called and all of the bodies have been subsequently updated, it's time to adjust the positions of our display objects. The next six lines of code simply update the *x* and *y* coordinates of the two paddles and the puck.

With only the update function in place, our game would run just fine since all of the heavy lifting is done by Box2D. However, as is, we have no way of knowing when a player lands the puck in their opponent's goal. If you recall from the *Game* class, we called a method named *checkForCollisions* that does just that.

```
public function checkForCollisions():void
{
    for ( var collision:b2Contact = mPhysicsEngine.
      GetContactList(); collision; collision = collision.
      GetNext() )
    {
        mCollisionBodies[0] = collision.GetFixtureA().
          GetBody();
        mCollisionBodies[1] = collision.GetFixtureB().
          GetBody();
        if ( mCollisionBodies.indexOf( mPuck ) > -1 &&
          mCollisionBodies.indexOf( mGoal1 ) > -1 )
        {
            if ( mConfig.mPlayer2ScoreCallback != null )
            {
        mConfig.mPlayer2ScoreCallback();
        break;
            }
        }
    }
```

```
                             if ( mCollisionBodies.indexOf( mPuck ) > -1 &&
                               mCollisionBodies.indexOf( mGoal2 ) > -1 )
                             {
                                    if ( mConfig.mPlayer1ScoreCallback != null )
                                    {
                                   mConfig.mPlayer1ScoreCallback();
                                   break;
                                    }
                             }
                      }
               }
```

Box2D stores all collisions calculated in a particular step in essentially an internal array. The information about when two objects touch and the associated forces is stored in a *b2Contact* object. Instead of giving us access to an array to iterate through, we have to get at this collision data in an unusual way. Basically, calling *GetContactList* on the world object returns the first collision it calculated (rather than an actual list). If there are none, it will return null. Once you have this collision, to get the next one, you must call the *GetNext* method of the contact object. This continues through all remaining collisions until eventually *GetNext* will return null. This is why we have such a nonstandard *for* loop; once the collision variable is null, the loop will end. For each contact object, we check to see if the two bodies in the collision are the puck and either of the goals. If the puck is touching Player 1's goal, Player 2 scores and vice versa. At this point, we run the callback function specified in the configuration earlier and let the game logic take over. We also assume that no further collisions need to be considered, so we *break* from the loop to prevent unnecessary object creation. Now we need to allow the controller class to update the positions of the paddles. This is done through the following methods:

```
public function setPlayer1Position( _x:Number, _y:Number ):void
{
       mPlayer1Joint.GetTarget().Set( _x / DISTANCE_RATIO, _y /
          DISTANCE_RATIO );
}

public function setPlayer2Position( _x:Number, _y:Number ):void
{
       mPlayer2Joint.GetTarget().Set( _x / DISTANCE_RATIO, _y /
          DISTANCE_RATIO );
}
```

Both work exactly the same way, setting the target of each associated mouse joint to the touch coordinates passed. Updating this target will make the joint react by exerting a force on the paddle.

This force will then translate to the puck when they collide. The final method we'll look at in this class is the *reset* function. This will reset all of the moving bodies to their original coordinates: exactly what you'd want to do after a player scores.

```
public function reset():void
{
        mPlayer1.SetPosition( mPlayer1Origin );
        mPlayer1Joint.SetTarget( mPlayer1Origin );
        mPlayer2.SetPosition( mPlayer2Origin );
        mPlayer2Joint.SetTarget( mPlayer2Origin );
        mPuck.SetPosition( mPuckOrigin );
        mPuck.SetLinearVelocity( new b2Vec2() ); // Stop puck in
            case it is in motion

        mConfig.mPlayer1.x = mPlayer1.GetPosition().x *
            DISTANCE_RATIO;
        mConfig.mPlayer1.y = mPlayer1.GetPosition().y *
            DISTANCE_RATIO;
        mConfig.mPlayer2.x = mPlayer2.GetPosition().x *
            DISTANCE_RATIO;
        mConfig.mPlayer2.y = mPlayer2.GetPosition().y *
            DISTANCE_RATIO;
        mConfig.mPuck.x = mPuck.GetPosition().x * DISTANCE_RATIO;
        mConfig.mPuck.y = mPuck.GetPosition().y * DISTANCE_RATIO;
}
```

We use the origin positions we stored during setup to reset the paddles and puck. We also force the velocity of the puck to 0 in case it was moving when *reset* was called. Finally, we simply adjust the display objects exactly the same way we did in the *update* method.

Ready to Build

We're done! We've covered all of the code that is in this example. If you have an Android device setup for debugging, you should be able to plug it into your computer and publish this game directly to it. You should notice very smooth motion and reaction to touch input. There are definitely optimizations that would need to be made for mobile if you were to start using lots of dynamic objects. In fact, for mobile development Adobe recommends the use of a different version of Box2D. It is actually the original C++ version of the library, run through a piece of Adobe software called Alchemy. Alchemy turns libraries of C and C++ code into Flash SWC files. These SWC libraries can then be included in your projects and tend to perform much faster than traditional ports. There is a link to the alchemy port of Box2D on www.flashgamebook.com.

You may be asking at this point "Why would you have not just used that version of the library?" I used the open source, traditionally ported version because it is updated more often (as of this writing) and it allows those interested in digging further to examine the entire source tree. The Alchemy process leaves no exposed code, and even if it did, it would likely not be as readable as a line-by-line port. Because the syntax is slightly different in a few cases, switching to the Alchemy version is not as simple as swapping out library references. However, it would make an excellent exercise to port this air hockey game to the Alchemy version ... an excellent exercise for you, my dear reader, that is.

Conclusion

You've reached the end of the examples in this book, congratulations! I hope you feel empowered to take on a Flash game of your own, regardless of the platform. Also, don't forget that there are additional bonus chapters and appendices available on www.flashgamebook .com, covering topics such as localization into other languages, JSFL Flash IDE scripting, creating back-end services with PHP, security, and more. Simply download them to your computer and continue reading!

AFTERWORD: FLASH'S FUTURE IN GAMES

In the afterword of the first edition of this book, I challenged my readers to do something different and original with their Flash games to help legitimize it as a gaming platform. That feels a little unnecessary, 18 months later, with all that has happened with multiple new platforms and Adobe's recent open commitment to supporting game developers with features such as hardware acceleration and controllers. The platform *is* legitimate for games and none of us have to prove that any longer. Instead, we need to push Adobe to improve the toolset and platform.

Obviously, I'm a big proponent of Flash (or it wouldn't make much sense for me to write this book), but I'm also mindful that it may someday be relegated to the fate of Shockwave and other high-level development platforms. The Apple versus Adobe debacle showed that Flash is not impervious to criticism (and that some of it is very valid). You may someday not be able to use Flash to reach a particular platform—and that's okay! As Keith Peters said at one point on his blog when talking about Apple's stance, "Be a professional. Learn a new language." I agree with this philosophy wholeheartedly. At the same time, Flash still has quite a bit of life left in it, and the community needs to be vocal with Adobe to demand that they keep Flash up to par with the expectations of its competitors and users. They will listen, and if they want Flash to survive, they will evolve.

I hope this text has been helpful to you, and I hope that you'll take a few minutes to leave feedback on this book's Web site, www.flashgamebook.com. It means a lot to me to hear comments, both positive and critical, and helps me improve my writing for future editions and other books. Thanks for your support.

INDEX

Page numbers in *italics* indicate figures and tables